FROM SLAVE SHIP
TO SUPERMAX

PATRICK ELLIOT ALEXANDER

FROM SLAVE SHIP TO SUPERMAX

Mass Incarceration, Prisoner Abuse, and the New Neo-Slave Novel

TEMPLE UNIVERSITY PRESS

Philadelphia • Rome • Tokyo

TEMPLE UNIVERSITY PRESS
Philadelphia, Pennsylvania 19122
www.temple.edu/tempress

Library of Congress Cataloging-in-Publication Data

Names: Alexander, Patrick Elliot, 1983– author.
Title: From slave ship to Supermax : mass incarceration, prisoner abuse, and
    the new neo-slave novel / Patrick Elliot Alexander.
Description: Philadelphia : Temple University Press, 2017. | Includes
    bibliographical references and index.
Identifiers: LCCN 2017012896 (print) | LCCN 2017045777 (ebook)
    | ISBN 9781439914168 (e-book) | ISBN 9781439914144 (cloth : alk. paper)
    | ISBN 9781439914151 (paper : alk. paper)
Subjects: LCSH: American fiction—African American authors—History and
    criticism. | American fiction—20th century—History and criticism. |
    African American prisoners in literature. | Imprisonment in literature. |
    Slave trade in literature.
Classification: LCC PS153.N5 (ebook) | LCC PS153.N5 A3985 2017 (print)
    | DDC 813/.5409896073—dc23
LC record available at https://lccn.loc.gov/2017012896

∞ The paper used in this publication meets the requirements of the American National
Standard for Information Sciences—Permanence of Paper for Printed Library Materials,
ANSI Z39.48-1992

Printed in the United States of America

9 8 7 6 5 4 3 2

For my Lord and Savior, Jesus Christ

For the liberation-minded learning communities

thriving behind razor wire at OCC and Parchman

For Dad and Mom

Remember those in prison,

as if you were there yourself.

Remember also those being mistreated,

as if you felt their pain in your own bodies.

—Hebrews 13:3

Contents

Acknowledgments

I owe the very existence of *From Slave Ship to Supermax* to imprisoned students with whom I have had the honor of sharing my love of learning and liberation through the courses in African American literature that—over the course of my doctoral studies and assistant professorship—I have taught at Orange Correctional Center (OCC) in Hillsborough, North Carolina, and Mississippi State Penitentiary in Parchman, Mississippi. Without their provocative inquiries and superb readings of *The Autobiography of Malcolm X*; the "Letter from Birmingham Jail," by Dr. Martin Luther King Jr.; the oratory of Fannie Lou Hamer; and the fiction of James Baldwin, Toni Morrison, and Ernest Gaines, I never would have asked myself questions such as these: *What does incarceration look like in contemporary African American fiction? How attuned are African American novelists to issues of interest to incarcerated people—such as political repression, racial bias, and prisoner abuse? Can the narrative techniques of James Baldwin, Toni Morrison, Charles Johnson, and Ernest Gaines help us trace continuities between the social control logic of slavery and the increasingly cruel forms of punishment that jailed and imprisoned men and women confront and resist in our contemporary epoch of racialized mass incarceration?* From inside the prison classroom, these students helped me "get" the urgency that surrounded my writing of this book. *From Slave Ship to Supermax* is most definitely for them.

I am immensely grateful for the genius and encouragement of Maurice Wallace, my dissertation director at Duke University, who offered extensive feedback on this book, even in its humble beginnings. An ever-ready interlocutor, Maurice also joined me in teaching African American literature behind bars throughout my graduate career. His counsel on the page and in the prison classroom fueled the process of writing, revising, and expanding *From Slave Ship to Supermax*. Words cannot adequately convey how beholden I am to Maurice for his insightful comments and support throughout this book's long journey to completion.

I am also grateful to Priscilla Wald, Ian Baucom, Wahneema Lubiano, and Tara T. Green, members of my dissertation committee who offered illuminating perspective on the earliest iteration of *From Slave Ship to Supermax*. Karla FC Holloway, Fred Moten, Sharon Patricia Holland, Nina Billone Prieur, and Ashley Lucas were also incredibly helpful readers in the germinal stages of my writing. In addition, I am indebted to Christina Chia, June Hee Kwon, Eric Brandom, Elizabeth Shesko, SherAli K. Tareen, and Youngmi Cho, colleagues at Duke's Franklin Humanities Institute who invested countless evenings of conversation that led to the early development of the manuscript. Our many discussions profoundly shaped the evolution of this book.

If *From Slave Ship to Supermax* succeeds in exhibiting an interdisciplinary scope, it is because of the pathbreaking critical prison studies scholarship of Dylan Rodríguez and Vikki Law, my mentors and scholar-activist friends who believed in this project from the very start. Dylan's generous comments during this book's middle stage of development matched his warm acceptance of my invitation for him to deliver a keynote address at the first Rethinking Mass Incarceration in the South conference at the University of Mississippi in 2014. That address would deeply inform my final set of manuscript revisions. The stirring keynote that Vikki generously gave on the final evening of that conference, our ensuing discussions, and her careful review of my writing have also greatly improved the final product. I am also indebted to Vikki for acquainting me with *Tenacious*, the incarcerated women's zine for which she serves as co-editor and whose contributors are featured in Chapter 2.

Humbled is too inadequate a word to describe how I feel in the presence of my colleagues at the University of Mississippi, who took time out of their own busy research, teaching, and service schedules to read and comment on *From Slave Ship to Supermax* in its various phases of near-completion. Deborah Barker, Leigh Anne Duck, Cristin Ellis, Ann Fisher-Wirth, Jaime Harker, Katie McKee, Peter Reed, Annette Trefzer, and Jay Watson all imparted a wealth of constructive ideas, for which—along with their morale-boosting conversations—I am very appreciative. Among those outside the University of Mississippi to whom I extend my thanks are Robert J. Patterson and Erica Edwards, colleagues whose stellar scholarship and thought-provoking discussions broadened my perspective on a version of Chapter 1 that I presented at the College Language Association Convention in Lexington, Kentucky, in 2013. I treasure Brenda V. Smith's expertise and every precious conversation that we shared in this book's final season of revision. Badia Sahar Ahad's thorough review of my initial book proposal will always mean the world to me. And I will always be grateful to Sara Cohen at Temple University Press for her instantaneous interest in my book and to the press's anonymous reviewers for their substantial feedback.

That so many university students helped me wrestle through ideas that would become central to *From Slave Ship to Supermax* means a great deal to me. I am grateful to the undergraduates who were brave enough to take "Prison and the Literary Imagination," my upper-level course on African American literature and the criminal justice system, which I have taught at both Duke University and the University of Mississippi. I am also grateful to the master's and doctoral students who have taken my "Black Voices from Prison" seminar on the writings of imprisoned intellectuals. This book is better because of our lively discussions about policing, punishment, and the prison-industrial complex.

I cannot adequately thank the benefactors of the University of Mississippi College of Liberal Arts Summer Research Grant, the Katherine Goodman Stern Fellowship, the Franklin Humanities Institute Dissertation Fellowship, and the Duke Graduate School Summer Research Fellowship. Without the consistent financial support that I received, I simply would not have had the time or intellectual energy that this book demanded.

Friends and loved ones make the journey to complete anything not only possible but also enjoyable. Church family and young adult ministry teams at Third Baptist Church in Youngstown, Ohio, Union Baptist Church in Durham, North Carolina, and Brown Missionary Baptist Church in Southaven, Mississippi, fed my soul during the many years of writing, reflection, and revision. A. J. Rice, Wallis C. Baxter III, Dave Nickel, Miles Parker Grier, Ashon Crawley, Cynthia Greenlee-Donnell, Lorien Olive, Sarah Higginbotham, Michael Stanton, Tamara Extian-Babiuk, Solomon Burnette, Gabe and Mary DesHarnais, Jan Dodds, Alice Denson, Joy Turner, Soji Sajuyigbe, Will and Donica Revere, and Jack and Goodwyn Bell offered their reassurance during moments of writing when I felt particularly alone. Reginald Patterson was a listening friend on those days when my writing seemed more rambling than researched argument. Lloyd Garrison—whose shining example of scholarship and mentorship initialized my immersion into African American literary studies—was always available, lending constructive criticism and an understanding awareness at every stage. Charles Freeman and Ángel Gallardo were my prayer warrior partners from the start of this book to its finish. Otis Westbrook Pickett and Allison Curseen have spent more years serving with me in prison education programs and prison ministry than anyone; the depth of their friendship and their investment in this book's potential for social transformation will always warm my heart. Marques Richeson's faith, humor, and shared passion for the work of prison abolition made the book-writing process feel like the most logical extension of our many rich dialogues. I am ever grateful to Tanya Nichols for her heartfelt prayers, which I know availed much during the months that I spent finalizing this book.

My two brothers, Michael Alexander-Ramos and Nolan Alexander, were my most dependable sources of sidesplitting laughter on the many occasions that revision blues made me want to holler and throw up both my hands. My father, Dale Michael Alexander, and my mother, Dwendolyn Alexander, were—and are—my spiritual anchors. The constancy and potency of their prayers and love—and their belief in this book—motivated me to persist through draft after draft during all hours of day and night. Above all, God and His sweet Holy Spirit have given me inner peace, sure-footed direction, and abiding hope while writing this book that was never mine to write alone.

FROM SLAVE SHIP
TO SUPERMAX

Introduction

Antipanoptic Expressivity and the

New Neo-Slave Novel

> As a slave, the social phenomenon that engages my whole con-
> sciousness is, of course, revolution. . . . Anyone who passed the civil
> service examination yesterday can kill me today with complete
> immunity. I've lived with repression every moment of my life, a re-
> pression so formidable that any movement on my part can only bring
> relief, the respite of a small victory or the release of death.[1]

Exactly 140 years after Nat Turner led a slave rebellion in southeastern Virginia, the U.S. carceral state attempted to silence another influential Black captive revolutionary: the imprisoned intellectual George Jackson. When guards at California's San Quentin Prison shot Jackson to death on August 21, 1971, allegedly for attempting an escape, the acclaimed novelist James Baldwin responded with a prescience that would linger in the African American literary imagination: "No Black person will ever believe that George Jackson died the way they tell us he did."[2] Baldwin had long been an advocate for Jackson, and Jackson—as evident from his identification with the slave in the block quotation above—had long been a critic of social control practices in the criminal justice system reminiscent of slavery. Jackson was a well-read Black freedom fighter, political prisoner, Black Panther Party field marshal, and radical social theorist who organized a prisoners' liberation movement while serving an indeterminate sentence of one year to life for his presumed complicity in a seventy-dollar gas station robbery. He first exposed slavery's vestiges in the penal system in *Soledad Brother*, the collection of prison letters he published in 1970. *Soledad Brother*'s searing critique of an emerging prison-industrial complex would win Jackson an international, intergenerational readership, as Dan Berger has observed: "*Soledad Brother* . . . constituted a metacommentary on the growth and racialized expansion of the carceral state from the viewpoint of its victims. Writing from the shadows of society, in the wake of civil rights legislative victories, George Jackson was a voice of protest for a new generation. . . . From beyond the grave, [he] . . . inspire[d] prisoners to write . . . and organize."[3] When Jackson was laid to rest on August 28, 1971—exactly eight years after the iconic Black activist-preacher Dr. Martin Luther King Jr. delivered his "I Have a Dream" speech at the nation's capital—it was clear that his literary voice and liberationist vision had done much more than ignite a groundswell of political activism behind bars. Jackson had also deeply moved people who lived hundreds of miles beyond the isolated terrain of mass-based racialized punishment to which he had been warehoused for years on end. Thousands of fist-raised mourners would pay homage to Jackson's life, literature, and legacy inside and outside St. Augustine's Episcopal Church in Oakland on that late August afternoon.[4] Two weeks later, Jackson's assassination would spark the Attica prison rebellion in New York, yet his literary genius had already reframed the content and context of contemporary African American literature. Through *Soledad Brother*, Jackson had electrified the literary imagination of James Baldwin.

Baldwin was so impressed with *Soledad Brother* that he planned to turn it into a motion picture.[5] Previously, in his bestseller *The Fire Next Time* (1963), Baldwin had declared that endemic racism in the justice system amounted to "a criminal power" and "another means of holding Negroes in subjection."[6] Poring over the pages of Jackson's *Soledad Brother*, Baldwin encountered the racial-historical context of his famed statements anew, for Jackson had meticulously theorized Blacks' routine confrontations with racial bias, economic exploitation, police brutality, and prisoner abuse as constituting a "modern variety of chattel slavery."[7] Baldwin also read about the years of solitary confinement, beatings, and unsubstantiated indictments that Jackson had endured after guards targeted him for radicalizing fellow imprisoned men and establishing political solidarity with readers around the globe. Outraged, Baldwin seized an opportunity to speak at a rally for Jackson in England four months before his death at the hands of the state. There, Baldwin decried a hyper-punitive logic of "law and order" in the United States that he linked to a long history of racial terror inside and outside the prison system: "*We are the victims* and we are the result of a doctrine called white supremacy, which came into the world God knows how many years ago."[8] Baldwin's words seemed an anticipation of Jackson's in his posthumously published text, *Blood in My Eye*: "Born to a premature death . . . *that's me, the colonial victim*."[9] Throughout the early 1970s, Baldwin continued to champion Jackson's cause, perhaps in

The funeral of George Jackson, the widely read imprisoned intellectual and Black Panther Party field marshal whose writings captured the interest of James Baldwin, was held at St. Augustine's Episcopal Church on August 28, 1971. Jackson's casket was wrapped in a Black Panther flag. (Photograph © 2016, Stephen Shames/Polaris Images.)

response to Jackson's unexplained and unprosecuted killing by prison guards at age twenty-nine. In 1974, Baldwin published *If Beale Street Could Talk*, a novel that revived both his admiration of Jackson and his prescient condemnation of the nation's (in)justice system. This intrinsically racist and abusive system of punishment would, after the turn of the century, lead the world in incarceration, imprisoning one in every ninety-nine U.S. adults and more Black men than had been enslaved in 1850.[10]

That Baldwin's *Beale Street* has yet to be explored in the context of his career-spanning critiques of the justice system and his engagement with the lives and literature of imprisoned intellectuals, activists, and writers such as Jackson, Malcolm X, Angela Y. Davis, Huey P. Newton, and Bobby Seale points to a blind spot in scholarship on prison in American studies, Black studies, and African American literary criticism. On the one hand, there are a growing number of scholars who study the complexities of narrative expression as they have emerged from the voices of men and women confined to the contemporary U.S. prison. In particular, Margo V. Perkins, Joy James, Michael Hames-García, Dylan Rodríguez, Dan Berger, Mechthild Nagel, and Lisa M. Corrigan have traced striking historical continuities between the institution of slavery and today's criminal justice system through their analyses of autobiographies authored by iconic imprisoned intellectuals such as Jackson, Davis, Assata

Shakur, and Mumia Abu-Jamal. Perkins, James, Hames-García, Rodríguez, Berger, Nagel, and Corrigan have thus begun the important work of critically translating carceral knowledges of the mass incarceration era: they have demonstrated how contemporary explorations of racialized state violence become more lucid when viewed through the literary lenses of some of the most socially isolated writers in the Black radical tradition.[11] Still, critical discourse has not yet explored the profound social commentary of non-imprisoned authors who write about prison—authors whose literary works are often indebted to the narrative techniques and critiques of the justice system of the aforementioned political prisoners and less well-known imprisoned writers. Moreover, while Tara T. Green importantly contextualizes her edited collection *From the Plantation to the Prison: African-American Confinement Literature* (2008) as "open[ing] new avenues of inquiry into confinement literature" in light of the past half century's exponential rise in incarceration and its impact on the writing and reception of African American literature, there remains a scarcity of scholarship that considers the place of fiction in contemporary explorations of racial bias, police intimidation, prisoner abuse, and premature death in the justice system.[12] *From Slave Ship to Supermax* builds on Green's work (even in its title), proposing that (1) mass incarceration is the most critically underexplored allusive framework for the contemporary African American novel; and (2) the increasingly repressive forms of mass-based bodily immobilization and incapacitation that a disproportionately Black population confronts while warehoused in contemporary U.S. prisons (perhaps seen most egregiously in today's supermax prisons) are traceable to the state-sanctioned racial terror, gendered social control, and global capitalist greed that mass-produced slave ship social orders and slave plantation economies during the 1600s, 1700s, and 1800s.[13] With the prison-industrial complex as its backdrop, this book examines how late twentieth-century African American novelists depict forms of discipline prototyped during the Transatlantic Slave Trade and slavery—including geographically withdrawn isolation, sexual intimidation, institutionalized rape and torture, indefinite solitary confinement, and public execution—as timeless practices of racialized social control.

In this book, I argue that the disciplinary logic and violence of the Middle Passage and slavery haunt depictions of the contemporary U.S. prison in African American fiction works authored by Baldwin, Toni Morrison, Charles Johnson, and Ernest Gaines. It is my contention that these African American novelists show us how social control practices that structured carceral life on slave ships and slave plantations have long, post-Emancipation afterlives that find their most pronounced manifestation in the hyper-policed Black ghettoes, male-staffed women's prisons, and disproportionately Black death row populations of post–Civil Rights U.S culture. Accordingly, this book should be understood as a nod to Avery F. Gordon's premise in *Ghostly Matters: Haunting and the Sociological Imagination* that haunting is "a way in which abusive systems of power make themselves known and their impacts felt in everyday life, especially when they are supposedly over and done with."[14] I extendedly unpack Gordon's conception of haunting in relation to imprisoned women's routine confrontations with sexual abuse by male prison guards in Chapter 2. But for now, let me underscore that her critical understanding of haunting makes apparent not only how the white supremacist logic of an *institution* from the repressed past (slavery) has infiltrated an *institution* in our present (prison) but also how disciplinary continuities between captive life in the Transatlantic Slave Trade, slavery, and prison—as depicted in Baldwin's *If Beale Street Could Talk* (1974), Morrison's *Beloved* (1987), Johnson's *Middle Passage* (1990), and Gaines's *A Lesson Before Dying* (1993)—illuminate a heretofore un-theorized Black carceral aesthetic. This unique aesthetic constitutes, I argue, a new narrative tradition within the African American literary tradition. To clarify: since slavery was not entirely abolished by the Thirteenth Amendment but, rather, was recodified through its exception clause as a condition of rights-lessness, social isolation, and state-sanctioned punitive harm reserved for the prisoner (the amendment states, "Neither slavery nor involuntary servitude, *except as a punishment for crime*, whereof the party shall have been duly convicted, shall exist within the United States, or any place subject to their jurisdiction"), the literary representation of this seamless continuity in legalized terror production before and after Emancipation, as it appears in works of fiction by Baldwin, Morrison, Johnson, and Gaines, historicizes captive characters' disturbing testimonies of prisoner abuse or carceral violence. Thus, during the final three decades of the twentieth century—decades in which the U.S. prison population soared and reports of prisoner abuse skyrocketed—these novelists cast a light on the centuries-spanning experience of Black captive *bodies in pain* (to invoke Elaine Scarry), pain that is institutionalized rather than inadvertent, disciplinary rather than aberrant.

This book aims to illuminate the extent of this centuries-spanning experience of carceral pain by building on recent scholarship in African American literary studies that focuses on the slave ship as a point of origin in a lineage of mass-based systems of white supremacist social control and corporeal constraint—a lineage whose current endpoint is the contemporary U.S. supermaximum-security prison, where disproportionately Black and mentally ill imprisoned populations are held in six-by-eight-foot cells that feature windowless, mattress-less, solitary confinement for 23½ hours a day, meals slid through cell door portals, and no human contact or mental stimulation. In particular, this book is in dialogue with Dennis Childs's recent study, *Slaves of the State: Black Incarceration from the Chain Gang to the*

Penitentiary. Throughout the study, Childs conceives of the slave ship as a primal site in a genealogy of mass-based authoritarian control that stretches back beyond the birth of the modern penitentiary to the Transatlantic Slave Trade's system of large-scale racialized confinement, corporeally constricting architectures, and experimentalist forms of living death. Childs emphasizes the centrality of state-sanctioned racial terror in the making of carceral pain throughout his discussions of this "Middle Passage carceral model," which he conceptualizes as "a paradigm of racial capitalist internment that necessitates a shifting of white-subject-centered penal historiography.... [F]or the African and those of African descent, the modern prison did not begin with Jeremy Bentham's Panopticon, the Walnut Street jail, or the Auburn System, but with the coffles, barracoons, slave ships, and slave 'pens' of the Middle Passage."[15] Resonating with Childs's interest in complicating a "Western philosophy of imprisonment" by "remapping . . . the carceral through the lens of epochal race terror," Chapters 2 and 3 show how the ubiquity of unpoliced and unpunished prisoner abuse in the increasingly geographically withdrawn prisons of our contemporary epoch is inextricably linked to the logic and impunity of white supremacist social control that led white slave ship captains and crewmen to routinely and sadistically restrain, beat, rape, torture, and debase African captives within the remote, maritime environment of the slave vessel.[16] Moreover, as I illustrate in Chapter 2, with reports of sexualized state violence on the rise in increasingly male-staffed U.S. women's prisons, this book is interested not only in the centrality of racial terror in the mass-production of centuries-spanning carceral pain but also in how foundationally and relatedly terror is gendered on the slave ship and in today's women's prisons.

This book is also in conversation with scholarship in the emerging field of critical prison studies—particularly, Dylan Rodríguez's *Forced Passages: Imprisoned Radical Intellectuals and the U.S. Prison Regime*. I argue that Baldwin, Morrison, Johnson, and Gaines accomplish in fiction what Rodríguez reveals so many imprisoned intellectuals as having achieved in their autobiographical writings. Like Jackson, Davis, Shakur, and Abu-Jamal, the African American novelists I examine link the social control logic of slavery's past to the sadistic and routine violence that typifies post-slavery imprisonment. For this reason, I perform my analyses of the slavery/prison "hauntings" of Baldwin, Morrison, and Gaines in relation to their under-discussed engagements with imprisoned writers, activists, and survivors of prisoner abuse and thereby offer an interdisciplinary reframing of discourse on these novels. Thus, from this book's start to its finish, I read the racially codified enslavement-incarceration continuum in contemporary African American fiction in the context of critical prison studies discourse on imprisoned (radical) intellectualism. In addition, I make the case that, through their involvement in the intellectual and cultural production of imprisoned people and through their depictions of racial terror as a formative rather than an exceptional dimension of U.S. culture, Baldwin, Morrison, Johnson, and Gaines expand free society's view of a contemporary prison system in which the institutionalization of secrecy has functioned to routinize the experience of prisoner abuse and mass-produce a condition of slavery behind bars. In a move similar to critical prison studies scholars such as Rodríguez, these novelists, by privileging the first-person testimonial perspectives of abused captive characters in their fiction works, have amplified the systemically muted voices of actual imprisoned men, women, boys, and girls who combat racially discriminatory sentences, prisoner abuse, and premature death and who literarily organize against these forms of state-sanctioned repression.

Finally, this book also intentionally intersects discourse on prison in African American literature with human rights scholarship. I show throughout the ensuing chapters how Baldwin, Morrison, Johnson, and Gaines appropriate fictional narrative as a viable form of social justice advocacy for imprisoned people and thereby challenge prevailing ideas regarding the mediation of narrative voice and victim representation in prisoners' rights discourse and human rights literature—an issue that Kay Schaffer and Sidonie Smith discussed in their 2004 study, *Human Rights and Narrated Lives: The Ethics of Recognition*. Moreover, this book tells the story of how these novelists create captive characters that craft narratives in crafty ways that illustrate what I discuss in ensuing sections of this Introduction under the rubric of "anti-panoptic expressivity": a confined human being's unforeseeable act of speaking truth to unmediated institutional power while being held within a carceral locale premised on the dispossession of voice, racial terror, social isolation, and racialized premature death. Baldwin, Morrison, Johnson, and Gaines, that is to say, demonstrate the radical utility of the African American novel during our contemporary epoch in which prisoner abuse has been widespread and generally documented in ways that marginalize the voices of abuse-surviving imprisoned people. The most widely circulated stories of prisoner abuse appear in reports published in the human rights literature of advocacy organizations such as Human Rights Watch, Amnesty International, and the Death Penalty Information Center. These mainstream narratives of prisoner abuse tend to shock and awe because they emphasize the harrowing reality of prisoner abuse over the subjectivity of abuse survivors. Despite their well-intentioned attempts to evoke affective appeal, human rights reporters generally depict men, women, and children who confront state violence behind bars as victims only, often eliding these abuse survivors' critical interpretations of their mistreatment. These reporters, in other words, ironically reinforce prevailing conceptions of imprisoned people as people who lack agency even as they insist on and appeal for their access to "human rights." Throughout this book, I argue that novels by Baldwin, Morrison, Johnson, and Gaines sharply contrast with the truncated, victimization-focused narratives that typify the mainstream prisoner abuse stories appearing in the literature of human rights organizations. These contemporary African American novelists foreground the unabridged, resistance-laden, redress-seeking first-person testimony of abused captives and thus make apparent how actual imprisoned writers can and do offer narratives critical of the justice system in their own voices and thereby transform the exploitative environments to which they are confined into generative sites for reconstituting the self and refashioning ideas about community, freedom, and human rights. Moreover, this book demonstrates how Baldwin, Morrison, Johnson, and Gaines speak to and beyond the con- straining representational parameters that surround "human rights" discourse more fundamentally: precisely because these novelists depict abused captives who articulate the insufficiency of pursuing justice within relatively narrow legal conceptions of "human rights," they offer a fiction-framed portal into the "real" world of imprisoned intellectualism whose occupants constantly re- imagine alternative paths for achieving restitution and radical social trans- formation. It is in this way that—during the past half century in which the state has severely penalized imprisoned writers who have sought to call into question abusive practices in the justice system—the narratives and narrative techniques of Baldwin, Morrison, Johnson, and Gaines can be understood as amplifying their social critique and affirming their humanity at one and the same time.

"I question America": Hamer's Testimony and the Prisoner Abuse Narrative in African American Literature

"She's telling it like it is! She's saying, prison is not *like* slavery—it *is* slavery!" I am having a moment of déjà vu as I listen to students in a Mississippi prison classroom articulate an interpretive framework that I had first witnessed imprisoned students at Orange Correctional Center in Hillsborough, North Carolina, introduce when they dissected a famous speech delivered by Fannie Lou Hamer. Hamer was a Black sharecropper-turned-civil-rights-orator from rural Mississippi whose liberationist struggle against Black disenfranchise- ment and white supremacy in June 1963 resulted in her subjection to sexual assault and jailhouse beatings by white patrolmen—acts of state violence that left her with permanent kidney damage, a lifelong leg injury, and a nearly blinded left eye. Interestingly, at both of these men's prisons, the postsecondary students whom I had the privilege to teach and learn from emphasized Hamer's evocation of enslavement as a critical lens for grasping the historical continuities that undergirded the racial terror that shaped her confrontations with prisoner abuse as she describes them in her oft-anthologized "Testimony Before the

Credentials Committee." Hamer, co-founder of the Mississippi Freedom Democratic Party, delivered this oration at the 1964 Democratic National Convention in Atlantic City, New Jersey. On this particular in-prison teaching day, I am at Parchman, Mississippi's plantation-style state penitentiary, which the Pulitzer Prize–winning historian David Oshinsky has described as "the closest thing to slavery that survived the Civil War."[17] The oldest prison in the state, Parchman is located less than fifteen miles from where Hamer lived. I am co-teaching a history and literature course with my friend Otis Westbrook Pickett titled "Justice Everywhere: The Civil Rights Stories of Martin Luther King Jr., Fannie Lou Hamer, and Barack Obama." We have invited a number of students who are part of the University of Mississippi Prison-to-College Pipeline Program (PTCPP) to be as candid as they desire during a close reading discussion of Hamer's oratory. The ensuing hours of textual analysis are so full of illuminating dialogue that neither we nor our students can find a fitting way to conclude class. Perhaps sensing this, several students cluster around me at the lectern as our time to bid farewell hastens. They urge me—with each reference they make to passages from Hamer's testimony that they have highlighted in blinding yellow—to heed their assertions about slavery's vestiges in the contemporary justice system. I am all ears.[18]

The most vocal PTCPP students argue that Hamer calls to mind the institution of slavery in her testimony through the emphasis that she places on incarcerated Black men striking her with blackjacks under the command and overseeing presence of sadistic white male authorities. The students insist that while these white men are obviously patrolmen, they act like nineteenth-century slave masters: they yank up Hamer's dress and—as Hamer reveals in later speeches—fondle her without fearing the slightest threat of punishment. The students also remind Dr. Pickett and me of what they learned when they read *For Freedom's Sake*, Chana Kai Lee's seminal biography on Hamer. These white patrolmen were not only acquitted of conspiracy charges. They were also protected from *any* punishment by law, because state policemen had coerced Hamer, at gunpoint, to sign a confession stating that she had been harmed not by the patrolmen but by her fellow Black activists during their confinement in the Winona, Mississippi, jail. That the state so callously criminalized Hamer and other Blacks for white men's abusive treatment of her was not a racist incident *like* slavery, the students remarked. It was a racist practice signifying slavery's perpetuity. Other PTCPP students then chime in, making the case that Hamer testified of being punished by the state *like a slave* for her disturbance of Jim Crow society's "peace." As these students see it, while Hamer did not break any official laws on the books, she had transgressed the South's unwritten law of white supremacy: she had refused to stay in her socially designated "place" of racial and gender inferiority. These students reiterate that Hamer's mere interest in voting was a crime, an audacious assertion that she had a citizen's voice in a de facto segregation world that had labeled her a *sub-citizen*. Following this line of thinking, Jim Crow society's overseers—white patrolmen—were the first to discipline Hamer, the recalcitrant second-class citizen, by recovering two forms of punishment from the antebellum era: physical violence and sexual harm. Hamer thus exposed the justice system's reliance on slavery-era punitiveness nearly one hundred years *after* the abolition of slavery.

On my drive back to Oxford, Mississippi, that day, I could not stop thinking about the PTCPP students' perceptive perspectives on slavery's vestiges in the contemporary justice system. Indeed, Hamer had evoked the memory of slavery in her testimony to effectively incriminate the state before the eyes of the television-viewing U.S. public. Indeed, Hamer had exposed the disturbing hypocrisy of U.S. democracy. This was the hypocrisy of slavery's perpetual reinstatement "in the land of the free." This was the hypocrisy of routine, unchecked, state-sanctioned anti-Black violence and discrimination in the post–*Brown v. Board of Education* era—hypocrisy as old as the infamous exception clause in the Thirteenth Amendment. It was a hypocrisy that Hamer voiced most explicitly at the conclusion of her riveting, eight-minute testimony by way of one the most indicting rhetorical questions posed during the Civil Rights Movement: "All of this on account of we want to register, to become first-class citizens. . . . I question America. Is this America, the land of the free and the home of the brave, where . . . our lives be threatened daily, because we want to live as decent human beings, in America?"[19]

Hamer's oratory and PTCPP students' critical translation of it in the context of an increasingly repressive world behind bars inspired me to trace anew the beginnings of a distinct literary tradition. In this tradition, jailed and imprisoned orators, writers, and intellectuals draw from personal experiences of incarceration, the narrative form of testimony, and the long history of slavery (beginning with the Transatlantic Slave Trade and slavery, and continuing with the Jim Crow racial caste system and lynching) to condemn the existence and expansion of the prison-industrial complex. I had previously seen this tradition as having emerged from autobiographical writings published in the post–Civil Rights era by George Jackson and Angela Y. Davis, political prisoners who—as I discuss in Chapters 1 and 2—are very forthcoming in the parallels that they draw between racialized state violence and white slaveholders' infliction of terror on recalcitrant slaves. After a more careful retrospective glance, I began to see that Hamer actually preceded Jackson and Davis (and even Malcolm X and Alex Haley, with their publication of *The Autobiography of Malcolm X* in 1965) in literarily revealing and resisting the state's post-slavery practice of slavery-era discipline and punishment. It is my contention that Hamer's oratory (which I examine at length later in this Introduction), the slavery-allusive narrative frameworks that Jackson and Davis incorporate into their autobiographical writings on prison life, and the profound associations between slavery-era terror and post-slavery imprisonment articulated by captive characters in the late twentieth-century novels of Baldwin, Morrison, Johnson, and Gaines point to two untheorized narrative traditions within the African American literary tradition: a tradition of prisoner abuse narratives, and a tradition of neo-abolitionist novels. I now turn our focus to these interlocking traditions.

Prisoner Abuse Narratives in Contemporary African American Literature

> When a worldwide furor erupted after the abuses at Abu Ghraib, where members of a generation that grew up on electronic games gave vent to their sadistic impulses by humiliating prisoners of war, I, along with many African-Americans, wondered how long it would take for the public to become outraged by the Abu Ghraibs that exist in this country. Most telling in this scandal was that one of those involved in these abominable acts was a former American prison guard.[20]

Although I have referred to Hamer's testimony at the Democratic National Convention as focused on *prisoner abuse*, that term did not begin circulating regularly in public discourse until the early 2000s in the wake of the notorious prisoner abuse scandals at U.S. war prisons in Iraq; Guantánamo Bay, Cuba; and Afghanistan—and, as the quotation from Ishmael Reed above reveals, in contemporary African American novelists' responses to them. In this book, I definitely intend to call to mind this prevailing conception of prisoner abuse because the widespread visceral reactions to it have ignited rare and vital discussions among writers, activists, and scholars in fields such as law, human rights, and critical prison studies. Along these lines, this book, as a whole, is a nod to the important legal studies work of Brenda V. Smith, Kim Shayo Buchanan, and Colin Dayan, for it takes as its premise the critical under-standing that they and a growing number of scholars who study prisoner abuse abroad and at home have expressed: prisoner abuse is not an aberration—as news media coverage of the aforementioned prisoner abuse scandals seemed to convey—but a norm in U.S. jails, prisons, juvenile detention facilities, and immigration detention centers.[21] Prisoner abuse is one of the state's most secret, *legally facilitated* practices of racial terror and gendered social control. Thus, I conceive of prisoner abuse, in the most fundamental sense, as the state's opportunistic and systemic incapacitation of people who are criminalized, arrested, jailed, imprisoned, or otherwise detained—including the physical, sexual, psychological, and medicinal exploitation of men, women, and youth who are held in some form of state custody by police officers and corrections employees (e.g., stop-and-frisk policing, beatings, and other forms of corporal punishment; rape, sexual abuse, and sexual intimidation; sensory deprivation and enforced nudity; the introduction of electric shock, stun belts, restraint chairs, indefinite solitary confinement, extraordinary rendition, and premature death on the body; medical neglect or harm; and the shackling of pregnant women under state supervision).[22] Again, while most twenty-first-century discussions of prisoner abuse understandably evoke images of U.S. war prisoners who suffer attacks from snarling dogs and sexually abusive military personnel, or who find themselves hooded, robed, and "strung with electrical wiring" while standing atop boxes, this book refuses to think about abuse behind bars in such a reductive, exceptional, and allegedly "un-American" manner.[23] Instead, I talk about prisoner abuse as a persistent symptom of homegrown terror, which is how it has been discussed by the nation's foremost scholar of literature from prison, H. Bruce Franklin (among others):

> By the end of the twentieth century, when the prison had become a major political weapon of the corporate state, torture designed to dehumanize had become the norm. . . . Gone from the so-called "penitentiary" or "correctional facility" is any pretense of reformation or rehabilitation. *In the typical American prison, degradation, brutalization, and even overt torture are the norm.* Beatings, electric shock, prolonged exposure to heat and even immersion in scalding water, sodomy with riot batons, nightsticks, flashlights, and broom handles, shackled prisoners forced to lie in their own excrement for hours or even days, months of solitary confinement, rape and murder by guards or prisoners instructed by guards—all are everyday occurrences.[24]

I add that this book aims to complicate the relative ease with which critical discourse has relegated the experience of prisoner abuse to the geography of the prison proper. Even by way of its title, *From Slave Ship to Supermax* insists on investigating prisoner abuse in a historical context that includes and is inflected by the Middle Passage and slavery. One need not be in prison, in other words, to be systematically isolated and abused in ways that are continuous with the state's routine incapacitation of the contemporary U.S. prisoner or prisoner of war. Building on the pioneering critical prison studies scholarship of Dylan Rodríguez, I view prisoner abuse as a historically rooted, nation-defining, white supremacist practice of social control that begins with the racial violence of the Transatlantic Slave Trade and slavery and continues with lynching, the violent enforcement of the Jim Crow racial caste system, and, contemporaneously, extrajudicial execution by law enforcement, racialized mass incarceration, and capital punishment.[25] Thus, in this book I show how prisoner abuse must also be understood as the calculated immobilization, exploitation, debasement, debilitation, injury, and killing of confined people by agents of institutional power in *any* authoritarian regime—be it the physical and sexual violence to which white captains and crewmen subject the Africans they kidnap and confine on slave ships in Morrison and Johnson's contemporary reimaginings of slavery; the violent premature death that white male proponents of Jim Crow justice expedite for the wrongfully convicted Black male protagonist in Gaines's *A Lesson Before Dying*; or a racist police state's collaborative efforts to incriminate and incarcerate a young Black father-to-be for showing race pride in Baldwin's *If Beale Street Could Talk*. The disciplinary continuities between captive life in slavery and in prison that Baldwin, Morrison, Johnson, and Gaines depict in their novels fit squarely within this second conception of prisoner abuse, a conception that might be understood as conveying the "ghost of slavery" variety of racialized punishment that Colin Dayan speaks of in her important legal studies work *The Story of Cruel and Unusual:*

> If the methods of punishment used in the United States today—the death penalty, prolonged solitary confinement, extreme force, and psychological torture—seem barbaric by our standards and by those of the rest of the so-called civilized world, this can be traced to the colonial history of the legal stigmatization and deprivation of a group considered less than human. . . . The ghost of slavery still haunts our legal language and holds the prison system in thrall.[26]

Prisoner abuse narratives—whether they are autobiographical, like Hamer's speech, or fictional, like Baldwin's novel—are unabridged testimonial stories published from the Civil Rights era to the present that focus on experiences of incarceration burdened with the very "ghost of slavery" of which Dayan speaks. These narratives constitute a viable narrative tradition, and that tradition is entirely distinct from what has been broadly termed "prison literature." On the one hand, the claim could be made that *any* narrative written from or about prison is a prisoner abuse narrative. As the contemporary African American writer John Edgar Wideman observes in his reframing of Supreme Court Justice Roger B. Taney's infamous opinion in the 1857 Dred Scott case (Taney states, "Blacks have no rights which the white man [is] . . . bound to respect") in *Brothers and Keepers*—the acclaimed memoir he published in collaboration with his imprisoned brother Robby in 1984—the combination of prison employees' access to near total impunity and the prison's geographically withdrawn setting makes today's facility a no-man's land where state power is often administered abusively: *"Prisoners have no rights that the keepers are bound to respect* [is] . . . the motto of the prison. . . . [K]eepers run prisons with little or no regard to prisoners' rights because license to exercise absolute power has been granted by those who rule society. . . . You, the custodians, formulate whatever rules . . . you require to keep prisoners in captivity."[27] Removed from the immediate presence of judiciary oversight, the prison is a carceral locale whose isolation from free society often affords correctional officers unbridled discretion in their enforcement of law and order; thus, its very existence perpetually (re-)creates the possibility for imprisoned peoples' encounters with unchecked physical and psychological harm to be disturbingly ordinary. Indeed, *any* writing they produced from such a space could be termed a "prisoner abuse narrative."

Wideman's point notwithstanding, I make the case throughout this book that prisoner abuse narratives are defined not by their emergence from within hyper-punitive "correctional" settings so much as by their reference to the penal facility as an occasion for contesting a centuries-spanning experience of racialized social control. Put differently, I resist using the term *prison literature* in this book not only because literary works most commonly classified as "prison literature," "prison writings," or "prison narratives" were not conceived of as such by their authors but also because they might be better understood as "*anti*-prison narratives." Following Rodríguez's important assessment of "the problem of prison writing" in his work on imprisoned radical intellectuals, I submit that the uncritical categorization of many late twentieth-century imprisoned and formerly imprisoned writers' works that are critical of the justice system—such as *The Autobiography of Malcolm X* or *Soledad Brother*— as "prison literature" would likely make their authors turn over in their graves.[28] In the case of Malcolm and Jackson, such a slapdash categorization of their work would give them a reason to abandon their graves with indictments more scathing than they ever made while they were alive, for their autobiographical narratives (which I would most definitely term "prisoner abuse narratives") depict, but also decry, captive life in the correctional facility and in the larger U.S. carceral state. When read as prisoner abuse narratives, *The Autobiography of Malcolm X* and *Soledad Brother* diverge sharply from the conventional history of American "prison writing" which, as Franklin has shown, beckons non-imprisoned readers to gaze on a prisoner voyeuristically, whether through (1) picaresque confessional narratives in which imprisoned authors plead with their audience to understand and forgive them for their pre-incarceration criminality; (2) sensationalist dramas in which unrepentant convicts glorify their past and present perpetuation of violence and drug trafficking; or (3) trite conversion narratives in which hardened criminals recount how the experience of punitive isolation has positively transformed them into law-abiding (unquestioning of the state) citizens.[29]

Malcolm and Jackson reject these constricting narrative frameworks in their autobiographies. Their works testify to both the prevalence of state violence behind bars and their tactical resistance of such abusive treatment. Narratives published by authors imprisoned in the late twentieth century, such as Rubin "Hurricane" Carter, Angela Y. Davis, Assata Shakur, Mumia Abu-Jamal, and Robert Hillary King, similarly adopt an oppositional discourse that reveals the contemporary U.S. prison to be a terrain of struggle and economic exploitation where poor Black and Brown people wrestle against discriminatory laws and political repression agendas that render them raw material for an ever-expanding system of mass incarceration.[30] Drawing on legal scholarship, court cases, historical studies of slavery, and the conventions of the fugitive slave narrative genre, Malcolm X, Jackson, Carter, Davis, Shakur, Abu-Jamal, and King all launch radical "anti-prison" critiques that critical prison studies scholar Joy James has discussed under the rubric of "contemporary insurrectionist penal-slave narratives": "Contemporary insurrectionist penal-slave narratives, such as Abu-Jamal's *Live from Death Row* or Assata Shakur's *Assata: An Autobiography*, can question the very premise of rehabilitation, indicting the state and society and contextualizing or dismissing individual acts of criminality by nonelites, the poor and racialized, to emphasize state criminality or the crimes of elites."[31]

I make the case in this book that the accounts of "state criminality" authored by jailed orators such as Hamer or political prisoners such as Jackson and Davis and enslaved or incarcerated characters in novels by Baldwin, Morrison, Johnson, and Gaines all constitute prisoner abuse narratives. What I term a *prisoner abuse narrative* is a testimonial story that a confined human being creates and selectively circulates to expose (1) the ordinariness of unchecked physical violence, sexual exploitation, or state-sanctioned premature death within a site of mass-based captivity; and (2) the racial-historical precedents for such practices (especially the Transatlantic Slave Trade and slavery). Importantly, a prisoner abuse narrative is not a victimization narrative that catalogues harm and emphasizes subjugation; rather, it is an account of utter defiance that illustrates how confined people resist authoritarian torment, reclaim their wounded bodies and psyches, establish desired community and political solidarity, and thereby undermine the asymmetries of power characteristic of carceral environments governed by a white supremacist disciplinary logic.[32] Resonating with what James calls Abu-Jamal's and Shakur's "contemporary insurrectionist penal-slave narratives," and what Margo V. Perkins has classified as "political autobiography" in her study of Davis's and Shakur's texts, prisoner abuse narratives—whether they emerge in autobiographical, oratorical, or fictional form—combat and subvert individual and institutional attempts to silence the confined "noncitizen" and thus alter, even if only temporarily, those geographies of containment fraught with punishment practices that are reminiscent of slavery and what the social theorist Michel Foucault has famously described as a panoptic gaze.[33] Such antipanoptic expressivity, I argue, can be traced (at least) to Hamer's oratory.

Antipanoptic Expressivity in Contemporary
African American Literature

Prisoner abuse narratives defy panoptic logic. I now wish to reveal how this defiance happens, for it is my contention throughout this book that the antipanoptic expressivity that Hamer and other abused captives evoke in their meditations on Black confinement cast long shadows on contemporary novels by Baldwin, Morrison, Johnson, and Gaines—the fictional prisoner abuse narratives that I examine in the ensuing chapters of this book. In *Discipline and Punish: The Birth of the Prison* (1975), Foucault investigates the disciplinary function of institutional power in modern European and American prisons and in free society; free society, he argues, has become increasingly carceral. One of Foucault's more famous discussions in *Discipline and Punish* focuses on an architecture of surveillance that is also a system for routinizing large-scale social control: the British philosopher Jeremy Bentham's Panopticon. Even at the level of structure and spatial arrangement, the Panopticon ensures prison guards' perpetual visual objectification of confined people. As a disciplinary edifice, the Panopticon is constituted by an "annular building" with many rows and levels of cells and a centralized watchtower with "windows that open onto the inner side of the ring" out of which unseen seers oversee cell dwellers with an uninhibited line of vision.[34] Confined people are so fixated on the intensity of this all-seeing panoptic gaze that they anxiously police their behavior as if a guard were actually keeping watch over them in their solitary cells. Yet the Panopticon is not only a mechanism of institutional power that aims to facilitate self-governance within prisons (or hospitals, asylums, and so forth); it is also the state's chosen method for dispossessing confined human beings of voice—and thus a means whereby the state perpetuates a climate in which mass-based domination and prisoner abuse can occur in secret. In Foucault's words, a prisoner is totally objectified by this panoptic gaze, for "he is seen, but he does not see; he is the object of information, *never a subject in communication. . . .* And this invisibility is *a guarantee of order.*"[35] We must remember that, given the size of the employee population at a jail or prison, innumerable prospective unseen seers are working at any given facility. Panoptic gazers need not be standing within an observation tower at Stateville Correctional Center in Illinois—which currently houses the only architectural panopticon in the United States—to enforce panoptic repression. The contemporary facility's employees/unseen seers can and do exploit the geographically withdrawn nature of their unsupervised supervision of imprisoned people to suppress voices and abuse bodies they deem a threat to the institutional status quo. It is this second, more covert system of panoptic silencing—the state's simultaneous institutionalization of secrecy and dispossession of voice—that prisoner abuse narratives fundamentally undermine.

Prisoner abuse narratives subvert some of the state's most routine practices of voice dispossession, such as its censorship of imprisoned writers and its increased outlawing or hyper-surveillance of interviews with them. The journalist Cristina Rathbone has compellingly revealed the prevalence of these practices—practices that I see as panoptic in every way. Rathbone confronted frequent opposition from the Massachusetts Department of Corrections (DOC) when she attempted to interview women imprisoned at MCI-Framingham for her book *A World Apart: Women, Prison and Life Behind Bars* (2005). In the book, Rathbone discusses the great lengths to which prison administrations across the nation go to dispossess imprisoned populations of voice:

> Almost every major periodical in the country has had to shelve prison stories because access was denied. Despite attempts by press organizations to rally against such restrictions, the trend to exclude media from prisons continues to grow apace with the system itself. In 1998, for example, California, which has the nation's third-largest prison system, banned all face-to-face interviews with, as well as confidential correspondence to, every inmate in its system. Arizona followed suit. Pennsylvania maintains a blanket ban on all news-media contact with inmates, as does South Carolina. . . . Alaska insists on officials monitoring interviews. . . . Mississippi states that consideration will be given only to media requests to develop stories "portraying rehabilitative efforts."[36]

Rathbone adds that in the case of Massachusetts, the DOC permitted her entry into the prison only after the intervention of the American Civil Liberties Union and nine months of waiting. Still, that did not stop MCI-Framingham staff from putting up administrative barriers: "For the first couple of months, correctional officers routinely kept me waiting for hours before allowing me into the visiting room. Sometimes they wouldn't let me in at all, citing failure on my part to provide . . . previously unnecessary paperwork. . . . [P]eople at the DOC were determined to do all they could to keep me from discovering the worst of their practices."[37] In light of Rathbone's observations and what I have discussed throughout this Introduction regarding the well-concealed practice of prisoner abuse in domestic U.S. penal institutions, it is important to note that legal efforts to keep justice-seeking media representatives and activists outside of prison have greatly diminished the possibility of imprisoned people's testimonies of routine guard-on-prisoner rape, sexual assault, and torture—and their resistance against such state violence—from ever reaching free society. Franklin has spoken to this point quite powerfully: "The prison's walls are designed not only to keep the prisoners in but to keep the public out, thus preventing observation or knowledge of what is going on inside. Unknowable to all but prisoners and guards, the prison thus becomes a physical site where the most unspeakable torture can continue without any restraint."[38]

Prisoner abuse narratives destabilize this panoptic enforcement of voice dispossession within and among imprisoned communities. The authors of prisoner abuse narratives find ways, often clandestinely, to speak truth to power. In so doing, they counteract their carceral condition of systemic silencing. Their intentional creation of oppositional speech and an in-prison literary counterculture affords them, if only temporarily, the opportunity to be something other than the object of an immobilizing, panoptic gaze. The literary scholar Michael Collins has made a case for conceptualizing this literary counterculture as an "antipanopticon" in the context of his work on the formerly imprisoned Black Arts Movement poet Etheridge Knight:

> Knight act[s] as an antipanopticon surveilling United States society and justice to look into the souls not only of prisoners but also of the whole tradition that locks them in. To power his redefinitions [of crime and criminality], Knight borrows authority from . . . the black-power and black-arts movements and their project of redefinition and counterhegemonic communication. . . . At least in his stanzas, the poet can defeat the panoptic apparatus.[39]

From Collins's vantage point, the imprisoned Knight—who, while confined, regularly exchanged correspondence with and was visited by the Pulitzer Prize–winning poet Gwendolyn Brooks—turned to literary expression critical of the justice system as a way to join his voice with revolutionary Black speakers outside Indiana State Prison who astutely passed judgment on the unseen seers (especially in the U.S. carceral state) who had passed judgment (and enforced racially discriminatory confinement) on him and other men held there. Knight and the other imprisoned contributors to his edited collection *Black Voices from Prison* (1970) moved people outside of prison literarily while removing themselves from the panoptic discipline of a maximum-security facility designed for their immobilization and silencing. Thus, through improvisational literary expression, Knight and his carceral writing team actualized what was arguably unforeseen and unforeseeable speech: imprisoned men's published critique of racial bias and the abuses of power they witnessed and experienced in the justice system. This otherwise unknown community of writers locked away in a high-security Indiana prison not only spoke in a way that received a hearing; they also exuded—in their testaments, poetry, and essays—the mass-based, unlicensed movement and antipanoptic expressivity that I argue is characteristic of the prisoner abuse narrative.

Throughout this book, I build from Collins's ideas about Knight's anti-panopticon in my theorization of prisoner abuse narratives and antipanoptic expressivity. I define *antipanoptic expressivity* as a confined person's un-anticipated act of speaking truth to power while he or she is dispossessed of voice and contained within any site premised on a white supremacist disciplinary logic, authoritarian rule, gendered social control, or premature death. Thinking back to Knight, at one level, he and his mostly Black carceral writing team unpredictably undermined the maximum-security prison's ever-present panoptic gaze by their very creation of a literary movement within a space whose power dynamics were designed to prevent the mobilization of their bodies *and political-intellectual voices*. But at another level, Knight and the contributors to *Black Voices from Prison* succeeded in insurrectionist communal writing within and against an even larger system of deindividuation and social control that traces its roots to the slave ship holds of the Transatlantic Slave Trade era—a system of *racialized* carceral power that predated and has always outstripped the regulatory force of the Foucauldian panoptic gaze. When Knight's work is (re-)read in this context, many of his most famous poems in *Black Voices from Prison*, such as "The Idea of Ancestry," "Hard Rock Returns to Prison from the Hospital for the Criminal Insane," "Cell Song," and "He Sees Through Stone," shatter the seeming invincibility of a panoptic gaze because the content and style of these works evoke the signal-song duplicity, mass-based recalcitrance, and political solidarity that effuse from (supposedly silenced) enslaved men and women in their spirituals and work songs. Knight's poems thus reflect his carcerally expressive consciousness of Blacks' long history of covert resistance to unchecked state power and a panoptic gaze that Joy James rightly defines as having been shaped as much by racial terror and gendered social control as by architectural design: "Panopticism and the policing gaze are also informed by racial and sexual bias. . . . Ignoring disenfranchised ethnic minorities policed by both the state and dominant castes, Foucault . . . allows the representative [disciplined] body, which [he] bases on a white male model, to appear as universal."[40] Indeed, because Foucault makes no reference to the prevalence of *racialized* punishment or the history of *racialized* carceral power (e.g., the Transatlantic Slave Trade, slavery, the Jim Crow racial caste system, lynching, or the prison system as an emerging prison-industrial complex) in his study of the modern prison's disciplinary development, he also fails to consider the possibility that those people who confront a panoptic gaze find (and have always found) ways—small and large—to evade or undermine its impact. In the words of Dylan Rodríguez: "For all his profound insight . . . Foucault never quite examines whether and how the captive body/ subject also, perhaps inevitably, attempts to dissipate, appropriate, resist, absorb, and rearticulate [the panoptic apparatus's] power relations."[41] Frustrating *racialized* carceral power relations is rich, antipanoptically expressive work—and it is that work, I argue, that distinguishes prisoner abuse narratives, whether they are autobiographical, as we see with the published works of Malcolm X, Davis, Jackson, Shakur, Abu-Jamal, and King; oratorical, as we see with Hamer's 1964 testimony; or fictional, as we see with the character Caleb Proudhammer's recollection of life on a prison farm in Baldwin's novel *Tell Me How Long the Train's Been Gone* (1968).

Hamer's Prisoner Abuse Narrative

> I was carried . . . into another cell where they had two Negro prisoners. The state highway patrolmen ordered the first Negro to take the blackjack. . . . And [he] began to beat. And I was beat by the first Negro until he was exhausted. . . . The state highway patrolman ordered the second Negro to take the blackjack. The second Negro began to beat. . . . I began to scream and one white man got up and began to beat me in my head and tell me to hush. One white man—my dress had worked up high—he walked over and pulled my dress [up], I pulled my dress down, and he pulled my dress back up.[42]

As shown in the block quotation above, antipanoptic expressivity infuses Hamer's oft-anthologized testimony of racialized prisoner abuse and sexualized state violence. I offer now a heretofore untheorized reading of her oratorical undermining of racialized carceral power and the panoptic gaze.[43] At one level, Hamer, a Black woman who was no stranger to the state's use and abuse of her body (she was the victim of a forced hysterectomy and the target of white vigilantes' gunfire in Ruleville, Mississippi), very conscious-ly evokes the memory of slavery when she tells of the degradation and debilitation to which she is subjected in a twentieth-century jailhouse. Perhaps the most striking image in Hamer's testimony is the first one that captured the eyes of my students at Parchman. At the midpoint of her address, Hamer recounts a contemporary southern jail's slavery-reminiscent enforcement of Black-on-Black punishment: she paints an age-old picture of white men who answer to no one as they oversee and order around captive Black men who, under threat of violence, mete out disciplinary pain on the body of a captive Black woman. The actions of these unseen (over)seers— these white patrolmen whose panoptic watchtower-like positions as civilian protectors with badges conceal from public record the reality of their crimes of assault and battery and sexual abuse against Hamer—call to mind a scene from the Academy Award–winning film *12 Years a Slave* (2013), based on the slave narrative by Solomon Northup of the same title. Northup was a Black male slave who, under threat of violence from a white slave master, brutally beat a Black female slave named Patsey. Yet just as Northup literally testified of this experience in 1853 to put slavery on trial through the form/forum of the slave narrative, in 1964 Hamer invited a national audience and the court of public opinion to indict the white supremacist justice system that facilitated her state-sanctioned beating and sexual assault through the form/forum of her prisoner abuse narrative. Again, while jailed Hamer had been the object of panoptic interrogation—an "object of information, but never a subject in communication," as Foucault would have it. Along these lines, Hamer recalled that one of the patrolmen "asked me where I was from," then retorted, "We are going to check this," and upon verifying her Mississippi address, disparaged her: "You are from Ruleville, all right. . . . We are going to make you wish you was dead." Yet by using national television as her witness stand during the Democratic National Convention—by conveying to a diverse and sizeable viewing audience an image of white patrolmen as contemporary slave masters who exploit a location removed from society to inflict terror on a law-abiding citizen—the criminalized Hamer ironically exposed the criminality of the justice system. "All of this on account of we want to register, to become first-class citizens," she quipped. Her ensuing "I question America" should thus be understood as antipanoptic expressivity, for this Black female activist who—from the panoptic-gazing vantage point of the patrolmen—was supposed to be politically neutralized after her incarceration became (if only temporarily) an all-seeing "I"/"eye" who, with innumerable television-watching witnesses across the nation, oversaw the unjust administration of justice by so-called defenders of justice. Thus, through the very presentation of her prisoner abuse narrative, Hamer undermined the docilizing force of racialized carceral power and reclaimed her institutionally abused Black body for the purpose of social conscience pricking and radical social transformation.[44]

And yet Hamer's testimony is also a prisoner abuse narrative because it makes use of the jail cell as a space for issuing a historically rooted critique of racialized social control in the U.S. carceral state. Hamer's speech, in fact, might be the first widely accessed work of rhetorical resistance to a condition of sexualized state violence in contemporary women's jails and prisons that I discuss more fully in Chapter 2. Sexualized state violence is a disciplinary holdover from the Transatlantic Slave Trade whose proliferation in women's correctional settings has resulted from the passage of Title VII of the Civil Rights Act of 1964. On the one hand, Title VII paved the way for female correctional officers to be able to work in men's prisons, but on the other, it sanctioned male guards to oversee women held in state custody—and thus have unsupervised access to jailed and imprisoned women's cellblocks, restrooms, cells, *and bodies.* Hamer delivered her testimony just one month after the Civil Rights Act *effectively institutionalized* this male supremacist practice of sexualized state violence in women's facilities. In the wake of the law's passage, Hamer publicized the government's reinstatement of the rape culture to which European captains and crewmen subjected captive African women on seventeenth-century slave ships. Hamer thus defiantly spoke out against this racial-historical condition of sexualized state violence, a condition that would become increasingly concealed and thus disturbingly prevalent in the criminal justice system in ensuing decades. Of particular note is Hamer's exposure of the systemic nature of this culture of harm. Hamer called on her audience to witness not only her confrontations with sexualized state violence but also those of her female comrades. Sexual overtones pervade Hamer's recollection of her fellow activist Annell Ponder's screams. "I began to hear the sounds of licks and screams," Hamer stated. "I could hear the sounds of licks and *horrible* screams. And I could hear somebody say, 'Can you say 'yes, sir,' nigger? Can you say 'yes sir?' And they would say other horrible names."[45] Hamer's unrelenting exposure of the wounded humanity of *multiple* Black women held in the unsupervised state custody of white men evoked viewers' sympathy not only toward Black people's status as sub-citizens (the Black female activists Hamer mentions were all, like her, criminalized for their participation in a voter registration workshop) but also toward Black *women* and their historically denied status as women. As a fellow activist watching Hamer deliver her address remarked, "Half the [credentials] committee being women, [Fannie] had a tremendous impact. Lot of women were crying after she finished." Hamer herself was crying, telling a reporter—antipanoptically— "I felt just like I was telling it from the mountain."[46]

What also distinguishes Hamer's testimony as a prisoner abuse narrative is her refusal to present her confrontation with sexual abuse and brutal beating in the framework of a victimization narrative. Throughout her testimony, Hamer emphasizes how she and other jailed Black female activists strove to reclaim their bodies within a male supremacist environment that was fundamentally designed for their brutalization. For instance, Hamer highlighted the resistance of Ponder toward the jail guard who called her "nigger" and asked her to say "yes, sir." Hamer gloried in Ponder's verbal dexterity, noting that she replied sardonically to the request, "I don't know you well enough." Similarly, Hamer was careful in explaining to a nation of viewers how she preserved her bodily integrity while *five* men—three white patrolmen and two Black male prisoners—nearly beat her to death and sexually harmed her. She described a quick maneuver that she made as a means to lessen the blows she was receiving: "I began to work my feet." Later, she made a point of articulating how she resisted sexual harm at the precise moment a white patrolman tore at her dress: "One white man . . . walked over and pulled my dress [up;], I pulled my dress *down*."[47] In sum, Hamer's 1964 testimony is a shining example of a prisoner abuse narrative, for while she makes evident a racial-historical condition of gendered social control that would come to define the lives of far too many women held captive in the emerging prison-industrial complex, she also emphasizes the reality of women's strategic acts of opposition to such control—acts that Victoria Law, an award-winning scholar who writes about the contemporary women's prison, defines as "resistance behind bars."[48]

"I picked up my pitchfork": The Emergence of the Neo-Abolitionist Novel in Contemporary African American Fiction

Like Hamer, contemporary African American novelists have used the narrative form of testimony, the narrative style of antipanoptic expressivity, and the narrative framework of the Middle Passage and slavery to convey disciplinary continuities between the carceral violence that enslaved people confronted and decried in centuries past and the racist and abusive justice system that jailed and imprisoned people have combated from the 1960s to the present. At one level, the sheer volume of incarcerated characters in contemporary African American fiction who endure and contest physical aggression, psychic harm, unprosecuted injury, and premature death at the hands of policemen, jail and prison guards, chain gang officers, military personnel, or other agents of social control bespeaks the subfield's investment in exploring how Black bodies receive, resist, and recover from a long history of racialized carceral power. For instance, in addition to the works of fiction by Baldwin, Morrison, Johnson, and Gaines that I examine in this book, novels such as Donald Goines's *White Man's Justice, Black Man's Grief* (1973), Alice Walker's *Meridian* (1976), Gayl Jones's *Eva's Man* (1976), Sherley Anne Williams's *Dessa Rose* (1986), and Walter Mosley's *The Man in My Basement* (2004) reflect this investment. But what distinguishes the league of African American fiction writers who are the focus of this book is that their confined characters (1) record their routine confrontations with racialized harm in the form of extended first-person, testimonial narratives; and (2) bring to light literary practices that thrive, clandestinely, among imprisoned intellectuals in the world behind the razor wire—literary practices that make a case for radical prison reform or prison abolition.[49]

Baldwin is the first member of this league of neo-abolitionist novelists. I examine *If Beale Street Could Talk* (1974) at length in Chapter 1, but for now I will draw attention to *Tell Me How Long the Train's Been Gone* (1968), the first of Baldwin's relatively neglected, antipanoptically expressive works. Although *Tell Me How Long* has received notable attention in a small body of twenty-first-century scholarship, including the important analyses by Lynn Orilla Scott, Aaron Oforlea, and D. Quentin Miller, the novel has only recently been examined in the context of Baldwin's growing vexation with the criminal justice system during the second half of his career.[50] While Baldwin focuses *Tell Me How Long* on the complicated love affairs and artistic life of Leo Proudhammer—a Black bisexual actor raised in Harlem who has suffered a heart attack—he also makes apparent how police harassment on the streets of New York City and prisoner abuse behind bars are disturbingly common aspects of Black life. Early in *Tell Me How Long*, readers discover that Leo shares much more than friendship with his older brother Caleb. He also shares his experience of encountering white policemen who racially profile, incriminate, and intimidate young Black men. One evening, white policemen arrest Caleb on trumped-up charges, and he is forced to do hard labor at a geographically withdrawn plantation prison in the Deep South. Scott rightly calls Caleb's experiences at the prison "an episode that reads like a neoslave narrative," for in the context of the rest of the novel the prison-farm section demonstrates how Caleb has been confined to a different place *and time*.[51]

What is essential about Baldwin's depiction of such confinement for my analysis is (1) his rendering of it in the first-person testimonial, selectively circulated form of a prisoner abuse narrative; and (2) the narratological shadow that Hamer—an actual Black woman who oratorically reflects on punishment practices reminiscent of slavery that characterized her Civil Rights–era jailing in rural Mississippi—casts on the fictional Black prisoner Caleb's account of unchecked physical violence and sexual intimidation on a southern prison plantation. I begin by focusing on the former point. Halfway into Baldwin's novel, the character Caleb recounts a raw, unabridged, self-fashioned story of prisoner abuse before his chosen audience—his younger brother, Leo. Throughout his narrative, Caleb emphasizes historical continuity between the sadistic harm that characterized slaveholders' disciplinary treatment of Black people during slavery and the racial violence that he suffers at the hands of the state in the narrative present of the novel—which is the twentieth century, an epoch many decades beyond the signing of the Emancipation Proclamation. Caleb's references to routine whippings, extended hours of fieldwork, and a white prison guard who insists on public appraisals of incarcerated Black men's bodies (treatment that calls to mind the putatively antiquated auction block) make evident the extent to which prison authorities intend to make Caleb and other prison-farm captives feel like twentieth-century slaves:

The [prison] farm I was on, down yonder. They used to beat me. With whips. With rifle butts. It made them feel good to beat us; I can see their faces now. There would always be two or three of them, big mother-fuckers. The ringleader had red hair, his name was Martin Howell. Big, dumb Irishman, sometimes he used to make the colored guys beat each other. And he'd stand there, watching, with his lips dropping, his lips wet, laughing, until the poor guy dropped to the ground. And he'd say, That's just so you all won't forget that you is niggers and niggers ain't worth a shit. And he'd make the colored guys say it. . . . The first time I saw this red-haired mother-fucker, I was in the field, working. He was on a horse. He come riding up, and stopped and watched me. But I just kept on working. Then he yells out, Hey, Sam! but I just kept on doing what I was doing.[52]

Like Hamer's testimony, Caleb's prisoner abuse narrative references slavery not only to provide an imagistic framework for historicizing Black carceral pain but also to register how fundamentally racialized harm operates as a logic of social control in "correctional" settings. Along these lines, Baldwin's Caleb draws attention to the way in which white guards' sense of pleasure commingles with the terror that they unleash on captive Black men, whom they often command to terrorize one another with the whip. Like the notorious white slave master Captain Anthony who gleefully scourges Aunt Hester in the opening chapter of Frederick Douglass's 1845 narrative, the white guards who order Caleb around "feel good" when they beat bound, unarmed, and therefore defenseless Black field laborers. They feel so good, in fact, that they giggle while overseeing the whippings. Moreover, Caleb notes that—in eerily similar phraseology as Hamer's when she recalls a white jail guard asking Ponder, "Can you say, 'yes, sir,' nigger?"—it makes white guards like Howell feel especially good to remind the Black prison farm workers about the relationship between their status as criminals and their socially designated "place" of racialized expendability: "you is *niggers* and *niggers* ain't worth a shit."

Caleb goes on to describe how these scenes of racial spectacle function on the prison farm as they did on the slave plantation. The scenes are designed to inflict collective psychological injury on the disproportionately Black captive population to ensure their submissiveness to the white men in charge. Caleb intimates that his spirit is broken by routinely witnessing and experiencing such racialized exemplary punishment: "He'd make the colored guys say . . . [']No, Mr. Howell, we ain't worth shit.['] The first time I heard it, saw it, I vomited. But he made me say it, too. . . . That hurt me more, hurt me more than his whip, more than his rifle, more than his fists."[53] Howell eventually links his devaluation of Black life and the racial epithet "nigger" to the threat of rape when Caleb informs him—with an antipanoptically expressive flourish that matches Ponder's rejoinder, "I don't know you well enough," to the guard who demands that she identify herself as a subservient "nigger"—of the proper way to call his name: "My name ain't Sam. . . . My name is Caleb Proudhammer, mister, and I'd appreciate it if you'd let me get on with my work."[54] Affronted, Howell remarks: "*Nigger,* if my balls was on your chin, where would your prick be?"[55] Caleb recounts responding by arming himself: "I picked up the pitchfork. I didn't do nothing, I just picked up the fork. But the horse kind of jumped. And this red-haired mother-fucker, he looked surprised, and he looked scared, and he was having a little trouble hanging on to his horse. I knew he didn't want me to see that."[56] Of course, Caleb's unforeseen defiance only increases Howell's interest in teaching him his "place." Howell eventually locks Caleb away in the prison farm's version of a Security Housing Unit—a rank, rat-infested "jail inside the jail" to which he is confined in windowless isolation for nearly the entirety of each day.[57] During this stint of indefinite solitary confinement, Caleb provocatively links his struggles against prison authorities with his ancestors' confrontations with slave masters: "[Howell] made me feel like I was my grandmother in the fields somewhere and this white mother-fucker rides over and decide to throw her down in the fields. Well, shit. You know. I ain't my grandmother. I'm a man. . . . I ain't about to be raped."[58]

In the end, Caleb does not defeat Howell; however, like Hamer, he uses both his body and antipanoptic expressivity to undermine the penal in-stitution's attempts to render him a docile twentieth-century slave. Most fundamentally, Caleb makes a point of telling Leo about his resistance against Howell's rape attempts: "[Howell] said something about my mama and my daddy and he come up to me and touched me on the behind . . . and . . . I picked up the big heavy pot I was washing and I threw the water all over him and I beat him over the head with the pot. As hard as I could. As hard as I could. . . . I was trying to kill him . . . and he knew it, too."[59] In the ensuing brawls between Caleb and Howell, Caleb does not downplay the fact of the wounding and degradation that he suffers. Still, like Hamer, Caleb places emphasis in his prisoner abuse narrative on how well he preserves a recalcitrant Black body that guards seek to panoptically oversee and violently subdue in a geographically withdrawn southern facility: "I ducked," "I battled him to the bars," "I made that mother scream."[60]

Caleb's nine-page prisoner abuse narrative in *Tell Me How Long the Train's Been Gone* is the precursor to what I describe throughout this book as the neo-abolitionist novel. Neo-abolitionist novels are prisoner abuse narratives in extended fictional form. They are Black fiction's centuries-spanning, first-person testimonial accounts of institutionalized suffering. They are stories of Black repression and Black resistance. They are narratives that profoundly link racialized state violence in the contemporary prison with slaveholding U.S. society's disciplinary use of terror on Black captive bodies during the Transatlantic Slave Trade and slavery. But neo-abolitionist novels are not only that. During our current epoch, in which, as Schafer and Smith note, "the State can and does regulate personal storytelling as part of punishment [and] State regulations control what kinds of access activists have to inmates and their stories," neo-abolitionist novels also illuminate the suppressed political-intellectual thought, unforeseen resistance, and literary genius of abuse-surviving men and women behind bars who literarily strive, often clandestinely, to end mass incarceration as the reflexive mode of response to the unresolved social problems that mass-produce prisons and prisoners.[61] I thus argue that the fiction of Baldwin, Morrison, Johnson, and Gaines—fiction that is often shaped by these authors' personal engagement with the intellectual and cultural production of prisoner abuse survivors—challenges legal measures designed to dispossess imprisoned people of voice at a moment in which their voices could not matter more.

I add, finally, that because neo-abolitionist novels implicitly (and, at times, explicitly) push for the abolition of slavery's vestiges in the criminal justice system, they are the new neo-slave novels. "Neo-slave narrative" is a term that, for the past three decades, has categorized a subgenre within African American literary studies in which authors of the post–Civil Rights era reimagine the historical experience of slavery in fictional form. Yet in light of my attention to slavery's carceral contemporaneity, I argue that the time is ripe for a redefinition of this subgenre.

This book is intended to expand and complicate conventional discussions of neo-slave narratives. It is my contention that the emphasis that Baldwin, Morrison, Johnson, and Gaines place on the Transatlantic Slave Trade and slavery's interrelation with post-slavery (or post-slave trade) carceral life in their novels opens up vast and underexplored terrain of analysis—terrain rife with lived experiences of enslavement that persist in contemporary U.S. prison life. And yet, my theorization of the new neo-slave narrative—the neo-abolitionist novel—is still indebted to scholars such as Bernard Bell, Ashraf H. A. Rushdy, Elizabeth Ann Beaulieu, Angelyn Mitchell, and Arlene R. Keizer, who have all convincingly defined what neo-slave narratives are and why we call them what we call them. Bell first coined the term in 1987 and attributed it to "residually oral, modern narratives of escape from bondage to freedom."[62] More than a decade later, Rushdy described neo-slave narratives as "contemporary novels that assume the form, adopt the conventions, and take on the first-person voice of the antebellum slave narrative" in the context of the Black Power Movement's push for radical social change.[63] Though Beaulieu and Mitchell importantly focus on narratives written by women in their studies of neo-slave narratives, their overarching critical frameworks are quite similar to Bell's and Rushdy's. For Beaulieu, the neo-slave narrative is "the slave narrative of the twentieth century [and] the inevitable outgrowth of both the civil rights movement and the feminist movement."[64] Mitchell's notable contribution to the discussion includes conceiving of these narratives as "liberatory narratives" because of their emphasis on freedom rather than enslavement.[65] More recently, Keizer has examined how what she calls "contemporary narratives of slavery" take into account how "Caribbean and Black British writers have also turned back toward slavery as a touchstone for present-day meditations on the formation of black subjectivity."[66] By shifting the discussion of neo-slave narratives to the field of critical prison studies, it is my intention to highlight even more ways in which slavery's carceral contemporaneity shows up in these narratives, as a handful of scholars—most notably, Dennis Childs—are beginning to do.[67] Moreover, I examine in this book three modes of antipanoptic expressivity through which neo-abolitionist novels articulate captives' endurance and resistance of Middle Passage and slavery-era terror in post-slavery carceral life. In Chapter 2, I analyze the mode of *survival testimony*; in Chapter 3, I discuss the mode of *rehabilitative address*; and in Chapter 4, I conceptualize the *revivifying narrative* as a mode of antipanoptic expressivity that scholars in the field of critical prison studies often discuss under the rubric of imprisoned (radical) intellectualism.

Plan of the Book

Chapter 1 argues that Baldwin's late-career fiction reflects his personal engagement with the carceral life, literature, and social theory of George Jackson and Angela Y. Davis, two Black intellectuals who were also political prisoners during the Black Power era. Given the extent of Baldwin's advancement of Jackson's and Davis's work, I examine *If Beale Street Could Talk* in the context of critical prison studies scholarship and make a case for how Baldwin accomplishes in fiction what many imprisoned intellectuals achieve in their autobiographical works. In *Beale Street*, Baldwin alludes to the social control logic of slavery's past to situate Blacks' confrontations with racialized state violence in our contemporary epoch in a more complete historical context. Baldwin's novel also foreshadows the rapid expansion of a fundamentally racist and abusive prison-industrial complex and pays homage to the intellectualism of its earliest captives.

Toni Morrison's *Beloved* is the focus of Chapter 2. While scholars and critics have thoughtfully examined the chain gang camp as a site of post-slavery racialized incarceration and sexual violence in this neo-abolitionist novel, I argue that the contemporary U.S. women's prison informs *Beloved*'s narrative development in an even deeper way. Drawing from Morrison's personal engagement with Davis's writings from jail, Avery F. Gordon's conception of haunting, and the legal scholarship of Brenda V. Smith, I make the case that testimonies of sexual abuse in the contemporary women's prison haunt Black female characters' recurring stories of confrontations with rape in *Beloved*. I build my argument from the profound irony that Title VII of the Civil Rights Act of 1964, although intended to champion gender equity by creating opportunities for female correctional officers to work in men's prisons, institutionalized male correctional officers' unsupervised supervision of incarcerated women and thereby reinstated the rape culture that European crewmen established and enforced on slave ships as a means of socially controlling the African women they kidnapped and enslaved during the Transatlantic Slave Trade. With its focus on rape as white men's trusted pre- and post-Emancipation tool of racial terror and gendered social control, *Beloved* reveals how the recent surge in accounts of sexualized state violence in women's prisons indicates that the sexual abuse of incarcerated women is not an aberration, as it is often portrayed in news media discourse and human rights literature, but historically rooted, systemic harm. By also examining *Beloved* alongside the work of the historian Danielle L. McGuire, the Black expressive culture scholar Geneva Smitherman, and the critical prison studies scholar Victoria Law, I demonstrate how Morrison's fictional Black women— as with actual women who confront routine sexual abuse by male guards in the contemporary prison—turn to the narrative form of testimony to expose the gendered nature of their harm and resistance within male supremacist carceral spaces premised on racialized confinement and sexualized subjection.

In Chapter 3, I continue my chronological examination of the neo-abolitionist novel by analyzing how writings on state violence in maximum- and supermaximum-security prisons by men imprisoned in the late twentieth century haunt associations that Charles Johnson makes between slave ships and prisons in his novel *Middle Passage* (1990). Drawing from Gordon's conception of haunting, the imprisoned intellectual Mumia Abu-Jamal's essays, Colin Dayan's legal scholarship, and Dylan Rodríguez's critical prison studies work on the Middle Passage, I argue that the routine and cruel nature of violence on the novel's slave ship alludes to the climate of state-sanctioned sadism and institutionalized suffering that is confronted daily and voiced literarily by actual imprisoned men in the high-security prisons of our current epoch. These men make reference to slave ships in their writings to register a repressive genealogy of punishment from which they speak their own social truths. Thus, building from Chapter 2, the chapter illustrates further how, in the neo-abolitionist novel, the slave ship emblematizes historical continuity between the Transatlantic Slave Trade and the incapacitation-focused contemporary prison.

Chapter 4 argues that, through his provocative depiction of a wrongfully convicted Black man's diary writing from death row in *A Lesson Before*

Dying, Ernest Gaines introduces to African American fiction what Rodríguez has theorized in critical prison studies scholarship as an *imprisoned radical intellectual*. As a whole, the chapter links the critiques of the criminal justice system made by the incarcerated characters in Gaines's oeuvre to his extratextual articulations of slavery's vestiges in the post-slavery South's system of racialized incarceration—vestiges that include racial bias, economic exploitation, prisoner abuse, and premature death. Revisiting Gaines's repeated requests while writing *Lesson* to visit with a man on death row at Angola penitentiary (Louisiana's slavery-reminiscent plantation prison); his under-discussed witnessing of imprisonment on death row and the execution of prisoners as a young writer; and his prolonged reflection on the botched electrocution and re-execution of Willie Francis, a Black adolescent from his home state, I make the case that Gaines portrays his unlettered Black male protagonist in *Lesson* in the narratological shadow of Francis. Before his second electrocution, Francis, a semiliterate Black Louisianan, wrote a widely read account of his initial encounter with and survival of the electric chair and the state's ensuing (but unsuccessful) attempts to defame him. Gaines's Black Louisianan protagonist similarly establishes himself as an astute critic of a racist justice system in the death row diary that he passes on to a learning community in a Black schoolhouse on the morning of his execution. Like Francis's pamphlet *My Trip to the Chair*, the very existence of this fictional protagonist's diary undermines the criminal/post-slavery slave identity that the justice system has assigned to him and thus provides an antipanoptic counter-narrative to the story that jail administrators have constructed for his incarceration on death row: "This ain't no school."[68]

Of principal focus in this book's Epilogue is the way in which Gaines's *Lesson* depicts, with startling timeliness, a movement that unites imprisoned and non-imprisoned people against the deprivation of education in the prison system. Revisiting the attempts of the novel's townspeople to secure learning opportunities for Gaines's death row protagonist during his incarceration, as well as the resistance of the punishment-minded jail administration to their efforts, I make a case for conceptualizing *Lesson* as a meditation, in part, on the ongoing national debate about the place of arts and education initiatives behind bars. It is this book's concluding contention that the institutionalization of educational deprivation in the contemporary U.S. prison—a practice that intensified after Congress eliminated Pell Grants for imprisoned learners in 1994 and thus ended public funding for postsecondary prison education programs—recovers a form of mind-numbing terror from the era of slavery and constitutes a new terrain of prisoner abuse on which the neo-abolitionist novel(ist) has joined the imprisoned student in resistance.

1

Talking in George Jackson's Shadow

Neo-Slavery, Police Intimidation,
and Imprisoned Intellectualism in Baldwin's
If Beale Street Could Talk

Prison preoccupied the literary imagination of James Baldwin. Yet his biographer David Leeming is one of the few to notice that "prisons *and* prisoners were a significant part of Baldwin's *personal* experience."[1] Even the most cursory glance at Baldwin's published works and interviews bear out Leeming's important observation. In his essay "Equal in Paris" (1955), Baldwin reveals that during his time in France, he was "arrested as a receiver of stolen goods and spent eight days in prison."[2] While confined, Baldwin witnessed, with great shock, another incarcerated man's bleeding and wounding go unattended, intentionally, by prison staff. In his longer essay *No Name in the Street* (1972), Baldwin reflects on frequent prison visits that he made to his friend Tony Maynard, a Black man who suffered violent treatment from guards after he was falsely charged with the murder of a white U.S. Marine.[3] Baldwin's advocacy for Black political prisoners, in particular, deeply informed his writings and public addresses throughout the 1970s and included actions such as aiding in the release of the imprisoned Black Panther Party co-founders Huey P. Newton and Bobby Seale.[4] In 1970, Baldwin was so outraged by the appearance of Angela Y. Davis, the Black revolutionary and advocate for political prisoners, in handcuffs and mock mug shot posture on the cover of *Newsweek* magazine that he published an open letter in the *New York Review of Books* in which he deemed her jailing a continuation of slavery and a foreshadowing of a racialized epidemic of mass incarceration at one and the same time: "Only a handful of the millions of people in this vast place are aware that the fate intended for you, Sister

Angela . . . and for the numberless prisoners in our concentration camps—
for that is what they are—is a fate which is about to engulf them, too."[5] When
Baldwin spoke out about racism in the criminal justice system on the *Dick
Cavett Show* in 1973, he won widespread admiration among imprisoned
Black communities, receiving "so many letters from them that he determined
to arrange a Christmas version of [his musical drama] 'The Hallelujah
Chorus' that would . . . tour American prisons."[6] Finally, in 1982, Baldwin
published a letter in which he insisted that "artists and prisoners have more
in common with one another than have servants of the State."[7]

Indeed, Baldwin was a stranger neither to witnessing nor to writing about
prisons and prisoner abuse. Yet Baldwin's oeuvre has not been examined
extensively in the context of his engagements with the literature and life
experiences of imprisoned men and women.[8] This chapter focuses on
Baldwin's understanding of prisoner abuse and police intimidation as interrelated racialized social control functions of the contemporary U.S. carceral
state and pays careful attention to how his historicizing of racialized state
violence in fiction is shaped by his admiring engagement with the writings of
imprisoned intellectuals. Baldwin, I contend, alludes to the human chattel
condition(ing), disciplinary violence, and economic exploitation that typified
the institution of slavery in his Black Liberation Movement–era short stories
and novels to situate his Black working-class characters' subjection to racial
profiling, police brutality, wrongful incarceration, indefinite solitary confinement, prisoner abuse, and premature death in racialized historical context. Focusing mostly on Baldwin's novel *If Beale Street Could Talk* (1974), this
chapter explores how Baldwin, inspired by the narrative techniques of the
imprisoned intellectual George Jackson, links a repressive logic of racial
terror from the era of antebellum slavery with the state's practice of white
supremacist social control in the contemporary criminal justice system. I
argue that, by incorporating Jackson's conception of neo-slavery into the
allusive framework for *Beale Street*, Baldwin elucidates the predictability—
rather than the aberrant nature—of Black men's hyper-criminalization,
incarceration, and brutalization by the state. *Beale Street* thus exemplifies well
what I theorized in the Introduction as a neo-abolitionist novel: with this
work, Baldwin becomes the first canonical African American writer to
construct a conceptual model of the prison-industrial complex in fiction that
privileges the narrative viewpoint of its captives while also making apparent
slavery's vestiges in the contemporary U.S. criminal justice system.

My point of departure for this chapter is Baldwin's career-length consideration of racial terror as a state-sanctioned social control function of
pre- and post-slavery American life—and the relationship of this instru-
mentalist terror to Blacks' recurring encounters with state violence in the
late twentieth (and twenty-first) century. This contextualization establishes

a broader framework within which my reading of criminalization and punishment in *Beale Street* might be understood.

Baldwin's Literary Eyewitnessing of Racialized Social Control in the Justice System

Baldwin's witnessing of the physical, psychological, and spiritual harm that the criminalized Black body endures at the hands of the state shows up prominently in his nonfiction works. In his book-length essay *No Name in the Street*, for instance, Baldwin's assessment of wounds that prison guards inflict on his former driver and bodyguard Tony Maynard—a wrongfully incarcerated Black man—is characteristically disturbing and damning: "Tony had been beaten, and beaten very hard; his cheekbones had disappeared and one of his eyes was crooked; he looked swollen above the neck, and he took down his shirt collar, presently, to show us the swelling on his shoulders. And he was weeping. . . . I had never seen him weeping."[9] Baldwin lingers with photographic precision on the expanse of Maynard's battered and bruised body, revealing, on the one hand, the crushing corporeal impacts of unchecked, racialized state terror on Black life, and, on the other, a courtroom-style exhibition of state criminality. Baldwin thus manages to juxtapose, here and throughout his body of work, the wounded humanity of the Black criminal/noncitizen—in this case, Maynard—with the unprosecuted aggression of the state. Baldwin elucidates this tension further in an earlier essay collection, *The Fire Next Time*. There, he argues that contemporary policemen's unquestioned racial bias and "criminal power"— their frequent exploitation of state-issued authority to intimidate and harm (rather than protect) unarmed men, women, and children who are disproportionately Black—is a continuation of the social control logic of slavery in the contemporary moment, "another means of holding Negroes in subjection."[10] Still, it is in his fiction that Baldwin best illuminates this point.

In Baldwin's fictional works, jailed and imprisoned characters are usually young, Black, and male, and they are also commonly victims of state violence. Their plights often begin with subjection to routine police intimidation. Richard, a twenty-two-year-old self-educated Black man who shows up only as a minor character in Baldwin's novel *Go Tell It on the Mountain* (1953), provides a shining example of such a plight—and he is, arguably, Baldwin's archetypal victim of prisoner abuse. From the moment Richard appears in the novel, his ostentatious race pride foreshadows his abusive treatment in a racist criminal justice system: "I just decided me one day . . . no white son-of-a-bitch *nowhere* [will] never talk me down, and . . . make me feel like *I* [am] dirt. . . . Shit—he weren't going to beat my ass."[11] One Saturday night,

Richard's leisurely wait at a New York subway station is interrupted by "two colored boys [who] come running down the steps," his unexplained search and seizure by white men, and his being falsely accused of robbing a nearby store.[12] Despite Richard's insistence on his absence from the scene of the crime—"But *I* wasn't there! Look at me . . . I wasn't *there!*"—the white storeowner identifies him as one of the four thieves: "You black bastards . . . you're all the same."[13] After being handcuffed and taken to the city jail, Richard refuses to sign a confession acknowledging his culpability in the robbery, which earns him a beating from police interrogators that is so severe he can "hardly walk" the next day.[14] Richard is jailed following this incident, but he is eventually found innocent of the robbery and freed. Yet Richard is so shaken by the state's unrestricted power to racially profile, humiliate, criminalize, and punish that he commits suicide the night after his release.

Richard's post-incarceration trauma, as well as the state's violation of his Fourth Amendment and Eighth Amendment rights, is unsettling enough to make one wonder whether this fictional character's plight was a reflection of Baldwin's run-ins with the state.[15] In his essay "Down at the Cross," in *The Fire Next Time*—published a decade after *Go Tell It on the Mountain* was released—Baldwin reveals that Richard's subjection to police aggression was, in fact, semiautobiographical: "When I was ten . . . two policemen amused themselves with frisking me, making comic (and terrifying) speculations concerning my ancestry and sexual prowess, and for good measure, leaving me flat on my back in one of Harlem's empty lots."[16] White policemen habitually harassed Baldwin during his formative years in New York City, where, over the past six decades, racialized police intimidation and police brutality have remained notorious practices—as the cases of Johnson Hinton, George Whitmore Jr., Eleanor Bumpurs, Yvonne Smallwood, Tracy Brock, Abner Louima, Amadou Diallo, Marcus Ferguson, Andre Burgess, and Eric Garner have all shown us.

Richard's story, though, does more than illustrate Baldwin's interrogation of police violence, racial bias, and racialized prisoner abuse. Richard's story also bespeaks Baldwin's skill with using fiction in the service of justice advocacy. By representing prisoner abuse in *Go Tell It on the Mountain* as a violation of civil/human rights interconnected with police aggression, Baldwin participates in a specific literary tradition in which authors relate the unjust treatment of people behind bars to the practice of unprosecuted state violence in so-called free society.

H. Bruce Franklin reminds us that this tradition began in the midnineteenth century when imprisoned writers, who had grown largely uninterested in mass-producing confessional narratives and sensationalist crime stories, started writing poems and autobiographical works that linked the routine and unpunished harm to which prison guards subjected them with the ordinariness of police misconduct. These early "political prisoner" writings included poems such as "The Prisoners in Jail," a piece in which white anti-rent activist Mortimer Belden remarks that guards "seize upon prisoners" and "do as they please" while "sheriffs . . . all hell they don't fear . . . bring [men] in guilty if they prove themselves clear."[17]

Richard's testimony of police brutality in *Go Tell It on the Mountain* updates this tradition, as do stories of police intimidation and jailhouse beatings in Baldwin's later fictional works "Going to Meet the Man," *Tell Me How Long the Train's Been Gone*, and *Beale Street*. In these works that Baldwin published throughout the late 1960s and early 1970s, racialized historical context profoundly shapes his representations of state violence. Baldwin frequently alludes to the racial terror so central to the maintenance of white supremacy during the era of slavery to historically contextualize the recurring nature of anti-Black police intimidation and prisoner abuse in late twentieth-century U.S. culture. To take the example of Baldwin's story "Going to Meet the Man" (1965), a white sheriff displays "peculiar excitement" as he unleashes his cattle prod on a jailed Black adolescent who is already wounded. It turns out that this criminalized Black youth is a Civil Rights activist whom Baldwin describes as a "boy roll[ing] around in his own . . . blood . . . as the [sheriff's] prod hit his testicles."[18] The intense pleasure that accompanies this white sheriff's infliction of disciplinary violence on a captive Black male body recalls the attitudes and actions of nineteenth-century slaveholders whose greatest delight often came from experimenting with methods of torture on enslaved men, as Harriet Jacobs reveals unforgettably in her slave narrative, *Incidents in the Life of a Slave Girl* (1861).[19] In Baldwin's novel *Tell Me How Long the Train's Been Gone* (1968), white policemen stop, frisk, and seize without cause two unarmed Black boys—including one who is but ten years old. The elder boy, Caleb, bemoans the futility of taking down the officers' badge numbers by situating the Black youths' contemporary confrontation with racialized police intimidation— particularly the policemen's unquestioned racial bias and near-total impunity—in the context of slavery-era manifestations of white supremacist power (a past he evokes in his reference to "a long time ago"):

> You know a friendly judge? We got money for a lawyer? Somebody they going to *listen* to? You know as well as me they beating on black ass all the time, all the time, man, they get us in that precinct house and make us confess to all kinds of things and sometimes even kill us and don't nobody give a damn. Don't nobody care what happens to a black man. If they didn't need us for work, they'd have killed us all off a long time ago.[20]

Building from this racial-historical interrogation of state violence in *Tell Me How Long,* Baldwin depicts in *Beale Street* the Black girlfriend of a jailed Black man who associates his routine encounters with police intimidation and prisoner abuse with the disciplinary harm meted out on recalcitrant slaves. Throughout the novel, Baldwin's female narrator-protagonist illustrates how a purportedly abolished system of racial terror underlies the state's ordinary (mis)treatment of criminals—and those who are prejudicially labeled as such.

Taking into consideration Baldwin's career-length critique of police intimidation and prisoner abuse, as well as his immersion in the intellectual and cultural production of imprisoned activists, I argue in the sections that follow that Baldwin makes a case for prison abolition in *Beale Street.* Throughout the novel, Baldwin pushes literarily for an end to mass incarceration, state violence, and racist policing by admiringly drawing from the narrative techniques of George Jackson. It is my contention that Jackson's centuries-spanning model of white supremacy as a form of social control—as outlined in *Soledad Brother*—deeply informs narrative development in Baldwin's novel. Jackson conceptualizes his and other Blacks' recurring confrontations with racial profiling, economic exploitation, police violence, and prisoner abuse as constituting "the new slavery, the modern variety of chattel slavery."[21] An inspired Baldwin alludes to Jackson's slavery metaphor to illustrate how police intimidation and prisoner abuse are not aberrations, despite their frequent representation as unusual, isolated incidents in mainstream news media and even human rights discourse. Thus, in *Beale Street* Baldwin reveals how state violence—a seeming deviation in the just administration of punishment in the justice system—is both a racist practice reflective of America's age-old, constitutive logic of white supremacist social control and state power's guised attempt to contain and constrain the corporeal and social movement of Black life more than a hundred years after the legal abolition of slavery.

The Baldwinian Witnessing of the Black Political Prisoner George Jackson

Leeming has called *Beale Street* "Baldwin's prison parable, a fictionalization of his prison concerns during the 1968–73 period."[22] Trudier Harris describes *Beale Street* as "one of the most striking representations of prison experience in African American literature," and Horace Porter reminds us that the novel, "while ostensibly a love story, dramatizes the travesty and inefficiency of the American justice system."[23] Baldwin himself declared that "the key to the book is the [U.S.] prison situation."[24] In light of these observations,

I submit that *Beale Street* offers us Baldwin's most probing look into racial profiling, police impunity, and racialized prisoner abuse. Foregrounding the role of racial bias in the false arrest and abusive incarceration of the Harlemite craftsman Alonzo "Fonny" Hunt, Baldwin's penultimate novel provides provocative commentary on an epoch of political repression and state violence. In a Civil Rights and Black Power Movement era in which the Federal Bureau of Investigation's Counterintelligence Program (COINTELPRO) bent—or, more precisely, broke—the law to systematically criminalize, incarcerate, and exterminate hundreds of Black political activists (many of whom Baldwin knew personally), Baldwin initially conceived of *Beale Street* as a novel about "a black revolutionary in an American jail whose pregnant wife gives birth to their son at the instant [he] is slain."[25] While Fonny, the novel's central Black character, is not affiliated with any of the revolutionary organizations that COINTELPRO targeted, his plight and persona are not far removed from that of the "black revolutionary" who preoccupied Baldwin's original vision for the book.

Fonny is, in fact, regularly targeted by white policemen because of his race, gender, and what Richard Majors and Janet Mancini Billson might call his "cool pose"—his "expressive performance that helps [him] counter stress caused by social oppression and racism," his appropriation of "posing and posturing to communicate power, toughness, detachment, and style."[26] Throughout the novel, Fonny's direct stare into the eyes of law enforcement officers and his accompanying stoic postures can be understood as constituting both a coping mechanism and brazen resistance to the status quo. As Fonny is ceaselessly scrutinized by white policemen on the streets of New York City, his eyes very intentionally convey defiant speech and are, as Harris has argued so superbly, weapons.[27] In the language of the novel's narrator, "Fonny looked straight at [Officer] Bell [and] Bell looked straight ahead. *I'm going to fuck you, boy,* Bell's eyes said. *No you won't,* said Fonny's eyes. *I'm going to get my shit together and haul ass out of here.*"[28] To grasp further the complexity of Fonny's stylized displays of ocular opposition to New York City policemen, we would do well to recall the work of Maurice Wallace on spectragraphia in his award-winning book *Constructing the Black Masculine: Identity and Ideality in African American Men's Literature, 1775–1995.* That is to say, Fonny is best understood as one who is spectragraphically monitored: he is a young Black man who is both seen and unseen through an unrelenting, *racialized* police gaze. Thus, Fonny's ritualized expressions of Black masculinity before state power also frame him—in every sense of the word. On the one hand, Fonny's stinging one-liners and penetrating glare go unnoticed by most New Yorkers because they have no bearing whatsoever on public safety. Yet Fonny's self-assured demeanor becomes punishable at the precise moment that white policemen see it as posing a threat to their unspoken racial superiority. So

Fonny's *perceived* aggression, despite being conveniently and prejudicially invented by law enforcement officers, is codified as transgression. Fonny's *perceived* aggression both captures the attention of white policemen and facilitates his capture. Yet the threat that "cool-posing" Fonny presents to white policemen reveals not Black crime/criminality but, rather, white (male) self-anxiety, which is another phenomenon that Wallace discusses compellingly: "Black men have come to embody the inverse picture necessary for the positive self-portrait of white identity."[29]

As the novel opens, Fonny is described as a "bad nigger" who is known by a no-nonsense, Black revolutionary swagger.[30] In addition to being recognized as a Black man who frequently "raised his fist" and "always . . . stood up," Fonny refuses to be berated by Officer Bell, an unabashedly racist white policeman.[31] Moreover, for Fonny the Harlem ghetto is indeed the police state famously described by the Harlem resident and formerly imprisoned Black freedom fighter Malcolm X.[32] A far cry from peacekeeping civilian protectors, the policemen who patrol Fonny's side of town are combative racial profilers—or, in the words of Tish Rivers, Fonny's wide-eyed, nineteen-year-old Black lover—"the worst cops." When Fonny takes a long walk one evening, for instance, he is watched both by "the cop car parked on the corner, with the two cops in it, [and] other cops swaggering slowly along the sidewalk." "Cool-posing" Fonny's subjection to such intense racialized surveillance bespeaks the policemen's white supremacist reframing of what Michel Foucault has theorized under the rubric of "Panopticism." Fonny frequently confronts a *racialized* panoptic gaze in the novel, so much so that it evokes the ire of Tish after she shares an enjoyable dinner with Fonny at his favorite Spanish restaurant: "There was a patrol car parked across the street from our house."[33]

And yet Fonny is not alone in encountering such routine and racialized police intimidation. As a child, Tish was warned that "the [city] police would come and put [her] in the electric chair." Moreover, Fonny's friend Daniel Carty, a "big, black boy" who is repeatedly arrested on trumped-up charges, remarks that white policemen are "always passing by" his neighborhood in Harlem. The police incessantly circle the block in search of Black bodies they can put away downtown, and, according to Daniel, they achieve a sexualized pleasure—they "com[e] in their pants"—when they manage to do so. Daniel's observation seems a bit overstated, yet readers later discover that Fonny's nemesis, Officer Bell, has murdered a twelve-year-old Black boy and, having escaped legal penalty, "walk[s] the way John Wayne walks, striding out to clean up the universe." It thus comes as no surprise that when Fonny and Tish move into a new neighborhood downtown, Fonny insists that she be especially wary of those policemen who claim to be her guardians: "We live in a nation of pigs and murderers. I'm scared every time you out of my sight."[34]

Fonny's unconcealed disdain for a mostly white police force, and his momentary trip to make a cigarette purchase that takes Tish "out of [his] sight" foreshadow his racially motivated arrest. Fonny becomes the object of Officer Bell's murderous intentions following a public altercation in which an Italian storeowner verbally defends Fonny and onlookers mock Bell. One afternoon while Fonny is "up the street, just around the corner" at a convenience store, Tish, selecting tomatoes at a local market, is sexually assaulted by a "young, greasy Italian punk," a white boy who grabs her buttocks, blocks her path, and refuses to release her arm while demanding that she comply with his repeated sexual advances: "Hey, sweet tomato. *You* know I dig tomatoes."[35] While Tish calls out to the approaching Officer Bell for help, Fonny catches a glimpse of the scene and rescues Tish from the white boy's threats with his fast fists. When Bell arrives on the scene, he bypasses Tish's white male assailant and focuses his energy on accusing Fonny of neglecting the safety of his girlfriend. Moreover, Bell interrogates Fonny before a growing crowd, repeatedly calls him "boy," and assures him that he and the local police will "take [him] down . . . for assault and battery."[36] Suddenly, an Italian storeowner interrupts Bell, recounts with precise detail the sexual assault that Tish suffered at the hands of the white boy, and questions Bell before jeering onlookers: "What would *you* do if a man attacked *your* wife? If you have one."[37] Blushing with shame, Bell attempts to flee the scene. As he leaves, Bell attempts to recover his pride, announcing to Fonny, "Be seeing you around." Fonny's retort, "You may . . . and then again you may not," so enrages the white policeman that he "intend[s] to kill Fonny."[38]

Bell jump-starts this murder plot when he receives word that Victoria Rogers, a young, married Puerto Rican woman, has been raped. Bell immediately accuses Fonny and arrests him. Pending a guilty verdict, Fonny faces the death penalty. Despite testimony from Tish and Daniel that Fonny was with them at the time of the rape, and despite conflicting details in Bell's eyewitness report (curiously, he was the crime's only witness), Rogers's alarming testimony—later revealed to have been coerced by Bell and other white policemen—seems to seal Fonny's fate:

> *Mrs. Victoria Rogers . . . declares that on the evening of March 5, between the hours of eleven and twelve, in the vestibule of her home, she was criminally assaulted by a man she now knows to have been Alonzo Hunt, and was used by the aforesaid Hunt in the most extreme and abominable sexual manner, and forced to undergo the most unimaginable sexual perversions.*[39]

In sum, Fonny's adoption of cool pose and his subjection to the police's racialized panoptic gaze (and, of course, his public framing through racial

stereotypes such as that of the Black brute who lingers in the backdrop of
Victoria Rogers's coerced testimony) leads to his criminalization and abusive
treatment by law enforcement and, later, jail guards.

In his essay on the figure of the embattled craftsman in Baldwin's oeuvre,
Houston Baker goes as far as calling Fonny a "political prisoner."[40] Baker's
reading, the only published essay on *Beale Street* to date to make such a bold
claim, merits careful reconsideration. If we consider Fonny's adoption of
cool pose from the perspective of Officer Bell, we might interpret his unabashed expressions of race pride, his speaking out of turn, and his open
defiance of Bell's state-issued authority as all constituting transgressions of
an unwritten racial law. Concerning this implicit law, Jared Sexton has
argued that from the antebellum era of slave hunting—an era in which white
patrollers pursued alleged runaway or recalcitrant slaves—to policing in the
post–Civil Rights era that is typified by racialized intimidation and premature death, Black people have been racially profiled and expected to
display utter submissiveness before white state power.[41] It is with such a
historical precedent of unchecked racial terror in mind that Bell decides that
Fonny's insubordination necessitates and sanctions his criminalization and
violent treatment by law enforcement, the courts, and even jail guards. Thus,
to resituate Baker's claim alongside Angela Davis's writings on political
repression, Fonny *is* a political prisoner. As Davis points out, while political
prisoners are formally tried for criminal acts, their perceived culpability has
everything to do with how they express their political viewpoints. More to
the point, people like Fonny are arrested, tried, and convicted because they
are belligerent social agitators—because they have "*violated the unwritten
law* which prohibits disturbances and upheavals in the status quo of
exploitation and racism."[42] Davis's point notwithstanding, Fonny is also the
spitting image of the one political prisoner whose life story captivated
Baldwin: George Jackson, the charismatic Black revolutionary who insisted
that he was routinely subjected to state violence because of his race pride,
political beliefs, and perceived aggressiveness.[43]

Baldwin was, in a word, transfixed by Jackson. Baldwin spoke at rallies in
the United States and abroad in support of Jackson's prison liberation
movement, referenced Jackson in his writings, and even compared Jackson's
mother to the mother of Christ.[44] Jackson was a radical social theorist, a
member of the Black Panther Party, and—thanks to the publication of *Soledad
Brother: The Prison Letters of George Jackson* by "the nation's largest publisher
of paperbacks"—one of America's most widely read imprisoned intellectuals.[45]
Jackson's charge at age eighteen as an alleged accomplice in a seventy-dollar
gas-station robbery landed him in prison with an indeterminate sentence of
one year to life. After being introduced to radical philosophy and the Black

Liberation Movement by the imprisoned revolutionary W. L. Nolen, Jackson dedicated his years behind bars to studying African American history and Marx, raising imprisoned men's political consciousness, and fighting an unsubstantiated indictment that he had killed a white prison guard. Interestingly, he was quite familiar with Baldwin, whom he referenced in *Soledad Brother:* "The reactionary, repressive forces presently at work will bring things to such a crisis soon that Baldwin's warning of 'The fire next time' must soon be borne out with all its sinister accompaniments."[46] Following his alleged escape attempt in 1971, Jackson was shot dead by guards at San Quentin prison. Competing narratives emerged regarding the true reasons behind his killing. Baldwin's written response to the tragedy, as Brian Conniff reminds us, would produce "the most frequently cited quote related to Jackson's death."[47] Long before insiders confessed that Jackson's shooting was part of prison guards' "mission to kill George Jackson," Baldwin wrote: "No Black person will ever believe that George Jackson died the way they tell us he did."[48] While Baldwin did not embrace Jackson's Marxist ideology, he was, as Randall Kenan points out, fascinated with Jackson, "so taken with Jackson's writing and his story that he wanted to make a film based on Jackson's life."[49] Baldwin never made the film. Yet his characterization of Fonny Hunt as a Black political prisoner—and, as we shall see, a slave—reflects his serious engagement with Jackson's narrative project in *Soledad Brother.*

"Born a slave in a captive society": Jackson's Slave Metaphor

Baldwin's depiction of Fonny in *Beale Street* is a meditation, at least in part, on Jackson's slave metaphor in *Soledad Brother,* a metaphor that serves as a clarifying illustration of the efficiency with which the U.S. carceral state economically exploits, prejudicially criminalizes, physically abuses, and socially controls Black people. When Jackson, writing from a solitary cell in one of the nation's worst prison systems, calls to mind the historical past of slavery in his work's opening letter, he makes an intervention that is literary and political at one and the same time:

> Blackmen born in the U.S. and fortunate enough to live past the age of eighteen are conditioned to accept the inevitability of prison. For most of us, it simply looms as the next phase in a sequence of humiliations. Being born a slave in a captive society and never experiencing any objective basis for expectation had the effect of preparing me for the progressively traumatic misfortunes that lead so many blackmen to the prison gate. I was prepared for prison. It required only minor psychic adjustments.[50]

From a literary perspective, Jackson consciously alludes to the slave narrative genre by introducing his work as so many enslaved authors began theirs: by asserting "I *was* born," by documenting the reality of his socially neglected birth and human life. Jackson speaks the truth of his aliveness to proponents of institutional power, for to become a published writer while behind bars and thus establish a record of his humanity (as opposed to his criminality) is to declare that he is *not* a systemically silenced and disciplinarily dehumanized slave of the state but a proud practitioner of antipanoptic expressivity, to recall my language from the Introduction. Relatedly, as Tara T. Green aptly noted in *From the Plantation to the Prison*, "Solitary confinement created within Jackson the desire to find his voice in writing. His voice is an expression within the state confinement that challenges the system designed to render prisoners voiceless and powerless."[51]

From a political perspective, Jackson's insistence that he was "born a slave in *a captive society*" makes evident specific ways in which his physical and social mobility have been consistently circumscribed by white supremacist power. Growing up in Chicago's Troop Street Projects in the 1940s, Jackson was the target of relentless acts of racial profiling, the product of segregated schooling, and the inheritor of destitution so severe that stealing was—initially, anyway—his strategy for avoiding starvation. As Dylan Rodríguez points out, Jackson "recognized his own incarceration as the *logical* outcome of a collective plight. The destiny of human expendables, surplus people left to languish under the advance of white-supremacist capital, was death, addiction, unemployment, and mass warehousing or social liquidation."[52] For Jackson, then, economic inequality (represented particularly by Blacks' forced tolerance of underpaid labor, racist hiring practices, and subsequent unemployment), inferior education, police harassment, incarceration, and prisoner abuse all represent phases "in a sequence of humiliations" reserved for this "surplus" population. Prison and the routinized intimidation and abuse that Jackson and any number of men suffer there thus constitute an "inevitability," the result of being read as "a slave" in a white supremacist culture that views certain groups as not only socially inferior but also fundamentally superfluous.

Moreover, like the slave revolt leader Nat Turner he so highly esteemed, Jackson sees himself as a Black man who, by virtue of affirming the possibility of his humanity, is unjustly punished by the state for asserting self-determination against those who reserve those privileges for themselves. Jackson writes, then, not only to attain a voice but also to break free from a repressive social structure—a "captive society" that grooms Black men for prison. In his letters, Jackson often makes this argument in figurative terms, such as, "I don't want to raise any more black slaves."[53]

Jackson's use of slavery as a metaphor for contemporary manifestations of racialized social control defines his carceral aesthetics and distinguishes his writing style. Consider, for instance, Jackson's letter to his attorney, Fay Stender, dated April 17, 1970:

> Chattel slavery is an economic condition which manifests itself in the total loss or absence of self-determination. The new slavery, the modern variety of chattel slavery updated to disguise itself, places the victim in a factory[,] or[,] in the case of most blacks[,] in support roles inside and around the factory system (service trades), working for a wage. However, if work cannot be found in or around the factory complex, today's neoslavery does not allow even for a modicum of food and shelter. You are free—to starve. The sense and meaning of slavery comes through as a result of our ties to the wage. You must have it, without it you would starve or expose yourself to the elements. . . . If you're held in one spot on this earth because of your economic status, it is just the same as being held in one spot because you are the owner's property.[54]

Jackson's discussion of "chattel slavery" here can be traced to an earlier note that he wrote to Stender in which he refers to himself as an "old slave trying to deal with his environment," and to a letter from May 1968 addressed to his mother, Georgia, in which he conceptualizes the constrained social mobility that they and nominally free Blacks endure as a post-slavery chattel condition: "Our change in status from an article of moveable property to untrained misfits on the labor market was not as most think a change to freedom from slavery but merely to a *different kind of slavery*."[55] The excerpt from Jackson's letter to Stender, in other words, reveals a synecdochical dimension to his chattel slavery-as-racialized social control metaphor. The letter shows us how Jackson, by implicitly linking "the new slavery" of Blacks' systemic underemployment, labor exploitation, and job termination to mass-based, racialized criminalization and incarceration (recall that Jackson was imprisoned indefinitely for his alleged complicity in stealing a whopping seventy dollars), circumscribes a historical context broad enough simultaneously to tell his life story and that of many other pre- and post-Emancipation slaves. Jackson makes this point apparent later in the letter when he describes such "neoslavery" in exactly the same terms as he defined "chattel slavery": "Neoslavery is an economic condition, a small knot of men exercising the property rights of their established economic order, organizing and controlling the lifestyle of the slave as if he were in fact property. Succinctly: an economic condition which manifests itself in the total loss or absence of *self*-determination."[56]

By establishing the institution of slavery as his letter collection's narrative framework and thus rendering comprehensible the systemic nature of his and other Blacks' repeated encounters with economic exploitation, under-education, police intimidation, and prisoner abuse, Jackson also makes a political maneuver reminiscent of enslaved autobiographers. He condemns the system (rather than just the people) responsible for his confinement in ways that can expedite its abolishment. Jackson issues an indictment against the entire U.S. carceral state, repeatedly making the case that he has "in-herited a neoslave existence" and is but one "runaway slave"—one of the many fugitives of a centuries-old white supremacist social order—who has been "captured and brought to prison . . . because [he] couldn't adjust" to lingering forms of racist, capitalist plantation humiliation.[57]

But Jackson was, of course, no choirboy. As he confesses at the beginning of *Soledad Brother,* "I could play the criminal aspects of my life down some but then it wouldn't be me. . . . In effect, I lived two lives, the one with my mama and sisters, and the thing on the street."[58] During his formative years, Jackson was truant and often tangled with the police. When Jackson's father transferred his Post Office job to Los Angeles in the hope of giving young Jackson a new start in life, Jackson accumulated a number of robbery convictions, which landed him in the California Youth Authority detention camp.[59] Still, although Jackson's penchant for petty theft was undeniable, this is not what led to his subjection to state violence and indefinite punitive isolation in prison. Jackson's identification with the slave is meant to head off this conclusion to suggest a more primary reason for his abusive incar-ceration—namely, his transgression of unwritten racial laws.

Consider, for instance, why Jackson says he regularly skipped school and thus became an easy target for police who would harass him: he "couldn't adjust" to an unofficial law of "separate and equal." While Jackson grew up in the North where segregation was not legally upheld or militaristically enforced, he was still made to feel the psychic pain of racial isolation during his elementary schooling in the 1940s and 1950s. At the Catholic mission that he attended, Jackson (like his siblings and other Chicago Blacks) was fenced out of a spacious garden that was understood by all as a whites-only zone:

> St. Malachy's was really two schools. There was another school across the street that was more private than ours. "We" played and fought on the corner sidewalks bordering the school. "They" had a large grass-and-tree-studded garden with an eight-foot wrought iron fence bordering it (to keep us out, since it never seemed to keep any of them in when they chose to leave). "They" were all white. . . . The white students' yard was equipped with picnic tables for spring lunches, swings, slides, and other more sophisticated gadgets. . . . For years we had only the very crowded sidewalks and alley behind the school.[60]

As we read Jackson's letters, it becomes hard to distinguish between the version of racial segregation that he confronted in the urban North and the Jim Crow racial caste system that the poet Maya Angelou depicts with similarly disturbing precision as she reflects on her 1940s-era schooling in rural Arkansas in her acclaimed autobiography *I Know Why the Caged Bird Sings* (published a year before the release of Jackson's *Soledad Brother*): "Unlike the white high school, the Lafayette County Training School [for Negroes] distinguished itself by having neither lawn nor hedges, nor tennis court, nor climbing ivy. Its two buildings . . . were set on a dirt hill with no fence to limit either its boundaries or those of bordering farms."[61] Indeed, given the racism implied by St. Malachy's "two schools," Jackson did not see much reason to attend the Catholic mission. The mission resembled more an institution of social control that Jackson "couldn't adjust to" than a site of learning. Interestingly, Jackson relates the police harassment that he suffers as a youth to the racialized isolation that he experiences at St. Malachy's: "I stopped attending school regularly, and started getting picked up by the pigs more often. . . . These pickups were mainly for 'suspicion of' or because I was in the wrong part of town."[62] On more than one of these pickups, Jackson would be subjected to what he called "oak-stick therapeutics"—violent thrashings in which a policeman would "pop [him] behind the ear with the 'oak stick' several times."[63] While Jackson "wasn't caught for breaking any laws" when picked up as truant, he was, on almost every one of these occasions, a victim of unchecked and unpunished police violence.[64] Jackson had become a target for Chicago police largely because he refused to attend a racially segregated school—because, in his language, "aggression on the part of the slave means crime."[65]

A similar situation transpired when Jackson was in prison. Jackson, along with Fleeta Drumgo and John Clutchette, were Black men whom guards at Soledad Prison identified as militant and influential activists. Collectively known as the Soledad Brothers, the three were accused of killing Opie G. Miller, a white guard whose racist views were well known and who, as Rodríguez reminds us, "*assassinated* the widely respected black prison boxing champion, mentor, legal activist, and political organizer W. L. Nolen in January 1970 (as well as black prisoners Cleveland Edwards and Alvin Miller)."[66] On the one hand, Jackson's culpability could legitimately be seen as probable since Nolen was Jackson's first and closest prison comrade. In addition, Jackson was quite candid in expressing his exasperation with the racist attitudes and actions of Soledad guards. For instance, in *Soledad Brother*, Jackson remarked, "The great majority of Soledad pigs are southern migrants" who fail to "stop the many racist attacks; they actively encourage them."[67] Moreover, Jackson was candid in describing the debilitating consequences of this custodial arrangement: "I am very tired of waking up each morning wondering if I will be . . . insulted, humiliated, injured, or even done to the death today."[68] Still, no concrete evidence was ever produced to indicate that Jackson, with the help of Drumgo and Clutchette, had tossed Miller over the third-tier railing of the prison. Jackson, however, was charged with this heinous crime, and before any verdict was reached in the controversial Soledad Brothers trial, prison officials punished him with indefinite solitary confinement and routine beatings.

Unsurprisingly, even in the years before his alleged murder of the white prison guard—years in which Jackson successfully organized a prisoners' liberation movement and spoke up for Black and white comrades who had been victimized by guards—guards singled out Jackson for mistreatment. The journalist Min Yee notes that "a San Quentin guard nearly broke Jackson's kneecap" because Jackson tried to thwart the institution's attempts to torture an imprisoned white man who had spoken up for the rights of Black men in custody.[69] In a letter to his mother dated November 13, 1965, Jackson wrote, "All of the officers here have preconceived notions about my patterns of behavior. Consequently, it is somewhat hard for me to avoid falling under suspicion for almost every misdeed perpetrated by a black."[70] The author and activist Eric Mann, who worked with the Soledad Brothers Defense Committee, points out that Jackson's routine abusive treatment was a tried and tested tool of institutional discipline: "Prison authorities put George through this excruciating torture to make an example of him. . . . It got to a point where [they] were so afraid of George's influence that any black prisoner who gave [him] the black power salute . . . was thrown in the hole."[71]

Aggravated by his relentless revolutionary activities, Soledad prison administrators confined Jackson to a six-by-eight-foot strip cell in the prison's O wing *for years.* There, Jackson was unprotected from wet weather, restricted to washing his hands once every five days, and locked away for all but thirty minutes of a given day.[72] Years of living without regular human contact took a toll on Jackson. All throughout *Soledad Brother,* he writes of this toll: "I am living very badly now and just to stay alive is an ordeal"; "I am holding off the ill effects of the concentration camp as best I can"; "I'm just locked down and forgotten"; "To be alone constantly is to torture normal men."[73] At one point in Jackson's epistolary narrative, the pain of his isolation is disturbingly palpable: "Try to remember how you felt at the most depressing moment of your life, the moment of your deepest dejection. . . . That is how I feel all the time, no matter what my level of consciousness may be, asleep, awake, in between."[74]

Ironically, Jackson's extended periods of isolation, which psychiatrists such as Terry A. Kupers have shown to be responsible for the serious mental disorders of thousands of prisoners, did not isolate him from the realm of indictment.[75] Again the target of prison guards' racially motivated allegations in 1967, Jackson is stunned: "They have accused me of leading something when all the evidence points to the contrary. . . . I never raised my hand against an official. In fact, in all the seven years I've been here I have never attacked an official."[76] In ensuing letters in *Soledad Brother*, Jackson remarks that he was criminalized, harassed, and beaten by guards at Soledad and San Quentin "just because I want[ed] to be my black self, mentally healthy, and because I look[ed] [at] anyone who addresse[d] me in the eye."[77] Moreover, he states that because he, Nolen, Drumgo, Clutchette, and other politically conscious prisoners "attempted to transform the black criminal mentality into a black revolutionary mentality," they were "subjected to years of the most vicious reactionary violence by the state."[78] Routine beatings aside, Jackson spent seven of his ten years of imprisonment in solitary confinement and confronted guards who frequently destroyed his personal effects, threw human waste in his cell, and pitted him against imprisoned white men (who were also armed) purely for their own entertainment. Racial segregation within the prison only intensified Jackson's struggles behind bars, as Dan Berger has noted: "Jackson inhabited a world even more sharply polarized by race than the neighborhoods he had once called home. The few sanctioned social spaces inside the prison were segregated, and white prisoners and guards regularly attacked black prisoners."[79]

Jackson returned in his later letters to the slave metaphor that he employed at the opening of *Soledad Brother* as a way of situating his confrontations with false indictment, political repression, and state violence in racialized historical context. Beyond describing his subjection to guards' attacks with a plantation lexicon—"I have felt the sting of the knout"; "The lash affects me for sure"—Jackson evoked the memory of the Transatlantic Slave Trade in his letters:[80]

> My recall is nearly perfect, time has faded nothing. I recall the first kidnap. I've lived through the [middle] passage, died on the passage, *lain in the unmarked shallow graves of the millions who fertilized Amerikan soil with their corpses; cotton and corn growing out of my chest.* . . . I feel all that they ever felt, but double. I can't help it; there are too many things to remind me of the 23½ hours [a day] that I'm in this cell. Not ten minutes pass without a reminder.[81]

Jackson's internalization of the slave's physical and psychological wounding is gripping—and painful. In particular, his sustained attention to the relationship between routinized punishment ("the lash affects me for sure") and the Black captive body recalls the descriptions of beatings in the autobiographical narratives of formerly enslaved men and women such as Frederick Douglass, William Wells Brown, Harriet Jacobs, and Elizabeth

Keckley. On the one hand, given the kind of literature that Jackson pored over—texts that chronicled the routine suffering and violently punished resistance of enslaved persons such as W.E.B. Du Bois's *The Souls of Black Folk*, Philip Foner's *Frederick Douglass: A Biography*, and Herbert Aptheker's *Documentary History of the Negro People in the United States*—the appearance of the brutalized slave in Jackson's letters is, arguably, quite foreseeable.[82] Yet the racialized violence and guards' impunity that surround Jackson's bodily affliction make the comparisons of his abusive confinement to the common treatment of enslaved persons anything but hyperbole.

I am arguing that Jackson's reference here particularly to the slave's tacit expendability and unattainable restitution in the "Amerikan" judicial system (note Jackson's satiric, Ku Klux Klan–allusive spelling of "American")—"I've . . . lain in the unmarked shallow graves of millions who fertilized Amerikan soil with their corpses; cotton and corn growing out of my chest"—renders comprehensible the profound *systemization* of his victimization. Prison administrators, after all, frequently labeled Jackson expendable, as the following Soledad official's report makes evident: "As we are trying to make room for South Facility inmates, [Jackson] should be considered *expendable* on the basis of his record here and the circumstances of his transfer."[83] The deposition of Allan Mancino, a white man who was also imprisoned at the facility and had loose ties to a white supremacist prison gang, makes plain the reality of Jackson's expendability in the eyes of white Soledad prison guards: "[Captain Moody] . . . *asked me directly if I would kill George Jackson.* He said he did not want another Eldridge Cleaver [here]."[84] Later in *Soledad Brother*, Jackson writes that just as the slave lived and died under the unmediated authority of an owner who would "hold it in one square yard of the earth's surface [and] . . . beat it, work it, maim it, fuck it, [and] kill it," the unbridled discretion afforded contemporary prison guards facilitated their holding of imprisoned people "in one spot" where they "beat and maim us" [and] even "murder us and call it justifiable homicide."[85] Thus, for Jackson, the tacit expendability of the racialized prisoner, guards' use of violence as a social control strategy, and the near-total impunity afforded offending officers all represent vestiges of slavery's system of discipline and punishment in the contemporary criminal justice system.

Jackson's slavery metaphor elucidates how prisoner abuse in the California prison system in which he was tormented was not aberrant but reflective of an age-old practice of racialized social control, as the critical prison studies scholar Joy James has observed: "The aim of the abuse [was] the mental and physical deterioration and, ultimately, annihilation of 'deviant' bodies—particularly black bodies in resistance to the prison structure."[86] The prison system's culpability in racializing and institutionalizing prisoner abuse has now been substantiated by extensive evidence revealing that Jackson was not alone in his subjection to unchecked physical and psychic harm at Soledad and other California facilities. After excavating prison records, formal inspection reports, stories from imprisoned men's family members, and the men's own testimonies, outside investigators have discovered that hundreds of men imprisoned at Soledad confronted guards' racial slurs; had their food contaminated with glass, urine, and fecal matter; and were coerced to engage in guard-staged racial fights.[87] By cultivating an atmosphere of perpetual violence, confusion, and fear, prison employees at Soledad and San Quentin *systematically* subdued "deviant" or otherwise expendable Black bodies. Jackson's ability to frame the disciplinary nature of such abuse in the racialized historical context of slavery, as well as his allusion to the slave in his discussions of Blacks' repeated encounters with economic exploitation and police harassment in free society, profoundly shape Baldwin's characterization of Fonny Hunt as a prisoner-slave.

From Jackson's "New Slavery" to Baldwin's "Bad Nigger" Prisoner-Slave

> I looked around the subway car. It was a little like the drawing I had seen of slave ships. Of course, they hadn't had newspapers on the slave ships, hadn't needed them yet; but, as concerned space (and also, perhaps, as concerned intention) the principle was exactly the same.
>
> —TISH, *BEALE STREET*

In *Beale Street*, as in Jackson's prison letters, "slave" is anything but a convenient indexical term for unquantifiable Black bodily affliction. By using the word "slave" in *Beale Street*, Baldwin situates contemporary scenes of Black economic exploitation and racialized state violence in the historical context of slavery. Inspired by *Soledad Brother,* Baldwin fundamentally uses the term "slave" to register historical continuities between past and present forms of state-enforced Black deprivation and social immobility. As Lynn Orilla Scott notes in her reading of Baldwin's novel, Tish, an impoverished Black teen growing up in a cramped Harlem ghetto, should be understood as "historicizing the present to suggest the continuity of oppression in black life" when, reflecting on her sole means of transportation, she compares the New York subway to slave ships.[88] It is my contention that Baldwin also uses the term "slave" to describe Fonny's encounters with racial profiling, police intimidation, and prisoner abuse in the novel. By comparing Fonny to a recalcitrant slave, Baldwin builds on Jackson's "neoslavery" conception of racialized social control: Baldwin's figurative engagement with the rebellious, antebellum-era bondman brings to light how racialized state violence becomes a predictable outcome of Black resistance to the state's *endemic* racism rather than a forgivable response of law enforcement officers to allegedly incorrigible Black men and boys.

In the first section of *Beale Street*, Baldwin's narrator, Tish, calls to mind the social control–based schooling experience that the neo-slave George Jackson chronicles in *Soledad Brother*. Tish describes Fonny's former vocational school as a place where Harlem's disadvantaged adolescents are corralled, ordered around, and taught "to be slaves."[89] Presumed by those who run the school to be "dumb," Fonny and his classmates come to understand themselves as expendable as teachers and staff direct them to "work with their hands" for hours on end and make "useless things" that "nobody's ever gonna buy."[90] The school, fittingly described by Scott as "an institution of social control," is too much for Fonny: Tish comments that "Fonny didn't go for it *at all*."[91] He is already one of those "kids [who] had been told they weren't worth shit" from birth, so when school administrators make workhorses of Fonny and other impoverished Black teens so "they don't get smart," Fonny sees them as training him and his ghettoized peers to continue mindlessly down a path of economic exploitation.[92] Accordingly—to recall Tish's language— Fonny refuses to be a slave.

As Brady Thomas Heiner and Ariana Mangual have observed, "The school in communities of color [often] functions as a repressive apparatus of the State; it operates to supply bodies to the prison industrial complex. . . . The goal of these institutions is to produce subjects [who] will readily accept their exploitation in the economic system."[93] Incensed by the "repressive apparatus of the State" that his vocational school represents, Fonny drops out, but not without making a radical political statement on his way out the door. During his last week at the school, Fonny steals "most of the wood from the woodshop" to begin a career as a craftsman; he tactically resists institutional exploitation by taking from those in power to empower himself.[94] While Fonny is not charged for theft, the oppositional politics that precipitated his act of stealing—what Tish calls Fonny's "passion"—makes him a marked man:

> Fonny had found something that he could do, that he wanted to do, and this saved him from the death that was waiting to overtake the children of our age. . . . That same passion which saved Fonny got him into trouble and put him in jail. For, you see, he had found his center, his own center, inside him: and it showed. He wasn't anybody's nigger. And that's a crime, in this fucking free country. You're suppose to be *somebody*'s nigger. And if you're nobody's nigger, you're a bad nigger: and that's what the cops decided when Fonny moved downtown.[95]

Fonny's assertion of race pride and self-determination at the school and in a city that his father describes as being "in the hands of white men" marks him as a "bad nigger" and is, in and of itself, an offense.[96] Tish is thus accurate in her assessment that it will be only a matter of time before Fonny will get "into trouble" officially and wind up "in jail." Jackson, in *Soledad Brother*, is the archetypical recalcitrant slave who is born into "a captive society" and taken to prison because he cannot adjust to a "modern variety of chattel slavery"; likewise, the more frequently Fonny-the-"bad nigger" resists state initiatives to make him into a "slave," the more likely is his brutal castigation by the forces of a white supremacist police state.[97]

Wrongful incarceration is, in fact, Fonny's exemplary punishment—his most fundamental experience of prisoner abuse. Officer Bell, the police department, the prosecution, the courts, and the jail guards work together, in a systematic manner, to ensure that Fonny will fall to his knees before the state and white civil society. In light of Officer Bell's earlier threat to Fonny— "*I'm going to fuck you, boy*"—Trudier Harris describes the state's calculated incrimination of Fonny as "symbolic rape," as Bell "us[ing] the system to 'fuck' [Fonny]."[98] Bell launches an accusation of rape against Fonny and orchestrates false testimony through Victoria Rogers. Law enforcement officers then make sure that Fonny is the only Black male in a police lineup after they hear that Rogers was allegedly raped by a young African American man. When news leaks out that Fonny's Black friend Daniel will provide the defense with exculpatory evidence, the district attorney's office indicts Daniel on trumped-up charges and ensures that he is "held incommunicado" and beaten senseless by prison guards.[99] Then Fonny's bail is set so high that his impoverished Black father takes to stealing to get him released and ultimately commits suicide. Finally, when Fonny is singled out for sexual abuse at the Manhattan Detention Center (better known as the Tombs), his resistance earns him time in solitary, as well as regular beatings from guards.

By the novel's end, it is clear that Officer Bell has launched a felony accusation against Fonny not because of his genuine concern about Rogers's rape but because Fonny refused to reply "yes, sir" when Bell called him "boy" and because Fonny publicly shamed him—a white male authority—when the policeman bid him a foreboding farewell. The summation of Fonny's plight by Ernestine, Tish's sharp-tongued older sister, speaks directly to the prejudicial nature of his incrimination: "If Fonny were white, it wouldn't be a case at all."[100] Fonny is made an example of by Bell and the state because— as in the case of the vocational/plantation school—he refuses to be a slave; he refuses to submit to an unwritten law of racialized social control. Fonny's indefinite solitary confinement and jailhouse beatings are thus predictable— not aberrant—occurrences. They result from Fonny's fundamental rejection of a system of racial subjugation that was purportedly abolished with the passing of the Thirteenth Amendment in 1865. This is why, near the end of *Beale Street*, Tish relates Fonny's subjection to indefinite solitary confinement with striking matter-of-factness: "[Fonny] is not here for anything he has done. . . . He is placed in solitary for refusing to be raped. He loses a tooth, again, and almost loses an eye. . . . He is fighting for his life. . . . He [is] so skinny; he [is] so bruised: I almost cried out."[101] For Tish, Fonny's predicament is saddening but not at all surprising. In truth, she has told much of the story of Fonny's plight when she first brings it up on the fourth page of the novel: "He's very proud, and . . . that's the biggest reason he's in jail."[102]

Fonny's assertion of race pride and self-determination is the root cause of his routine torment in jail. Like Jackson's refusal to follow an unwritten racial law of Black submissiveness to white supremacist power in free society and behind bars, Fonny's resistance of prisoner-on-prisoner rape is not interpreted by jail administrators as mere self-defense. Rather, they read his defiance as out-and-out noncompliance with their agenda of racialized social control—and thus, grounds for further brutalization. As revealed in a tearful testimony offered by Daniel, the act of rape among jailed and imprisoned male populations—an act that the legal scholar Kim Shayo Buchanan identifies as reflecting "institutional actors [who] condone and legitimize sexual abuse"—is often a tool of racial degradation.[103] Buchanan's point becomes particularly lucid in *Beale Street* when Tish recounts how Daniel processes his witnessing and experience of prisoner-on-prisoner rape: "[Daniel] was crying. He was talking again, about his time in prison. He had seen nine men rape one boy: and *he* had been raped. He would never, never again be the Daniel he had been."[104] A victim of both wrongful conviction and institutionalized rape, Daniel tells Fonny that jail guards' and administrators' feigned ignorance of his sexual victimization was their way to reinforce racial hierarchy behind bars: "They were just playing with me, man, because they could. . . . They can do with you what they want. *Whatever they want.* And they dogs, man. I really found out, in the slammer, what Malcolm [X] . . . was talking about. The white man's got to be the devil. He sure ain't a man. . . . The *worst* thing—is that they can make you so fucking *scared*. Scared, man. *Scared*."[105]

Ultimately, like Jackson's acts of resistance, Fonny's opposition to the jail's attempts to break him leaves him among the most damnable of Black captives in a white supremacist society. He is yet another twentieth-century Nat Turner, yet another revolutionary whose unabashed expressions of Blackness and liberationist struggle make him vulnerable to both state-sanctioned violence and premature death. Thus, through Fonny, Baldwin helps us to see how Black men come to be expendable in the eyes of the law and how easily state officials can cripple Black men who challenge their perceived racial superiority. The association that Baldwin makes between Fonny-as-"bad nigger"/political prisoner-slave and Jackson as archetypical recalcitrant slave presents an incisive critique of a U.S. criminal justice system and nation plagued by a long, violent history of white supremacist social control.

Yet Baldwin's allusion to the slave throughout *Beale Street* also offers us a critical lens through which to decipher the radical political sensibilities of Tish, the novel's most developed Black female character, who consistently resists the state's enforcement of racial terror and gendered social control against her. The intersection of racism and sexism in the administration of discipline and punishment is a subject that I take up at length in my examination of Toni Morrison's novel *Beloved* in the next chapter. But for now, we must remember that Tish, *Beale Street*'s narrator-protagonist, is a young Black woman who both relates and *relates to* Fonny's confrontations with the New York City police. Tish, like Fonny, is targeted by a white policeman who subjects her to unmediated intimidation and unpunished bodily harm because she contests his presumed racial authority. Unlike Fonny's opposition, though, Tish's struggles against police aggression are also overtly sexualized.

Tish's unprosecuted assailant is, of course, Officer Bell. He remembers Tish as not only Fonny's lover but also the outspoken co-conspirator in his own moment of greatest public humiliation: Tish, after all, interrupted Bell during his interrogation of Fonny by declaring that Fonny was "not a boy, Officer," just before the Italian storeowner disparaged Bell's protective abilities as a policeman and as a husband.[106] In retaliation, Bell often makes a point of sending Tish his most reproachful and lustful looks when he is out walking the beat: "After that day at the vegetable stand, I saw Bell everywhere, and all the time. . . . Sometimes I was with Fonny when I crossed Bell's path, sometimes I was alone. . . . When I was alone, [Bell's] eyes clawed me like a cat's claws, raked me like a rake."[107]

One evening leading up to his arrest of Fonny, Bell stalks Tish on a city street. Tish presumes that her petty shoplifting has made her the object of Bell's intense policing. But she quickly gathers that Bell's surreptitious patrolling has everything to do with his desire to remind her of his and the state's agenda to deal a punitive deathblow to Fonny *and* her for openly challenging his unwritten racial authority as a white policeman. After declining Bell's disingenuous offer of help to carry her package, Tish turns, only to have Bell, much like the Italian boy who had hunted her down weeks earlier, block her path and sexually assault her:

> I tried to keep moving, but he was standing in my way. . . . I can still see us on that hurrying, crowded twilight avenue, me with my package and my handbag, staring at him, he staring at me. I was suddenly his:

a desolation entered me which I had never felt before. *I watched his eyes, his moist, boyish, despairing lips, and felt his sex stiffening against me.* "I ain't a bad guy," he said. "Tell your friend."[108]

Ever the verbal ironist, Bell later remarks that Fonny and Tish "ain't got to be afraid" of him, yet the very point of his act of sexual harassment of Tish is to strike disciplinary fear into her heart and Fonny's.[109] Bell means to avenge Tish and Fonny's checking of his unspoken racial authority by intimidating Tish in a distinctly gendered way. The racial-historical precedent for Bell's attempts to neutralize the political praxis of a recalcitrant Black man through unmediated sexual intimidation of that man's female comrade is slavery.

When we recall Baldwin's Jackson-inspired reframing of Fonny as recalcitrant slave throughout *Beale Street*, Bell becomes a more contemporary version of the slave master figure that Davis examined in "Reflections on the Black Woman's Role in the Community of Slaves," an essay she published while she was being held as a political prisoner. In it, Davis argues that the plantation's most feared white male authority was often most affronted by the potential threat that enslaved Black women posed to him in their role as housekeepers, for their conceivable duplicity in meal preparation (e.g., poisoning food) and home maintenance (e.g., burning the house down) not only could prove lethal to members of the enslaving class but could also inspire their insurgent Black male counterparts toward an all-out slave rebellion. Davis makes the case that beyond enforcing his control over Black women's sexuality and reproductive autonomy, the master's rape of enslaved women was a tool of terror intended both to reinforce their purportedly "natural" place of racial and gendered inferiority and to wound the masculinist pride and resistance sensibilities of the plantation's enslaved men:

> In its political contours, the rape of the black woman was not exclusively an attack upon her. . . . In launching the sexual war on the woman, the master would not only assert his sovereignty over a critically important figure of the slave community, he would also be aiming a blow against the black man. . . . [T]he master hoped that once the black man was struck by his manifest inability to rescue his women from sexual assaults of the master, he would begin to experience deep-seated doubts about his ability to resist at all.[110]

In his sexual assault of Tish, which, of course, goes unpunished, Bell recovers this strategy of gendered social control and racial-political repression. Bell, the twentieth-century version of the slave master analyzed by Davis, subjects Tish to the same sexualized racial terror that enslaved women encountered during the antebellum era when white men sought simultaneously to discipline Black women and Black men who they deemed recalcitrant. Tish, like Fonny, is thus a contemporary slave, although Baldwin does not explicitly use the term "slave" to describe her. Tish's characterization as slave is traceable to the Jackson-inspired slave metaphor that frames Baldwin's construction of Fonny's plight and to Baldwin's statement of gratitude to Davis—whom he praised in "An Open Letter to My Sister, Angela Davis" before *Beale Street* was published—for helping him begin "to apprehend . . . of the uses to which we could put the experience of the slave."[111]

And yet it is Tish and Fonny's collective resistance of what Jackson and Davis reveal to be the state's slavery-era tools of racial terror that Baldwin emphasizes in *Beale Street*. The first-person storytelling of state violence that Baldwin employs through Tish as narrator makes apparent his use of fiction to affirm the humanity and amplify the political-intellectual voices of all people who are targeted and subjected to stop-and-frisk, racial profiling, police brutality, wrongful conviction, discriminatory sentencing, and racialized prisoner abuse. This point becomes evident first in how Tish testifies about Officer Bell's act of sexual assault. There is no third-person omniscient narrator, justice advocate, or sympathetic minor character who recounts what Tish suffers. Tish herself testifies. Tish tells readers her own story of Bell's abusive treatment—and her resistance. When Bell remarks to Tish, after sexually assaulting her, that she needs to tell Fonny not to be afraid of him, she emphasizes how she uses her voice and mind to reclaim her body. Tish tells us that she replies a defiant "I'm not afraid" and a dismissive "good-night" to Bell; then, taking advantage of a "hurrying, crowded twilight avenue," she darts past him. Moreover, Tish reveals, "I blotted [the act of sexual assault] out of my mind."[112] Because Baldwin clearly privileges Tish's narrative point of view throughout *Beale Street*, she can be understood as a victim of police violence who is not a victim only. That is, while she is not denying the fact of her victimization, Tish does not reduce her testimony to the experience of being victimized. She highlights her verbal dexterity when Bell confronts her, as well as her preservation of bodily integrity. Tish thus conveys to readers the reality of Bell's act of sexual assault and the reality of her resistance to it. To recall my language from the Introduction, Tish shows herself to be a knowledgeable practitioner of antipanoptic expressivity.

Tish is careful to do the same in her relation of Fonny's encounters with police intimidation and racialized prisoner abuse. At the beginning of the novel, reflecting on Fonny's wrongful incrimination and subjection to state-sanctioned rape at the Tombs jail, she tells readers, "I'm not ashamed of Fonny. If anything, I'm proud. He's a man. You can tell by the way he's taken this shit that he's a man."[113] Tish concludes the novel by emphasizing how Fonny, whistling as he works on one of his wood sculptures, remains mentally free despite being physically confined, routinely beaten by jail guards, and tried for a crime that he did not commit: "They beat him up, but they didn't beat him. He's beautiful."[114] Moreover, in a move that calls to mind Jackson's practice of writing letters to family while imprisoned, Tish draws attention to how Fonny focuses on his enduring connection with human life even while he is confined to a dehumanizing jail environment where his attempts to build community and maintain meaningful relationships are systemically constrained. Tish highlights, for instance, that Fonny reads the books she has given him, sketches on the paper she brings him during her jail visits, greets and bids her farewell by raising his fist in a Black Power salute, and projects a hopeful demeanor when they discuss the expanding size of their unborn child. She observes that, for Fonny, "the growth of [our] baby is connected with his determination to be free."[115]

Baldwin's narrator Tish thus teaches us the critical importance of conceptualizing victims of police aggression and prisoner abuse as human beings and critical thinkers. At one level, Tish reveals, through the very existence of her narrative on anti-Black state violence in New York City (which constitutes the entirety of the novel), the frequently unacknowledged presence and significance of her voice and humanity as victim, survivor, and empathetic witness of police intimidation. At another level, though, Tish shows, through her use of Jackson's recalcitrant slave metaphor, the incisive social critique that even the best-intentioned human rights advocates overlook or delete in their desire to cast victims of state violence as desperately needing help. As with the characters in the late twentieth-century African American novels that I examine in ensuing chapters, Tish, by refusing to reduce her accounts of racialized state violence to the fact of Blacks' systemic victimization, wrests those accounts from the lens of objectification that so often characterizes human rights literature. Tish infuses herself and Fonny with the vitality of subjective experience and antipanoptic expressivity. In the end, then, Baldwin's narrative technique in *Beale Street* demonstrates that remarkable method of witnessing that he preached and practiced throughout his life: "To know how justice is administered in a country . . . one goes to the unprotected—those, precisely, who need the law's protection most!—and *listens* to their testimony."[116]

Conclusion: Baldwin's Tish and Survival Testimony

With the important exceptions of independent news-media discourse and We Charge Genocide—an initiative that Chicago residents describe as "a grassroots, inter-generational effort to center the voices and experiences of young people most targeted by police" in their city—most extended narratives on police intimidation in the United States during the past two decades (especially those that focus on the New York City Police Department) have appeared in special reports published within the field of human rights literature.[117] These reports include Amnesty International's *United States of America: Police Brutality and Excessive Force in the New York City Police Department*, Human Rights Watch's *Shielded from Justice: Police Brutality and Accountability in the United States*, and the United Nations' *In the Shadows of Terror: Persistent Police Brutality and Abuses of People of Color in the United States*.[118] On the one hand, I applaud the authors of these reports. Their detailed coverage of state violence helps to raise public consciousness about subject matter that sorely needs widespread attention. By reconstructing hundreds of stories of police brutality from investigations and trial records from the 1980s–2000s, the reports have revealed the disturbing ordinariness of police misconduct in dozens of U.S. cities, including New York, Los Angeles, Philadelphia, Chicago, and Detroit. Their authors also pay careful attention to the frequent racialization of police aggression and make evident the near-total impunity that the state grants to law enforcement officers who beat, choke, shoot, torture, and sexually assault alleged criminals or suspects. Consider, for instance, the following passage from the Amnesty International report:

> The overwhelming majority of victims in many areas are members of racial or ethnic minorities, while most police departments remain predominantly white. Relations between the police and members of minority communities—especially young black and Latino males in inner city areas—are often tense, and racial bias is reported or indicated as a factor in many instances of police brutality. . . . The disciplinary sanctions imposed on officers found guilty of brutality are frequently inadequate, and officers are rarely prosecuted for excessive force. The "code of silence"—in which officers fail to report brutality or cover up abuses—commands widespread loyalty, contributing to a climate of impunity. Although there has been pressure on police departments to become more publicly accountable in recent years through independent oversight mechanisms, these remain inadequate or wholly absent in many areas.[119]

This passage alone demonstrates the important justice system critique that these advocacy reports perform. The authors very explicitly make the case that racial bias, the lenient punishment of offending officers, and the near-nonexistence of effective "independent oversight mechanisms" have created a "climate of impunity" that is so far-reaching that police violence should be understood not as an aberration but as a tried-and-tested practice of racialized social control.

Still, despite the vital social commentary that the authors of these reports provide, they tend to emphasize the state-sanctioned harm that criminalized people of color face at the expense of the illuminating testimonial narratives they tell about enduring, surviving, critiquing, resisting, and creatively organizing against state violence. This is not a criticism of these authors' reports so much as it is my candid observation regarding the representational hindrances that victims of state violence encounter because of conventions specific to the field of human rights literature. As Kay Schafer and Sidonie Smith discuss in *Human Rights and Narrated Lives*, human rights reporters often trim victims' testimony or narrate it using a third-person point of view to make its condemnatory content appear legitimate and to establish affective appeal for victims with an audience of prospective justice advocates:

> Official reports strategically deploy personal testimony to achieve political ends. . . . Victim testimony is often thematized in different sections of a report, or juxtaposed against perpetrator testimony, or segmented to document specific human rights violations. Thus, the voice, structure, style, intentions, and ownership of an individual story can be appropriated to and subordinated by the larger intentions of the reporting commission.[120]

I argue that because of their impetus to represent "victim testimony" of police misconduct in ways that reflect the "larger intentions of the reporting commission," these well-meaning reporters—even as they illuminate how state violence functions as a racialized social control practice—ironically reinforce a condition that I described in the Introduction as the dispossession of the state violence sufferer's voice.

Despite their laudable intentions, these reporters recover a style of representing victimization within a constricting framework continuous with the narratological practices of the antebellum era. In the mid-nineteenth century, white antislavery activists held abolitionist rallies in which they would attempt to move audiences to advocate for the end of slavery by exhibiting the corporeal injury of formerly enslaved men and women. These northern white abolitionists did not honor the testimonial voices of slavery's survivors. They did not consider whether these men and women desired to speak for themselves and thus critically interpret their lives and wounds in the context of their own personal experiences, their resistance philosophies, or the racial terror of the slave plantation. In an essay titled "Scene . . . Not Heard," Houston Baker expounds on such representational punitiveness, reconceiving the abolitionist rally as a "scene of violence" in which white antislavery activists ironically repressed the expression of "slave truth":[121]

The slave—even when he or she is a "fugitive" from southern violence—is expected to remain *silent*. At northern abolitionist rallies . . .
the fugitive becomes the "Negro exhibit." She silently turns her naked
back to the audience in order to display the stripes inflicted by the
southern overseer's whip. Blacks in white-abolitionist employ were
required always to earn the right—by silent display—to tell their
stories. And even when blacks were permitted to tell their stories, the
interpretation of their narratives—no matter how effective a slave's
oratory—was the exclusive prerogative of their white-abolitionist
employers.[122]

It is against this particular tradition of representational punitiveness—one
that I argue is still very much with us today in the state violence–storytelling
practices that we see in the field of human rights literature—that *Beale Street*
evinces its radical utility.

In *Beale Street*, the two characters Baldwin depicts as slaves of a white
supremacist police state—Tish and Fonny—possess an unmediated antipanoptic expressivity. Their subjection to state violence is never once chan-
neled through the voice of a well-meaning justice advocate—not even, for
instance, through the voice of the novel's socially conscious white lawyer, Mr.
Hayward. Because Baldwin foregrounds the testimonial narrative production
of a young Black woman (Tish) who has witnessed anti-Black state violence
and endured and resisted it personally, he makes evident how victims of
police aggression and prisoner abuse cultivate their own discourse of cultural
critique and reclaim their abused bodies. Although she is a fictionalized
survivor of state violence, Baldwin's Tish reveals three points that are
understated or entirely excluded from the cited human rights reports on
victims of state violence: (1) racial profiling and unchecked police aggression
are racialized social control practices that operate on a historical continuum
with the disciplinary violence to which slave masters subjected enslaved
people; (2) Black women—not just young Black men—are white policemen's
recurring targets for racial and sexual intimidation; and (3) despite the
relative underrepresentation of their subjection to police brutality in the
mainstream news media and even scholarly discourse, Black women often
use narrative as a way to combat state violence, as can be seen recently in the
emergence of #SayHerName, a gender-inclusive racial justice movement that
illuminates the systemic nature of police violence against Black women.[123]

First, as Tish uses the recalcitrant slave metaphor to describe Fonny's
victimization by the police, she is developing a sophisticated discourse of
cultural critique—a discourse that offers a racial-historical lens through
which readers can view the routine confrontations that she and Fonny

endure with Bell and other New York City law enforcement officers. Put simply, Tish casts Blacks' acts of resistance against police intimidation and prisoner abuse in the novel as age-old scenes of enslaved people's opposition to antebellum-era terror, restaged scenes of insurgency that find their precedent in the historical experience of slavery. Tish's pedagogical turn to the slave past reflects a narratological trend that emerges not in human rights reportage on police brutality but in autobiographical writings on neo-slavery in the justice system published in the past four decades by iconic Black imprisoned intellectuals such as George Jackson, Angela Y. Davis, Assata Shakur, Mumia Abu-Jamal, and Robert Hillary King. In other words, through his character Tish, Baldwin shines a light on a literary practice in the contemporary prison that would continue to develop in the years following the publication of *Beale Street* and illuminates anti-Black state violence as reflecting not an aberration but, rather, a constitutive element of the state's long-standing commitment to racialized social control.

Let me also emphasize that, by privileging Tish's viewpoint, Baldwin makes evident a literary practice that figures prominently among writers confined in contemporary U.S. women's jails and prisons. What I examine under the rubric of *survival testimony* in Chapter 2 is a narrative in which women who survive sexualized state violence expose the disciplinary nature of such violence in their own voices to indict the male supremacist systems of control that are responsible for their harm and to reclaim their abused bodies. Baldwin portrays Tish as a practitioner of survival testimony, for beyond illustrating the racial terror and gendered social control agendas that undergird the police intimidation that she endures (a point that some human rights reporters convey through their stories about female victims of state violence), he also depicts her as exuding a testimonial sensibility that anticipates the antipanoptic expressivity of Black female characters in the fiction of Octavia Butler, Toni Morrison, Sherley Anne Williams, and J. California Cooper. The novel's emphasis, that is to say, is on Tish's radical vocality, on her unrelenting commitment to make known the unforeseeable bodily reclamation and desired community that systemically silenced women have achieved since the era of slavery by speaking truth to proponents of unchecked white supremacist and male supremacist power.

In sum, it is worth remembering that when Fonny first encounters police intimidation in Baldwin's novel, it is Tish who interrupts Officer Bell in an attempt to help Fonny reclaim his body. It is Tish who places her body between Fonny's and Bell's before declaring to the white policeman that Fonny is "not a boy."[124] It is Tish who retorts to Officer Bell that she is "not afraid" of him while keeping her body from his reach.[125] It is Tish who uses words to honor the assaulted body and humanity of her beloved Fonny as he routinely confronts state violence: "[Fonny] hates it [in jail], you can see that.

And he should. But he's very strong. And he's doing a lot of reading and studying. . . . Fonny is working on the wood, on the stone, whistling, smiling."[126] Baldwin's decision to foreground Tish's voice and resistance thus shows us the difference that engaging contemporary African American neo-abolitionist novels can make in our conceptualization of people who, like Tish and Fonny, are subjected to the racist machinery of the criminal justice system, on the one hand, and, on the other, actively immersed in speaking their own truths to institutional power. While human rights reporters generally truncate testimony by victims of state violence, following narrative conventions in their field, Baldwin, an empathetic witness, helps readers to see and to hear these victims as survivors—as living, breathing, justice-seeking critical thinkers who use the narrative form of testimony to combat their carceral condition and reclaim their bodies. In the next chapter, I consider the far-reaching implications of Baldwin's *Beale Street* and other neo-abolitionist novels that privilege the testimonial perspectives of Black female characters who are confined to carceral environments governed by both racial terror and institutionalized sexual violence.

2

Middle Passage Reinstated

Whispers from the Women's Prison
in Morrison's Beloved

Eighteen seventy-four and whitefolks were still on the loose. Whole towns wiped clean of Negroes; eighty-seven lynchings in one year alone in Kentucky . . . *black women raped by the crew.*[1]

It is unchecked sexual violence that most fundamentally circumscribes the carceral lives of Black women and girls who appear in Toni Morrison's contemporary narrative of slavery, *Beloved* (1987). Into the twenty-first century, Morrison's Pulitzer Prize–winning novel continues to be an unsettling read, not least because it depicts the recurring sexual victimization of nominally "free" Black women in the post-slavery epoch as inextricably bound to the far-from-antiquated gendered social control methods of the Middle Passage and slavery. This point is evidenced in the passage from the novel quoted above, in which Morrison links the rape that her "free" Black female characters routinely suffer at the hands of "whitefolks" in 1874 with the sexual violence that white crewmen regularly unleashed on enslaved African women on seventeenth-century slave ships.

This point is also evidenced through the "unspeakable thoughts, un-spoken" that eventually are spoken by Sethe, the protagonist and runaway slave woman in *Beloved* who, as a schoolboy named Nelson Lord recalls, was jailed at one time in her life—"*locked away* for murder."[2] In the post–Emancipation Proclamation narrative present of the novel, Sethe, now an ex-slave and non-incarcerated "free" Black citizen, challenges her love interest—a former slave and chain gang captive named Paul D—to grasp how white men's routine instrumentalization of racial terror and unchecked sexual violence against "free" Black women functions to confine her and her daughter Denver to their house on 124 Bluestone Road, despite their almost decade-long status as "free" subjects in the seeming safety of post-slavery Cincinnati, Ohio: "Feel how it feels to be a coloredwoman roaming the roads with anything God made liable to jump on you. Feel that."[3] The novel's narrator eventually reveals that Denver, a Black female adolescent who never spent a day of her life enslaved, inevitably "feels" the sexual intimidation that typifies this "coloredwoman" carcerality when she steps outside their house one morning in April 1874, for only the third time in her life: "Beyond her, voices, male voices, floated, coming closer with each step she took. Denver kept her eyes on the road in case they were whitemen. . . . *Suppose they flung out at her, grabbed her, tied her.* They were getting closer."[4]

Later, when Beloved—the ghost of Sethe's deceased oldest daughter who appears throughout the novel in the form of a young Black woman—tells Sethe that she cannot remember much about her past but does recall that she "*knew* one whiteman" sexually, Sethe surmises that Beloved has "been *locked up* by some whiteman for his own purposes, and never let out the door."[5] For Sethe, Beloved's insinuation of a traumatic sexual past immediately calls to mind the story a Black man recounted about "a girl *locked up* in a house with a whiteman over by Deer Creek [who] . . . [f]olks say . . . had [been] . . . in there since she was a pup."[6] Sethe then remembers even more accounts of "free" Black women's sexual victimization by white men in the years following Emancipation. In particular, she reflects on the troubling testimony of Ella, a "free" Black woman who had once disclosed to Sethe that white men had confined her to a house indefinitely for the sole purpose of rape: "It was two [white]men—a father and a son—and Ella remembered every bit of it. For more than a year, they kept her *locked up* in a room for themselves. 'You couldn't think up,' Ella had said, 'what them two done to me.'"[7]

These passages from *Beloved* reveal a disturbing condition of carceral torment and gendered social control that originated during the Transatlantic Slave Trade—a racial-historical condition whose long, post-slavery afterlife I examine at length in this chapter. To again invoke Sethe, I am speaking of a "coloredwoman" carcerality condition typified by male supremacist deployments of sexual harm on the bodies of "locked-up" Black women and girls. In this chapter, I am particularly interested in exploring how and why the state-sanctioned disciplinary use of sexual violence on the Black female body—a distinctly *gendered* form of Transatlantic Slave Trade terror and slavery-era social control designed to wound Black women and girls psychically, debase them corporeally, and exploit them capitalistically—persisted during and well after *Beloved*'s post-slavery present of 1874. Morrison's novel is haunted, I contend, by not only the sexual violence of the Middle Passage and slavery but also its resurgence in the post-1964 women's prison. The rape culture that Morrison depicts in her famed novel as fundamentally organizing interactions between white men and Black women on slave ships and slave plantations, and within post-slavery U.S. society, is but a nar-ratological refraction of the legally facilitated practice of guard-on-prisoner rape in the women's jails, prisons, juvenile facilities, and immigration de-tention centers of our contemporary epoch whose populations are dispro-portionately Black.

To situate in historical context my claim about how profoundly slavery's carceral contemporaneity haunts *Beloved*, let me point out that Title VII of the Civil Rights Act of 1964 ironically made it legal for female correctional officers to work in men's prisons and for male officers to work in women's prisons—and thus have daily opportunities to exercise unchecked authority over the privacy, sexual autonomy, and reproductive freedom of women and girls held in penal institutions all over the nation. In the words of the investigative reporter Silja J. A. Talvi, "In the rest of the Western world, women prisoners are guarded only or primarily by other women because of existing international standards. This was also true in the United States until the passage of the 1964 Civil Rights Act and the 1972 Equal Employment Opportunity Act, both of which integrated the workforce but also moved men into more direct contact with female prisoners."[8] The Sentencing Project, based in Washington, DC, has tracked the impact of such male supremacist containment statistically, reporting that "women in prison are more likely than are men to be victims of staff sexual misconduct. More than three quarters of all reported staff sexual misconduct involves women who were victimized by male correctional staff."[9] From the vantage point of Brenda V. Smith, a legal scholar who has spent much of her career studying the role of law in facilitating abusive conditions in women's prisons, the "sexual abuse of women in prison . . . [is] a more contemporary manifestation of slavery."[10] Assuredly, when one considers that today's male prison guards are generally *unsupervised* as they oversee imprisoned women undress, shower, sleep, and use the bathroom and *unpunished* as they sexually abuse these "locked-up" women, it becomes easier to grasp how effortlessly they have been able to enforce a system of abuse behind bars that perpetuates the gendered violence so intrinsic to slavery's functioning—and so routinely depicted in *Beloved*. Because of the systemic, unpoliced, and mostly unpunished nature of this state violence, I conceptualize it throughout this chapter as a legally sanctioned instrument of white supremacy—as a contemporary iteration of what Saidiya Hartman has insightfully identified as an entire "discourse of seduction" that legitimated the sexualized subjection of enslaved women for centuries.[11] This critical lens—one that makes unequivocally clear how the slave ship's captain, the slave master, and the prison guard exist in a disciplinary lineage premised on the use of rape as a social control weapon on the bodies of captive women—shows that contemporary corrections officers' routine and mostly unprosecuted rape of women in custody is no aberration. This lens reveals more fully the alarming interrelations between present and past in Morrison's contemporary narrative of slavery. It shows how sexual abuse has been a timeless tool of terror wielded against women confined within social orders premised both on white supremacy and patriarchal dominance—social orders that include eighteenth-century slave ships and slave plantations, as well as contemporary jails and prisons and "free world" American society.

Drawing on Morrison's personal engagements with the lives and literature of imprisoned women, sociologist Avery F. Gordon's conception of haunting, and Smith's legal scholarship, I argue in the sections that follow that the increasing number of testimonies of sexual violence from the contemporary U.S. women's prison haunt the depiction of rape in *Beloved* in both the slavery era and the post-slavery-era. Moreover, I make the case that, by depicting women in her novel who craft and exchange testimonial narratives in which they condemn their subjection to disciplinary rape, Morrison reveals these captive women's will to survive, reclaim their bodies, and build community in the midst of such gendered social control—and, in so doing, shines a light on contemporary imprisoned women's literary practices around the issue of sexualized state violence. It is also my contention in this chapter that careful engagement with testimony as a narrative form in Black women's neo-abolitionist novels—novels such as *Beloved*—can help us to conceptualize anew conventional stories about sexual abuse in women's jails, prisons, juvenile facilities, and immigration detention centers. We frequently encounter these stories in the human rights literature published by advocacy organizations such as Human Rights Watch and Amnesty International. Because the reporters who write these stories rarely foreground the perspectives of abuse survivors, they tend to neglect survivors' critical understandings of their experiences of abuse and thus inadvertently reintroduce the silencing literary conventions that Black female rape survivors faced in nineteenth-century abolitionist print culture.[12] Indeed, as Breea C. Willingham has argued in her work on incarcerated Black female writers, "Despite their sustained presence in prisons and jails, the voices of black women are often excluded from discussions about the criminal justice and corrections systems."[13] Morrison, however, by foregrounding the profound social commentary of her Black female characters through their unabridged testimonies of rape in *Beloved*, rescues her sexual abuse survivors from such social scientism. Morrison imbues them with the vitality of subjective experience and thus joins prison abolitionist scholar-activists such as Victoria Law in illuminating testimonial literary practices that actual incarcerated women establish, clandestinely, to achieve a measure of agency and restitution in the contemporary women's facility, where sexualized state violence is disturbingly ordinary.

"It's [about] national amnesia": Morrison's Literary Eyewitnessing of Sexualized State Violence in the U.S. Women's Prison

Beloved is not only the story of a fugitive slave named Sethe being haunted by Beloved—the ghost of the infant child she killed with a handsaw in a desperate (and, as some critics argue, damnable) act of maternal love aimed at undermining the efforts of slave catchers who intend to capture, humiliate, and control her and all of her other children for the rest of their lives. *Beloved* is, in other words, much more than the fictional retelling of the story of Margaret Garner, the runaway slave woman who ended the life of her two-year-old daughter in 1856 under precisely the same white supremacist danger and duress. In fact, the contextual scope of Morrison's fifth novel exceeds what many critics have focused on over the past three decades. Its framing includes, but goes beyond, (1) a resurrection of disremembered people, experiences, expressive cultures, and architectures from the Middle Passage and slavery;(2) a reconstruction of U.S. history and historical fiction; (3) a testament to African cosmology and culture; and (4) the spectral bridge between personal memory and a traumatic historical past that is too often repressed.[14] *Beloved* is, most fundamentally, a novel about the ceaseless, male supremacist instrumentalization of sexual harm on the bodies of enslaved and "free" Black women and their long history of resistance to such racial terror and gendered repression.

As Sabine Sielke has observed, while "sexual violation looms large in Morrison's work, beginning with *The Bluest Eye* [and] running through *Tar Baby*," it "return[s] with particular vehemence in *Beloved*, a text literally haunted by the history, memory, and trauma of rape."[15] For Mae Gwendolyn Henderson, acts of bodily reclamation and remembering in the novel are deeply connected to its Black female characters' confrontations with racial violence and sexual endangerment during the Middle Passage, slavery, and Reconstruction: "Morrison seeks to repossess the African and slave ancestors after their *historical* violation (figured in *Beloved* as physical rape)."[16] Moreover, as Pamela Barnett has argued, Morrison emphasizes in *Beloved* both the ordinariness of Black women's subjection to sexual violence, and—through the character Sethe—their preventive responses to trauma that they know will follow their daughters' encounters with such disciplinary harm: "For Sethe, being brutally overworked, maimed, or killed is subordinate to the overarching horror of being raped and 'dirtied' by whites; even dying at the hands of one's mother is subordinate to rape."[17] Indeed, throughout *Beloved* Morrison makes a point of revisiting scenes from pre- and post-Emancipation Black life that are painful to witness—scenes in which white men deploy rape and sexual intimidation against Black women, as well as Black men, to teach them their "natural" place of inferiority in an American society premised on the violent enforcement of racist and sexist hierarchies.[18]

These scenes abound in *Beloved*. There is Sethe's mother-in-law, Baby Suggs, an enslaved Black woman who is manipulated into "coupling with a straw boss for four months in exchange for keeping her third child with her."[19] There is Stamp Paid's betrothed lover, an enslaved Black woman named Vashti, who is "gone all night" for an entire year in which she is subjected to routine rapes by their master—rapes that culminate in her untimely death.[20] And, of course, there is Sethe, the escaped slave woman who repeatedly testifies of her confrontation with sexual violence on a slave plantation in Kentucky. Sethe's violation—a forced "milking," which she later discovers is witnessed by her enslaved husband who goes mad as a result—foreshadows her act of infanticide, as well as her decision to confine her only living daughter (Denver) to 124 Bluestone Road: "I am full God damn it of two boys with mossy teeth, one sucking on my breast the other holding me down, their book-reading teacher watching and writing it up."[21] Thus, from start to finish Morrison's *Beloved* exposes how unchecked sexual violence functions as a tool by which white men maintain racial hierarchy and patriarchal dominance during the Middle Passage and slavery and after its ostensible abolishment in 1865 with the passage of the Thirteenth Amendment.[22]

In an interview with *Time* magazine in 1989, Morrison intimated this very point: "[*Beloved*] is about something that the characters *don't want* to remember, I *don't want* to remember, black people *don't want* to remember, white people *don't want* to remember. . . . It's [about] national amnesia."[23] The novel, that is to say, is not about an inability on the part of its author, its characters, or its readers "to remember" the reality or purpose of sexualized anti-Black violence. Rather, *Beloved* makes evident a nation's *selective* amnesia about such violence—its *not wanting* to recall and bear witness to the historical consequences and traumatic effects of a system of gendered white supremacist social control that did not end with the outlawing of slavery. It is in this sense that Morrison's novel is what Linda Krumholz calls a "personal reckoning with the history of slavery."[24] As such, I am proposing that we revisit *Beloved* as a narratological case study of slavery's *unending* past—a past that includes Black women's unrelenting confrontations with state-sanctioned sexual harm during the Middle Passage, slavery, Reconstruction, the Civil Rights era, and our current epoch of racialized mass incarceration.

"Both men managed to grab me": Angela Y. Davis, the Women's Prison, and Scenes of Sexual Subjection in *Beloved*

One scholar who is uniquely positioned to aid us in conceptualizing just how tactically men in power use sexual violence as an instrument of racial terror in *Beloved* is Angela Y. Davis. A Distinguished Professor Emerita of History of Consciousness at the University of California, Santa Cruz, and renowned anti-prison activist, Davis was jailed in U.S. women's facilities in the 1970s for her political beliefs and activities. Morrison visited Davis during her incarceration. Moreover, Davis's autobiography, which described her fifteen months behind bars, was one that Morrison edited during her tenure at Random House. Drawing from her arrest and incarceration, as well as her public lectures, essays, and pathbreaking critical prison studies texts such as *Are Prisons Obsolete?* and *Abolition Democracy: Beyond Empire, Prisons, and Torture*, Davis has often made evident how the gendered social control agendas that slaveholders established and enforced on plantations have served as racial-historical precedents for contemporary women's confrontations with unchecked sexual violence in the justice system. Davis became a target of such violence at least as early as 1969, the year that Governor Ronald Reagan rushed to fire her from her professorship at the University of California, Los Angeles, when he learned of her political affiliation with the Communist Party. As Dan Berger notes, "Much of the hate mail that Davis received in the wake of the revelation of her membership in the Communist Party contained openly racist threats of sexual violence."[25] Less than a year after opening that slew of letters laden with racial hostility and sexual intimidation, Davis shared Sethe's (and Margaret Garner's) experience of being a Black woman on the run from the nation's fiercest proponents of white supremacy: Davis became one of the most hotly pursued fugitives in U.S. history.

Davis became one of the FBI's Ten Most Wanted Fugitives when J. Edgar Hoover—the bureau's longtime director and overseer of the politically repressive and lethal Counterintelligence Program responsible for the covert destruction of the Black Panther Party (and other liberationist groups and leaders)—placed her on the agency's pursuit list in August 1970. After her high-profile arrest in New York City two months later, Davis was charged with the capital offenses of conspiracy, kidnapping, and first-degree murder. The state's extensive criminalization of Davis stemmed from her solidarity with the imprisoned intellectual George Jackson and the Soledad Brothers, Black political prisoners whose plight I discussed in Chapter 1. Davis's case quickly became an international cause célèbre. In 1972, an all-white jury acquitted her of each of these charges. But, as Davis makes clear in her self-titled autobiography, the "unknown perils of being a fugitive" forever marked her.[26] In her narrative, Davis discusses how, in the course of striving to outwit and outpace her criminalizing pursuers before her arrest in October 1970, she came to empathize with her many enslaved ancestors who had narrowly escaped the prison of slavery:

> My life was now that of a fugitive, and fugitives are caressed every hour by paranoia. Every strange person I saw might be an agent in disguise, with bloodhounds waiting in shrubbery for their master's commands. Living as a fugitive means resisting hysteria, distinguishing between the creations of a frightened imagination and the real signs that the enemy is near. *I had to learn how to elude him, outsmart him.* It would be difficult, but not impossible. Thousands of my ancestors had waited, as I had done, for nightfall to cover their steps, had leaned on one true friend to help them, had felt, as I did, the very teeth of the dogs at their heels. . . . The circumstances that created my hunted state were perhaps a bit more complicated, but not all that different.[27]

While Davis clearly alludes to the experience of the fugitive slave to situate her subjection to unfounded criminalization, violent capture, and abusive incarceration in a more complete historical context, her framing of such racialized torment as also representing a *gendered* vestige of slavery in the contemporary justice system ("I had to learn how to elude *him*, outsmart *him*") is continuous with her more recent observations on the justice system.

In *Are Prisons Obsolete?* Davis argues that the Jezebel stereotype—a view perpetuated by white society that African-descended women are "naturally" lascivious temptresses with overactive libidos—figured prominently in the era of slavery as a supposedly logical explanation for white slaveholders' routine rape of Black women. Davis contends that contemporary male prison employees have recovered the Jezebel stereotype to legitimate their gendering of harm—their sexualization of state violence—against imprisoned women. Davis states, "The coerced sexual relations between slave and master constituted a penalty exacted on [Black] women, if only for the sole reason that they were slaves. In other words, the deviance of the slave master was transferred to the slave woman, whom he victimized. *Likewise, sexual abuse by prison guards is translated into the hypersexuality of women prisoners.*"[28] In a later interview, in 2014, Davis observed, "The prison-industrial complex reminds us that we live with the *ghost of slavery*. Punishment was used in the aftermath of slavery in order to reinstitute slavery."[29] If we pair Davis's observation about "the ghost of slavery" with her earlier remark about the racist and sexist logic that undergirds guard-on-prisoner rape in contemporary women's prisons ("*sexual abuse by prison guards is translated into the hypersexuality of women prisoners*"), it becomes even more apparent how Morrison's *Beloved* is as much a case study as it is a fiction.

To comprehend *Beloved* as a centuries-spanning case study in (Black) women's confrontations with male supremacist containment and unchecked sexual violence, let us recall that the novel, which one critic described as being concerned with "the histories of women who endured the Middle Passage, where the institutionalized rape of enslaved women began," hit bookstands in 1987, precisely when reports of male prison employees' sexual victimization of imprisoned women and girls skyrocketed.[30] In 1990, for instance, California's *Orange County Register* disclosed that a male correctional officer who had raped ten women behind bars in the 1980s was eventually fired but never prosecuted.[31] In 1992, a *Los Angeles Times* reporter revealed that nearly two hundred women imprisoned at Georgia Women's Correctional Institution testified of guards who, throughout the 1980s, routinely subjected them to rape, forced pregnancies, forced abortions, and off-site prostitution.[32] In 1994, a U.S. Department of Justice investigation of two Michigan prisons uncovered that "nearly every [imprisoned] woman interviewed reported various sexually aggressive acts of guards."[33] Then, in 1996, Human Rights Watch's now widely referenced report *All Too Familiar: Sexual Abuse of Women in U.S. Prisons* uncovered evidence of male guards' habitual rape of imprisoned women in California, Georgia, Illinois, Michigan, New York, and the District of Columbia. Unsurprisingly, Human Rights Watch later found that "virtually all of the women who were interviewed for *All Too Familiar* and who had lodged complaints of sexual harassment or abuse have suffered some form of retaliation by the accused officer, his colleagues, or other inmates. . . . [These] incarcerated women have no protection, no recourse, and nowhere to hide."[34]

More recently, in 2004, a small group of incarcerated girls confined to a Colorado facility populated mostly with incarcerated adolescent boys confronted—beyond a carceral environment whose majority-male captive population made it sexually endangering—routine rape by adult male employees, leading to a string of pregnancies. As Silja J. A. Talvi notes, "After the pregnancies, guards went to the extent of forcing the girls to take birth control pills. The girls were also threatened with violence against them *and their family members* if they spoke out against the abuse."[35] In 2010, the National Prison Rape Commission published a report that found incarcerated girls as constituting the population most susceptible to sexual abuse behind bars. The report discussed, by way of example, a juvenile facility in Alabama where "pervasive misconduct . . . beginning in 1994 and continuing through 2001 led 49 girls to bring charges that male staff had fondled, raped, and sexually harassed them."[36] In 2014 and 2015, the Alabama prison system made headlines again when national news reporters disclosed that women confined at Julia Tutwiler Prison in Wetumpka testified of male guards who had "raped, beaten, and harassed [them] . . . *for at least 18 years*" and who had also coerced the women to undress for "a New Year's Eve strip show."[37] Over the past three decades, similar testimony of male guards' disciplinary use of sexual intimidation and rape against imprisoned women and girls has appeared in the literature of human rights organizations such as Amnesty International, the American Civil Liberties Union, Just Detention International (formerly Stop Prison Rape), and Grassroots Leadership; in narratives by imprisoned women (such as the Black freedom fighter Assata Shakur's autobiography); and in the scholarly and journalistic publications of Davis, Talvi, Cristina Rathbone, Victoria Law, Jodie Michelle Lawston and Ashley E. Lucas, and Robin Levi and Ayelet Waldman.[38]

Given the curious surfacing of these contemporary testimonies of sexualized state violence in the same historical moment as the release of Morrison's contemporary narrative of slavery, they cast time-bending shadows on enslaved and nominally "free" Black women's accounts of rape that recur throughout *Beloved*. I am arguing that these testifying contemporary imprisoned women reveal—with the moral force of courtroom witnesses—two points: (1) there are myriad ways in which male prison employees exploit Title VII of the Civil Rights Act of 1964 to subject women in custody to routine sexual harm; and (2) such opportunistic treatment of women deemed less than citizens in our present epoch reinstates the unspoken law of white supremacy that sanctioned the rape of women deemed less than human in the nineteenth-century U.S. past depicted in *Beloved*. If examined through this centuries-spanning case study lens, then, *Beloved* is a novel as much about Black women's and girls' vulnerability to sexual, corporeal, and psychic pain during slavery as it is a critical reconsideration of the post-slavery legal precedents that facilitate and fuel male prison employees' practice of unchecked sexual violence against captive women of all races in the contemporary women's prison.

The latter point becomes even more apparent when we take into account Morrison's personal engagements with the literature and lives of contemporary imprisoned women and how these engagements inform her novel's depictions of Black women's confrontations with unchecked sexual violence. Before publishing *Beloved*, Morrison worked for nearly two decades at Random House, where she edited two narratives about contemporary women's imprisonment: Gayl Jones's novel *Eva's Man*, published in 1976, and Davis's autobiography, published in 1974.[39] The former work curiously takes as its subject a Black imprisoned woman's recollections of sexual abuse. The latter chronicles (among other things) how Davis combated the gendered violence and racialized harassment of jail guards while she was held as a political prisoner in New York and California in the early 1970s. Morrison not only was familiar with Davis's (carceral) life story during that time frame and after; for more than four decades, she has been Davis's close friend. Morrison visited Davis while she was confined within the Marin County Jail in San Rafael, California, and has seized opportunities to share in public talks with her—as she did at "Literacy, Libraries, and Liberation," their lecture on literary production and learning in the epoch of mass incarceration at the New York Public Library in 2010.[40] Morrison has even shared Davis's experience of being criminalized by the state. In 1998, the Texas Department of Criminal Justice (which has permitted Ku Klux Klan literature in its prisons) banned Morrison's novel *Paradise* from Texas state prisons for its "information of a racial nature" and alleged potential to incite riots— outrageous assessments that Morrison, firing back, described as constituting "an extraordinary compliment" to the counterhegemonic content that typifies her oeuvre.[41] In a recent interview, Morrison testified of the great distance that she has traveled, literarily and personally, with Davis: "Working with Angela was sui generis, and I didn't just edit her book. I went on her book tour with her."[42] Comparative close readings of the close friends' works make evident the extent to which Davis's abusive treatment at the New York Women's House of Detention casts its time-bending shadow on the pages of *Beloved*. Of particular interest to me is Davis's autobiographical transcription of one especially harrowing strip search—a search whose middle-of-the-night terror (re-)plays in the dark of many scenes of male supremacist containment and sexual subjection in the fictional narrative of slavery that her book's editor published years later.

In part one of *Angela Davis: An Autobiography*, Davis recounts participating in a "massive demonstration" that "was spearheaded by the bail fund coalition and the New York Committee to Free Angela Davis," an ingenious protest that succeeds in uniting the voices of non-incarcerated activists outside of the House of Detention with those of incarcerated demonstrators.[43] The jail administration wastes no time in retaliating: a white female guard storms Davis's cell and shoves her before a white female deputy warden. Davis writes, "She bluntly informed me that I should prepare for a strip search. I angrily refused."[44] Upon Davis's repeated refusals to be searched, the deputy warden changes her strategy. The receiving room where jail guards have now detained Davis undergoes its most shocking transformation as the deputy warden calls on additional, high-ranking women officers and two *male* guards to "break" the recalcitrant Davis:

> Out of the corner of my eye, I caught a glimpse of two men in guard's uniforms *approaching me from behind. This was the first time I had seen male guards in the House of D.* My mind flashed back to what the sisters had said about these "last resort" guards—the jail's riot squad—who were always on for situations where force was deemed

Right: Angela Y. Davis walks and talks with Toni Morrison on March 28, 1974. Morrison also visited Davis during her incarceration at Marin County Jail in San Rafael, California, in the early 1970s. (Photograph © Jill Krementz, March 28, 1974, New York City; all rights reserved.)

Below: As part of a New York Public Library lecture with Davis on October 27, 2010, Morrison reads from the Texas Department of Criminal Justice's letter from 1998 banning her novel *Paradise* from Texas state prisons. (Photograph by Jori Klein/© The New York Public Library.)

necessary. *Realizing why they were there, I jumped up, took a battle stance and prepared to defend myself.* One of them grabbed my arm. I kicked him. When the other man came to his aid, they both knocked me to the floor. By the time I could get up, the deputy warden and some of her female helpers were in on the action—*as if two male prison guards weren't capable of subduing me.*[45]

That we learn in previous paragraphs that it is just after 3:00 A.M. when female officers yield total access of Davis's body to two male guards whom Davis describes as "approaching [her] from behind" and later "knock[ing] [her] to the floor" is worth careful consideration. To say it plainly, when Davis tells us that she is compelled to take a "battle stance" against fast-approaching male guards at nighttime, she is expressing her desperate attempt to "defend [herself]" against the imminent threat of state violence that is sexual as well as physical in nature. As the "jail's riot squad," these male guards—who ordinarily work at a prison (not at the pretrial confinement site that is a jail)— eagerly make use of the unbridled discretion that the female officers have granted them. They apply excessive force against Davis without consequence. The results of such asymmetrical power dynamics were well known in the House of Detention, especially since other special-duty male guards had already injured other Black women jailed there, as Davis noted in a letter she wrote to a fellow political prisoner, Ericka Huggins, during her incarceration: "At the time of my arrest, the whole building was astir. . . . [A] sister . . . was so badly beaten by male guards that she had to spend two or three weeks in Bellevue Hospital."[46] The male guards' free rein in commandeering Davis to the strip search thus initializes her subjection to forms of male supremacist containment and sexual intimidation that will haunt Morrison's depiction of Sethe's subjection to slaveholders' acts of sexualized harm in *Beloved*. Although Davis does not disclose in her autobiography whether the male guards sexually assaulted her, this scene is one that undeniably reveals the normalization of sexualized state violence in women's jails and prisons, especially as we reconsider what Davis has written elsewhere about the nature of strip searches.

In *Abolition Democracy*, Davis makes the case that, because of their re-curring and intrusive performance, strip searches constitute "the routin-ization of sexual abuse" behind bars.[47] During these full-body searches, incarcerated women are forced, under threat of punishment, to remove their clothing while they bend over and expose their vaginal and rectal areas, often in full view of other guards and incarcerated women for whatever length of time the overseeing guard deems necessary. It is clear from the passage quoted above that Davis, despite the political significance of her "battle stance," is physically attacked (at the very least) by the male guards to the point of having to submit to this sexually abusive procedure. Davis *does* disclose her forced submission to the procedure by tellingly stating that the male guards are "capable of *subduing* her" without "the deputy warden and some of her female helpers" beating her. She later expounds on the intensity of male supremacist containment that she confronts as she attempts to resist the search: "Both men managed to grab me, each one seizing an arm. They bent each arm upward behind my back in a hold that was impossible to break. Bruised and breathless, there was nothing I could do to prevent them from *locking* the handcuffs."[48] Although Davis does not provide details of what ensued between her and the male guards after this moment, beyond remarking that she was "shoved, protesting into a side room" while clothed in nothing but a "sleeveless, cotton jail dress," her testimony of being *locked* into a carceral locale typified by unchecked, middle-of-the-night male authoritarian control is a record of sexual intimidation that casts a time-bending shadow on the "routinization of sexual abuse" accounts told by or about Black female characters in *Beloved*— characters such as Vashti, Ella, and Sethe.[49]

Sethe, like Davis, is a Black woman who is firmly *locked* within the ground zero of a male supremacist social order. Like Davis, Sethe will eventually be locked up in jail for her unforeseeable recalcitrance—her act of infanticide against her Black daughter Beloved, an act that the state interprets as more spiteful than inhumane. Sethe, after all, has not only killed her child. She has also deprived the plantation economy of years of potential capital (a developing slave) capable of reproducing capital (more slaves). Sethe also shares with Davis a more fundamental confinement: she is also perpetually reminded that she represents the ultimate race and gender subordinate within a culture premised on her subjection to patriarchal dominance and white supremacy. Put simply, Sethe is locked into an antebellum U.S. culture that is a sexually repressive prison for Black women and girls. Thus, since the slave plantation—rather than the women's facility—serves as a primal site for disciplinary rape in Sethe's epoch, it is within a barn on the Garners' Sweet Home estate in Kentucky (rather than in jail) that Sethe is subjected to sexual assault by white men who intend to "break" her and ensure that she will not flee the premises (as other slaves have begun to do). Like Davis, Sethe is sexually victimized by *two* men whose patriarchal privilege grants them authority over and above that of the white woman in power at Sweet Home, a mistress named Mrs. Garner. The two white men are nephews of schoolteacher, a sadistic white slave master who has replaced the deceased Mr. Garner as the head of the plantation. In a move that calls to mind the invitation by the House of Detention's female *jail* officers to male *prison* guards to have open season on Davis, schoolteacher's two white nephews disregard Mrs. Garner's requests that they ensure the safety of her female house slaves—a safety that made her house what Baby Suggs describes as a haven on the plantation "where nobody knocked her [or any other female house slaves] down (or up)."[50] Sethe, despite being one of the Garners' house slaves, is subjected to sexual harm from schoolteacher's two white nephews. Sethe recalls this harrowing encounter in a conversation with her Black lover, Paul D: "Those boys . . . took my milk. . . . Held me down and took it. I told Mrs. Garner on em. She had that lump and couldn't speak but her eyes rolled out tears. Them boys found out I told on em. Schoolteacher made one open up my back and when it closed it made a tree. It grows there still."[51] Paul D, inattentive to the gendered nature of degradation that typifies Sethe's forced milking, is stunned only by Sethe's beating, which she has described as schoolteacher "open[ing] up [her] back." Paul D exclaims, "They used the cowhide on you? . . . They beat you and you was pregnant?"[52] As Paul D rushes to make sense of the visible scars of Sethe's suffering (the "tree" on her back) from his myopically masculine worldview. Sethe's repeated references to her less visible confrontation with sexual assault go unheard: *And they took my milk!*"[53] Like Davis, Sethe intimates that it is not only the noticeable effects of physical violence but also the ineffable wounds of sexual assault that make the everyday lives of Black women in male supremacist social orders so painful.

This intense scene helps to illustrate how, from yet another angle, *Beloved* can be understood as a case study of slavery's unending past. Sethe, after all, is disturbed by the trauma of this *pre*-Emancipation encounter with sexual harm throughout the *post*-slavery epoch that constitutes the novel's narrative present: even as a "free" citizen in 1874, Sethe cannot stop recounting her forced milking or the hold that it continues to have on her body and being. Even within the so-called freedom of her post-Emancipation house on 124 Bluestone Road, Sethe expresses repeatedly to her daughter Denver how deeply the dehumanizing acts of schoolteacher's nephews still shatter her self-image. On one occasion, Sethe explains to Denver that her forced milking has left her with not only a desecrated body but also an untreated psychic wound—a wound to her selfhood so profound that she sees her identity as interchangeable with that of a farm animal: "It was took from me—they held me down and took it. Milk that belonged to my baby. . . . [T]hey handled me like I was the cow, no, the goat back behind the stable because it was too nasty to stay in with the horses."[54] Later, Sethe tells Denver that her recurring remembrances of her susceptibility to state-sanctioned sexual assault before and after the abolition of slavery has led her to confine Denver to their house: "No undreamable dreams about whether . . . a gang of whites invaded her daughter's private parts, soiled her daughter's thighs, and threw her daughter out of the wagon. . . . This and much more Denver heard [Sethe] say from her corner chair."[55]

Sethe's traumatic recollections of her forced milking on the Sweet Home plantation also deepens her critical understanding of the impunity that surrounds white men's sexual abuse of Black women in the post-Emancipation era. Sethe is noticeably apprehensive, for instance, when her back-from-the-dead daughter Beloved (who appears to Sethe throughout the novel in the form of a young Black woman) struggles to recount her past: Beloved seems to recall only having been "snatched away" from those close to her and having experienced a sexual encounter with "one whiteman" immediately thereafter.[56] Sethe insists that Beloved's inability to clearly identify her origins or remember the details of this sexual encounter with an unnamed white man signifies that "Beloved had been locked up by some whiteman for his own purposes, and never let out the door. She must have escaped to a bridge or someplace and rinsed the rest out of her mind."[57] Sethe's apprehensiveness deserves careful attention, for it is both the lived reality of Black women's subjection to disciplinary rape in the post-slavery epoch and the words of Beloved's own testimony of sexual violence during the Middle Passage past that makes her presence in the novel so haunting. To reiterate: we must not forget that Beloved, in Morrison's own words, is both the ghastly, grown-up manifestation of the infant daughter that Sethe killed and "a survivor from a true, factual slave ship."[58] Moreover, as Avery Gordon points out, Beloved is the kind of ghost whose "double voice speaks not only of Sethe's dead child, but also of an unnamed African girl lost at sea. . . . [T]he ghost that is haunting [Sethe] is haunted herself."[59] That this abuse-surviving African girl/ghost named Beloved is so forthcoming in her unsettling testimonies of sexual victimization during and after a middle passage—and, moreover, that even Sethe's mother's friend Nan articulates detailed accounts of rape on a slave ship—is, at one level, a testament to Morrison's facility with illustrating the centuries-spanning nature of Black women's confinement to carceral locales typified by phallocentric intimidation and unchecked sexual violence. At another level, though, the prevalence of such intimidation and violence in Morrison's novel renders all the more visible one of the slave ship's most disturbing contemporary referents: the geographically withdrawn women's prison where male supremacist containment is perfectly legal and where a disproportionately Black population of captive women and girls have found themselves, like Beloved, "snatched away," "locked up," and sexually abused without recourse. It is this reinstated slave ship social order that deeply haunts *Beloved*.

"All of it is now": *Beloved's* Haunted Slave Ships, the Women's Prison, and a New Slave Ship Social Order

For Gordon, the author of *Ghostly Matters: Haunting and the Sociological Imagination*, the novel *Beloved* teaches us much about haunting. Gordon focuses the latter portion of her book on Morrison's acclaimed work, but her study as a whole develops a theory of haunting. From Gordon's vantage point, haunting offers us a social lens through which we can grasp how covert and overt forms of systemic oppression have facilitated the commodification, confinement, and premature death of people and communities deemed expendable in a globally capitalistic U.S. culture. Haunting functions as a kind of racial-historical magnifying glass for people who, in Gordon's words, seek "to understand modern forms of dispossession, exploitation, repression, and their concrete impacts on the people most affected by them and on our shared conditions of living. This mean[s] trying to comprehend the terms of an always already racial capitalism and the determining role of monopolistic and militaristic state violence."[60] Yet Gordon does not conceive of haunting as mere acquiescence to the academic exercise of exploring "subjugated knowledges"—those discredited discourses that Michel Foucault famously describes in *Society Must Be Defended* as being produced by people and groups relegated to the realm of political inconsequence by the dominant culture. Gordon also understands haunting as placing an ethical demand on the haunted. Haunting challenges people who find themselves most disturbed by oppression's long history to participate actively with past and present disenfranchised groups in the project of amplifying their voices and catalyzing a socially transformative "something-to-be-done" in the broader culture.[61] From this angle, haunting can be understood as socially disruptive speech and actions that compel the dominant culture to confront the ineffable and the unspeakable. Haunting is a pedagogy of the *repressed*, a way that subjugated speakers undermine forms of social control that have been known and felt by those people whom the state has rendered unknowable, as Gordon explains at length:

> Haunting is one way in which abusive systems of power make themselves known and their impacts felt in everyday life, especially when they are supposedly over and done with (slavery, for instance). . . . What's distinctive about haunting is that it is an animated state in which a repressed or unresolved social violence is making itself known, sometimes very directly, sometimes more obliquely. I [am using] the term *haunting* to describe those singular yet repetitive instances when . . . the over-and-done-with comes alive, when what's been in your blind spot comes into view. Haunting raises specters and it alters the experience of being in time, the way we separate the past, the present, and the future.[62]

As I have argued throughout this chapter, sexualized state violence—in its pre- and post-Emancipation forms—is the "unresolved social violence" that haunts *Beloved*. Again, Morrison's enslaved and "free" characters' recurring confrontations with the Middle Passage and slavery's primary instrument of gendered repression—unchecked sexual violence—blur the demarcation of the antebellum and post-slavery epochs. Perhaps Beloved, more than any other character in the novel, emblematizes what Gordon describes as haunting, for Beloved's centuries-spanning subjection to routine and unpunished forms of sexual harm fundamentally "alters . . . the way we separate the past, the present, and the future."[63]

Described by the novel's narrator as "disremembered and unaccounted for," the African girl/ghost Beloved ceaselessly testifies of being haunted by a social control condition that transcends time and place.[64] Beloved recounts that on multiple occasions and in different historical contexts "*ghosts* without skin"—menacing white crewmen on slave ships—have raped her.[65] On the one hand, Beloved, in expressing that she regularly combats crewmen's acts of digital rape (at the very least), identifies the slave ship as the site that initializes and defines her struggle against white men's unchecked sexual violence: "Beloved said . . . when she cried there was no one. That dead men lay on top of her. That she had nothing to eat. *Ghosts without skin stuck their fingers in her and said beloved in the dark and bitch in the light.*"[66] On the other hand, Beloved contextualizes this war that she wages against sexual harm—presumably harm that, as Gordon would have it, is "supposedly over and done with"—as part of not only a distanced slave ship past but also a more immediate, post–Slave Trade present:

> *All of it is now   it is always now* . . . I watch him eat   inside . . .
> I am going to be in pieces   he hurts where I sleep   he puts his
> finger there.[67]

Just following this scene of Beloved's timeless, "always now" susceptibility to phallocentric intimidation and unchecked sexual violence, a scene whose use of the present-tense verb form implies that Beloved's endurance of digital rape is rather commonplace ("he hurts where I sleep   he puts his finger there"), Beloved reminds readers of just how contemporarily this unnamed "he" sexually "hurts" her. Beloved discloses that she suffered very similar sexually abusive treatment by an unnamed white man during her post-slavery confinement to his house. Beloved, that is to say, corroborates Sethe's supposition that she has been subjected to sexual abuse as much in the post-Emancipation present as in the Middle Passage past. In Beloved's own words, "Where are the men without skin? . . . Can they get in here? . . . One of them was in the house I was in. He hurt me."[68]

Beloved's labeling of her routine encounters with rape as both past and present—as part of her daily confrontation of terror on the antiquated slave ship (*"Ghosts without skin stuck their fingers in her and said beloved in the dark and bitch in the light"*) and her ongoing vulnerability to sexualized state violence in post-Emancipation Ohio ("All of it is now it is always now," "One of [the men without skin] was in the house I was in")—makes evident her representative embodiment of a long history of Black women's uniquely raced and gendered carceral conditions. This is a history that extends even beyond the domain of Beloved's fellow sufferers of sexual abuse in the novel's story world—sufferers who include Sethe, Baby Suggs, and Ella and others, such as Nan and Sethe's mother, who are "taken up many times by the crew" during their transatlantic captivity.[69] I am arguing that when testimony of disciplinary rape in Morrison's novel is recast under the lens of Gordon's haunting concept, Beloved also seems to cry out on behalf of actual imprisoned women and girls—a disremembered and unaccounted for community of female sufferers who serve as her referents within the criminal justice system in the contemporary moment of *Beloved*'s release to the reading public. As these women and girls confront behind bars the same disciplinary condition of male supremacist containment faced by their enslaved ancestors, they articulate the "something-to-be-done" that ghostly presences always demand, as Gordon notes: "The ghost is . . . (like Beloved) pregnant . . . with the something to be done that the wavering present is demanding. This *something to be done* is not a return to the past but a reckoning with its repression in the present."[70]

Beloved as a whole calls for such a "reckoning with . . . repression in the present" of its abusive mass incarceration publication moment. Morrison's depictions of Beloved and the slave ship make apparent the sexualized subjection that typifies the confinement of today's imprisoned women and girls. In Morrison's novel, slave ships, beyond being architectures of racial isolation, stand in for the geographically withdrawn women's facilities of our current epoch in which survivors of sexual abuse—much like Black female captives on slave ships in *Beloved*—refuse to be hushed. From this angle, testimony of sexual victimization throughout *Beloved* returns readers to the primal site of sexualized state violence—the slave ship—while also calling to attentive readers' minds the women's prison, the more contemporary architecture of mass-based racialized confinement in which a half-century-old law has reinstated the male supremacist supervision, sadistic violence, and rape culture that characterized slave ships' social order.

The legal scholarship of Brenda Smith has come closest to elucidating the overarching point I wish to make about the complex nature of *Beloved*'s contemporary carceral hauntings. I am arguing that Morrison's novel not only traces how the disciplinary violence of slavery's past haunts our post-Emancipation/mass incarceration present; it also reveals how the repressed reality of institutionalized rape in our mass incarceration present haunts our retrospective view of slavery's purported past. To some degree, Smith explicates this point in "Sexual Abuse of Women in United States Prisons: A Modern Corollary of Slavery." There, she unpacks the irony represented by the passage of the Title VII of the Civil Rights Act of 1964—the law I mentioned at the outset of this chapter that has effectively stationed female correctional officers in men's prisons and male correctional officers in women's prisons. Observing that "a congruency of both sexual abuse of women in prison and women in slavery is that sexual abuse was and is used as a tool of oppression," Smith also states:

> Staff—primarily male—have exploited the prison setting as an op-
> portunity to abuse women prisoners. . . . *Like slaves*, women pri-
> soners have few means to protest these sexual relations. . . . While
> there is legal protection in the modern context for sexual abuse of
> women in custody, women prisoners still have little choice about
> whether to become sexually involved with correctional staff. *Like
> slaves*, women prisoners are often wholly dependent upon correc-
> tional staff for their lives and livelihoods. Correctional staff, *like slave
> owners*, determine the ways in which women will serve their time:
> where they will be housed; where they will work; how much contact
> they will have with the outside; what they will eat; and how they will
> be clothed. . . . *Like slaves* who lacked freedom of choice, women
> prisoners must often use their sexuality to negotiate within the pri-
> son system.[71]

Given my argument about the centuries-spanning way in which unchecked sexual violence haunts *Beloved*, Smith's examination of historical continuities between women's confrontations with rape in prison and on the plantation is important to unpack at length. Smith is not only re-visioning sexual abuse in women's facilities through the lens of slavery; she is also challenging us to reconceptualize slavery from the vantage point of contemporary women's imprisonment. Beyond making the case that "like slaves," imprisoned women suffer under a system of sexual abuse and unchecked male authority, Smith reveals, through a telling shift in phrasal construction, how much more vivid the phallocentric opportunism of nineteenth-century "slave owners" appears when it is juxtaposed with the behavior of contemporary male prison employees: "Correctional staff, *like slave owners*, determine the ways in which women will serve their time." Smith's insertion of the comparative expression "like slave owners" *after* her mention of "correctional staff" at the start of this sentence bespeaks much more than syntactic variation. Smith's rearrangement is, in fact, a telltale sign that the unbridled discretion and near-total impunity that surround the abusive treatment of women in custody constitute a timeless bond between the plantation and prison as male supremacist social orders.

Again, Smith is not simply expressing a "congruency" between slavery and prison by highlighting male authorities' sexually abusive methods of gendering discipline in the two institutions. She is also making the case that the more disturbing historical continuity between the antiquated slave plantation and the contemporary women's prison is that the efficacy of mass-based control in both institutions *relies on* the perpetual and unquestioned supplying and sanctioning of male supremacist overseers. To clarify: while male prison employees in the women's prison are indeed legally accountable for acts of sexual misconduct and are threatened with imprisonment or high fines for such acts, most offending officers are politely censured by prison staff; even when they are fired, they are rarely prosecuted, as Davis, Talvi, Victoria Law, and Joy James have all discussed extensively.[72] Moreover, because of laws such as the Prison Litigation Reform Act of 1996, which restricts imprisoned women from effectively issuing complaints against offending members of the correctional staff, what also happens, as the longtime journalist Alan Elsner has pointed out, is that incarcerated women's grievances about sexual abuse are rejected while administrators continue to perpetuate a climate of guard-on-prisoner rape by disregarding guards' sexually explicit remarks toward and unauthorized searches of women in custody.[73] Such institutional indifference toward the sexual victimizers of imprisoned women of the current epoch—indifference that human rights organizations define as the United States' tolerance of torture—resumes the uncontested impunity enjoyed by sexually abusive male slave owners of centuries past.[74] To recall Smith's syntax, slave masters were indeed the male prison guards of their day. They reveled in the free rein that they had to wield unrestricted power over the sexual autonomy and reproductive activity of women deemed less than women. Today, the mere presence of armed men who make up between 50 percent and 80 percent of staff in women's prisons reminds us that slavery is not as archaic as many have imagined. Slavery is, both from Smith's discerning vantage point and my own, a centuries-spanning system of discipline typified by racialized confinement *and* unchecked sexual violence—a system of white supremacist, male supremacist social control that laws such as Title VII of the Civil Rights Act have effectively reinstated in women's jails, prisons, juvenile facilities, and immigration detention centers.[75]

Smith's elucidating examination of the interconnectedness of past and present forms of sexualized state violence deserves an even closer look in light of my reading of *Beloved*. Morrison's novel, with its emphasis on African-descended women's subjection to rape on slave plantations *and slave ships*, suggests that the slave vessel's captain and crewmen—rather than the slave plantation's master and overseer—are the oldest "ghostly" incarnations of the women's prisons' male prison guard. First, we must recall that throughout the novel, Beloved speaks of "ghosts without skin"—more than one white crewman—who sexually abuse her during a middle passage. Unlike the sexual violence that Sethe suffers at the hands of schoolteacher's nephews on the Sweet Home plantation, Beloved's emphasis on the anonymity *and innumerability* of her sexual abusers—and the fact that "there was no one" to hear her cries (let alone the possibility of a Mrs. Garner to advocate for her)— points to a secreted sadism and masculinist opportunism that link slave ship crewmen to the male prison guards of our current epoch.[76] The scholar-activist Anannya Bhattacharjee has discussed this centuries-spanning phallocentric pride as an extension of free society's patriarchal dominance in male supremacist carceral spaces:

> In an environment characterized by isolation, authoritarian control, and an active philosophy of dehumanization, rape and harassment serve as the ultimate opportunity for guards and others to assert their authority. Needless to say, the predominance of male guards and medical personnel makes women's prisons an especially potent site for use of rape as a tool for reinforcing male control of women's bodies.[77]

I submit that—as with the men in today's women's prisons who seize their remoteness from the condemnatory eyes of the judiciary to routinely rape and impregnate imprisoned women—*the fact that more than one "ghost without skin" rapes Beloved on the geographically withdrawn slave ship* suggests that throughout history, male groups given limitless power to dominate women in isolated locales of confinement have often exploited such opportunities to sexualize social control.[78] The award-winning maritime historian Marcus Rediker underscores this point. After emphasizing that "the relationship between sailors and slaves [was] *predicated* on . . . the rape of women [slave ship] captives," Rediker observes the following: "The geographic isolation of the ship, far from the governing institutions of society, was both a source of and a justification for the captain's swollen powers."[79]

The "ghosts without skin" of the Middle Passage past and our mass incarceration present—slave ship crewmen and male prison guards—savor their "swollen powers," powers that have always gendered the enforcement of social control and sexualized the experience of terror in locales of mass-based captivity. Put simply, male supremacist "ghosts without skin" have haunted Beloved, Black women, and imprisoned women for too long. The practice of male authoritarian containment in the women's prison and the repression of male officers' rape of far too many contemporary Beloveds demand an ethical response. In the antipanoptically expressive testimonial vernacular of Morrison's survivors of unchecked sexual violence, we witness such a response: the story-world's illumination of a carceral world of literary resistance that approximates what Gordon calls haunting's socially transformative "something-to-be-done."

"You she gave the name of the black man": Survival Testimony as Resistance to Past and Present Forms of Unchecked Sexual Violence

What Gordon calls the "something-to-be-done" of haunting shows up in Morrison's *Beloved* in a form of Black vernacular expression that is as condemnatory as it is communal: testimony. By adopting an incriminating, in-group, first-person, call-and-response-laden expressive style throughout the novel, the enslaved, formerly enslaved, and nominally free Black women in *Beloved* effectively put the institution of slavery—and the centuries-spanning practice of male supremacist containment—on trial. Through testimony, Morrison's Black women speak unspeakable stories of repression and resistance. Their clandestine, stylized dialogic exchanges thus constitute much more than the attainment of voice. They are also unforeseeable expressions of agency, telltale signs of what I theorized in the Introduction as antipanoptic expressivity. Given the vast system of subjugation that Morrison's women confront, testimony in *Beloved* can be understood as an oppositional discourse through which they orally undermine the panoptic, racist, sexually disciplining gaze that normalizes their gendered confinement within the social orders of the slave ship and the slave plantation. In sum, testimony is the narrative form to which Black female characters in Morrison's novel turn to create alternative narratives about their subjection to unchecked sexual violence: through testimony, they can critically assess their abusive treatment *and* defiantly declare their will to live and reclaim their bodies at one and the same time.

Testimony in *Beloved* is best understood as socially disruptive speech, to again recall Gordon's concept of haunting. Such speech in the novel is typified by nonlinearity and rejection of Western standards of grammar—so it comes as no surprise that its transcribed appearance on the page has often baffled Morrison's readers. For many critics of *Beloved*, the testimonies of Black female characters are "scattered perceptions," "perplexing interior monologue[s]," and "fragmented narration[s]," clear indications of the "untellability" of Black women's subjection to rape during the Middle Passage, slavery, and Reconstruction.[80] In a sense, these critics' views call to mind those of Stamp

Paid, the Black male Underground Railroad conductor in Morrison's novel. Stamp Paid runs away from Sethe's house when he overhears her and other abuse survivors speaking in "undecipherable language" that approximates "the mumbling of the black and angry dead."[81] To say it plainly, Stamp Paid flees what he chooses not to take the time and cultural sensitivity to comprehend. Although Stamp Paid and some critics of *Beloved* myopically conceive of Black female characters' testimonies as the "undecipherable language" of the dead, such orations actually make evident a literary practice that amplifies the socially disruptive speech of the living. Morrison has described testimonial expressivity in *Beloved* as "literary archaeology"—the kind of discourse that exhumes the historically unrepresented interior life of a silenced and marginalized population (in this case, enslaved women) through the power of memory and imagination.[82] It is through Morrison's literary archaeology that a long history of Black women's confrontations with unchecked sexual violence receives a full hearing. It is through this truth-telling practice that fictional Black women in *Beloved* can, as the late Barbara Christian argued, "probe those terrible spaces that nineteenth-century slave narrators could not write about" and alter official histories that generally have excluded women's accounts of enduring *and resisting* institutionalized rape.[83] It is through Morrison's practice of literary archaeology that Beloved, Nan, Sethe, Sethe's mother, and Ella—captive women in *Beloved* who are routinely subjected to rape—articulate themselves as human beings who have indeed been sexually victimized within slave ships, plantations, and geographically withdrawn houses but whose lives and identities are not reducible to those experiences of victimization.

Testimony in *Beloved* is thus a radical act of subjectification. Through their clandestine practice of testimony—whether locked within 124 Bluestone Road or elsewhere—Morrison's Black female characters identify themselves outside of print culture's reductive narrative frameworks of victimization precisely because they "define themselves by relating and explaining their experience[s to one another]," as Cynthia Hamilton has observed.[84] As with the discursive space that Mae Gwendolyn Henderson has discussed under the rubric of "speaking in tongues" in relation to Black feminist cultural production, women in *Beloved* experience revelation, survival, and healing by uniting to create narrative that is at once interlocutory and evasive—unreservedly dialogic among its practitioners and unabashedly distrustful of the supervisory intentions of the dominant culture—of the white supremacist and male supremacist culture to which they are most fundamentally confined.[85]

Beloved and Nan, a friend of Sethe's mother's, are especially interlocutory and evasive when they testify about what Hamilton calls the "unspeakable subject [of] . . . rape of the slave by a white man who ha[s] her in his power."[86]

Before offering their testimonies, Nan and Beloved both make a point of "stealing away" from male overseers, plantation duties, and Black men in their community. By calling Nan's and Beloved's actions "stealing away," I mean to equate them with actual enslaved people's flights from plantation life to attend praise meetings, quilting parties, and dances—flights that were, in fact, acts of resistance. Saidiya Hartman speaks to this point in *Scenes of Subjection: Terror, Slavery, and Self-Making in Nineteenth-Century America*: "'Stealing away' designated a wide range of activities. . . . It encompassed an assortment of popular illegalities focused on contesting the authority of the slave-owning class and contravening the status of the enslaved as possession. The very phrase 'stealing away' played upon the paradox of property's agency and the idea of theft."[87] Nan "steals away" from her plantation duties so she can talk with young Sethe about Sethe's mother's and her own subjection to unchecked sexual violence on the slave ship and how the strategic lovemaking of Sethe's African mother and African father (and the resulting conception and birth of Sethe) undermined that particular system of gendered social control. Nan does not begin to testify until she is sure that she and Sethe are alone. Later in the novel, Beloved also waits patiently to disclose her confrontation with rape on a slave ship with her desired audience. Beloved refuses to divulge the terror that she experienced in the transatlantic until Sethe has entered the house on 124 Bluestone Road and "locked [the door] tight behind her," and Stamp Paid has "abandoned his efforts to see about Sethe."[88] Once Beloved, Sethe, and Beloved's sister Denver have succeeded in "stealing away" from Stamp Paid's probing male gaze, Beloved decides to talk freely about her experiences on the slave ship, as the novel's narrator reveals: "When Sethe locked the door, the women inside were free at last to be what they liked, see whatever they saw and say whatever was on their minds."[89]

As contemporary incarcerated women maneuver past surveillance systems and censorship policies to selectively create and circulate zine writings and newsletters on sexualized state violence behind bars, they "steal away" in a manner that carries on the interlocutory and evasive narrative tradition of Nan and Beloved, Morrison's captive female characters whose gendered subjection is (recalling my overarching argument in this chapter) haunted by the very existence of today's male supremacist U.S. women's prison. While zines have always been what Danielle Maestretti describes as inexpensively produced, "self-published, self-assembled booklets that reflect the whims and desires of the person putting them together," she also reminds us that "in the case of prisoner zines, that usually means giving men and women behind bars a voice, and a lifeline to their peers and the outside world. [Zines are] typically distributed to and read by prisoners themselves, but a handful of copies find their way to prison activists, legal professionals, and members of the alternative media."[90] When incarcerated women self-publish accounts about their own and other women's confrontations with sexual intimidation and sexual violence in the criminal justice system and distribute them, clandestinely, from facility to facility—and thus "speak" as a critically thinking collective—they use zine dissemination and newsletter writing as a means of radically transforming terrains of (gendered) punishment *and* themselves at one and the same time. Like the enslaved Nan's forbidden flight from her slave plantation duties to create a mother-like moment of dialogue with young Sethe, imprisoned women's undercover collaboration in composing and circulating zines and newsletters are acts of resistance that fundamentally subvert their institutionally defined identities. As they write and publish about the disciplinary nature of unchecked sexual violence in the world behind the razor wire, those who are deemed *women prisoners* by the state declare—if only through their in-group production and distribution of the condemnatory written word—that they are *women*. It should thus come as no surprise that prison administrators often place imprisoned women who write, circulate, or receive these insurrectionary writings in solitary confinement. These administrators know that the zines and newsletters that incarcerated readers publish and exchange often include accounts of male guards' sexual misconduct and can be produced in court as evidence of prisoner abuse and lead to lawsuits. As Victoria Law observes in *Resistance Behind Bars: The Struggles of Incarcerated Women*, "In some instances, merely the fact that women [in custody] are able to have their words printed is seen as threatening [to jail and prison administrators]."[91]

I am arguing that contemporary imprisoned women also engage in dialogue about their subjection to sexualized state violence in the narrative form that Nan and Beloved know so well: testimony. As the award-winning historian Danielle L. McGuire so ably discusses in *At the Dark End of the Street: Black Women, Rape, and Resistance—A New History of the Civil Rights Movement from Rosa Parks to the Rise of Black Power*, from the era of slavery to our current epoch of mass incarceration, testimony has been the form of in-group truth telling that Black women have relied on to expose and oppose racialized social control and male supremacist containment. Through testimony, Black women have revealed both how white supremacy regularizes their encounters with rape and how they have resisted these encounters and reclaimed their bodies.[92] Further, as the prize-winning Black expressive culture scholar Geneva Smitherman has observed, the aim of testimony has often been not only to publicize harm but also to humanize the harmed: "To testify is to tell the truth through 'story.' . . . Testifying . . . is not plain and simple commentary, but dramatic narration and a communal reenactment of one's feelings and experiences. Thus, one's humanity is reaffirmed by the group and . . . her sense of isolation diminished."[93] Taking this idea one step further in a foreword to *Inside This Place, Not of It: Narratives from Women's*

Prisons, a collection of incarcerated women's accounts of abuse behind bars, Michelle Alexander, the acclaimed author of *The New Jim Crow: Mass Incarceration in the Age of Colorblindness*, discusses the survival-focused expressivity of these "personal narratives":

> These are personal narratives not only of suffering, but of human dignity and survival against all the odds. Hope flickers, even through recollections of . . . institutional abuse. . . . [M]others, daughters, sisters, [and] wives . . . tell you stories that are nearly unbearable to read, and yet their courage, dignity, and perseverance compel us to imagine how their lives would be different—how *we* would be different—if we responded to their experience with genuine care, compassion, and concern.[94]

The accounts of unchecked sexual violence that zine-writing contemporary imprisoned women and Morrison's enslaved and formerly enslaved women exchange among themselves are testimonies in the senses that McGuire, Smitherman, and Alexander outline. These accounts—which I refer to hereafter as *survival testimonies*—are *not* narratives of victimization. On the contrary, they emphasize abuse survivors' will to survive by attending to (1) the political significance of abuse survivors' assertions of bodily reclamation or desired community while confined within male supremacist social orders; and (2) abuse survivors' critical understandings of how institutionalized sexual violence functions within an overarching system of dehumanization. In the ensuing sections of this chapter, I trace the development of survival testimony in *Beloved* and in the zine and newsletter writings from contemporary women's prisons that haunt Morrison's famed novel.

Nan's Survival Testimony

Nan's account of Sethe's mother's and her own confrontations with rape on the slave ship offers us an important first example of survival testimony. Nan shares her testimony with young Sethe one evening as she is "holding her with her good arm":

> "Telling you. I am telling you, small girl Sethe," and [Nan] did that. [Nan] told her that her mother and Nan were together from the sea. Both were taken up many times by the crew. "She threw them all away but you," [Nan said]. "The one from the crew she threw away on the island. The others from more whites she also threw away. Without names, she threw them. You she gave the name of the black man. She

put her arms around him. The others she did not put her arms around. Never. Never. Telling you. I am telling you, small girl Sethe."[95]

Nan's testimony is clearly one that she repeatedly calls her own ("*I am telling*"). It is also one that Nan shares selectively. Nan frames her testimony as an important chapter in young Sethe's family history and accordingly imparts it *only* to Sethe ("I am telling *you*, small girl Sethe"), who, following the untimely death of her mother, claims Nan as her surrogate mother: "Nan was the one [Sethe] knew best, who was around all day."[96] By circumscribing the range of her listening audience, Nan is able to testify genuinely—"to tell the truth through 'story,'" as Smitherman would have it. Nan tells the abuse story she wants to tell *how* she wants to tell it and *to whom* she wants to tell it.

In contradistinction to the nineteenth-century slave narrative tradition that scholars such as James Olney, John Sekora, William Andrews, and Molly Abel Travis have discussed, no white amanuensis authenticates Nan's survival testimony.[97] Nan tells a free story because, in the realm of Morrisonian literary archaeology, she is able to speak candidly about the severity of sexual harm on the slave ship—and the reality of enslaved women's resistance to it. Nan's story is in no ways subjected to abolitionist print culture's stifling conventions—conventions that made it hard for formerly enslaved narrators to tell their stories as fully as they desired because of prohibitions (for instance) against explicit accounts of enslaved women's confrontations with rape. Nan's testimony reads nothing like the distanced, third-person, voyeuristic description of male supremacist harm that the white slave ship captain-turned-abolitionist John Newton includes in his pamphlet *Thoughts upon the African Slave Trade* of 1788:

> When the [African] women and girls are taken on board a ship, naked, trembling, terrified, perhaps almost exhausted with cold, fatigue, and hunger, they are often exposed to the wanton rudeness of white savages. *The poor creatures cannot understand the language they hear, but the looks and manners of the speakers are sufficiently intelligible.* . . . [Their] resistance or refusal would be utterly in vain, [for] even the solicitation of [their] consent is seldom thought of.[98]

Unlike Newton's pamphlet, Nan's account of institutionalized rape contains what I have identified as defining elements of survival testimony: assertions of bodily reclamation and desired community by a survivor of a male supremacist system of confinement. Perhaps the most important and complicated details of Nan's testimony are those that underscore Sethe's mother's assertions of bodily reclamation. On the one hand, Nan does not shy away from disclosing the fact of Sethe's mother's and her own routine subjection to rape on the slave ship. Along these lines, of particular importance here is that young Sethe recalls that Nan and her mother were both "taken up *many* times by the crew." Yet Nan's primary focus is on their resistance. When Nan speaks of Sethe's mother, she tells Sethe: "*She threw* them all away but you. The one from the crew *she threw* away on the island. The others from more whites *she also threw* away. Without names, *she threw* them." Four times in Nan's short testimony, Sethe's mother is not, as could be syntactically anticipated, a sentence's direct object. She is, rather, the subject. Readers thus discover not only the harm that was done to Sethe's mother but also Sethe's mother's actions as a result of being harmed. As Claudine Raynaud has noted in her examination of this passage, "Repetitions abound, language stutters, meaning hides, appears, against a tragic compulsive gesture of rejection."[99] Nan depicts Sethe's mother as one who repeatedly "did *not* put her arms around" her sexual aggressors—"Never. Never."

I add here that, given Nan's emphasis on infanticide as a viable (and even somewhat heroic) strategy of resistance to white crewmen's disciplinary practice of rape, the decision of Sethe's mother to throw overboard the babies that she bears following her rapes is not just combative—it is also cruel. Yet we must remember that Nan tempers this seeming cruelty with her emphasis on the affections that Sethe's mother offers to an *African* man who fathers a child she *does* name: "You she gave the name of the black man." Through this remarkable employment of juxtaposition, Nan helps us to understand infanticide as a complicated assertion of bodily reclamation within the slave ship's male supremacist social order. In other words, given the dire, sexually repressive circumstances before Sethe's mother, her act of infanticide might be understood as an enslaved woman's last-ditch effort to demonstrate a measure of reproductive freedom in a system that denied her that autonomy. One must remember that, after all, the slave ship was the precursor to the slave plantation—the transatlantic predecessor of the social control regime premised on what Black feminist scholars such as Bibi Bakare-Yusuf call "the violent subjection of the slave[-woman] . . . into an entity that could produce and reproduce the property necessary for accumulating [white] wealth."[100]

Nan's account of routine, male supremacist rape is also what I have termed a survival testimony because it foregrounds assertions of desired and unforeseeable community that she and Sethe's mother established while confined to the slave ship at sea. Consider: even when Nan begins her testimony, she refuses to impart to young Sethe images of herself or Sethe's mother as isolated victims. She leaves out of her account's introduction the fact that brutal kidnapping, separation, and captivity preceded the friendship that she forged with Sethe's mother. Nan instead begins her testimony with the emboldening observation that she and Sethe's mother were "*together* from the sea." In other words, Nan emphasizes how the interpersonal bond that she shared with Sethe's mother halved the pain of the slave ship's system of bondage, rape, and kin separation—a familial and cultural separation that the scholar Orlando Patterson has described as "natal alienation" in his comprehensive work on slavery.[101] From Nan's viewpoint, she and Sethe's mother cannot be remembered as victims only. Rather, they are longtime friends ("[Nan] told Sethe that her mother and Nan were together *from the sea*"), tender lovers of Black men ("She put her arms around [the black man]"), and proud mothers ("Without names, she threw [the babies born from the repeated rapes]. You she gave the name of the black man. . . . I am telling you, small girl Sethe").

These images of bonding alone demonstrate Nan and Sethe's mother's incredible attainment of desired community. But Sethe's recollection of the bond that Nan and her mother share merits even closer examination. Sethe's phraseology—that the two women were "together *from the sea*"—bespeaks her attentiveness to the profundity of Nan's antipanoptic expressivity. Nan has clearly succeeded in getting young Sethe to grasp that she and Sethe's mother *unexpectedly* managed to establish kinship in a regime that was fundamentally designed to isolate them. Nan and Sethe's mother's development of a friendship on a ship full of strangers (strangers whose kidnapping from various regions of West Africa likely means that they do not speak the same language), as well as their preservation of such companionship in a setting whose landlessness, the award-winning historian Stephanie Smallwood reminds us, "did not figure in precolonial West African societies as a domain of human (as opposed to divine) activity," are revolutionary accomplishments.[102] So Sethe's paraphrased remembrance of Nan's choice of words—"together from the sea"—thus reveals that even in a maritime environment that was, as Smallwood points out, aimed at "reducing African captives to an existence so physically atomized as to silence all but the most elemental bodily articulation, so socially impoverished as to threaten annihilation of the self [and] the disintegration of personhood," Nan and Sethe's mother found ways to express and experience desired community.[103]

Relatedly, Nan's emphasis on the love that Sethe's mother offers to Sethe's father while they are both confined on the slave ship also illustrates the attainment of desired community that typifies survival testimony. Nan revels in the intimacies that Sethe's mother and an enslaved African man share on the slave ship: "She put her arms around him. The others (the white crewmembers) she did not put her arms around." Nan juxtaposes these tender embraces that Sethe's mother offers to Sethe's father with the complete absence of affection she shows toward the white crewmen and, in so doing, stresses the fact of Sethe's mother's resistance to their routine rape of her and other African women on the male supremacist slave ship. Nan's attention to the lovemaking of Sethe's parents garners additional political significance when it is examined in historical context. As historian Deborah Gray White has observed in her seminal work on slavery, enslaved women "did not generally travel the middle passages in the holds of slave ships but took the dreaded journey on the quarter deck."[104] Further, unlike the enslaved men, who were usually bound and stowed away for hours on end in the cargo hold, female captives made their trip across the Atlantic unshackled—but only so they would be "easily accessible to the criminal whims and sexual desires of [white] seamen."[105] Given this gendered isolation, the fact that Sethe's mother and father even managed to make love on the slave ship is yet another revolutionary accomplishment. Nan's emphasis on their embraces thus celebrates the attainment of desired community accomplished by Sethe's mother in a regime premised on enslaved African women's *and men's* bodily immobilization and gendered subjection.

Marianne Brown's Survival Testimony

A survival testimony appears within the pages of a contemporary incarcerated women's zine that resembles—or, rather, haunts—the very one expressed by Morrison's Nan. It is to that zine testimony that I now draw our focus.

Barrilee Bannister is one of the founders of the incarcerated women's zine, *Tenacious: Art and Writings from Women in Prison*. She was imprisoned at Coffee Creek Correctional Facility in Oregon and organizes against prisoner abuse. During one period of her incarceration, Bannister was sent to a *men's* private prison in Arizona, where she was denied food until she "consented" to perform oral sex on a male guard. Bannister then decided that the time had come to put up a fight—and turned to the condemnatory power of testimony. As Victoria Law, who co-founded *Tenacious*, has pointed out, Bannister connected with seventy-eight other women who had been subjected to sexual harm by male employees at the prison, "contacted the media and launched a lawsuit, which resulted in [her own and the other imprisoned women's] return to Oregon, a public apology and the firing and disciplining of many of the involved guards."[106] Bannister fittingly describes her contributions to the *Tenacious* zine with pugilistic imagery: "Writing [for *Tenacious*] is my way to escape the confines of prison and the debilitating ailments of prison life. It's me putting on boxing gloves and stepping into the rin[g] of freedom of speech and opinion."[107]

Bannister's association of zine writing with public prizefighting brings us back to Smitherman's conception of testimony as "dramatic narration and a communal reenactment of one's feelings and experiences." Bannister's observation, in other words, helps us to understand that, for imprisoned women, the practice of zine writing—like Nan's practice of "stealing away" from plantation duties for the purpose of in-group testimony—represents a political act. Bannister's words provide us with a useful backdrop for thinking through the following survival testimony, which was submitted to *Tenacious* by Marianne Brown, a woman imprisoned at the Edna Mahan Correctional Facility for Women (EMCFW) in New Jersey. This facility once held the Black freedom fighter Assata Shakur (a former political prisoner who escaped to Cuba, where she has obtained political asylum), and it is one women's prison where, as the *Star-Ledger* of Newark reported in 2004, guard-on-prisoner rape has been anything but an aberration: "Three times in the past three years . . . correctional officers have been hauled into criminal court for sexual misconduct with inmates. . . . In the six years before that, internal investigations identified five other correctional officers who had had sex with inmates, one of whom got pregnant. One officer went to jail. . . . [T]he rest were fired . . . [and] their cases were never made public."[108] I reproduce Brown's testimony from *Tenacious* at length here:

MAKING HISTORY INSIDE PRISON WALLS

Around the year 1993 or 1994, me and my Christian sisters in the maximum-security compound of Edna Mahan Correctional Facility for Women (EMCFW) began to pray about several injustices being done to prisoners by the government. The New Jersey State Department of Corrections no longer works at correcting the problems. Though we are in a "correctional facility," it is run as a penal institution to punish and harass and oppress. . . . We have witnessed and endured here a lot of abusive authority, power issues. . . . I have seen unnecessary physical violence towards the women in this place. Thank God I was not one of their victims. My Christian sisters and myself would meet three to five days a week, sometimes in the yard, sometimes in the game room to study God's word, pray, talk about [these] issues and to be of one mind in prayer. . . . Abusive authority—verbal, physical, and/ or sexual abuse instead of the proper positive authoritative power [are often] used. . . . When an officer gets into trouble, if there are no pending charges, instead of firing them, they are transferred to a different location and promoted. Who does that? The government with all their corrupt cover-ups! Before being an inmate myself, I would have never believed all of this! Then, in 1998, we knew God was moving and beginning to clear out some of the corruption in the prison system. State correctional officers were getting fired, transferred, sent to rehabs and even given jail time. Some of those who believed they were above the law and untouchable now were humbled by God. . . . A lot of officers were having sexual relations with inmates. One female inmate, after giving an officer oral sex, went and spit out his semen in a plastic bag and mailed it out. Well, his DNA he couldn't deny and he was gone fast![109]

It is telling that Brown begins her survival testimony the way Nan begins hers. Even in her testimony's first sentence, Brown rejects the identity of an isolated victim. Her opening statement informs *Tenacious* readers that they will be reading a story that follows the path of "me and my Christian sisters." Just as Nan's account of sexual terror on the slave ship begins with an assertion that she and Sethe's mother were "together from the sea," Brown's survival testimony is introduced with the emphasis on her own and other women's attainment of desired community within a system designed to "punish and harass and oppress" and keep them separated from one another. In fact, Brown's account reveals that it was her very achievement of friendship with "Christian sisters" in custody that inspired her to immerse herself in intensive prayer and organizing against a culture of "abusive authority" exemplified by the routine practice of male supremacist rape in this women's prison: "*My Christian sisters and myself* would meet three to five days a week, sometimes in the yard, sometimes in the game room to study God's word, pray, talk about [these] issues and to be of one mind in prayer."

Beyond this, when we remember that Brown's "Making History Inside Prison Walls" is a zine article that gets distributed mostly among incarcerated women, the language surrounding her attainment of solidarity with other women imprisoned at the EMCFW conveys subtle defiance. As with the phrasing that conveys Nan and Sethe's mother's unforeseeable friendship in a maritime prison ("together *from the sea*"), Brown's use of juxtaposition—"me and my Christian sisters *in the maximum-security compound*"—makes evident that she and other women imprisoned at the EMCFW have intentionally undermined a system of control premised on "unnecessary physical violence" and their interminable isolation from the possibility of human community. Moreover, Brown's testimony models for her larger audience of *Tenacious*-reading incarcerated women the shifts (however temporary) in carceral power dynamics that can follow women's pursuit of desired community while they are in custody. That is to say, because Brown situates her observation that "state correctional officers were getting fired, transferred, sent to rehabs and even given jail time" as the end result of her own and other imprisoned women's corporate prayer and collective organizing against a system of rape ("My Christian sisters and myself would meet three to five days a week ... to study God's word, pray, talk about [these] issues and to be of one mind in prayer"), she makes evident to her entire readership of incarcerated women that their commitment to unite in resistance against sexualized state violence can lead to punitive measures against offending officers and, ultimately, ameliorate prison conditions. Brown's survival testimony is thus what the scholar Anne Folwell Stanford, who is also an instructor at the Cook County women's jail, would call "dangerous because it proclaims a making and remaking of selves despite state attempts to confine, fix, and stabilize identities as 'inmates.' . . . It proclaims a 'we' within the confines of the razor wire and disrupts the individualistic discourse and practice on which any system of oppression depends."[110]

Brown's testimony also resonates with Nan's because it focuses mostly on the way in which women reclaim their bodies within an abusive, male supremacist system of confinement. Throughout her account, Brown highlights actions that women imprisoned at the EMCFW take, even on an individual level, to protect themselves from male prison staff's unchecked access to their bodies. In particular, Brown makes a hero of the imprisoned woman who confiscates the semen of a male guard who coerced her to perform oral sex on at least one occasion. Just as Nan testifies of Sethe's mother undermining the system of reproductive control on the slave ship by disposing of the babies that resulted from rape by crewmen, Brown glowingly makes known this unnamed woman's reversal of the gender-repressive carceral power dynamics that a male guard has exploited for sexually abusive ends. Like Sethe's enslaved mother, this imprisoned woman not only rejects the seed that an opportunistic male authority forcibly implanted in her; she also subverts (if only temporarily) a comprehensive system of sexual harm that is endemic to the male supremacist regime to which she is confined.

Armed with a package of this male guard's seminal fluid—indisputable biological evidence of his illegal behavior—Brown over time is able to find some recourse in the same legal system that facilitated his abuse of her by its sanctioning of cross-gender supervision in a male supremacist environment. Along these lines, we must recall that this imprisoned woman did not just "spit out his semen"; ironically, she, an ostensible criminal, "mailed out" to state authorities the sperm of this state enforcer of law as proof of *his* criminality. Brown's scornful tone throughout this section of the testimony is unparalleled—"Some of those who believed they were above the law and untouchable now were humbled by God"—and it underscores how unforeseeably this imprisoned woman temporarily "plays God," for it is she who brings about the punishment and relocation of this seemingly omnipotent authoritarian: the male guard. It is this imprisoned woman—this rights-less noncitizen—who makes a way out of no way for herself and establishes some level of legal recognition of her right to bodily integrity. In Brown's eyes, this prison-confined, sexually victimized woman, like Sethe's mother on the slave ship, has temporarily succeeded in resisting her victimizer: "Well, his DNA he couldn't deny and he was gone fast!" It is thus clear that Brown's account of the culture of sexual abuse at the EMCFW is a survival testimony. Throughout the account, Brown emphasizes how women behind bars attain desired community and bodily reclamation in a manner that is continuous with that of Nan and Sethe's mother within *Beloved*'s maritime prison—within Morrison's reimagined slave ship social order that is indeed haunted by the sexual abuse experiences and survival testimonies common to the contemporary gendered social control terrain that is the U.S. women's prison.

Beloved's Survival Testimony

In chapter 22 of *Beloved*, Beloved shares her survival testimony with Sethe and Denver, who listen to every word after locking the doors of their house on 124 Bluestone Road. Beloved recollects her subjection to rape on the slave ship, which she identifies as being typified by mass-based, male supremacist, racialized confinement when she references the state of "always crouching" in which she finds herself while held there—a state of being perpetually tight-packed, crammed into carceral spaces where she "watch[es] others who are crouching too" and witnesses these fellow Africans disappear when "men without skin push them through with poles" until they "fall into the sea":[111]

> I am standing in the rain falling   the others are taken   I am not taken
>   I am falling like the rain is   I watch him eat   inside I am crouching to keep from falling with the rain I am going to be in pieces   he hurts where I sleep   he puts his finger there   I drop the food and break into pieces . . . there is no one to want me to say me my name.[112]

Nowhere else in the novel does Beloved's syntax appear as it does here—in spaced-out, stream-of-consciousness form. To recall Smitherman's conception of testimony, Beloved is not offering "plain and simple commentary, but dramatic narration and a communal reenactment of [her] feelings and experiences." She is, with every seeming pause, with every staccato utterance, inviting her sympathetic circle of listeners inside 124 Bluestone Road to affectively experience her pain and affirm her humanity. This moment of testifying is an opportunity for healing for Beloved—a chance to halve the isolation that she feels surrounding her subjection to and memory of rape during the Middle Passage. Scholarly assessments of Morrison's *Beloved* have been curiously hesitant in articulating Beloved's agonizing remembrance in this passage as definitively constituting a recollection of rape, yet Beloved's phrases "he hurts where I sleep   he puts his finger there" plainly convey harm that is sexual in nature (digital rape at the very least).[113]

Moreover, elsewhere in the novel Beloved uses similar but much more explicit language to articulate her subjection to sexual abuse during her transatlantic confinement: "[Beloved] said when she cried there was no one. . . . Ghosts without skin *stuck their fingers in her* and said beloved in the dark and bitch in the light."[114] On the one hand, Beloved speaks of her experience of rape on the slave ship as an intense physical and psychic wounding: she describes her reflexes as impaired ("I drop the food"), her body as aching (she "break[s] into pieces"), and her name as sullied ("there is no one to want me to say me my name"). On the other hand, Beloved's description of such harm does not constitute the whole of her testimony, or even the majority of it. Instead, Beloved, like Nan and Brown, emphasizes her will to survive and establish desired community while confined within a geographically withdrawn, male supremacist regime.

To fully grasp what makes Beloved's account a survival testimony, we must revisit the beginning of chapter 22, which can be imagined as Beloved's extended introduction to her confrontation with rape. As with Nan's and Brown's testimonies, Beloved does not open hers with any reference to victimization. Rather, she begins by proudly declaring her name and her closeness with Sethe (Beloved here refers to Sethe as "she" and, in her recollection of life on the slave ship, references Sethe as "the woman with my face"): "I AM BELOVED and she is mine. . . . I am not separate from her   there is no place where I stop   her face is my own and I want to be there in the place where her face is."[115] "I AM BELOVED" is the only phrase that appears in capital letters in Beloved's entire testimony. As with Nan's emphasis early in her account on the "together[ness]" that she shares with Sethe's mother "from the sea," as with Brown's focus in her opening sentence on the unforeseeable friendships that she forges with other women imprisoned at the EMCFW ("me and my Christian sisters *in the maximum-security compound*"), Beloved's emphasis on her name and her connectedness to Sethe in the first paragraph of her testimony convey her attainment of desired community within a sexually abusive, male supremacist carceral locale in which isolation from kin is the norm. Beloved's name, after all, is a relational one, synonymous with "dearly loved," "dearest," "adored," "treasured," "cherished," "admired," and "revered," and the fact that she states it in the context of a mother-daughter bond before, during, and after her subjection to sexual terror on the slave ship—"she is mine" and "I am not separate from her"—is a sign that even as Beloved discloses the fact of her rape, she does not define herself by her rape experience. She is not an isolated victim but a beloved survivor. Relatedly, in the two chapters that precede Beloved's testimony— chapters in which Beloved's mother, Sethe, and sister, Denver, offer testimonies of their own—the opening words are "BELOVED, she my daughter," and "BELOVED is my sister."[116] Again, "BELOVED" is the only word to appear in capital letters. Beloved's emphatic restating of her name at the start of her testimony—"I AM BELOVED"—thus reminds her listeners (and readers) that in spite of the routine sexual victimization that she confronts on the slave ship, her identity cannot be reduced to that experience of being victimized. Although Beloved's subjection to institutionalized rape has left her feeling, understandably, as though "there [wa]s no one to want her" or "say [her] name," Beloved's references throughout her testimony to Sethe and "the woman with my face" (who either is or emblematizes Sethe) bespeak her assurance that she is dearly loved, cherished, and desired by her mother.

The Middle Passage experience that Beloved recollects is also a survival testimony because she emphasizes her attainment of desired community on the slave ship from the account's start to its finish. Most notably, Beloved shifts the focus in her testimony from her own confrontation with male supremacist containment and rape on the slave ship to how she survived such harm, in part, by sympathizing with a fellow sufferer. To say it plainly, Beloved spends the vast majority of her account of abuse eulogizing an enslaved African she refers to as "my own dead man."[117] Beloved's discussion of this man—compared with her four-phrase articulation of rape—is quite lengthy:

> his teeth are pretty white points . . . he is fighting hard to leave his body which is a small bird trembling   there is no room to tremble so he is not able to die   my own dead man is pulled away from my face I miss his pretty white points . . . I love him because he has a song when he turned around to die I see the teeth he sang through   his singing was soft . . . he locks his eyes and dies on my face . . . there is no breath coming from his mouth and the place where breath should be is sweet-smelling   the others do not know he is dead   I know his song is gone   now I love his pretty little teeth instead.[118]

From a historical perspective, one must remember that, as Smallwood has observed, enslaved men and women on the slave ship had to face "the trauma of death, and the inability to respond appropriately to death."[119] Slave ship captains generally kept enslaved men and women from performing any ceremonial practices related to the passing of their kin, using force when necessary.[120] Crewmembers would often hurl their dead bodies overboard like pieces of trash.

When considered from this historical context, Beloved's verbalizations of belonging and possession—"*my own* dead man"—as well as the drawn-out homage that she pays to this African man ("I miss his pretty white points"; "I love him because he has a song when he turned around to die I see the teeth he sang through his singing was soft") are not only moving remembrances; they are also antipanoptic expressions of defiance. They are war-waging words, words that articulate the African girl/ghost Beloved's attainment of desired community with an African man within a slave ship social order typified by crewmen's sexually manipulative arrangement of gendered isolation—an arrangement that Beloved describes this way: "the [enslaved] women are away from the [enslaved] men and the [enslaved] men are away from the [enslaved] women."[121] Beloved, mentally admiring the teeth, stature, resistance, song, and humanity of a perishing African man, succeeds in memorializing him while he and she are confined within a social order that prohibits end-of-life ceremonial practices and intends for the imminent threat of physical and sexual harm to discipline the thought patterns of its captives. Beloved's surreptitious staging of a ceremony that she and all slave ship captives were forbidden from performing thus reminds her listening female kin (and readers) that her testimony of sexual victimization during a middle passage cannot be reduced to the fact of her victimization. While the eulogy that Beloved offers "her own dead man" in no way diminishes the pain that she experienced during and after her confrontations with unchecked sexual violence, it does demonstrate how Beloved's unforeseeable attainment of desired community with another slave ship captive helped to facilitate her survival.

Beloved also illustrates an element of survival testimony that I have yet to discuss in an example: an abuse survivor's discussion of how her subjection to institutionalized sexual violence functions within an overarching system of dehumanization. Beloved takes great pains to indicate how rape constituted but one manifestation of dehumanization that she and other enslaved Africans suffered in the floating dungeon that was the slave ship. She reveals that she and other captives were also forced to imbibe the urine (which she refers to as "morning water") of white crewmembers ("men without skin," recall, is Beloved's way to label crewmembers as "white"), and suffered the relentless attacks of ship rats while tightly packed in cramped spaces: "the men without skin bring us their morning water to drink . . . small rats do not wait for us to sleep   someone is thrashing but there is no room to do it in . . . we cannot make sweat or morning water so the men without skin bring us theirs."[122] Mistreatment of the enslaved Africans is so pervasive that Beloved later insists, "We are all trying to leave our bodies behind."[123]

This statement expresses Beloved's understanding of the main aim of the men who govern the slave ship's social order: the utter dehumanization of captives. Implicit in Beloved's very expression of the collective pursuit of a fugitive existence by her and other enslaved Africans is her understanding that captains and crewmen on slave ships have interests that go even beyond enforcing gendered social control in a transatlantic prison: these white men intend both to commodify captive Africans as chattel for the booming plantation slavery enterprise and facilitate their systemic expulsion from the realm of human community. As Smallwood reminds us, the infliction of bodily pain and injury on slave ship captives was a disciplinary strategy that captains and crewmen used to ensure that "an African body [would become] fully alienated and available for exploitation in the American marketplace."[124] Beloved's statement "we are all trying to leave our bodies behind" implies her awareness of such capitalistic exploitation. She and other enslaved Africans know that the routine nature of their subjection to rape and forced urine intake and exposure to scavenging rats are calculated acts designed not simply to torment them, but also to sear into their psyches a white supremacist logic of their purportedly "natural" inferiority and thus serviceability to the whims and demands of the enslaving culture. Indeed, Beloved's use of the present tense as she describes these terrors, as well as her employment of understatement—her refusal to use words that might register the harm inflicted on Africans as aberrations—convey their systemic nature. Beloved thus depicts her rape on the slave ship not as an isolated incident, but as the predictable outcome of living as a captive in a geographically withdrawn regime premised on the enforcement of dehumanization. Beloved ably demonstrates how survival testifiers do not reduce their recollections of abuse to the fact of their individual victimization but, instead, think critically about its institutional character.

M.S.'s Survival Testimony

A survival testimony that appears in the pages of *The Fire Inside*, the news-letter of the California Coalition for Women Prisoners, haunts Beloved's. *Fire Inside* writers are mostly imprisoned women, but the newsletter also receives contributions from people in free society. Law has called *The Fire Inside* "an exception to the limited distribution of prisoner-made media. It boasts a circulation of over 2,000 and has an online archive accessible to anyone with an Internet connection."[125] Diana Block, Urszula Wislanka, Cassie Pierson, and Pam Fadem of The Fire Inside Collective emphasize that the newsletter "allows a conversation to occur among people who otherwise would have great difficulty connecting with one another within and between different prisons, as well as across the walls."[126] The following survival testimony was submitted to *The Fire Inside* by M.S., a woman imprisoned at the Central California Women's Facility (CCWF) in the rural town of Chowchilla. The CCWF is the largest and most severely overcrowded women's prison in the nation. It is a facility that has been reported as func-tioning "at 180 percent capacity," where "eight women pack into cells built for four," nearly 70 percent of correctional officers are men, and—as women once imprisoned there have testified—medical neglect and sexual abuse are commonplace.[127] For instance, Beverly Henry, confined at the CCWF for years, has reported to the *Huffington Post*, "I have watched 17 women die in 1 year. . . . Guards have sex and [imprisoned] women are harassed by the guards. . . . Women get pregnant; babies are born: These things happen here and the guards are responsible."[128] Relatedly, Johanna Hudnall discloses in *Razor Wire Women: Prisoners, Activists, Scholars and Artists*, "In 1997, while incarcerated at the Central California Women's Facility in Chowchilla, I was raped by a staff member of the California Department of Corrections and Rehabilitation. I was . . . mocked by the investigating sergeant. . . . He continuously tried to coerce me into saying that another inmate had assaulted me."[129] What follows is M.S.'s survival testimony as it appeared in *The Fire Inside*:

ABU GHRAIB TORTURE BEGAN AT HOME

It was not a surprise to me that the scandal in Iraq's prison involved people who were guards in a U.S. prison. Most of the Abu Ghraib abuses happen in every prison in California: harassment, degradation, the inhumanity in treating prisoners. The worst is the plain arbitrariness of the guards. The staff here is not helpful in almost any situation. We see abuses of helpless people every day. If you try to stand up for yourself, you go to jail (segregation unit, or SHU). The only thing they don't do here is put naked prisoners in pyramids or put hoods on us. Otherwise, what I saw in Iraq is what happens here every day. They say that this kind of treatment is against the rules. They have rules they are supposed to follow here, too. But they don't. The Geneva Convention should apply as a human standard in all situations. The belittling is constant and at all levels. Recently, I was standing in line for sanitary pads; the white women in front of me got 10 pads each. I got three. When I asked if race had something to do with getting an inadequate number of pads, the guard made a scene and said I disrespected her. We can get strip searched at any time for no reason at all, and many of us do. They feel this is normal, anything they do to us is "normal." I had not heard that there were women held at Abu Ghraib, but I can just imagine the treatment they suffered. The incidents underscore the importance of people who stand up when something is not right. It was the soldier who blew the whistle who is the real hero. I had a situation when a staff member abused me. It was only because another staff member stood up for me that I can say *I no longer suffer his abuse.* I need to speak out about it, because the staff member who was harassing me was also harassing others. If I don't

speak the truth about it, then I am allowing the things that got me
here to continue to chain me.[130]

Just as Beloved recalls how she and other enslaved Africans on the slave ship
were not only raped by crewmen but also forced to imbibe their urine and
endure attacks by ship rats, M.S. enumerates the myriad forms of dehumanization—in addition to sexual abuse—to which staff at the CCWF
subject her and other imprisoned women. M.S. opens her testimony with the
statement that "Abu Ghraib abuses happen in every prison in California:
harassment, degradation, the inhumanity in [guards'] treat[ment] [of]
prisoners. . . . We see the abuses of helpless people everyday." While M.S.
later states that some of these "abuses" take the form of racial discrimination
in the distribution of sanitary pads and pointless strip searches, her linking
of everyday life at the CCWF with the notorious U.S. war prison in Iraq in
the early portion of her account ("What I saw in Iraq happens here everyday")
demonstrates her awareness that the system of dehumanization at the
California women's prison is continuous with the netherworld of nudity,
sodomy, dog siccing, electric shock, and sexual violence to which U.S. prison
guards subjected imprisoned people at Abu Ghraib in the early 2000s. As
with Beloved and her tight-packed fellow sufferers' wish for nothing more
than to "leave their bodies behind" on the slave ship, M.S.'s Abu Ghraib–
allusive disclosure of the CCWF staff's extensive commitment to inflicting
harm and humiliation on imprisoned women makes evident that they, like
the crewmen on Beloved's slave ship, seek to transform captives' bodies and
psyches to keep them from "standing up for [themselves]." Thus, by the time
M.S. testifies of her encounter with sexual abuse, she, like Beloved, has
made clear how such harm functions within an overarching system of dehumanization. Well before she mentions the "situation when a staff member
abused [her]," M.S., like Beloved, has established herself as a critically
thinking commentator on the institutional character—rather than exceptional nature—of unchecked harm in the male supremacist regime to which
she is confined.

As a survival testimony, M.S.'s account also demonstrates an antipanoptically expressive sensibility—a sensibility that bespeaks her will to
reclaim her body while held at the CCWF. First, in a narratological gesture
that parallels Beloved's, M.S. does not use the word "rape" to articulate
definitively the sexual nature of the "situation when a staff member abused
[her]." Rather, she makes another allusion to Abu Ghraib, a clear reference
to her awareness of the intensely concealed character of sadism that she and
other abuse survivors confront at the CCWF. A few sentences before this
phrase, M.S. remarks, "I had not heard that there were women held at Abu
Ghraib, but I can just imagine the treatment they suffered." The subtext here

is that since women *did* number among those held in an overseas carceral space where former domestic U.S. prison guards were torturing prisoners of war, the sexual abuse of imprisoned Iraqi women was an ordinary aspect of their always already dehumanizing experiences (as many sources confirm).[131] Thus, in a manner that recalls Fannie Lou Hamer's antipanoptic, testimonial rallying cry for fellow female activists in a rural Mississippi jail (as I discussed in the Introduction), M.S. indicts California state officials while also demonstrating literarily that they will not have the privilege of exploiting the geographically withdrawn nature of their male supremacist containment site to mute her exposure of them as proponents of a sexualized state violence that is a defining (rather than "anti-American") aspect of U.S. foreign *and domestic* punitive confinement.

Moreover, that M.S. tells us that she must "speak out" about this "situation when a staff member abused [her]" in prison to free herself of "the things that got [her t]here" in the first place signals that she was indeed abused *sexually* by a male staff member. Especially worth noting here is M.S.'s insistence that she "needs to speak out about" the abuse. M.S. spends very little time providing details about her sexual victimization but focuses instead on what is at stake when she publicizes it: "the staff member who was harassing me was also harassing others." M.S.'s seeming tangent ("I need to speak out about it") is as insurrectionary and verbally ironic as Beloved's clandestine funeral performance on the slave ship, for by M.S.'s very submission of this piece of writing to *The Fire Inside*, she *is* "speak[ing] out" about her abuse. Just as Beloved testifies to Sethe and Denver about her subjection to an extensive male supremacist system of sexual harm and her undermining of that system, M.S. has raised her voice to raise the consciousness of her (mostly) incarcerated readership about the reality of her sexual victimization *and* her resistance of it. M.S., that is to say, does not dismiss the fact of her abuse behind bars but chooses—perhaps for the sake of her incarcerated readers—to emphasize another one: the fact that she has reclaimed her body. Although her correctional officer abuser is not gone, in her words, "I no longer suffer his abuse."

Conclusion: A Sexualized State Violence Story to Pass On

In this chapter, I have made the case that, from the autobiographical prose of Angela Davis to the zine writings of Brown and M.S., Morrison's *Beloved* is deeply haunted by testimonies of unchecked sexual violence from the contemporary women's prison. Yet *Beloved* is also instructive for our rethinking of the politics of representation that shape conventional stories about jailed and imprisoned women's accounts of sexualized state violence. In the aftermath of the passage of Title VII of the Civil Rights Act of 1964, a

Middle Passage–era practice of authoritarian male supervision has typified carceral life in women's prisons, juvenile facilities, and immigration detention centers, and male corrections employees' rape of women and girls in custody has gone largely unknown and has rarely been portrayed in a manner that highlights abuse survivors' antipanoptically expressed resistance. Admittedly, the representation of sexualized state violence is an especially complex discursive site, and the important work of Sharon Daniel, Victoria Law, Jodie Lawston and Ashley Lucas, Robin Levi and Ayelet Waldman, Beth E. Richie, Rickie Solinger, Paula C. Johnson, Martha L. Raimon, Tina Reynolds and Ruby C. Tapia, and Beyondmedia Education's website "Women and Prison: A Site for Resistance" has reversed the trend in mainstream stories about the sexual victimization of women in custody to omit or simplify abuse survivors' expressed acts of resistance and critical understandings of guard-on-prisoner rape.[132] Nevertheless, Megan Sweeney is right to remind us that imprisoned women generally appear as "silent objects of cultural and political discourse," whether their accounts of sexualized state violence show up in the literature of human rights organizations such as Human Rights Watch and Amnesty International, in the news media, or in scholarly texts.[133]

According to Law, the relative inattention to women's rapidly increasing presence behind bars, and to their critical assessments of the sexual harm they experience at the hands of state officials while confined, can be attributed to persistent cultural narratives of the imprisoned body as one that is gendered male. Because of the influence of Hollywood and urban legend, the U.S. popular imagination's image of sexual violence in prison pictures a man who either actively combats the threat of gang rape from other imprisoned men or struggles not to drop a bar of soap while showering. Law makes the case that these male-centered images of sexual intimidation behind bars make it all the more difficult for people in free society to conceive of imprisoned women as routinely enduring and resisting rape by male prison staff:

> Although female incarceration has increased drastically during the past few decades, prevalent ideas of prisoners remain masculine: the term "prisoner" continues to conjure the image of a young, black man convicted of crimes such as rape or murder. . . . Because women do not fit this stereotype, the public, the politicians, and the media often choose to overlook them. . . . Such neglect leads to the definition of prison issues as masculine and male-dominated. . . . Articles about both prison conditions and prisoners often portray the male prison experience, ignoring the different issues facing women in prison. . . . [A]n occasional article spotlights the sexual abuse in female facilities.[134]

Law later remarks that even "activist-oriented publications mirror the mainstream media's masculinization of prison and prisoners," so much so that "women in prison receive much less support from both individual activists and prisoner rights groups" than imprisoned men.[135] The fact that Morrison's *Beloved* exists reminds us that slavery represents the origin of such cultural neglect of captive women's antipanoptically expressive resistance within confinement terrains premised on gendered social control—confinement terrains whose disciplinary lineage includes the slave ship and the slave plantation. Moreover, if, as Law notes, conventional news-media stories about imprisoned women are known for "dismissing . . . threats of sexual abuse by guards and . . . any actions that women [behind bars] take to address and overcome these concerns," Morrison, by foregrounding the voices and critical understandings of her enslaved and formerly enslaved Black female characters through their first-person accounts of unchecked sexual violence, undermines a long history of underrepresentation and misrepresentation of sexualized state violence, a history that includes our contemporary epoch.[136]

Along these lines, let us also recall that Black feminist scholars have well demonstrated that during slavery, the rape of enslaved women was either pityingly referenced in the pamphlets of white abolitionists (recall my earlier attention to the Reverend John Newton's pamphlet, "When the [African] women and girls are taken on board a ship, naked, trembling, terrified, perhaps almost exhausted with cold, fatigue, and hunger, they are often exposed to the wanton rudeness of white savages") or projected as an attack on Black masculinity, as in the slave narratives of Moses Roper, William Craft, and Josiah Henson. The result of this narrow representational landscape, as Frances Smith Foster has pointed out, was "a monolithic characterization of slave women as utter victims."[137] On the one hand, nineteenth-century enslaved women's narratives such as Harriet Jacobs's *Incidents in the Life of a Slave Girl* and Elizabeth Keckley's *Behind the Scenes, Or, Thirty Years a Slave and Four in the White House* were indeed instrumental in unsettling this "monolithic characterization," but, on the other, novels about the historical experience of slavery that Black women published in the late twentieth century, including Octavia Butler's *Kindred*, Sherley Anne Williams's *Dessa Rose*, J. California Cooper's *Family*, and Morrison's *Beloved*, more fully wrest enslaved women from their common depiction as "utter victims" in abolitionist print culture. Indeed, as Deborah McDowell has remarked, these imaginative retellings of enslaved women's lives that have emerged during the past half century in African American literature—at last free of white abolitionists' constraining conventions and Black male slave narrators' patriarchal narcissism—"shift the points of [narrative] stress from sexual victimization to creative resistance."[138]

With this centuries-spanning Black feminist literary history in mind, I submit that the representational impact of *Beloved* must not be underestimated. Morrison's acclaimed novel, a pre- and post-Emancipation narratological witness of confined women who endure *and* resist unchecked sexual violence, helps us to see better contemporary incarcerated women whose carceral debasement and defiance too often go unseen. *Beloved*, in the end, is a sexualized state violence story to pass on. It is a story about women who boldly testify of systemic repression and bodily reclamation, injurious isolation and unforeseeable community. It is the neo-abolitionist novel that challenges us to see survival testifiers, whether they are survivors of pre-Emancipation sexual abuse on slave ships and plantations or of post-Emancipation rape in geographically withdrawn houses and women's prisons, the way that so many of them see themselves: not as victims only, but also as friends, lovers, mothers, and resisters who discover new ways to live in spite of—or, rather, precisely because of—their abusive captivity.

3

"Didn't I say this was worse than prison?"

*The Slave Ship–Supermax Relation
in Johnson's* Middle Passage

Cringle smiled. . . . "Being on a [slave] ship *is* being in jail with the chance of being drowned to boot." . . . [F]rom within the [captain's] cabin, whose curtained windows were pulled shut, I heard the squeaking of mattress springs, then a stifled whimper, and at last a venereal moan so odd in its commingling of pleasure and complaint that I had, of a sudden, the vision of being not aboard a ship but instead a bordello. It made no sense then, those Venusian groans, that gasping yip of orgasmic strings, but soon enough it would. "Has he a woman aboard?" I looked to Cringle for an answer, but the mate wouldn't look me in the eye; he chewed the inside of his cheek and politely pulled the door shut. "Didn't I say this was worse than prison?"[1]

In the previous chapter, I made the case that contemporary imprisoned women's testimonies of sexualized state violence haunt the Middle Passage storytelling of enslaved and formerly enslaved Black female characters in *Beloved*. The story world of Toni Morrison's classic novel is disturbed, I argued, not only by the frequently hushed ghost of institutionalized rape from the Transatlantic Slave Trade's system of male supremacist containment via the slave ship but also by a successor specter—the largely unknown specter of guard-on-prisoner sexual abuse, which continues to plague the increasingly male-staffed women's prisons in our current epoch of racialized mass incarceration. In this chapter, I consider how Charles Johnson helps us to see, from yet another angle, how today's U.S. prison exists on a ghostly social control continuum with the putatively obsolete slave ship.

Throughout *Middle Passage*, his 1990 National Book Award–winning novel, Johnson reveals that as localities, both slave ships and prisons—by virtue of their extreme geographical isolation from the judiciary—afford those people granted the power to manage them the opportunity to do as they will with the bodies of captive people in a manner that is often hidden from public knowledge. As shown in the block quotation above, early in Johnson's novel a white crewman named Peter Cringle intimates that the unsupervised captain and crew of a slave ship at sea—like administrators and guards in a prison—can easily prototype and mass-produce cruelty on bodies trapped in an out-of-sight, out-of-mind locale. It is precisely because captives contained within the slave vessel and the penal facility are so far removed from the eyes of free society that these racialized confinement spaces are two of the most closely related sites of sadism and large-scale social control. Cringle asks, *"Didn't I say this [slave ship] was worse than prison?"* after forcing the naïve newest member of the crew—a freed Negro slave named Rutherford Calhoun—to listen in on what is clearly a contentious sexual encounter in the cabin of the ship's captain.[2] Cringle's refusal to reply to Calhoun when he asks him whether the captain has a "woman aboard" and his insistence that Calhoun overhear "a venereal moan [that is] . . . odd in its commingling of pleasure and complaint" introduce Calhoun to disciplinary activities that will be anything but exceptional for those deemed socially inferior or com-modifiable on this particular slave ship.[3] Cringle's comparison of the ship to a "worse than prison" kind of prison prepares Calhoun for comprehending both the quotidian nature of sexual violence, debilitation, and injury that the ship's captain and crew will inflict on enslaved Africans and the shamed demeanor of Tommy O'Toole, the young white cabin boy whom the skipper, Captain Falcon, has just raped: "A heartbreakingly handsome cabin boy came scrambling out [of Falcon's quarters], closing the door behind him, his jerkin unfastened, his face drained of color, and his eyes crossed by what he'd been through. . . . Cringle rubbed his face. . . . 'Are you and the captain finished, Tom?' . . . Now I was rivering sweat."[4]

As Calhoun tries to process Cringle's matter-of-fact phrasing of Tommy's subjection to forced sex with Captain Falcon in his question to the cabin boy, he is beyond stunned. Calhoun is "rivering sweat" not only because he has overheard what amounts to the captain's *routine* rape of Tommy—who appears before Calhoun with "his eyes low . . . shivering and rubbing his arms and standing bowlegged as if his bum was cemented shut by dried semen"—but also because Cringle has just apprehended Calhoun and is now preparing to take *him* to Falcon for due punishment.[5] Calhoun has conned his way onto Falcon's ship, hoping to escape either a "jail sentence" or a coerced marriage for outstanding debts that he accumulated as a jobless former slave living in pre-Emancipation New Orleans.[6] Fearing that he might share Tommy's plight—or worse—Calhoun desperately pleads with Cringle for "a word" that might earn him "favor with the captain."[7] Calhoun is clearly unsettled by the unknowable depths of terror that Falcon will mete out against him as a criminalized *Black* body trapped in this remote maritime netherworld. As Falcon has already established his authority among white crewmembers on the ship by his routine rape of Tommy, Calhoun cannot help but wonder the level of harm to which Falcon—who tells Calhoun moments later, "I don't like Negroes"—will subject him, especially since Calhoun is a former slave *and* a Black criminal on the run.[8]

The degradation and ineffable, sadistic harm that awaits Calhoun on this geographically withdrawn slave ship returns us to Cringle's question: "Didn't I say this [slave ship] was worse than prison?" I contend that Cringle's question is directed as much to *Middle Passage* readers as it is to Calhoun, for Cringle's seeming linkage of terror on an antebellum-era slave ship with the disciplinary machinations of the modern prison (the penitentiary was just coming into existence during the novel's narrative present of 1830) reminds Calhoun *and us* of the more contemporary landlocked referent for such open-sea brutality. Johnson, by repetitiously drawing social control parallels between the slave ship and the prison in the penological-historical moment of *Middle Passage*'s publication—the last decade of the twentieth century—establishes a chilling association between these two otherwise disparate confinement locales. I submit that as Johnson compares his fictive slave ship to a prison, he does much more than recast innovations in corporeal constraint that were designed to teach enslaved Africans their "natural" place of racial inferiority in a system of transatlantic captivity and New World slavery. Johnson simultaneously calls to mind the racial terror that prison administrators and employees mete out on bodies held captive within the remote site of large-scale confinement that today's imprisoned writers most frequently compare to the purportedly defunct slave ship social order: the supermax prison.

In the pages that follow, I examine how depictions of mass-based state violence that appear in contemporary imprisoned men's writings from U.S. maximum- and supermaximum-security prisons function as centuries-spanning meditations on disciplinary torment that haunt the slave ship-prison relation in *Middle Passage*. Specifically, I argue that the white captain and crewmen's prototyping of harm on the bodies of enslaved Africans confined within the novel's slave ship is shadowed—as made evident in the testimonies of its captive characters—by actual imprisoned men's literarily transposed confrontations with experimentalist and ritualized forms of racialized prisoner abuse in the high-security prison of the late twentieth century. These men allude to slave ships in their work to critically situate their encounters with institutionalized suffering in the penological-historical context of the Transatlantic Slave Trade. Drawing from the imprisoned intellectual Mumia Abu-Jamal's essays, Avery F. Gordon's conception of haunting, Colin Dayan's legal scholarship, and critical prison studies scholar Dylan Rodríguez's Middle-Passage-to-prison model of racialized captivity, I argue throughout this chapter that Johnson's novel makes apparent a system of dehumanization that began on the slave ship and persists in today's geographically withdrawn high-security prison. Ultimately, I make the case that the antipanoptic expressivity exuded in testimonies about this age-old system of dehumanization—testimonies offered by imprisoned men confined to high-security facilities and by Johnson's fictional slave ship captives—undermines the silencing social control agendas of proponents of institutional power. In the latter portion of the chapter, I trace the development of such antipanoptic expressivity within slave ship social orders of the past and the present, paying careful attention to how the narrator-narratee relationship in *Middle Passage* pushes readers toward socially transformative action in our current mass incarceration epoch in which the institutionalization of secrecy and increased investment in constructing supermax prisons make deployments of prisoner abuse by state and private prisons disturbingly ordinary.

"Rebellious nigger[s]" in a Withdrawn Carceral World: The Contemporary High-Security Prison as Reinstatement of the Slave Ship Social Order

> U.S. military authorities, politicians, and prison administrators seize on the usage of the phrase "the worst of the worst" to justify the barbarities practiced against prisoners. They use it to justify the isolation, abuse, and torture of prisoners in places like the federal lockup known as Marion Control Unit in Illinois, and in various such units in two-thirds of the states, and more recently—and infamously—at the U.S. military prisons in Guantánamo Bay, Cuba, Abu Ghraib, Iraq, and Bagram, Afghanistan.[9]

Mumia Abu-Jamal is perhaps the most widely published critic of the prison-industrial complex—and the high-security prison, in particular—who is currently in state custody. An award-winning Black radio journalist and former president of the Philadelphia chapter of the Association of Black Journalists, Abu-Jamal has spent most of the past three and a half decades in solitary confinement on Pennsylvania's death row. Widespread evidence of police corruption and prosecutorial misconduct surrounding Abu-Jamal's trial led to his becoming an international cause célèbre—and to the U.S. Supreme Court ruling his death sentence unconstitutional in 2011, although he remains imprisoned for life.[10] As shown in the block quotation above, from his work *Jailhouse Lawyers: Prisoners Defending Prisoners v. the U.S.A.* (2009)—one of the more than half dozen books he has published during his imprisonment—Abu-Jamal makes unflinching assertions about injustice in the justice system from the solitary cell. The literary scholar Brian Conniff understands Abu-Jamal's candid critiques of incarceration as exposing a wide range of human rights issues. In Conniff's words, Abu-Jamal uses "his encounters with the law as steps towards a broader conception of 'human rights,' one that reconnects the fate of the most marginalized, including inmates *on death row and in super-maximum prisons*, with the common good."[11] From my vantage point, Abu-Jamal pursues what Conniff calls the "common good" through his frank, trenchant, and antipanoptically expressive analysis of "U.S. military authorities, politicians, and prison administrators" who manipulate language to perpetuate a system of high-security confinement and large-scale dehumanization—a system that he classifies under the rubric of "U.S. *torture* centers"—that gives those in power near-total impunity.[12] Abu-Jamal's sensitivity to the state's practice of "characterizing . . . captives as the 'worst of the worst'" as "a pretext . . . to deflect criticism of official treatment" in both U.S. domestic and war prisons is notable, for his consideration of such rhetorical repression points to a long history of social control that precedes and prefigures today's maximum- and supermaximum-security prisons, a history in which discriminatory ideologies have been used to legitimate disciplinary violence.[13] This history stretches back to the antiquated slave vessel, especially as that vessel gets represented as a "worse than prison" space in *Middle Passage*.[14]

About halfway into Johnson's novel, Falcon, the white slave ship captain, uses the term "rebellious nigger" in a manner similar to the way in which Abu-Jamal argues prison administrators manipulate the "worst of the worst" ascription in the context of the contemporary high-security prison.[15] To rationalize ideologically his large-scale ransacking, kidnapping, enslaving, branding, beating, and tight-packing of unarmed and unassuming African men, women, and children, Falcon labels an unusually resilient group of them "rebellious nigger[s]"—dangerous Blacks who (allegedly) contain within their "nature" the potential to incite "slave insurrections."[16] Falcon, in other words, fabricates African criminality to make his acts of cruelty seem legitimate, even necessary. He seeks to convince his crew that some (and thus all) enslaved Africans can be understood ideologically as "naturally" criminal— as the "*black as Cain*" variety of subhuman imagined by eighteenth-century white Christians whom the Black poet Phillis Wheatley reprimands in her famous poem about the Middle Passage—and thus, the kind of murderous, God-cursed creatures who are deserving of the most brutal treatment.[17] Abu-Jamal similarly makes apparent how the state's branding of high-security prisoners as "the worst of the worst" criminals functions to sanction guards' unchecked violence against them. In fact, Abu-Jamal discusses such rhetorical repression in a manner that haunts Johnson's depiction of mass-based mistreatment on his nineteenth-century fictional slave ship: as with Falcon's self-serving practice of labeling the (supposedly) "untamed" captive African as "naturally" recalcitrant on Johnson's slave vessel, Abu-Jamal makes painfully clear that the high-security prison's captives are recodified as *criminally subhuman* by the state to "justify the isolation, abuse, and torture" that supervising authorities mete out against them.[18] Human Rights Watch has dubbed the brutal consequences of this type of recodification "Marionization" as a way to call attention to the U.S. supermax prototype, the U.S. Penitentiary in Marion, Illinois. For Abu-Jamal, such "Marionization" is best understood as "dehumanization *by design*."[19]

And yet Abu-Jamal is not alone in his assessments of high-security prisons as sites where state-sanctioned dehumanization is ideologically rationalized and perpetually innovated. After years of ethnographic research, the anthropologist Lorna Rhodes found maximum- and supermaximum-security prisons to be locales of "extreme confinement," specialized architectures of captivity typified by the indefinite solitary confinement and routine degradation of human beings whom prison administrators deem innately irrational or "naturally" delinquent.[20] The scholar and anti-prison activist Angela Y. Davis conceptualizes high-security prisons along similar lines, adding that the state's assessment of supermax prisoners as intrinsically criminal is also racialized. She states, "In the supermax prison, [the] . . . main function is to subdue and control 'problematic' imprisoned populations . . . composed largely of black men who, having been locked away in the most remote and invisible of spaces, basically are no longer thought of as human."[21] From another angle, the legal scholars Leena Kurki and Norval Morris have observed that this prevailing idea of high-security prisoners as barbaric, subhuman, or nonhuman has given rise to conditions in supermax prisons that are distinguished by "nearly complete isolation and deprivation of sensory stimuli"—living-death conditions legitimated by the state.[22] Thus, the very design of supermax facilities correlates to the "worst of the worst" label: once branded "worst of the worst" by state officials, any individuals in the contemporary prison system are subjected to an unlimited number of *years* in six-by-eight-foot Security Housing Units for 23½ hours a day, where they are fed through slots and prohibited human contact of any kind, including visits from family and friends, medical assistance, phone calls, mail correspondence, and reading material.

The case of Tamms Correctional Center Closed Maximum (C-Max) Security Unit in Illinois sheds more light on how such a twisted logic of justifiable torture has been used to explain away living-death conditions and rampant prisoner abuse in high-security facilities. Tamms, which opened in 1998, was a supermax located 360 miles from Chicago. Thanks to the tireless efforts of imprisoned and non-imprisoned activists, Tamms was shut down in 2013.[23] Yet as of June 30, 2009, 54 of the 247 men imprisoned at the supermax—the majority of whom were suffering from serious mental health illnesses—had been held in solitary confinement *continuously, for more than ten years*. Solitary at Tamms entailed a minimum of twenty-three hours of windowless isolation in one's cell; meals served through an unsanitary feeding slot; controlled water intake; limited access to health professionals; limited reading material; limited, non-contact visits with family and friends; limited opportunities for exercise in a concrete, walled-in yard; and a host of outright restrictions, including no telephone calls (except to one's attorney), jobs, group or educational programs, religious services, or recreational equipment. In addition, imprisoned men deemed disciplinary problems by corrections officers were placed in strip cells, where any possessions—including their clothes—were removed indefinitely. In the case of Faygie Fields, who suffered from schizophrenia before his arrest and imprisonment, subjection to indefinite solitary confinement and the living-death conditions at Tamms drastically worsened his mental illness, yet such treatment was rationalized by Department of Corrections officials who deemed him "among the 'worst of the worst,'" a man "trying to fake his way to easier time."[24] In his extensive examination of high-security prisons, the investigative reporter Lance Tapley notes that the state's callous infliction of such psychological pain on high-security prisoners is so commonplace that the very existence of maximum- and supermaximum-security prisons should be understood as torture, as state-sanctioned harm that far exceeds the language of "state violence" and the Eighth Amendment's forbidding of cruel and unusual punishment: "Even when mental suffering alone is considered . . . the prolonged solitary confinement of American [high-security] prisoners has increasingly been described by U[nited] N[ations] agencies or human rights organizations as cruel, inhuman, degrading, or *torture*."[25]

And yet, to add further insult to the profound psychic injury that psychiatrists and human rights organizations have shown Tamms and other supermax prisons to manufacture, reports of guards' commitment to experimentalist forms of unchecked violence against people confined within high-security facilities is also disturbingly ordinary. Michael James, a man held in a supermax in Maine, speaks to this point: "They beat the shit out of you. . . . They slam your head against the wall and drop you while you are cuffed. . . . There's a lot who shouldn't work here because they get a kick out of controlling people."[26] James is not alone in testifying to the state-sanctioned sadism that engenders a climate of prisoner abuse in high-security prisons. Vaughn Dortch is an African American man who has experienced racialized torment during his imprisonment at Pelican Bay State Prison, a California supermax complex where reports of abuse are so frequent that imprisoned people across the nation refer to the site as "Skeleton Bay."[27] Dortch told *60 Minutes* that the most egregious example of his suffering there in the early 1990s involved six guards who ripped his clothes off, yanked him out of his cell, and submerged him in a tub of boiling water for several minutes. Calling this a "Klan bath" in which they would transform Dortch into a "white boy," the guards "scrubbed him with a bristle brush until his skin started to peel away."[28]

The state's ideologically rationalized psychological torment, disciplinary brutalization, bodily debasement, and social isolation of the contemporary high-security prisoner reinstates the slave ship social order that Johnson's Peter Cringle describes as "worse than prison."[29] On the one hand, in *Middle Passage*, which was published during the supermax-building explosion of the 1980s and 1990s, Johnson assuredly has in mind a slave ship of the early nineteenth century, as, drawing from historical archives and literary works, he depicts Africans who have been forcibly removed from their homeland, confined to a locale "leagues from culture or civilization," "sardined belly-to-buttocks in [a ship's] orlop," and repeatedly beaten and raped by a white captain and crew.[30] Yet as I discussed by way of reference to Gordon's theory of haunting in Chapter 2, throughout the long, post-Emancipation era of perceived racial freedom in U.S. culture, the terror of the Transatlantic Slave Trade and slavery has persisted. The African American literary imagination of the *post*–Civil Rights era casts an eerie glance back at the slave ship precisely because that slave vessel's depiction is haunted—haunted not only by the male supremacist containment and unchecked sexual violence of women's prisons (as I discussed in Chapter 2) but also by the state's practice of (supposedly) justifiable torture in the slave ship–descended supermax. Contemporary Black fiction's reflective gaze at the slave ship is thus much more than retrospective; it also brings into view the current epoch of mass-based carceral cruelty—an epoch in which the state's increasing investment in the building of high-security prisons is burdened by vestiges of the Middle Passage's social control logic. Describing such haunting in the language of temporal dislocation, Gordon reminds us: "What's distinctive about haunting is that it is an animated state in which a repressed or unresolved social violence is making itself known, sometimes very directly, sometimes more obliquely."[31] In the case of Johnson's novel, this "repressed or unresolved social violence" is state torture as it is refracted through the contemporary carceral referent for the slave ship social order: the supermax, whose construction during the 1980s and 1990s, as the journalist Alan Elsner reminds us, was "the hottest trend in corrections."[32] Thus, the literarily reimagined slave ship disturbs because, as a large-scale, geographically withdrawn carceral social order that is typified by torture, it is as much the haunting fact of Johnson's literary production present as it is the historical fiction of *Middle Passage*'s narrative past.

Also relevant to this discussion is the Thirteenth Amendment, which states, "Neither slavery nor involuntary servitude, *except as a punishment for crime*, whereof the party shall have been duly convicted, shall exist within the United States, or any place subject to their jurisdiction." Put simply, by creating a *criminally* inferior subject against whom ever more forms of state violence can be legitimately and thus ceaselessly unleashed, the Thirteenth Amendment does not rescind but, rather, reinstates the instrumentalization of torment that typified slavery. To this point, the legal scholar Colin Dayan argues, "The Thirteenth Amendment marked the discursive link between the civilly dead and the slave or social nonperson. . . . This amendment . . . is essential to understanding how *the burdens and disabilities that constituted the badges of slavery took powerful hold on the language of penal compulsion*."[33] Let me clarify here that I am not equating the identity of the contemporary high-security prisoner with that of the slave ship captive in a one-to-one fashion. An enslaved man or woman on the slave ship (and on the slave plantation) entered a condition of perpetual captivity, disciplinary torment, natal alienation, economic exploitation, and social death not as a result of alleged criminal acts, but solely because of his or her corporeal use value in the emerging, global capitalistic enterprise of slavery. My association between nineteenth-century slave ship captives and the supermax captives of our contemporary epoch thus has everything to do with the sanctioning of torture to structure their experience of confinement—how, to recall Dayan's language, slavery's "burdens and disabilities" have come to be authorized by the state as rational methods for controlling people deemed intrinsically irrational. It is, in other words, the same disciplinary, citizen-slave binaristic logic on which modernity was established—what Dayan discusses under the rubric of the slave's "be[ing] made superfluous"—that legitimates the "extreme confinement" and routine brutal treatment of contemporary supermax prisoners.[34]

With such an abusive carceral present in its narrative backdrop, the description of *Middle Passage*'s slave ship by the captain of the vessel as a place where "there's not a civilized law that holds water" begins to take on new and unsettlingly contemporary meaning.[35] On Johnson's fictional slave ship and in the U.S. supermax, *white supremacist social control is the law*, and that law does, mind you, "hold water." More to the point, there is nothing extraordinarily exceptional about the routine dehumanization that imprisoned people combat in America's high-security prisons; nor are the abominable actions taken by Johnson's white skipper unlawful in the most fundamental sense. But in both cases, there is no *"civilized* law"—no semblance of respect, compassion, or protection for the essential value of human life—preserving those people who are (re-)codified as less than human. Falcon demonstrates this point well in his barbaric relegation of African and African-descended men, women, and children—those who are "free" and those who are not—to a realm of social extinction that the Black feminist scholar Hortense J. Spillers has discussed as "captive flesh."[36] Early in the novel, Falcon, whom the former slave Calhoun describes as "an American empire builder," manufactures a "captive flesh" realm on his slave ship *Republic* though his enforcement of a system of unwritten, *uncivilized* law. The law of the *Republic* is racial terror, through and through. That law achieves its governing power in part through the cannibalistic horror stories that Falcon creates and re-creates before Calhoun, and through Falcon's and the white crewmen's unrestricted access to contain *and* consume enslaved and non-enslaved Black bodies.[37] Along these lines, Falcon boasts unabashedly of barbecuing and feasting on a nominally free Black cabin boy whom he clearly views, on the basis of his eligibility of edibility, as less than human: "Now that I think of it, [Calhoun], you remind me of a colored cabin boy named Fortunata who was aboard my first trip to Madagascar. . . . We ate him."[38] Falcon, continuing this discussion with Calhoun about Fortunata, adds, "He tasted . . . stringy."[39] For Calhoun, witnessing Falcon's orgasmic pleasure as he brags of his reduction of Black humanity to edible "captive flesh" is far worse than taking in the frightening content of Falcon's cannibalistic story—and its implications for him as a "free" but apparently consumable Black male body: "Cannibalism at sea was common enough, I knew, but [Falcon] *enjoyed* telling this tale. . . . [Y]es, this above all else did Captain Falcon and his species of world conquerors thrive upon: the desire to be fascinating objects in the eyes of others."[40] Put simply, Falcon governs his transatlantic prison through racial terror—through the unending and sadistic recodification of Black humanity as "captive flesh." Falcon's storytelling thus becomes the sinister act that disciplines Calhoun—disciplines him in a manner approximating the impact of Falcon's rape of the white cabin boy Tommy O'Toole, which Calhoun was previously forced to overhear. Indeed, as Vincent Woodard has argued in *The Delectable Negro: Human Consumption and Homoeroticism within U.S. Slave Culture*, the devaluation of the Black body by a slave ship captain's actual or remembered performance of human consumption must be understood as an act of *sexualized* social control: "By asserting his power to eat and consume, the captain also asserts his phallic might and right of ownership."[41]

Falcon's proclivity for enforcing racial terror as law on the *Republic* is displayed not only in his eager consumption of the Black body but also in his craving to maim Black bodies—and thereby reinforce their relegation to the realm of "captive flesh." Throughout Johnson's novel, it is clear that Falcon revels in beating enslaved Africans to a bloody pulp ("He beat them until blood came"), keeping them "double-ironed," and tight-packing them into the ship's hull after branding them (often on more than one occasion), since they are—in his mind, anyway—nothing more than "captive flesh":[42]

> [Captain] Ebenezer Falcon was, as they say, a "tight-packer," having learned ten years ago from a one-handed French slaver named Captain Ledoux that if you arranged the Africans in two parallel rows, their backs against the lining of the ship's belly, this left a free space at their rusty feet, and that, given the flexibility of bone and skin, could be squeezed with even more slaves if you made them squat at ninety-degree angles to one another. *Flesh could conform to anything.*[43]

Again, it goes without saying that Captain Falcon is vicious, vile, and violent. Indeed, his actions appear uncivilized—as do those of his crewmen, whom Calhoun describes as a "blustering, braying gang of tormentors" who rape, castrate, force-feed, and sic dogs on the enslaved Africans.[44] And yet—as Falcon remarks elatedly—"there's not a *civilized* law that holds water . . . once you've put to sea."[45] In the eyes of European maritime law, no harm has been done to any human being because the enslaved Africans—like Calhoun and Fortunata—are read as not only "captive flesh" with a criminally subhuman nature ("rebellious niggers") but also prospective capital. Conceptualized in this manner, African men, women, and children confined within Falcon's ship have never been and can never be legal subjects. Even Calhoun eventually arrives at this conclusion: "They were . . . chattel, according to white men's laws."[46] Falcon and his crew, then, have broken no law by virtue of their despicable treatment of "free" and enslaved African people. The slave ship, although most certainly a site where unspeakable racial terror is unwritten, uncivilized law, is precisely where brutality's undisguised, everyday practice cannot be criminalized. Falcon's slave ship social order is a transatlantic manifestation of Giorgio Agamben's state of exception, a place where even the most fundamental sense of "civilized law" is suspended.[47] Put simply, the process in which proponents of authoritarian control fabricate captive people as less than people—as the "rebellious nigger" brand of subhuman and as property—began on slave ships like Falcon's, and, as scholars such as Colin Dayan and Orlando Patterson have observed, such fabrication also facilitated those people's alienation from human life, legal subjectivity, and legal protection. This tripartite condition of irreversible social extinction has been reinstated in the contemporary supermax prison where, as Dayan points out, "criminals are legally degraded [and] placed under disabilities very like those suffered by slaves," and acts of violence and humiliation practiced against the supermax prisoner proceed with guards' near-total impunity.[48] It is thus the high-security prison's everyday horror stories—stories such as Faygie Fields's, Michael James's, and Vaughn Dortch's, as well as those told by the imprisoned male writers I discuss later in this chapter—that haunt the abuse testimonies of Johnson's slave ship captives in *Middle Passage*.

As a way to ground Johnson's centuries-spanning representation of disciplinary torment in a critical prison studies context, I now draw attention to the work of Dylan Rodríguez. In the section that follows, I offer a reading of *Middle Passage* that is informed by Rodríguez's conception of transatlantic captivity as a specific "technology of violence" that links the Middle Passage past with our mass incarceration present.[49] Rodríguez makes a strong case for how the slave ship—as a mass-based, overcrowded capture site and system of dehumanization that the maritime historian Marcus Rediker has called "a seagoing prison"—has been central to the state's creation of "a blueprint for the carceral technologies of the landlocked U.S. prison," especially the contemporary supermax facility.[50]

"Respatialization of bodies": Re-viewing Johnson's *Middle Passage* through a Critical Prison Studies Lens

In *Forced Passages: Imprisoned Radical Intellectuals and the U.S. Prison Regime*, Rodríguez remaps the terrain of racialized confinement in the United States by insisting that the torment unleashed on captive bodies within slave ships, antebellum plantations, and contemporary prisons should be conceptualized as practices guided by a logic of white supremacist social control, not as tragic or exceptional incidents on the "un-American" stage of the nation's history. As a critical prison studies scholar, Rodríguez is interested in the precedents, legal and otherwise, that give rise to the emergence not of the nineteenth-century penitentiary but, rather, of a late twentieth-century "prison regime" that "*functions* through excess and violations, at times uncodified or nominally 'illegal,' though generally occurring within generously interpreted rubrics of institutional policy and protocol."[51] In his book's final chapter, "Forced Passages: The Routes and Precedents of (Prison) Slavery," Rodríguez theorizes the slave ship as the prison regime's closest disciplinary antecedent. The slave ship is itself, in Rodríguez's carceral conceptual framework, a "technology of violence" whose innovations in large-scale bodily immobilization and routine degradation represent a "genealogical lineage" for a contemporary prison regime that is "centrally focused on containing, controlling, and punishing the bodies of white civil society's unassimilables and incorrigibles."[52] Because Rodríguez's thinking about the slave ship and contemporary prison's interconnectedness is central to my reading of Johnson's *Middle Passage*, I offer here an extended excerpt from his chapter:

> There is a material kinship between the prison as a contemporary regime of violence and the structures of racialized mass incarceration and disintegration prototyped in the chattel transfer of enslaved Africans. . . . The Middle Passage was, at its spatial core, a site of profound subjective and communal disruption for captive Africans: manifesting an epochal rupture from familiar networks of kinship, livelihood, and social reproduction, the voyage was the threshold of geographic, subjective, and bodily displacement for the transatlantic imprisoned. . . . The prison has come to form a hauntingly similar spatial and temporal continuum between social and biological notions of life and death, banal liberal civic freedom and totalizing unfreedom, community and alienation, agency and liquidation, the "human" and the subhuman/nonhuman: [it is] a reconstruction of the Middle Passage's constitutive logic. . . . The contemporary prison, working within the genealogical lineage of the Middle Passage, constantly prototypes technologies premised on a respatialization of bodies and coercive reembodiment of spaces.[53]

Rodríguez's attention to the "respatialization of bodies" is particularly important to note as it provides an illuminating critical lens through which to consider the spatial consequences of what I discussed as rhetorical repression in the previous section of this chapter. That is to say, Rodríguez's interest in bodies that are respatialized—bodies that are degraded, disciplined, and crammed into restrictive carceral and social locales following a systematic process of recodification—offers another level of conceptual engagement with those captive people whom, as I have argued, are being conveniently labeled criminally subhuman to justify terror and expand the capitalistic enterprises of the slave trade and (contemporaneously) the prison-industrial complex. The contemporary high-security prison, in other words, is the most egregious example of what Rodríguez terms the *contemporary prison regime*, for it is there where the state nominally recodifies disproportionately Black, Brown, and mentally ill people as criminally subhuman bodies (they are labeled "the worst of the worst") to sanction the very prototyping of violence that legitimates their perpetual "respatialization."

Again, Rodríguez's spatial understanding of the contemporary prison regime as "a reconstruction of the Middle Passage's constitutive logic" merits our close attention because it offers a centuries-spanning articulation of bodily immobilization as a tripartite social control practice. I am arguing that bodily immobilization, from the massive Black kidnapping era of the Transatlantic

Slave Trade to the current mass warehousing epoch of "respatialized" bodies of color in the high-security prison, has been a way to teach a group of people deemed naturally subhuman or irreparably criminal that their attempts at physical, economic, and social advancement can be legitimately, habitually, and violently restricted by the dominant culture. Put simply, rhetorical repression—the careful manipulation of language by proponents of institutional power to distort and degrade the identities of captive people—plays a major role in the long history of the spatialization of social control. The scholar Lisa Guenther speaks to this point in her study of solitary confinement. Guenther has found that, while the label "worst of the worst" is often used to conjure images of "serial killers, rapists, and terrorists who pose an incontrovertible threat to society at large, and even to other inmates," *any* imprisoned person's perceived (or potential) opposition to known or unknown prison policies can lead to what Rodríguez calls his or her corporeal "respatialization"— his or her unexplained relegation to the high-security prison, Security Housing Unit (SHU), or Control Unit.[54] Guenther writes:

> Many inmates convicted of nonviolent crimes end up in Control Units because they have broken prison rules against fighting (which is sometimes unavoidable), refusing to work (for pennies an hour, or in some states for no wages at all), possession of contraband (which can include anything from weapons to spicy tortilla chips), or even self-mutilation or attempted suicide. Some inmates are placed directly into the SHU without having done anything to break the rules [but] . . . are presumed to be gang members or gang associates. . . . As a result, there is a disproportionate number of black, Latino, queer, and trans inmates held at the supermax level.[55]

From this angle, the "worst of the worst" label that I have discussed as a staple of spatialized social control—a label whose roots can be traced to the Middle Passage—sanctions harm that outstrips even the kind that is purportedly legitimated by one's courtroom conviction. Guenther makes evident that the mere mention of "the worst of the worst" in relation to a captive body (this body often has not transgressed laws or prison policy) stamps on that body perpetual permission for state infliction of concealed and unpunishable violence—or, in another manner of speaking, the kind of official brutality that Captain Falcon unleashes on "free" and enslaved Blacks in *Middle Passage* when he mentally marks them "rebellious niggers" or "captive flesh."

Throughout the rest of his "Forced Passages" chapter, drawing from a wide range of transatlantic and penological-historical archives, Rodríguez links what he calls the slave ship's innovative "technology of violence" with the pioneering forms of punishment that have come to typify the contemporary high-security prison. He begins with an articulation of how kid-napped Africans' painful experience of confinement on the slave ship was designed to reinforce their utility to enslavers who sought nonhuman/subhuman commodities against which their Western "humanity" could be measured. Rodríguez shows how the slave ship's social order functioned through the methodical and corporeally debilitating use of a specialized carceral architecture (e.g., packing enslaved Africans tightly in the ship's hull) and the routinizing of enslaved Africans' degradation (e.g., their subjection to frequent force-feeding, branding, forced "dancing," and rape). This sadistic combination of bodily immobilization and routine degradation meant that confinement on the slave ship would be both physically and psychically disciplinary: enslaved Africans would not only be held in place; they would also be taught their "place." In Rodríguez's words, "The Middle Passage was simultaneously a *pedagogical and punitive* practice that deployed strategies of unprecedented violence in order to 'teach' and coerce captive Africans in the methods of an incipient global ordering."[56]

The violent containment of human beings in individual SHUs within the contemporary high-security prison clearly bespeaks what Rodríguez terms "the coercive reembodiment of spaces."[57] Not only are these people the ones administrators and guards have classified as "the worst of the worst," today's yardsticks for the human and the subhuman/nonhuman; this select group of prisoners also experience the state's perpetual shoving of their bodies into specialized carceral architectures (windowless, electronically monitored, six-by-eight-foot steel and concrete holding spaces) for hours on end, and routine degradation. I am thus arguing, following Rodríguez, that the deepest "material kinship" of the slave ship and high-security prison lies in their multiply disciplinary operation—in how those people in authority at each site oversee the physical constraint and psychic agony of captive people (these are human beings who have been recodified as "rebellious niggers" or "the worst of the worst" and therefore subhuman) without ever being overseen and thereby establish a fiendishly ingenious system of dehumanization.

It is precisely this system of dehumanization—which Rodríguez terms "massive human departure"—that Johnson's *Middle Passage* captures so well, given its hauntingly explicit linkage of life on a slave ship with experiences that are "worse than prison."[58] Johnson's novel, while foregrounding the seafaring experiences of the formerly enslaved Calhoun from a New Orleans port to Senegambia and back, focuses on a middle passage that he records in a ship's log. Put differently, while Vincent O'Keefe is right to remind us that "*Middle Passage* restricts itself primarily to Rutherford's story," and while Elizabeth Muther aptly notes that Calhoun observes the routine suffering of the enslaved but "still tries to make the log his own," we must remember that Calhoun's log, which makes up the entirety of the novel, often takes on a life of its own, veering from the turmoil of his personal life to his empathetic interactions with the ship's captives, a proud African people called the Allmuseri.[59] Again, my reading of *Middle Passage* does not overlook many critics' observations regarding how self-absorbed Calhoun is in taking stock of the damage that the Middle Passage wreaks on him: he notes that the transatlantic journey turns his hair "sugah white," alters his language and vocal intonations, and leaves him realizing just how much his "body's range of motion [is] restricted."[60] But I argue that Calhoun is also attentive to the way in which captive Africans are deformed by their subjection to unchecked institutional power. To recall Rodríguez's language, Calhoun studies how the captain's and crewmen's daily maintenance of the bodily immobilization and routine degradation of the captive Allmuseri constitutes a "technology of violence" that is also a "massive human departure." At one point in the voyage, Calhoun's perception of such departure is especially sharp, for he makes the case that the enslaved Africans "were not wholly Allmuseri anymore. We had changed them. . . . The slaves' life among the lowest strata of Yankee society—and the horrors they experienced—were subtly reshaping their souls as thoroughly as Falcon's tight-packing had contorted their flesh. . . . No longer Africans, yet [they were] not Americans either."[61] Calhoun's ability to read the Allmuseri's treatment not as tragic or exceptional but as systemic—"*We* had changed them"—is precisely what makes Johnson's novel as much about slavery's past as our contemporary epoch's system of mass-based bodily immobilization and routine degradation in the supermax prison.

I am struck, then, by how deeply Johnson's protagonist thinks about the systemic denial of the enslaved Africans' essential humanity. Calhoun ponders so long on their condition that, in time, he comes to assent silently to Captain Falcon's statement early in the novel that "there's not a civilized law holds water" on the slave ship.[62] After eavesdropping on a crewmember who tirelessly trains ferocious dogs to attack the most recalcitrant of the enslaved Africans, Calhoun remarks: "This was not a ship; it was a coffin. . . . On the water, [we were] *leagues from culture or civilization*."[63] Throughout *Middle Passage*, Calhoun beckons readers to witness how captive life on the slave ship is "worse than prison"—indeed, a haunting refraction of everyday life in the supermax prison that Rodríguez provocatively theorizes as a present-day slave ship social order.

"Evidence of American crimes": Johnson's Haunting Literary Refraction of Carceral Life in the U.S. Supermax Prison

Like Rodríguez, Calhoun is intensely observant of two interrelated aspects of enslaved Africans' confinement on the slave ship: their bodily immobilization and the routine nature of their degradation. Let us first consider Calhoun's sensitivity to the bodily immobilization of the Allmuseri. Earlier in the chapter, I discussed how attentive Calhoun is to Captain Falcon's penchant for bodily torment—to the way in which Falcon actually takes pride in the many methods he discovers for "stowing" slaves in the hull of his ship. I now analyze the response of Calhoun and the Allmuseri to such bodily immobilization. The language surrounding these responses, I contend, is haunted by phraseology commonly used to discuss the bodily immobilization that contemporary supermax prisoners endure and resist.

Calhoun's initial reaction to the disturbing systemization of the All-museri's bodily immobilization on the *Republic* is laden with the language of Christian humanism and is uncritically focused on the evil of one man rather than the construction and mechanization of an evil disciplinary machine. Reflecting on a morning in which he notices that the captive Allmuseri are "unable to come up on their own" when the crew prepares to give them some air, Calhoun remarks: "So when they came half-dead from the depths, these eyeless contortionists emerging from a shadowy Platonic cave, they were stiff and sore and stank of their own vomit and feces. Right then *I decided our captain was more than just evil.* He was the Devil. Who else could twist the body so terribly?"[64] Calhoun's statement here, though showing his abhorrence of the quotidian nature of the enslaved Africans' extreme confinement, is ultimately fixated on Falcon's fiendishness. While I do not discount the reality of Falcon's sadism, it is evident that, at least initially, Calhoun, like many slave trade abolitionists (and contemporary prisoners' rights advocates), voices a simplistic, Christian-humanist indignation toward an *individual* actor rather than the *institutional* condition of racial terror and dehumanization that I have discussed throughout this chapter.

It actually takes a few more pages before Calhoun grasps more fully how the crew and even Calhoun himself have been complicit in maintaining a carceral social order whose greatest evil was not the tight-packing orders of one man (Captain Falcon) but, rather, the physical and psychic pain that a number of crewmen routinely wreak on the bodies of the Allmuseri. Let us again recall one of Calhoun's most chilling observations: "The Africans, I realized, were not wholly Allmuseri anymore. *We* had changed them. . . . The slaves' life among the lowest strata of Yankee society—and the horrors they experienced—were subtly reshaping their souls as thoroughly as Falcon's tight-packing had contorted their flesh."[65] The Allmuseri's corporeal constriction within a carceral architecture, Calhoun comes to realize, is difficult to view less because of the "evil" it reveals in Falcon or even in all those who comply with his "devilish" commands than because of how profoundly it deforms the Allmuseri. Subjected to daily overcrowding, perpetual darkness, suffocating containment, and pervasive contamination, the *Republic*'s captive Africans,

Calhoun later remarks, are "no longer Africans, yet not Americans either. . . .
[O]f what were they now capable?"[66] The Allmuseri have suffered too long to
be the same, spent too many sleeping and waking hours in a hull, manacled
while "rest[ing] on the laps of others, down there in scummy darkness foul
with defecation, slithering with water snakes" to return to who they once
were.[67] This later reaction of Calhoun to the tight-packing of captive Africans
in the cargo hold reflects his deeper understanding of how confinement on the
Republic functions: confinement is indeed constraint, but it is also constraint
that is carefully calculated, designed not only to detain but also to debase.
Calhoun's way to articulate this interplay between large-scale corporeal
constraint and mass-based psychological suffering is consistent with what
Rodríguez has discussed under the rubric of "massive human departure."
Moreover, the Christian-humanist phraseology within Calhoun's responses
("[Falcon] was the Devil"; Calhoun, Falcon, and the seamen "were subtly
reshaping their souls") calls to mind the words of the Reverend William
McGarvey, a Presbyterian minister and member of the Bay Area Religious
Campaign Against Torture who has described SHUs—the contemporary
carceral referents for the "worse than prison" spaces to which characters in
Johnson's novel allude—in a similar manner:

> What concerns us as people of faith is the destruction of the human
> spirit. *When human beings are subject to conditions that destroy who
> they are*, it is incumbent upon the whole faith community to call our
> culture and, yes, even our government to accountability. If we allow
> solitary confinement to continue in our society, especially when we
> have been informed of the harmful results, *what does that say about
> the kind of people we all have become?*[68]

Calhoun's attention to the Allmuseri people's routine degradation on the
slave ship provides us with a second look into his understanding of the
fiendish nature of systemic dehumanization within the *Republic*—and, by
extension, within the "worse than prison" supermaximum- and maximum-
security prisons that haunt Johnson's novel. No scene better captures Calhoun's perception of the centrality of degradation on the *Republic* than the
one that follows an uprising. When the Allmuseri take control of the ship
following the white crewmen's failed mutiny, they recount their sufferings
before Cringle—one of the few surviving crewmen—whom they have tied to
a chair. The Allmuseri men are preparing to kill Cringle because he is the
most convenient scapegoat for their wrath. They burn with resentment as
they recall the degradation that Captain Falcon and the rest of the crew have
inflicted on them:

Three of [the Allmuseri men] I recognized as warriors named Ghofan, Diamelo, and Akim. . . . They had reason, good reason, for seeing the last of the *Republic*'s officers dead. Akim, a wide, dark-fired man who was short but had the strength of three, squatted on his hams; he made them relive his sister's death five days after we set sail. Ghofan, a black who had been gelded, and then suffered the torture of the brand, pulled his shirt down to show them how [Captain] Falcon had burned in the initials *ZS* not once but three times until the impression was as clear as stigmata, or the markings on cattle. *Each man had his own atrocity to tell. If not brutality to them then a beadroll of humiliations the midshipmen had inflicted upon the [Allmuseri] women, two of whom had been raped, or on their children, and to this list Diamelo added the small but nonetheless violent assaults on their spirit— parading them naked for bathing before their own children, forcing them to eat by ramming fingers down their throats, answering their wild clawing from the hold with gales of laughter.* On and on the charges came, and with each accusation a finger was stabbed toward the mate.[69]

Calhoun's discussion of the harm that the Allmuseri experience on the *Republic* makes for distressing reading. While readers receive only secondhand testimony about the enslaved Africans' torment on the slave ship (from Calhoun), this passage is the first in Johnson's *Middle Passage* in which Calhoun's phraseology incorporates language that implies that the routine degradation of the Allmuseri men, women, and children should be understood as *abuse*: "the *torture* of the brand," "*atrocity*," "beadroll of *humiliations*," "*raped*," "violent *assaults*."

Calhoun is also meticulous in recording the widespread experience of such degradation among the Allmuseri. He writes, "*Each man* had his own atrocity to tell." Although Ghofan, Diamelo, and Akim initiate this courtroom-style testimony, *every other Allmuseri man present* testifies of actions the *Republic*'s captain and crew took to wound and disgrace them, including the "gales of laughter" that the white crewmen had directed at manacled Allmuseri who had feebly attempted to pull themselves up from the ship's hull. The Allmuseri men dramatize their sufferings as they enumerate them before a bound Cringle and an alarmed Calhoun. Akim "ma[kes] them relive his sister's death"; Ghofan "pull[s] his shirt down to show them" the multiple brands Falcon had burned into his flesh; other Allmuseri men jab condemning fingers in Cringle's face as they tell of their torment ("with each accusation a finger was stabbed toward the mate"). To recall language that has been central to my argument throughout, the Allmuseri men testify with an antipanoptic expressivity that recalls Fannie

Lou Hamer's nationally televised testimony—a testimony in which she put the justice system and the larger U.S. nation on trial through the power of her orated remembrance of racial terror and sexualized state violence. The Allmuseri men tender evidence of their habitual brutal treatment before a surrogate defendant (Cringle) and jury (Calhoun). Importantly, Calhoun— the ship's log keeper—later goes as far as labeling the white captain's and crew's routine degradation of the Allmuseri as "evidence of American crimes perpetrated on the Allmuseri."[70]

Also in line with Rodríguez's understanding of the methodical nature of the slave ship/contemporary high-security prison's maintenance of routine degradation, Calhoun later reveals that the Allmuseri were debased culturally by the enforcement of their nudity on the ship. He remarks that the captive Africans said the crewmen "had *abused*" them by stripping them naked before their children and in the fundamental sense that they frequently fixed their gazes on unclothed Allmuseri women with complete disregard for their (gendered) humanity: they did not "lower [their] eyes when they passed on to show proper respect."[71] Perhaps nothing makes more evident the in- stitutionalized character of degradation that the Allmuseri confront than Calhoun's struggles in the passage quoted above to keep track of the number and diversity of humiliating afflictions of which the Africans testify. Calhoun mentions castration ("Ghofan, a black who had been gelded"), repeated branding ("Falcon had burned [on Ghofan] the initials *ZS* not once but three times until the impression was as clear as stigmata"), sexual violence ("two [Allmuseri women] . . . had been raped"), and force-feeding ("forcing them to eat by ramming fingers down their throats"), but leaves unspecified the details on the "beadroll of humiliations" that Allmuseri women suffer in addition to rape. In the end, Calhoun makes the case that degradation is not an aberration but a sadistic *practice* on the *Republic*. It is but another method by which Falcon and the white crewmen systematically dehumanize people they have recodified as "rebellious niggers" and "captive flesh."

"Herded into the dark hold of a 'Christian' slaveship": Rehabilitative Address in Literary Writings from the Contemporary High-Security Prison

The Origins of Rehabilitative Address

"From the time of the first of our fathers were bound and shackled and herded into the dark hold of a 'Christian' *slaveship*—right on up to the present day, the whole experience of the Black man in America can be summed up in one word: prison."[72] These indicting words open *Black Voices from Prison*, the collection of poems, letters, testaments, and short stories that the Black Arts poet Etheridge Knight and other men published in 1970 while imprisoned at a maximum-security facility in Michigan City, Indiana. Knight's assertion, which appears in the collection's preface, intends to link economic and disciplinary continuities between the slave ship and the contemporary U.S. prison. In particular, Knight's reframing of Black imprisonment as reflecting not a racialized propensity toward crime but, rather, the perpetual recodification of criminalized Black bodies into raw material for large-scale, capital-driven American industries (slavery and mass incarceration) implies that both the fiendish economic agenda and social control logic of the Transatlantic Slave Trade have resurfaced most visibly in the prison in the post–Civil Rights era. In other words, for Knight punitive isolation at Indiana State Prison—which, for him, included stints in the Hole—is not *like* the Middle Passage; it *is* its very continuation. In a move that looks ahead to Rodríguez's conceptualization of "the contemporary U.S. prison regime" as a fundamentally white supremacist arrangement of social organization that constrains Black life behind bars and in the "domestic war zones" of so-called free society, Knight describes the utter predictability of his and other Black men's confrontations with state terror on both sides of the razor-wire fence:[73] "Prison is the ultimate oppression. And as with black people in the larger prison outside, the keepers try to hold the black inmates' *minds in chains* along with their bodies by making full use of a white educational system, a white communications system, a dead white Art, and the white Law."[74] For Knight, the "larger prison outside" reproduces the white supremacist model of social ordering that governs Black carceral life at its ground zero in Indiana State Prison—the same model that had ensured "the first of [his] fathers [would be] bound and shackled and herded into the dark hold of a 'Christian' slaveship" centuries earlier.

Yet Knight's allusion to the slave ship and his inclusion of a sardonic modifier ("Christian")—which exposes America's oft-celebrated doctrine of freedom as fundamentally hypocritical—also makes evident his understanding that the very state power that aims to dehumanize him has been undermined by his published critique. In Knight's words, "The soul-killing effect of a racist culture on black inmates has been greatly offset by the phenomenal rise in black consciousness."[75] When considered in the context of his entire preface to *Black Voices from Prison*, Knight's allusion to the slave ship thus exemplifies the antipanoptic expressivity that, as I have argued throughout this book, distinguishes narratives of prisoner abuse. The very existence of Knight's preface (and the *Black Voices from Prison* collection) constitutes Black captives' opposition to the state's practice of Middle Passage–reminiscent authoritarian control and racialized economic exploitation via the high-security prison and its ever-expanding capture, containment, and abuse of criminalized—and disproportionately Black and mentally ill—bodies. Moreover, what makes Knight's antipanoptic expressivity throughout *Black Voices from Prison* especially noteworthy is that he had previously spoken to a younger Black imprisoned man regarding his anxiety about the racial terror undergirding the panoptic surveillance that he and other Black men at Indiana State Prison perpetually confronted: "Of course, you / know that one says a poem or writes a column here in prison with the warden's eyeballs, hovering / over one's left shoulder, and with the Commissioner of Corrections' eyeballs glaring only a few inches above the warden's and finally with the Governor's eyes hanging like twin bulbs from the whole prison."[76]

For the sake of this chapter's concluding sections, let me point out that Knight's allusion to the slave ship constitutes a glare that defiantly contests the "Commissioner of Corrections' . . . glaring," as well as the intensely panoptic vision of the warden, the governor, and the state at large. Knight's literary glower is, in fact, an *anti*panoptic gaze—a gaze that undermines the racialized panoptic power of the maximum-security prison that he describes as ceaselessly threatening to constrain or contain any attempts that he and others make toward oppositional narrative production while held in (hyper-) punitive isolation. This antipanoptic gaze is one defining element of the *rehabilitative address* that characterizes writings from the contemporary high-security prison that haunt Calhoun's antipanoptic expressivity in Johnson's *Middle Passage*. I define "rehabilitative address" as a Middle Passage–allusive discourse that people or characters dispossessed of voice fashion to illuminate and eradicate the institutionalization of extreme bodily immobilization and degradation that generally characterizes captive life in isolated carceral geographies. Rehabilitative address bears some relation to what the literary scholar James Weaver has termed "rehabilitative storytelling" in his narratological examination of neo-slave narratives. Weaver takes J. California Cooper's novel *Family* (1991) as his example text and argues that rehabilitative storytelling is a mode in which a neo-slave narrative "insistently addresses its reader and emphasizes the potential for social rehabilitation within the reader's contemporary world."[77] As in Weaver's rehabilitative storytelling, the narrator-narratee relationship figures prominently in what I have termed *rehabilitative address*, for the person or character who confronts the Middle Passage (or neo–Middle Passage) in this mode of antipanoptic expressivity also turns to the "use of direct address . . . [and] closes the gap between narratee and reader by crossing the temporal boundaries between narrator and reader" while "situating readers in a position to confront the United States's slave past . . . as a source for social regeneration in the present."[78] The primary differences between Weaver's rehabilitative storytelling and rehabilitative address have everything to do with how readers arrive at "a position to confront" slavery's past and what constitutes the more concrete "social regeneration" for which rehabilitative address pushes. In the sections that follow, I show rehabilitative address to feature an antipanoptic gaze; dialogical immediacy with readers; and an appeal for social transformation related to the contemporary criminal justice system.

The Rehabilitative Address of Etheridge Knight and George Jackson

> Today, we are witnesses to a new high-tech slave trade. This new slave ship is known to many as "prison." The only difference in this slave ship is that it does not sail. Black men, Black women, and even Black children who are now tried as adults, are packed into this ship (cell) like sardines, and they are treated like animals, not humans. . . . These inmates are being confined in an 8' x 10' stand-up grave (called a cell), and most of their waking hours are spent rotting away like wood in salt water.[79]

> *Today I recognized a Slave ship*
> *One still in existence and used today*
> *It was packed to the max with racks of Blacks*
> *The sight of it took my breath away*
> *. . . I say today I recognized a Slave ship!*
> *But no sea was under it*
> *It was a modern day vessel going nowhere*
> *Like the one they got at Jarratt*
> *Oh sure, they fill the media with other ideas*
> *To obscure the clear sight of their plan*
> *But I can see and all the Brothers with me*
> *That we're headed for slavery again.*[80]

I have already discussed how Knight's preface to *Black Voices from Prison* illustrates the first element of rehabilitative address. In what follows, I examine how his preface demonstrates the final two elements of this mode of antipanoptic expressivity—that is, dialogical immediacy with readers; and an appeal for social transformation related to the contemporary justice system

Knight displays a dialogical immediacy with readers mostly near the end of his Middle Passage–framed preface. There, he abruptly eschews a third person point of view and assumes second-person address as he recalls his words from a conversation with "a friend in the outside world" while also directly engaging readers: "You will notice, I'm sure, that even though these letters *are* repetitions of often voiced injustices, they're not grievances, in the usual sense. They are indictments."[81] Knight's dialogical immediacy here sets the stage for his major appeal for social transformation in the preface. First, by momentarily replacing a distanced third-person perspective with a more intimate second person, Knight shrinks the geographical and relational distance between himself and readers. He invites readers to peer into high-security carceral life as peers rather than as voyeurs. This perspectival shift then paves the way for readers to take seriously the ultimate aim of the book's contributors: to legitimate the critical understandings of lawbreakers who critique law enforcers and the law. Thus, while Knight is indeed isolated by "prison walls and men behind the prison walls who permeate this society," he is also, even while confined to a maximum-security prison, much closer to the realm of the human than he was before due to his commitment to literary community building.[82] In this way, Knight's dialogical immediacy also illustrates the final element of rehabilitative address: an appeal for radical social transformation. By the final page of his preface, Knight has established affective identification with his reader as a result of having attained and maintained an antipanoptic gaze within the space of the high-security prison. He has grown so conversationally close to the reading public that he now speaks in slang: "*These cats* (most of them are under twenty-five) make no apologies for being who they are; and . . . they no longer accept whitey's definition of their selves. . . . And in spite of the tyrannical character of prison . . . they somehow manage to keep body and spirit intact. Prison usually breaks men, but not *these cats*; they are a new breed of convict."[83] Knight continues by posing a justice-seeking question: ". . . in the meantime, *what is going to happen to these young men here who might have been hewers of wood or climbers of high mountains?*"[84] It cannot be understated here that Knight's culminating interrogative cry to readers is also an outcry. While there is indeed something empowering about readers' joining Knight in admiring these young Black men who refuse to allow white supremacist maximum-security imprisonment to destroy them (Knight describes them as "no longer accept[ing] whitey's definition of their selves"), Knight's emphasis on their youthfulness and his query about their futures is most definitely an appeal for radical social transformation—a call for his now conversationally close readers to take action against the hyper-criminalization of Black male youth and the expansion of the high-security prison at one and the same time.[85]

Like Knight, George Jackson, whose premature death plight and anti-panoptically expressive fight I discussed in Chapter 1, was a practitioner of rehabilitative address. During the late 1960s and early 1970s, not many years before the supermaximum prison would establish itself as the new carceral standard for bodily immobilization and routine degradation, Jackson was confined to the maximum-security wing of California's Soledad prison.

Jackson was held in an annex within the prison that he referred to as "jail, within a jail," and he was isolated within a six-foot-by-eight-foot strip cell *for years*.[86] Jackson's cell was an early model for the spatialized social control and racial terror that would typify the supermax prisons and SHUs that would emerge and rapidly expand in the 1980s, 1990s, and 2000s. Reflecting on his interminable indefinite solitary confinement, Jackson alludes to the slave ship. Jackson's allusion, like Knight's, expresses his lived experience-based understanding of disciplinary continuities between the tight-packed hulls of slave ships of centuries past and the contemporary epoch's high-security prison. For instance, in his collection of prison letters, *Soledad Brother*, published in 1970, Jackson states: "I recall the first kidnap. I've lived through the [middle] passage, died on the passage. . . . I can't help it; there are too many things to remind me of the 23½ hours that I'm in this cell. Not ten minutes pass without a reminder."[87] As with Knight's allusion, the profound, racial-historical critique embedded within Jackson's allusion to the slave ship is best examined in the fuller context of his book.

Throughout *Soledad Brother*, Jackson rejects the command of submission to the soul-crushing carceral technologies of racialized social control that he confronts in the maximum-security prison, much like Knight and the young imprisoned Black men who fashion an oppositional discourse and demeanor to white supremacy, racialized panoptic power, and high-security confinement at Indiana State Prison. In Jackson's case, this specifically meant that he refused to allow the unending corporeal constraint that he faced within a high-security forerunner to the SHU to strip him of his humanity. It is in this context that Jackson's allusion to the slave ship, bolstered by his frequent identification with the recalcitrant slave throughout his letters, illustrates the elements of rehabilitative address. In a letter to his lawyer, Fay Stender, dated March 12, 1970, Jackson states, "You know we aren't even allowed to get angry. They took away my showering action (the half hour on the tier we were getting) on Monday. . . . No problem, however. There is a sink in my cell. Then I have my vocational work to do. I'll get lost in that for hours sometimes. [This o]ld slave trying to deal with his environment."[88] Jackson here demonstrates all three elements of rehabilitative address. First, he attains an antipanoptic gaze by deciding, despite losing his already limited opportunities to shower, to refresh himself through immersion in self-directed "vocational work," an action that can take his mind out of the cell, despite his body's subjection to forms of neglect, immobilization, and degradation that call to mind the personal Middle Passage journey to which he alludes elsewhere in the epistolary narrative. Moreover, as with Knight's writings in Indiana State Prison, the existence and tone of Jackson's written words serve notice on proponents of state power at Soledad prison, for he reveals in his letter that he is a recalcitrant slave—an "old slave *trying to deal with his environment*"—rather than one controlled by the state's repressive construction of that environment. Jackson also demonstrates the second and third elements of rehabilitative address in the letter. First, he establishes dialogical immediacy with readers (his readers include his lawyer and the larger readership of *Soledad Brother*, his collection of prison letters) through his incorporation of direct address: "*You know.*" Like Knight's second-person address, Jackson's "You know" is much more than conversational writing style. As a widely read imprisoned intellectual who often compared high-security confinement in California's prisons to life in Holocaust-era concentration camps, Jackson says "You know" as a way to bring readers into his seemingly unreal world of state torture and appeal to them for radical social transformation. Jackson's "You know" thus becomes an aperture for readers' affective identification with him as he passes off supermax-level dehumanization with stunning verbal irony: "No problem."

Since Jackson's assassination by guards at San Quentin in 1971, men such as Melvin Farmer have, in their own ways, carried on this tradition of alluding to the slave ship to document and decry quotidian torment in the high-security prison—to actualize rehabilitative address. To call to mind the quotations that started this section, the formerly imprisoned Farmer's astute assessment of the role of law in facilitating disproportionate numbers of young Blacks into supermax prisons where they are methodically "packed into this [slave] ship (cell) like sardines" and degraded—treated "like animals, *not humans*"—demonstrates an antipanoptically expressive understanding of how the high-security prison has dehumanization as its object and how this objective traces its roots to the extreme bodily immobilization and degradation of slave ship captives (a group of human beings deemed criminally subhuman). Likewise, by emphasizing the unforeseen antipanoptic vision of imprisoned Black men who decipher their overrepresentation in high-security prisons as reflecting an economically exploitative "slave ship" social order—"But *I can see and all the Brothers with me / That we're headed for slavery again*"—Rashi'd Qawi' Al-Ami'n offers a racial-historical framework for tracing disciplinary continuities between the slave ship and the supermax, and antipanoptically expressive resistance to both mass-based systems of racialized social control.

"No matter that in 1808 the [slave] trade was outlawed": Rehabilitative Address in Johnson's *Middle Passage*

It is my final contention in this chapter that the contemporary high-security-imprisoned writer's antipanoptically expressive mode of rehabilitative address casts its carceral shadow on the ship's log testimony of the socially confined protagonist in *Middle Passage*, Calhoun. The contents of Calhoun's log speak as much to our current epoch of the neo-slave ship social order/high-security prison as to the post–Slave Trade era.

Over the course of the novel, Calhoun, the freed Black slave and *Republic* crewman, is not treated as horrifically as the enslaved Africans. Yet the captain and crewmembers constantly remind Calhoun of his close proximity to the Africans, in terms of pigmentation and social status. At one point in the novel, Calhoun thinks through comments that convey this sentiment made by the slave ship's cook, a white alcoholic named Josiah Squibb. When the crew nears Africa's coast and slave trading is imminent, Squibb remarks, "These blokes don't know you're a sailor. And they don't care."[89] Squibb's words reveal whites' disdain of Calhoun's Black identity more politely than do Peter Cringle's, for it is Cringle who grumbles about Calhoun's allegedly intrinsic evil "nature"—and the fundamentally evil "nature" of his race—when they first meet: "Hoodlums, every one of them. . . . It's the Devil, I do believe, that sends us the bloody flux, contrary winds, and rumpots like these."[90] Calhoun also numbers among the least trusted and most despised of the otherwise all-white crew. For instance, the boatswain Matthew McGaffin, who contends that a devastating sea storm is evidence that "the ship was cursed by its black chattel and infernal cargo," calls Calhoun "a fugitive and a vagabond" and, later labels him a criminally subhuman "*thief*" in front of the entire crew as they draw up plans to mutiny.[91] McGaffin remarks, "It's in Calhoun's *nature* to be in places he ain't supposed to be."[92] Thus, Calhoun, though not cuffed and detained in the ship's hull, is very often made aware that he is seen as far less than a sailor—or human being. As a result, Calhoun sympathizes with the captive Allmuseri all the more and strives to avoid Captain Falcon, who makes his contempt for Calhoun and all African-descended people unequivocally clear in their first conversation: "I don't like Negroes. . . . You don't think too well, or too often."[93]

Given his routine confrontation with such unconcealed racial animosity, it comes as no surprise that Calhoun seizes on Falcon's request that he keep the ship's log. Log keeping gives Calhoun the unforeseeable opportunity to speak—to literally speak truth to power in the antipanoptically expressive mode of rehabilitative address. Tellingly, Falcon has ordered Calhoun to privilege his white imperialist perspective on the voyage in the log entries: "I want others to know the truth of what happened on this voyage. . . . Include everything you can remember, and *what I told you* from the time you came on board. . . . [Include] *things I told you* when we met alone in secret."[94] While Calhoun hesitantly agrees, he intimates to readers that what he will write will be shaped by his race and social status: "I promised myself that even though I'd tell the story (I know he wanted to be remembered), it would be, first and foremost, as I saw it, since my escape from New Orleans."[95] The *Republic*'s log entries constitute the entirety of the novel, which means that it is the antipanoptic gaze of Calhoun that pervades the text. At no moment is this gaze more antipanoptic than when it targets and condemns Falcon, thereby helping Calhoun to keep record of Falcon's *post–Slave Trade slave trading*: "No matter that *in 1808 the trade was outlawed*. Like so many others with a seaworthy ship and crew . . . Falcon turned to piracy himself, then to a contraband market that many these days served clandestinely."[96] Here, Calhoun demonstrates the first element of rehabilitative address: he literarily attains an antipanoptic gaze while trapped within the *Republic*'s slave ship social order. Importantly, Calhoun reveals what makes Falcon's and the white crewmen's abuse of the Allmuseri so reprehensible: their very capture of the Allmuseri transgresses laws that uphold the abolition of the Transatlantic Slave Trade, laws that *do* "hold water" in Calhoun's narrative present of 1830. *In the eyes of the law, the slave trade was obsolete in 1830 and had been since 1808.* At the novel's end, when Calhoun displays the final two elements of rehabilitative address—dialogic immediacy and the appeal for social transformation—this issue arises again. This time, Calhoun discovers that his creditor is a partial owner of Falcon's illegal slave vessel. With a telling shift in narrative perspective from a first-person point of view to second-person address ("you"), Calhoun gingerly pulls readers into the scene. After assuring his creditor, Papa Zeringue, that Zeringue's name is in the logbook as a joint slave trader, Calhoun directly addresses readers: "*I opened the logbook you presently hold in your hands. . . .* I tilted the book so that [Papa Zeringue] could see. . . . [I told Papa], 'Captain Falcon's logbook. . . . It would be tragic, don't you think, if it fell into the hands of [the prominent white abolitionist] William Lloyd Garrison.'"[97]

In both scenes, Calhoun pushes readers beyond merely witnessing the utter dehumanization of life on the slave ship. He intends for readers to consider their capacity to participate in (post–)Slave Trade abolitionism, perhaps most powerfully in the scene with Papa Zeringue, as Calhoun reminds us that his logbook is no longer just his, but also a shared record of centuries-spanning systemic dehumanization that we, as readers, "presently hold in our hands." Johnson's *Middle Passage*, in other words, is not only a novel about the ineffable terror of the Transatlantic Slave Trade. It is also a book about how we—as close readers of contemporary U.S. culture—respond to its afterlife, to those geographically withdrawn systems of mass-based bodily immobilization and routine degradation (and those who perpetuate them, such as Falcon and Papa) that have persisted, behind razor wire, long after its abolition. If Calhoun could use his words to actualize the obsolescence of one slave ship social order, is it not time that we join the more contemporary Calhouns (such as Knight and Jackson) who have striven literarily to abolish the slave ship carcerality that yet remains in our current epoch via the very existence of high-security prisons?

4

"tell them im a man"

*Slavery's Vestiges and Imprisoned
Radical Intellectualism in Gaines's
A Lesson Before Dying*

"Would it be possible for someone not kin of a condemned man who [is] not a minister of religion or his legal advisor to visit him on death row?"[1] This question was posed to a warden at Louisiana State Penitentiary/Angola prison in the 1980s *not* by a death penalty opposition group or radical prisoners' rights activist but, rather, by the African American novelist Ernest Gaines. On at least two occasions while writing his novel *A Lesson Before Dying*, winner of a National Book Critics Circle Award in 1993, Gaines requested that Angola penitentiary personnel grant him the opportunity to share his time, conversation, and presence with a death row prisoner. His requests were denied, yet their very utterance (and Angola's phrase-long appearance in the novel) reveal something about Gaines that remains underexplored in critical discourse: how his fiction emerges from and responds to increasingly punitive forms of racialized social control in the U.S. criminal justice system and carceral state.

While scholars such as Herman Beavers rightly remind us that Gaines "has consistently denied having an interest in writing protest fiction," I hold that there is something decidedly political about the questions Gaines asked.[2] At one level, Gaines's insistent requests to visit a man on death row while he was in the process of writing his most acclaimed work bespeaks his belief that men on death row are human beings who have stories that deserve to be heard in so-called free society. In addition, though, by striving to position himself as a listener to a man on death row at Angola prison, Gaines implicitly makes a political statement. Angola, after all, is a sprawling *plantation prison* in the state that for many years has imprisoned more people per capita than any other in the nation. The largest penal facility in the United States, Angola has been described as a vast punitive farmland where "long rows of men, mostly African-American, till the fields under the hot Louisiana sun. The men pick cotton, wheat, soybeans and corn. They work for pennies, literally. Armed guards, mostly white, ride up and down the rows on horseback, keeping watch."[3] The literary critic Dennis Childs calls Angola a "fully operational eighteen-thousand acre slave plantation—a place that first began converting black men, women, and children into chattel in the early nineteenth-century— and a geography that continues to perform such mass (in)human confinement."[4] Numerous scholars, activists, and former occupants of Angola attest that it is one prison where there is no question that the economic exploitation, political repression, unchecked sexual violence, and prisoner abuse that were so central to the disciplinary logic of racialized social control in slavery's past persist in the contemporary epoch.[5] That Gaines would repeatedly strive to meet with a condemned man at Angola reflects his tacit affirmation that men confined there have voices and lives that matter.

My fascination with this more political dimension of Gaines's *Lesson* can also be traced to the relatively small body of criticism that has considered the potential for social transformation through the death row diary written by his protagonist, a young Black man who has been sentenced to death in Jim Crow–era Louisiana and who combats wrongful conviction and premature death in a fundamentally racist justice system. To some degree, Beavers attends to this political work in his reading of the novel: "[*Lesson*] . . . utilizes allegory to posit *political* dissent . . . in the black community: how will we deal with increasing numbers of young black men who are either dead or incarcerated and slated to die. . . . Gaines's use of prison not only highlights a potential space of transformation and redemption[;] it likewise prefigures the manner in which the jail will become . . . a site from which to articulate *political* resistance."[6] Marcia Gaudet speaks to the political implications that undergird Gaines's incremental amplification of his death row prisoner's voice in *Lesson:* "The novel questions the ability of the legal and social systems to achieve justice. By giving voice to the stories of those traditionally unvoiced, it provides an alternate discourse."[7] Similarly, former Louisiana poet laureate Darrell Bourque makes the case that Gaines's fictional depiction of his protagonist attaining a voice while awaiting execution registers the political significance of all death row prisoners' voices and lives: "Giving [his death row protagonist] a voice fulfills a part of . . . Gaines' intent from the beginning of his writing career: to give voice to an unvoiced people so that they know they have the power to effect the affirmation of their existence by writing themselves into the broadest laws of the cultures and societies they live in."[8] From another angle, the literary critic John Lowe situates death row narrativity in *Lesson* in the context of Michel Foucault's work on the modern prison:

> Written description of the inmate, which begins with the legal cate-
> gory of criminal he or she inhabits, places the person under a grow-
> ing and increasingly restrictive written definition of personhood.
> As Foucault notes, this development in categorization radically re-
> stricted the possibilities of individuality, as one became grouped with
> others and described through the words and terms of the oppressor.
> . . . Thus, the brilliance of the device of [the] *death row diary* [of
> Gaines's protagonist], which inverts this method, restoring his
> individuality, voice, and also offering [him] security.[9]

In this chapter, I advance the work of Beavers, Gaudet, Bourque, and Lowe by offering the first extended analysis of Gaines's *Lesson* that reveals his long-standing interest in honoring the voices and social commentary of imprisoned people. It is my contention that in *Lesson* and throughout his body of work, Gaines's recurring depiction of characters who are critical of the justice system elucidates his esteeming of antipanoptically expressive Black carceral speakers who expose and oppose slavery's vestiges in the post-slavery South's system of incarceration—vestiges that show up as racial bias, economic exploitation, prisoner abuse, and premature death. I open the chapter by examining Gaines's depictions of the southern penal system in his early works of fiction. The incarcerated Black characters who appear in these works critique the law and the justice system in ways that provide a framework for my new reading of *Lesson*.

"Things haven't changed": The Vestiges of Slavery in Gaines's Prisons

Many of Gaines's fictional works testify to how slavery lives on in the twentieth-century prison. A fair number of his novels and short stories reveal the carceral conundrum implicit in the Thirteenth Amendment, the oft-celebrated statute that, as I note throughout this book, outlaws and legalizes slavery at one and the same time: "Neither slavery nor involuntary servitude, *except as a punishment for crime*, whereof the party shall have been duly convicted, shall exist within the United States, or any place subject to their jurisdiction." Gaines, who represents the fifth generation of a family of sharecroppers, grew up on a Louisiana plantation in Pointe Coupee Parish, and has remarked that for the 1940s-era Black characters he depicts in his works—as with Blacks who lived in the Deep South during that time—

slavery is nominally a thing of the past, but, yet and still, "things haven't changed."[10] In Gaines's fiction, the racially biased criminalization of Black men and women; the economic exploitation of these so-called Black convicts by state officials who lease their labor out to private companies, prison farms, and sharecropping plantations; and guards' and overseers' disciplinary instrumentalization of violence against these convicts signify the continuing presence of "the peculiar institution" in the post-Emancipation era.[11] Gaines, that is to say, makes a point of never depicting his Black characters' bouts with criminalization, incarceration, or prisoner abuse as tragic or exceptional occurrences. Rather, he depicts them as predictable outcomes of a long history of systemic racial repression in the South and the nation at large.

Consider, for instance, Gaines's representation of racial intimidation in "Three Men," a short story that he published in 1968. Throughout this brief work, jailed Black men assess how the contemporary southern prison functions as a system of social control continuous with the antebellum slave plantation. Perhaps most tellingly, Gaines's Black male protagonist, Proctor Lewis, wrestles with the racial punitiveness that surrounds his sentencing. As the story opens, nineteen-year-old Proctor has turned himself in and confessed to two white policemen that he has killed another Black man in self-defense during a bar fight. Proctor soon discovers that his sentence will be either a long stint at the state penitentiary or a longer stint working as a laborer for a white plantation owner: "They knowed how to get a man down. Because they had me now. No matter which way I went—*plantation or pen*— they had me."[12] Proctor's understanding of the historical continuities be- tween the racial terror so central to the institution of slavery and the racial- ized punitiveness directed toward him by the contemporary policemen ("*plantation or pen*—they had me") continues when, near the end of the story, he attends to wounds that white guards have inflicted on a fourteen-year-old Black boy for stealing cakes. Proctor is dismayed as the youth cries un- controllably. Another jailed Black man, also disturbed by such racialized state violence, calls the guards "a bunch of pigs—dogs—philistines."[13] While some of the men at the jail are shocked by the scene, Proctor refuses to be stunned: "I told myself . . . he ain't the first one they ever beat and he won't be the last one, and getting in it will just bring you a dose of the same medicine. . . . *I hated what the law had done.*"[14] Proctor's assessment of the power of unwritten *law*—the power afforded white male proponents of Jim Crow justice to practice unbridled discretion in their punishment of an unarmed Black male teenager—shows us just how attuned Gaines is to the prison system's appropriation of slavery's logic of racial terror and to incarcerated men's critical understandings of that logic.

An even closer examination of this particular scene reveals how the attack that this Black youth suffers at the hands of white guards is also a form of racialized exemplary punishment. Proctor's recollection of the beating's aftermath conveys his comprehension that the jail administration intends for him and the Black men and boys in his cellblock to be witnesses of a *pedagogical* act of violence. Proctor knows that jail guards are striving to teach him and other incarcerated Black males their place as (racial) subordinates in the justice system, the South, and the nation: "Nobody had said a word since the guards threw that little boy in the cell. Like a bunch of roaches, like a bunch of mices, they had crawled in they holes and pulled the cover over they head. . . . I didn't want to have to pull cover over my head every time a white man did something to a black boy."[15] Gaines thus makes apparent—through Proctor—that just as plantation overseers could, without legal punishment, use violence as a method of social control in the antebellum South, the near-total impunity afforded the contemporary jail or prison guard similarly functions to legitimate prisoner abuse as a tool of racialized discipline in the twentieth-century penal facility.

The observations of Gaines's jailed protagonist in "Three Men," as well as those raised by incarcerated characters in his novels *Of Love and Dust*, *In My Father's House*, and *A Lesson Before Dying*, illustrate his acute awareness of slavery's vestiges in contemporary punishment practices such as racial profiling, police brutality, and prisoner abuse. Yet in each of these works, Gaines places narrative emphasis on the revolutionary expressions of voice that imprisoned people cultivate while confined. Such expressions emanate from characters who realize what Gaines has described as "the importance of standing."[16] When Gaines says that these characters "stand," he means that they show their fellow sufferers and society that they refuse to be broken by racialized social control practices in the justice system or the Jim Crow South. Those Gaines characters that "stand" exude antipanoptic expressivity, to recall the language of the Introduction.

One particularly memorable instance of "standing" appears in Gaines's novel *Of Love and Dust* (1967). When one of its main characters, an incarcerated Black man named Marcus Payne, is bonded out of jail to the white plantation owner Sidney Bonbon, he "stands" by refusing to put on the fieldwork clothes and straw hat that sharecroppers are expected to wear. Marcus refers to the sharecropping wardrobe as "that convict shit."[17] Marcus's seemingly ludicrous decision to don a short-sleeve silk shirt, dress pants, and low-cut dress shoes as he picks corn in the scorching Louisiana heat is the first of his many ostentatious displays of antipanoptic expressivity. Marcus makes dressing extravagantly his common practice when he learns that white authorities on the plantation treat "bond people"—who curiously are all Black—with the same degradation and disdain that plantation owners and private corporations meted out on the disproportionately Black laborers they overworked in the convict-leasing system.[18] Marcus's decisions about his hard labor attire can be understood, then, as staged acts of nonviolent non-compliance to a social control system that demands that he and all ex-cons work faster, harder, and longer than their non-criminalized counterparts for no pay. As Marcus "stands" against the plantation/prison/Jim Crow status quo, he also contests a racial-historical condition of large-scale economic exploitation, a condition he states as being reserved for the "contented old slave."[19] Marcus's habit of overdressing is thus an act of political resistance, a way to communicate to both Jim Crow society and the Black community that he rejects the status of twentieth-century "slave," has a voice, and is, in his words, "a human being."[20]

Gaines recovers this depiction of an incarcerated Black man "standing" in opposition to vestiges of slavery in his celebrated sixth novel, *A Lesson Before Dying*. The "stand" of Jefferson, the novel's death-sentenced protagonist, is even more pronounced than Marcus's. A young, systemically undereducated Black man who has been falsely charged with murdering a white male grocer, Jefferson "stands" by writing and releasing to free society a death row diary that is critical of the justice system and his white public defender's preposterous claim that he is either a mindless and expendable hog or post-slavery chattel serviceable to the whims of a white supremacist social order—"a thing that acts on command, a thing to hold the handle of a plow, a thing to load *your* bales of cotton, a thing to dig *your* ditches, to chop *your* wood, to pull *your* corn."[21] Jefferson, like all Blacks in the Louisiana town in which he labors, is seen in the eyes of the novel's 1940s-era white civil society as "just another nigger" who is legitimately confined to the prison house of segregation, a racial caste system that reinstated the racist ideology and disciplinary logic of slavery in the South decades after the purported abolishing of "the peculiar institution."[22] Yet Jefferson, like Marcus, is marked doubly because the prosecuting attorney and state have labeled him, a young Black man, a criminal. Mere suspicion of Jefferson's culpability in a robbery that ended in a white man's death is grounds not only for his condemnation but also for his subjection to endless displays of racialized exemplary punishment that culminate in the spectacle of execution in the electric chair, as the novel's Black schoolteacher recounts: "A white man had been killed during a robbery, and though two of the robbers had been killed on the spot . . . [Jefferson], too, would have to die."[23] Jefferson confronts, under the quotidian practice of Jim Crow and the white supremacist logic of the justice system, forms of racial terror that constitute vestiges of slavery, obscuring his desired human identity and constraining his attempts at self-expression. Gaines has remarked that by composing all of Jefferson's diary entries in chapter 29 of *Lesson*, he hoped to show how an unlettered Black convict in Jim Crow society could still "within a few weeks of his death . . . identif[y] himself as a human being on trial. . . . He's trying to say something, to show who he is."[24] Before Gaines wrote chapter 29, he spoke at length about portraying Jefferson's process of voice attainment as a kind of "stand": "I know one thing. I'm going to have [Jefferson] give a very good speech before [the execution] happens. . . . He's going to stand up real tall and tell . . . what he thinks manliness is and citizenship [is] and what life is about."[25] Jefferson's "real tall" stand and "very good speech" are fully realized in the chapter's nine-page, phonetically transcribed, grammatically disobedient diary in which Jefferson, its electric chair-bound author, rejects his state-ascribed identities of hog, criminal, and slave: "tell them im strong tell them im a man."[26]

Yet what remains understated in many scholarly assessments of this revered "Jefferson's Diary" chapter of Gaines's *Lesson* is the extent to which Jefferson's diary-writing and diary-distributing labors are, in and of themselves, radical political acts.[27] To say it plainly, Jefferson's diary, the only titled chapter in *Lesson*, testifies to his unforeseeable insurgency. From death row, Jefferson interrupts the state's itinerary for his systemic silencing by using his pencil, notebook, and confrontation with racial bias, wrongful conviction, and racialized premature death to empower politically himself and a Black community bound in the prison of Jim Crow. A twenty-one-year-old semiliterate field hand, Jefferson seems the least likely of prospective agents of social change in the segregated plantation community to which he is also confined. As Gaines reminds us, "Jefferson is barely literate. He has never written a letter in his life. He was barely able to write his elementary school assignments. But now, with his pencil and his notebook, he tries to define his humanity—in the few days he has left to live."[28] As he embarks on a journey of literarily "defin[ing] his humanity" from death row, Jefferson becomes nothing short of a revolutionary. Through the power of the written word, Jefferson frames his struggle against the criminal justice system in the context of a godforsaken Jim Crow social order that he and the members of his Black community endure together: "it look like the lord work for wite folks cause ever sense i wasn nothin but a litle boy i been on my on haulin water to the fiel on that ol water cart with all them dime buckets an that dipper just hittin."[29] Ever insurgent, Jefferson concludes his diary by having "wite folks" work for him. In the culminating phrase of his final entry, Jefferson boasts—with telltale antipanoptic expressivity—that he, a condemned Black man, intends for a white deputy named Paul Bonin to deliver his diary to a Black schoolhouse: "im gon ax paul if he can bring you this [notebook]."[30]

I am arguing, from one angle, that because of the fictional character Jefferson's decisions to write and release to free society a death row diary that contests the white supremacist logic of Jim Crow society and his systemic silencing by the justice system, he shares political lineage with actual Black male writers who have synecdochically used their subjection to racial profiling, discriminatory sentencing practices, solitary confinement, and physical and psychological abuse behind bars as a platform for racial uplift. Like Dr. Martin Luther King Jr., the iconic Black civil rights activist and author of "Letter from Birmingham Jail," the Black radical social theorist George Jackson (whose life, literary work, and political praxis I discussed in Chapter 1) and Black middleweight boxer Rubin "Hurricane" Carter, Jefferson writes about his personal struggle against slavery's vestiges in the justice system and white supremacist America for the benefit of a larger Black community and thereby transforms his solitary cell into a political terrain of resistance, cultural critique, and social transformation.[31]

Given the racial-political particularities that surround his death row diary writing, I also submit that Jefferson bears striking resemblance to a figure that scholars in the emerging field of critical prison studies identify as an *imprisoned radical intellectual*.[32] In his groundbreaking work on that subject, Dylan Rodríguez argues that imprisoned radical intellectuals represent a distinct lineage of post-1970s revolutionary social theorists and creative expressionists who are "*politically* constituted by the [contemporary] prison's regime of bodily immobilization and bodily disintegration" and pedagogically minded—invested in defying their daily confrontation with increasingly punitive and violent forms of incarceration by cultivating "creative new languages and embodied spaces, visions, and fantasies of liberationist political struggle" that can engender large-scale social trans-formation.[33] By examining Jefferson's diary alongside Rodríguez's work on imprisoned radical intellectualism in the ensuing sections, I make the case that Gaines's Jefferson represents in contemporary African American fiction the brutally confined, "*politically* constituted" educator whom Rodríguez has contemplated so provocatively in the autobiographical and epistolary writings of late twentieth-century imprisoned authors. I demonstrate how Jefferson uses his political condition as premature death captive of a white supremacist society to expose under-discussed realities of racial injustice in the justice system and also destabilize conventional ideas about the presumed "nature" of (Black) criminals.

In the pages that follow, I trace the development of the "Jefferson's Diary" chapter in *Lesson* to the imprisoned radical intellectual "stand" expressed in the prisoner abuse narrative that shadows the novel's production: the death row prisoner Willie Francis's *My Trip to the Chair* (1947). Francis was a Black adolescent from Gaines's home state of Louisiana who became the first known victim of a botched electrocution in 1946. Francis's subsequent appeal for justice to the U.S. Supreme Court and narrative about his failed execution made headlines but did not release him from a second, and ultimately lethal, confrontation with capital punishment. Francis's plight and death row writing did, however, inspire Gaines's characterization of

Jefferson as one who seizes his political confrontation with racial bias, wrongful conviction, and premature death as an opportunity to attain a voice literarily and to radically transform his criminal identity.

Although Gaines initially claimed that he set *Lesson* in 1948 instead of 1947 precisely "because I didn't want anyone to compare those two stories," his statements in more recent interviews suggest his esteeming of Francis's and other condemned men's perspectives on "what [a] person must go through, the month before, the week before, then the night before [he must die]."[34] By critically revisiting Gaines's witnessing of death row imprisonment and execution as a young writer, as well as his confessed horror and fascination with the idea of death row narratives, my new reading of *Lesson* demonstrates just how profoundly Francis's plight and "stand" shadow Gaines's characterization of Jefferson. As imprisoned radical intellectuals, Jefferson and Francis both, I contend, use their political confrontations with systemic racial injustice to refashion their identities literarily—and, by extension, the identities of Black communities bound in the prison of Jim Crow.

This chapter also makes the case that *Lesson* is a neo-abolitionist novel that proves instructive for critical discussions about wrongful conviction and wrongful execution stories. We frequently encounter such stories in the human rights literature published by advocacy organizations such as the Innocence Project, the American Civil Liberties Union, and the Death Penalty Information Center. Human rights journalists rarely focus on how imprisoned or formerly imprisoned people interrogate their construction by the state as "born criminals" and thus tend to overlook how they view the justice system—and themselves. I argue that, by depicting in *Lesson* a condemned man whose death row diary reveals his unforeseen attainment of (antipanoptically expressive) voice and his subjective experience, Gaines counters this obscuring social scientism and thus demonstrates the radical utility of the neo-abolitionist novel in ongoing critical explorations of the justice system.

Gaines's Jefferson as Post-Slavery Slave and Imprisoned Radical Intellectual

> What the government wants is not just death, but silence. A "correct[ed]" inmate is a silent one.
>
> —Mumia Abu-Jamal, *Death Blossoms*

While it is most assuredly *not* a Richard Wright-esque protest novel, Gaines's *Lesson* is, from start to finish, a narrative that exposes and opposes racially discriminatory incarceration and white supremacy.[35] Readers of the novel, a *New York Times* bestseller and an Oprah's Book Club choice, will miss much of its jolting cultural critique if they focus on its allegorical allure at the expense of its commentary on how the ordinariness of racial terror in twentieth-century U.S. culture is a continuation of slavery's past. In the early pages of the novel, Grant Wiggins, a college-educated Black schoolteacher, is disturbed both by Jefferson's unfounded criminalization and swift death-sentencing and the fact that whenever he visits Jefferson, he witnesses the overrepresentation and youthfulness of "colored prisoners"—boys he describes as being "fifteen or sixteen years old," "children," and "in their late teens."[36] Such implicit representations of racial bias in *Lesson* are not arbitrary. They illuminate the mass-based criminalization of Black youth as a vestige of slavery's disciplinary logic: these depictions make evident the state's post-slavery method of keeping young Black men under the lock and key of white supremacist social control. Jason Stupp has thoughtfully unpacked Gaines's emphasis on white investment in the perpetuity of such control:

> Ernest Gaines's *A Lesson [B]efore Dying* is, first and foremost, a prison novel. This is worth stating . . . because . . . it has been read primarily as a novel about personal transformation and racial reconciliation. . . . *The plot . . . is driven by the looming execution of Jefferson. . . . We are made aware of the distinct and irredeemable loss of Jefferson as a person. . . .* If Jefferson's death is symbolic of anything, the lesson he imparts is more of a warning: *young black men will continue to be put to death by a state invested in the defense and perpetuation of white power.*[37]

Of course, what Stupp calls the "irredeemable loss of Jefferson as a person" begins long before Jefferson's electrocution in a crowded room at the novel's end. Jefferson's "irredeemable loss" is reflected first in his being born a racial subordinate in a Jim Crow society. Even prior to his wrongful incrimination, any attempt that Jefferson might have made to speak his truth to (white) state power would have been inconsequential because of the fact of his blackness in a sharecropping culture premised on the disciplinary logic of white supremacy. Jefferson is rendered politically mute and socially invisible long before he is disappeared by the racist machinery of criminal justice system—long before he is sentenced to civil death and biological death by an all-white, all-male jury. Jefferson's most fundamental "irredeemable loss" is thus his quotidian containment to Jim Crow and the systemic silencing—the dispossession of voice—that precedes and prefigures his subjection to racial injustice in the justice system.

Gaines portrays racial injustice as anything but aberrant in *Lesson*. His depiction of the endemic racism of the justice system begins with the novel's opening scene, in which Jefferson appears as an unwitting accomplice in a

rural drugstore robbery that ends in a deadly shootout between two of his
Black male acquaintances, Brother and Bear, and the white male storeowner,
Alcee Gropé. Jefferson, the only survivor of the gunfight, is so confused and
afraid that he never leaves the store. As he tries to decide on his next move,
he babbles to Gropé, the wounded white owner who is barely conscious yet
capable of murmuring an indignant "Boy?" to Jefferson as he nears death, "It
wasn't me. It wasn't me, Mr. Gropé. . . . You got to tell the law that."[38] Moments
later, Jefferson stuffs his jacket pocket with cash, takes a swig out of a whiskey
bottle, and is seen by two unnamed white men who enter the store. Given his
telltale appearance as a young Black man at a scene of interracial homicide
in the segregated South, Jefferson's repeated "it wasn't me" goes unheard by
the perishing white grocer who repeatedly calls him "Boy"; this foreshadows
the statement's irrelevance to the two unnamed white men who incriminate
him and the twelve white men who will sentence him to death. Moreover, as
Karen Carmean has observed, Jefferson's state-appointed white attorney aids
and abets this systemic silencing: "Jefferson's lawyer . . . doesn't ask Jefferson
to tell his [own] story, thus denying him voice."[39] Jefferson's dispossession of
voice is then reinforced by the white judge, who asks him—before passing
down a verdict of death by electrocution—whether Jefferson "had anything
to say before the sentencing" and by his godmother's bitter rejoinder, "The
law got him."[40] Even from the novel's opening, then, the "irredeemable loss"
of Jefferson is reflected both by his social invisibility and by the inconsequence
of his attempts at self-expression: the state is interested not in Jefferson
recounting his version of the story behind Gropé's murder but, rather, in
reminding him of his "natural" place of powerlessness in a white supremacist
social structure.

To add justice system insult to this Jim Crow injury, Jefferson's trial,
conviction, and execution collectively constitute a ritualistic lynching, as
Carlyle Van Thompson has argued.[41] First, as with the vast majority of
lynchings in the United States that took place from the late 1880s to the 1960s,
Jefferson is physiologically dissected and publicly shamed by a white man in
power. In this case, that white man is Jefferson's own lawyer:

> Gentleman of the jury, look at him—look at him—*look at this. Do*
> *you see a man sitting here? Do you see a man sitting here?* I ask you, I
> implore, look carefully—*do you see a man sitting here?* Look at the
> shape of his skull, this face as flat as the palm of my hand—look
> deeply into those eyes. Do you see a modicum of intelligence? Do you
> see anyone here who could plan a murder, a robbery, can plan—can
> plan—can plan anything? A cornered animal to strike quickly out
> of fear, a trait inherited from his ancestors in the deepest jungle
> of blackest Africa—yes, yes, that he can do—but to plan? . . . No,

gentlemen, this skull holds no plans. . . . What justice would there be to take this life? Justice, gentleman? *Why, I would just as soon as put a hog in the electric chair as this.*[42]

Perhaps as disturbing as the lawyer's obviously racist employment of nineteenth-century phrenology theories and reverse anthropomorphism is his public declaration of Jefferson's tacit expendability. In the mind of his public defender, Jefferson is not only as mindless as, but also as *disposable* as, a hog. Moreover, the extrajudicial harm and racial terror so characteristic of lynching are manifested in the court's neglect of Jefferson's Sixth Amendment right to an impartial jury and his subjection to death before a crowd of jeering whites, including some who tell their children that the state is "put[ting] an old bad nigger away."[43] Grant is incensed as he reflects on the disturbingly predictable nature of Jefferson's trial and verdict and their relation to the racialization of incarceration and premature death in the Jim Crow South:

> Twelve white men say a black man must die, and another white man sets the date and time without consulting one black person. Justice? . . . They sentence you to death because you were at the wrong place at the wrong time, with no proof that you had anything at all to do with the crime other than being there when it happened. Yet six months later they come and unlock your cage and tell you, We, us, white folks all, have decided it's time for you to die, because this is the convenient date and time.[44]

Jefferson offers his own, embittered commentary on such racial injustice during one of Grant's early visits. Confined to the all-Black section of a jail that is housed in a courthouse externally arrayed with Confederate flags and a Confederate statue, Jefferson articulates with distressing precision how the environment of racial intimidation and squalor in which he is entombed only exacerbates the reality of his unjust sentence: "I'm a old hog. Youmans don't stay in no stall like this. I'm a old hog."[45] Jefferson is warehoused in conditions that call to mind the supermax prisons I discussed in Chapter 3. For all but one hour a week, Jefferson is locked in a filthy solitary cell that is "roughly six by ten, with a metal bunk . . . a toilet without a seat or toilet paper" and a "single light bulb."[46] He is permitted but one shower a week, and—with the exception of occasional visits from Grant, his godmother, Miss Emma Glenn, and select members of the Black community—he has no human contact. In addition, Jefferson's white jailers, Deputy Clark and Sheriff Guidry, glory in enforcing his subjection to living death during his pre-execution confinement. Guidry, for instance, takes great pride in squelching every attempt that Grant and the Black community make to facilitate Jefferson's access to education during his incarceration: "Every moment for the rest of his life, he's going to know he's in jail, and he's going to be here till the end. This ain't no school."[47]

Much like James Baldwin's jailed Black male protagonist Fonny, whose predictable plight I examined in Chapter 1, Gaines's Jefferson is falsely charged and held in deplorable conditions behind bars as a result of the state's systemic—not aberrant—practices. As Kathryn Daley and Carolyn M. Jones observe in their reading of *Lesson*, "We are witnessing the violent workings of a *system* of oppression. The mechanisms of this *system*—either overt or covert—keep everyone in 'place.'"[48] Indeed, Jefferson's dispossession of voice, racially biased criminalization, public degradation, racially discriminatory sentencing, and psychically injurious confinement are all intended to teach him and members of his Black community their "place" of racial subordination in a white supremacist social structure. Jefferson is, in another manner of speaking, the local Jim Crow society's object of racialized exemplary punishment. His punishment, given its public nature and irreversibility, is intended as much to control the Black community socially as to shame him. Its efficacy is far-reaching. Infuriated both by Jefferson's predictable plight and the Black community's inability to alter it in any significant way, Grant confesses to his Black lover, Vivian Baptiste, that he does not "feel alive," then bemoans his and Jefferson's institutionally enforced powerlessness: "Suppose I was allowed [by Sheriff Guidry] to visit him, and suppose I reached him and made him realize that he was as much as man as any other man; then what? He's still going to die. The next day, the next week, the next month. So what will I have accomplished? What will I have done? Why not let the hog die without knowing anything?"[49]

From this angle, Jefferson's wrongful conviction and impending execution are not exceptional occurrences but foreseeable consequences of his being Black in a Jim Crow society whose slavery-reminiscent conception of humanity is premised on the systemic dehumanization of a racialized Other. Jefferson's unjust sentencing to death and imminent encounter with the electric chair thus constitute what I have theorized throughout this book as slavery's vestiges, residual tools of discipline from an age-old system of racialized social control that includes and exceeds the carceral locale of the penal facility and is typified by unchecked state violence, systemic silencing, bodily/social immobilization, and premature death.

The extent of Jefferson's subjugation makes his death row diary writing reflective of imprisoned radical intellectualism. To recall again Rodríguez's conceptual framework, imprisoned radical intellectuals wage political war against the contemporary U.S. prison and carceral state and affirm their humanity by creating and distributing their own critical corpus of art, literature, theory, and so on amid the institution's deployment of various forms of terror, such as guard-on-prisoner sexual abuse, racialized violence, torture, and indefinite solitary confinement. Whether they are high-profile figures affiliated with radical political movements (e.g., George Jackson, Angela Y. Davis, Assata Shakur, or Mumia Abu-Jamal) or less widely known activists (e.g., Viet Mike Ngo), from Rodríguez's vantage point, all imprisoned radical intellectuals conceptualize their confrontations with criminalization, incarceration, and prisoner abuse as interrelated experiences of white supremacist social control that collectively intensify the political and pedagogical force of their justice system–critical work:

> [Imprisoned radical intellectuals'] individual formation as imprisoned political subjects occurs in a context of systemized repression that, in turn, forces them to map out new "cognitive territories" within which ways of knowing, feeling, and living the experience of unmediated state violence create new spaces and political trajectories of dissent, radicalism, and antisystemic possibility. . . . [I]mprisoned radical intellectuals appropriate their conditions of confinement to generate a body of social thought that antagonizes and potentially disrupts the structuring logic of their own civic and social death.[50]

Given the magnitude of "unmediated state violence" that Gaines's Jefferson confronts in the segregated South and on death row, I argue that Jefferson, by his very act of writing, does much more than identify a coping mechanism, engage in self-actualization, or exchange a hog identity for a man status—as criticism on *Lesson* often overemphasizes. I contend that Jefferson becomes contemporary African American fiction's most shining example of an imprisoned radical intellectual. By composing and later releasing to free society a death row diary, Jefferson does much more than attain a voice and a sense of self-worth. To invoke Rodríguez, he also "create[s] new spaces and political trajectories of dissent, radicalism, and antisystemic possibility" and "generates a body of social thought" for his fellow Jim Crow detainees. He writes pedagogically—with notable antipanoptic expressivity—from the state's ground zero of systemic silencing: death row. Moreover, Jefferson politically alters the site of death row imprisonment and undermines his premature death status by using the written word to transform himself from an isolated and voice-dispossessed death row convict to a communally conversant pedagogue. Jefferson's unforeseeable performance of this political act—one capped off by his imparting of his diary to Grant and to the Black boys and Black girls he teaches—is the true triumph of *Lesson*'s concluding chapters. But I do not wish to romanticize Jefferson's literary activism. We must not forget that Jefferson's imprisoned radical intellectual "stand" is shadowed by what I discuss in the next section: Gaines's involuntary remembrances of real-life executions and his deep contemplation of the living death experiences of the twice-electrocuted Black teenager Willie Francis.

Gaines's Personal Witnessing of Condemned
Men's Dispossessed Voices

Gaines has been captivated by the experiences and expressive voices of
people on death row for much of his literary career. In his interviews with
the Academy of Achievement and the National Endowment for the Arts
(NEA), Gaines speaks at length about how his distanced witnessing of
condemned men's executions inspired him both to read literary works that
foreground their perspectives on capital punishment (e.g., Leonid Andreyev's
The Seven Who Were Hanged) and to pose the questions that would compel
him to write the "Jefferson's Diary" chapter of *Lesson*.[51] Reflecting on days in
his early writing career in which he lived in full view of California's notorious
San Quentin State Prison, Gaines tells an NEA interviewer that he was so
terrified by the frequency of executions that he was compelled to write. For
Gaines, writing about capital punishment from the viewpoint of the
punished became his way to both mourn and honor the men he witnessed
enduring the agony of state-sanctioned premature death:

> I was horrified by executions at, at, at San Quentin. They'd always
> happen on a Tuesday at ten o'clock in the morning. I used to just
> leave the house—my apartment—and walk to the ocean. I lived
> about four, four and half miles from the ocean. And so I'd go to the
> ocean just to get away from everything. I didn't want to see anybody,
> talk to anybody, until I [was] sure the execution was over. And then
> I would come back home and just sit there all day. And I think this
> is what drove me to writing *A Lesson Before Dying*. [I wrote] because
> of these nightmares and nightmares about execution. What did,
> what did a person go through, that week before, the day before, the
> night before, he was to die? W-w-what was in, w-what was, what was
> in his mind?[52]

During this segment of the video-recorded interview, Gaines's repetitions
("at, at, at San Quentin"), stammering ("W-what was in, w-what was"), and
trembling voice all indicate just how deeply his observation of these executions
affected him. Off-camera, Gaines remarked that his "nightmares and
nightmares about execution" became increasingly personal: he would
envision himself, his family members, and even his close friends walking to
their deaths in San Quentin's gas chamber.[53] In his interview with the
Academy of Achievement, Gaines added that he was sleep-deprived *for years*
because his mind was so flooded with thoughts of death-bound prisoners and
executions. Ironically, writing proved to be the only way that Gaines could
process these unsettling dreams: "Whenever there was an execution, I would

not write that day. I could not write that day. I couldn't do anything, [because I was] trying to imagine what this person was going through. . . . I realized that in order to try to get rid of this, to exorcise this, I had to try to write about it."[54] Gaines's writing of *Lesson* was thus, on the one hand, a therapeutic strategy for "get[ing] rid" of recurring mental images of executions. On the other hand, it was an empathetic gesture: through the process of composing the novel, Gaines amplified the dispossessed voices of the condemned by laboring to "imagine what this *person* was going through" on death row and in the execution chamber.

Gaines's prolonged contemplation of the humanity of men on death row profoundly destabilizes the disappearing function and social isolation of death row incarceration. The death row imaginings that shaped Gaines's writing of *Lesson* bespeak an intimacy that is, in fact, personal. The "Jefferson's Diary" chapter is a bit of a requiem to a Black youth who had been sentenced to death whose plight Gaines knew very well. In his lecture "Writing *A Lesson Before Dying*," Gaines reveals that the novel's plot and characterization shadow the real-life story of Willie Francis, a Black adolescent who suffered the first bungled electrocution in U.S. history. Francis—like Gaines—grew up in rural, Jim Crow Louisiana. In 1946, Francis received a death penalty conviction following his alleged murder of a white Cajun pharmacist in St. Martinville, Louisiana, and a trial so racially biased that generations of local Black *and* white townspeople expressed their outrage.[55] Francis had had no previous run-ins with the law, but, as the Pulitzer Prize–winning historian Gilbert King and legal scholar Deborah Denno have revealed, white policemen coerced the semiliterate Francis to write a murder confession in very formal and incriminating prose.[56] In lieu of fingerprints on a gun or biological evidence, Francis's forced confession was used to convict him—despite his obvious near-illiteracy. Francis was swiftly sentenced to death; then he endured the torment of a failed electrocution. When the state ruled that Francis would face execution again after surviving, he appealed to the U.S. Supreme Court, and battled—unsuccessfully—against what he and his legal team argued were constitutional violations: double jeopardy and cruel and unusual punishment. While Francis's case made national headlines throughout late 1946 and early 1947, the publicity did not release him from having to face another electrocution and a premature death. On a more positive note, Francis, with the help of a sympathetic prison visitor named Sam Montgomery, published *My Trip to the Chair*—his personal account of this disturbing experience with racialized prisoner abuse—just months before he was sent to the chair for his final, fatal execution on May 9, 1947.

In the "Writing *A Lesson Before Dying*" talk, Gaines reveals just how well he remembers Francis—and the systemic racial injustice that led to his murder charge, death sentence, and two electrocutions. Although Gaines avoids using Francis's name, he acknowledges that, while he was in the beginning stages of writing *Lesson*, Paul Nolan, a colleague at the University of Southwestern Louisiana (now the University of Louisiana, Lafayette), gave him material on Francis's case that unsettled him, touched him, and shaped his characterization of Jefferson:

> Paul told me he realized that . . . I might benefit by reading [about Francis's] case and that he had a lot of material about the case if I would like to do so. This particular case . . . appeared familiar to me. . . . [It] happened only a few miles from where I was now teaching and no more than seventy miles from where I had lived as a child and the area where most of my previous stories had taken place. There were so many similarities—the work, religion, the food the people ate, everything. . . . The stories (Francis's and Jefferson's) are different, [but] still *I . . . use some of the information from the [Francis] case. Both young men are black. Both nearly illiterate. Both were involved in the murder of a white man. . . . No defense witnesses were called in either case. Only white men served on the juries.*[57]

Although there is no evidence to date indicating that Gaines knew Francis personally, it is clear from Gaines's talk that he connected to Francis's story in a very personal way. Beyond his quick recognition of the particulars of Francis's case, Gaines made note of the close geographical and experiential proximity that he and Francis shared. Francis's execution, that is to say, took place in St. Martinville, "no more than seventy miles" from Pointe Coupee Parish, where Gaines had grown up. As Black male teenagers in Jim Crow Louisiana, where white supremacy rendered Black men of all ages prime targets for criminalization, incarceration, and (double) execution, Gaines intimates that he could easily have suffered Francis's plight: "[Francis's] case . . . could have happened in the parish where I grew up."[58] Thus, while writing *Lesson*, Gaines's extended reflection on the racialized prisoner abuse experience of Francis and the death row terrors of San Quentin's condemned men helped him, a writer in free society, to establish a bond of genuine connection with death-bound populations in the withdrawn world behind the razor wire.

I am arguing that, even as he drafted a novel about the waning months, weeks, and days of a death row convict's life, Gaines laid the groundwork for himself and his readers to both establish meaningful bonds with those in bonds and imagine the far-reaching possibilities for narrative produced by actual people who live entombed in a carceral condition typified by state-sanctioned premature death. In the process of writing *Lesson*, then, Gaines was grappling with questions that have shaped contemporary critical discourse on imprisoned intellectuals while also literarily honoring the dispossessed voices of death row prisoners. As I mentioned at this chapter's outset, Gaines, in preparation for what would become the "Jefferson's Diary" chapter of *Lesson*, had written to a warden at Angola prison on at least two occasions, seeking the opportunity to talk in person with a condemned man awaiting execution there. Despite his persistence, the state, of course, denied Gaines visitation privileges.[59] Yet this rejection only intensified Gaines's investment in contemplating how men sentenced to death lived—and inspired others to live—in the midst of imminent execution. Gaines sought out the testimony of people who had witnessed executions of prisoners at the state penitentiary and posed difficult questions to them and himself about this systemically silenced—and disproportionately Black—population:

> I want to know exactly what the prison cells looked like in the forties and fifties. I want to know what kind of clothes the prisoners wore, what kind of food they ate, what kind of exercise they took. I want to know if there were windows. . . . How did blacks communicate with each other when the guards were around? How can [I] make [my imprisoned protagonist] here a true human being?[60]

Gaines's interest in the covert forms of communication accomplished by imprisoned Black men in the presence of Angola's guards, as well as his curiosity regarding how his Black protagonist might affirm his humanity in Angola, reflects concerns that are foundational to scholarship on imprisoned radical intellectuals. As Rodríguez has shown, this lineage draws from the immediacy of these intellectuals' confrontations with the state's repressive system of social isolation, bodily immobilization, prisoner abuse, and premature death to answer the very question—"How can [I be] . . . here a true human being?"—that Gaines intends for his fictional convict to illuminate in a death row diary. Imprisoned radical intellectuals, Rodríguez reminds us, reconceptualize humanity, community, and freedom as a survival strategy for themselves *and* all people they perceive as captives abused under regimes of unchecked institutional power. Through their distinct corpus of intellectual and cultural production, they "critically envision (and sometimes strategize) the displacement or termination of the epochal American production of biological and cultural genocides, mass-based bodily violence, racialized domestic warfare, and targeted coercive misery."[61] These underground social theorists and creative expressionists, in other words, are the Harriet Tubman–like conductors of a more contemporary Underground Railroad, for as they produce and distribute magazines, newsletters, pamphlets, artwork, and zines critical of the justice system within and beyond prison walls, they also advance a mission that eclipses individualized notions of attaining voice or achieving justice. As Rodríguez teaches us, imprisoned radical intellectuals get free by getting others free. They create an oppositional knowledge base that, even in the face of premature death, revivifies their political subjectivity as well as that of fellow imprisoned people, Jim Crow detainees, or carceral state captives.

Gaines's Jefferson is one such imprisoned radical intellectual, for Gaines, who repeatedly returns to that question—"How can [I] make [my imprisoned protagonist] here a true human being?"—creates within him the capacity to answer it, to imagine from death row a survivor's conception of meaningful human life within a racist justice system, a Jim Crow society, and a U.S. nation typified by a white supremacist logic of social control. Jefferson's diary, in other words, affirms the political subjectivity of Gaines's fictional Black community as much as that of the actual condemned men whose secret, subversive literary practices ("How did blacks communicate with each other when the guards were around?") Gaines is determined to honor. Thus, in the "Jefferson's Diary" chapter of *Lesson*, we have an opportunity not only to witness Gaines make prose sing. If we study that chapter closely enough, we also have an opportunity to recognize Gaines's revivification of death row intellectuals' dispossessed voices.

Lesson's Revivifying Narrative and Its Shadow

The word *revivify* is often used to describe the actions that a government or grassroots collective takes to spark a depressed local, regional, or national economy. For my argument, it is important to retain this connotation of the word. To understand fully the *revivifying* work that Jefferson accomplishes through writing and releasing to free society a death row diary that is critical of the justice system, we must remember that revivification is *large-scale* regeneration. We must remember that when this captive of both a racist justice system and a racial caste system passes on to his socially and psychically depressed Black community a diary in which he asserts his newfound humanness and manhood—"tell them im strong tell them im a man"—he infuses new life and political vitality into an entire population that has been routinely and even violently deemed less than human by the state.

When we conceptualize revivification in this light, the very existence of Jefferson's diary refutes Grant's claims in the early pages of the novel regarding the extremity of voice dispossession, social invisibility, and political impotence that Jefferson and the Black community endure together: "Jefferson is dead. It is only a matter of weeks, maybe a couple of months— but he's already dead. . . . He's dead now. And I can't raise the dead. All I can do is try to keep the others from ending up like this—but he's gone from us. There's nothing I can do anymore, nothing any of us can do anymore."[62]

When Jefferson writes and releases his diary to free society, he radically undermines this "already dead" status that Grant has ascribed to him and the Black community. Jefferson literarily raises himself from the dead space that Jim Crow society has reserved for post-slavery slaves deemed civilly, socially, and biologically dead. Through his unforeseen but unrelenting commitment to producing a socially conscious collection of diary entries from a carceral space defined by these multiple forms of death, Jefferson revivifies himself and his fellow Jim Crow prisoners at one and the same time. Jefferson, in writing himself out of the status of isolated prisoner to become a community-focused pedagogue, transforms not one but *two* sites of state repression—a racialized death row and a white supremacist social order—into arenas of political struggle.

The nature of Jefferson's near-death, antipanoptically expressive revivification can be understood even more fully in the context of the scholar Sharon Patricia Holland's theorization of dead speakers in African American fiction and U.S. culture in her award-winning book *Raising the Dead: Readings of Death and (Black) Subjectivity*. Conceptualizing the space of death as both a realm of Black nonhumanity/subhumanity on which white culture delineates itself *as* culture and a terrain of embattled non-citizenship existing between the enslaved subject and the freed one, Holland opens the ears of her readers to late twentieth-century novels and films, such as Morrison's *Beloved* and Allen and Albert Hughes's *Menace II Society*, that they might "hear the dead speak in fiction . . . to discover in culture and its intellectual property opportunities for not only uncovering silences but also transforming inarticulate places into conversational territories."[63] For Holland, voice attainment happens within such "inarticulate spaces" because "dead" speakers make enlivening use of their confinement to social death. They use the dead spaces to which the state has assigned them to speak in ways that redefine speech and loosen the stranglehold that racialized social control has on them and others. In producing his death row diary during the days leading up to his electrocution by a repressive social order, Gaines's Jefferson similarly revivifies himself, the fictional Black community confined within a Jim Crow space of death, and even the real-life condemned men whose pre-execution narratives haunt Gaines. At the white supremacist ground zero that is death row, Jefferson embarks on a journey of narrative revivification that unmoors his and others' self-expression in ways that produce and reproduce new forms of speech, life, community, and humanity.

What I hereafter refer to as a *revivifying narrative* is a political resistance text laden with antipanoptic expressivity that a captive author directs to captive audiences to thwart two consequences of state-sanctioned premature death in the justice system: voice dispossession and apolitical conformity to racialized social control.[64] Accordingly, my ensuing reading of two revivifying narratives that shadow each other—the "Jefferson's Diary" chapter written by Gaines's fictional protagonist in *Lesson* and the real, historical death row prisoner Willie Francis's *My Trip to the Chair*—attends to ways in which the authors of these texts subvert the state's attempts to neutralize their political praxis in the time leading up to their executions. I examine how Jefferson and Francis use the written word to (1) undermine their condition of voice dispossession; (2) dismantle slavery's logic of racialized discipline; and (3) refashion their stigmatized identities.

Jefferson's Revivifying Narrative

When Gaines's protagonist chooses to see his unjust sentence as an opportunity to empower his fellow sufferers literarily in the prison of Jim Crow, he undermines his racial-historical condition of voice dispossession. It is at this moment that he displays the first element of a revivifying narrative. Jefferson begins the work of undermining his condition of voice dispossession after hearing Grant contextualize his confrontation with racial injustice in the courts and in prison as a display of white supremacist bravado—and anxiety:

> White people believe that they're better than anyone else on earth—and that's a myth. The last thing they ever want is to see a black man stand, and think, and show that common humanity that is in us all. . . . [Jefferson], I want you to chip away at that myth by standing. I want you—yes, you—to call them liars. I want you to show them that you are as much a man—more a man than they can ever be. . . . When I showed [Sheriff Guidry] the notebook and pencil I bought you, he grinned. . . . He believes it was just a waste of time and money. What can a hog do with a pencil and paper? . . . Look at me, Jefferson, please. . . . I need you. . . . I need you more than you could ever need me.[65]

Implicit in Grant's call for Jefferson to "stand," and, in his own voice, to reveal the fictitiousness of racial myth is a second charge: Grant also needs Jefferson to do the rigorous thinking that he cannot do, even though he is a well-educated Black man. Yes, Grant is the teacher by trade. Yes, he has been called out and called on by Tante Lou and Jefferson's godmother, Miss Emma, to "make [Jefferson] know he's . . . a man."[66] But Grant desperately needs Jefferson to teach *him* about manhood. As Gaines has stated, Grant, like Jefferson, is "a prisoner of his environment" who "hates the South" and "hates everything around him."[67] A Black instructor working at an understaffed and under-resourced one-room plantation schoolhouse in the segregated South, Grant, in his own words, is systemically coerced to "teach what the white folks around here tell me to teach."[68] Without Jefferson's response to his plea for intervention—"I need you more than you could ever need me"—Grant remains nearly as isolated as Jefferson, a point that he reveals to Jefferson during the latter portion of this scene: "I want to run away, but go where and do what? I'm needed here and I know it, but I feel that all I'm doing here is choking myself."[69] It is at this moment that Jefferson begins to empathize with Grant and others who share his and Grant's confinement to the Jim Crow system of mass-based racialized discipline. Jefferson comes to voice, as it were, by crying at length for the first time in the novel. Grant, stunned, states that long after he had stopped talking to Jefferson, he knew "something was touched, something deep down in [Jefferson]—because he was *still* crying."[70]

Again, this scene marks the beginnings of Jefferson's attainment of voice. Jefferson has finally begun to grasp the racial-historical imperative that necessitates his death row diary writing. Grant has helped Jefferson to see that the psychic survival of the Black community depends on whether or not Jefferson will choose to speak up for him and them literarily in the midst of his painful confrontation with racialized premature death. If Jefferson refuses to express opposition to his state-ascribed identities of "hog," criminal, and post-slavery slave, his acquiescence will reinforce the centuries-old disciplinary logic of slavery and the fundamental voice dispossession of his fellow Jim Crow prisoners. So as Jefferson cries, he surmises, with awe and with anguish, that his voice exists—and matters. Perhaps Jefferson also hears another revelation in Grant's continued affirmation: that he, the *unlettered* hog/criminal/post-slavery slave—not Grant—is best positioned to regenerate the Black community politically. Grant states: "You could give something to [your godmother], to me, to those children in the quarter. You could give them something that I never could. . . . The white people out there are saying you don't have it—that you're a hog, not a man. . . . I want to show them the difference between what they think you are and what you can be. To them, you're nothing but another nigger."[71]

Grant argues that if Jefferson writes and releases to free society a death row diary, it will be, in the most basic sense, documented counterevidence of Blacks' presumed racial inferiority. The diary's mere existence will be Jefferson's way to dispel the racist myth that Blacks have "no dignity, no heart, no love,"[72] and it will thus serve as the teaching tool that even the college-educated Grant cannot produce. Moreover, the diary will perform an educational function even after Jefferson's execution: it will remind Grant, Miss Emma, Tante Lou, the Black schoolchildren, and the entire Black community that if their most visibly unlearned and systemically silenced member can counter the myth perpetuated by whites of Blacks' "natural" irrationality, they all have enough spirit, intellect, and political vision to write themselves out of the fabricated hog/criminal/post-slavery slave status to which they have been reduced by Jim Crow society. In this way, Jefferson, in Grant's words, can be "bigger than anyone who has ever lived on [the sharecropping] plantation or come from th[eir] little town."[73]

Moreover, since Jefferson's diary will also be a Black convict's *written* work, it will also testify of the Black community's unforeseen rational thought and humanity. This notion of a Black author defying a Eurocentric worldview in which she or he is perceived as biologically incapable of having or transposing rational thought—this notion of an unschooled and perceivably unschoolable racial subordinate producing and circulating writing that humanizes him or her in the eyes of the dominant culture—resituates an argument that Henry Louis Gates has made famously in a nineteenth-century context to the twentieth-century prison. In *The Signifying Monkey*, Gates argues that even as enslaved and unlettered Blacks began to situate their literary practice outside Western traditions during the antebellum epoch, they also recognized that any writings that they chose to publish in an Enlightenment-minded U.S. culture would be read as a rallying cry for and irrefutable evidence of their unforeseen humanity.[74] A tearful Jefferson's decision to write a death row diary exudes a similar cry, one that Grant seems to intuit: "I cry, not from reaching any conclusion by reasoning, but because, lowly as I am, I am still part of the whole. Is that what [Jefferson] was thinking as he looked at me crying?"[75]

By chapter 28, Jefferson is expressing in his own words what Grant has begun to infer: Jefferson does see himself as "part of the whole" that includes the Black community and, more broadly, humanity. Jefferson thus begins his revivifying narrative *orally*:

> Y'all asking a lot, Mr. Wiggins, from a poor old nigger who never had nothing. . . . I'm the one got to do everything, Mr. Wiggins. I'm the one. . . . Me, Mr. Wiggins. Me. Me to take the cross. Your cross, nannan's cross, my own cross. Me, Mr. Wiggins. *This old stumbling nigger.* Y'all axe a lot Mr. Wiggins. . . . Who ever car'd my cross, Mr. Wiggins? My mama? My daddy? They dropped me when I wasn't nothing. Still don't know where they at this minute. I went in the field when I was six, driving that old water cart. I done pulled that cotton sack, I done cut cane, load cane, swung the ax, chop ditch banks, since I was six. . . . Now all y'all want me to be better than ever'body else. How, Mr. Wiggins? You tell me. . . . What I got left, Mr. Wiggins—two weeks? . . . That's all I got on this here earth. . . . I'm go'n do my best, Mr. Wiggins. That's all I can promise. My best.[76]

Though clearly frustrated by the weight of communal expectations and personal inadequacies that surround his literary labor of self-expression from death row, the orphaned, diploma-less, "stumbling nigger" Jefferson promises to give his "best" to Grant and the Black community as he takes on the role of representative author and imprisoned radical intellectual. Now, Grant, the teacher, remarks, "You're more a man than I am, Jefferson," and becomes his first and most inquisitive student.[77] Grant speaks to Jefferson with reverential hope as he considers the impact that Jefferson's literary contestation of his own voice dispossession will have on the Black community: "My eyes were closed before this moment, Jefferson. My eyes have been closed all my life. Yes, we all need you, every last one of us."[78]

In this same chapter, Jefferson displays the second element of a revivifying narrative in the opening pages of his diary: he writes in a way that dismantles slavery's logic of racialized discipline. Jefferson accomplishes this by composing a diary entry in which he incisively critiques the state's construction of him as hog. He writes, "*If I ain't nothing but a hog, how come they just don't knock me in the head like a hog? Starb me like a hog? . . . Man walk on two foots; hogs on four hoofs.*"[79] Jefferson's questions here call to mind a passage from the narrative of the formerly enslaved Black abolitionist Frederick Douglass. He reflects on his time at Colonel Lloyd's slave plantation, remarking that only when his white master deemed it necessary would he and other enslaved children have opportunities to nibble corn meal off dirt floors, without utensils, *like pigs*: "I suffered from much hunger. . . . Our food was coarse corn meal boiled. This was called MUSH. It was put into a large wooden tray and set down upon the ground. The [enslaved] children were then called, *like so many pigs, and like so many pigs* they would come and devour the mush . . . none with spoons. . . . [F]ew left the trough satisfied."[80] That Douglass emphasizes that his master controlled the food intake of enslaved children to the extent that he, one of the representative "many pigs," eventually "suffered from much hunger" is important to note in light of Jefferson's anticipation that the state would eventually "starb" (starve) him "like a hog"—or, as Douglass would have it, like a slave. What Jefferson's questions do, I am arguing, besides exposing the extent to which the prison system ordinarily functions like the slave plantation system (by making its captive Black body-turned-raw material docile through the institutionalization of undernourishment) is ironically reveal the irrationality of state officials who repeatedly refer to him as "hog"—white men such as Sheriff Guidry—but fail to consider how the small liberties they extend to him actually facilitate his undermining of that hog/slave status. Jefferson, though quite candid earlier in the novel about the deplorable conditions of his confinement (he compares his dilapidated cell to a pig stall), also realizes that he has not been starved or stricken by his institutional overseers, as hogs are, when their owners are preparing them for slaughter. The weightiness of Jefferson's words becomes apparent when we recall the nature of hog slaughters. In the weeks leading up to their slaughter, hogs are castrated, starved, and then rendered unconscious by gunshot wound or electric current.[81] Jefferson, speaking in loosely metaphorical terms (*"Man walk on two foots; hogs on four hoofs"*), intimates that instead of denying him the sustenance of communal fellowship and educational engagement in the time preceding his slaughter, jail administrators like Guidry call him a "hog" and yet—by extending him the freedom to be "fed" by the visitation of Grant and members of the Black community—ensure his political-intellectual sure-footedness.

To say it plainly, for the hog, strength must be diminished before slaughter. The so-called hog Jefferson, though, in recognizing the liminal freedoms that he can access on this particular death row—for instance, visitation by loved ones and the opportunity to build literacy skills with a Black male educator— attests to the jail administration's inadvertent investment in his personal and intellectual strengthening, pre-execution. Jefferson's diary is thus, even in its earliest entry, reflective of the second element of a revivifying narrative: by calling into question his state-ascribed hog/post-slavery slave status in this entry, Jefferson begins to free himself from the racist label designed to legitimate the condition of premature death to which he is subjected.

Jefferson continues this dismantling work in the entries that follow. To fully grasp how he does this, consider first the extent to which Jefferson is aware of his being relegated to a *specific* subhuman status—a status against which white patriarchal dominance is defined. In *Lesson*'s opening chapter, not only is Jefferson entered into court records as a "hog"; in classic lynching fashion, his purported manhood has also been refuted and ridiculed—held up in mockery before the eyes and ears of a majority white crowd. In this courtroom scene that frames the entire narrative, Jefferson's white defense attorney declares:

> Gentlemen of the jury, look at this—this—this boy. I almost said man, but I can't say man. Oh, sure, he has reached the age of twenty-one, when we, civilized men, consider the male species has reached manhood, but would you call this—this—this a man? No, not I. I would call it a boy and a fool. . . . He does not even know the size of his clothes or his shoes. . . . Mention the names of Keats, Byron, Scott, and see whether the eyes will show one moment of recognition. . . . Gentlemen of the jury, this man planned a robbery? Oh, pardon me, pardon me, I surely did not mean to insult your intelligence by saying "man"—would you please forgive me for committing such an error?[82]

I wish to emphasize here that "hog" is not the only stigmatizing label that Jefferson's attorney pins on him. Trial transcripts show that he has also referred to Jefferson as "boy," "fool," "it," "a cornered animal," "a thing that acts on command," "a thing to hold the handle of a plow," "a thing to load *your* bales of cotton," "a thing to dig *your* ditches, to chop *your* wood, to pull *your* corn," and "not much."[83] In other words, even as Jefferson's own defense lawyer publicly humiliates him, he also reminds his listeners that Jefferson is subhuman in a way that makes him *serviceable* to those men whom the state recognizes as human. By thus defining him as the kind of "thing" that is designed for the specific capitalistic benefit of southern white "gentlemen"— "a thing to dig *your* ditches, to chop *your* wood, to pull *your* corn"—Jefferson's attorney reminds everyone in the courtroom that Jefferson is not only not human; he is also post-slavery chattel. Jefferson, in this instant, becomes the most visible commodity against which "civilized" white men in the courtroom and the Jim Crow South can measure their patriarchal dominance and high-class fantasies. As with the witnessing of the severed Black penis during/after the lynching act—often a hands-on exhibition that signified both the scorn and negation of Black masculine self-expression—when Jefferson's lawyer calls for this public notation of Jefferson's absent manhood ("Gentlemen of the jury, look at this") and employs language of corporeal dissection to enforce this notation ("look at this—this—this boy," "see whether the eyes will show"), he metes out racialized exemplary punishment. Thus, even before his wrongful conviction and death sentence, Jefferson's very public experience of racial degradation implicitly reminds him and all trial witnesses that Black men, whether innocent or guilty of crime, are supposed to be powerless, voiceless, and nameless in a white supremacist social order.[84]

Throughout his death row diary, though, Jefferson writes against this logic that legitimates his and other Black men's subjection to racialized discipline. In the diary, Jefferson never once calls himself "old hog"—the term he ordinarily uses to refer to himself in conversations with his visitors throughout the novel—but instead declares "i got to be a man" and some form of "im strong" or "im gon stay strong" six times in four short pages.[85] Jefferson's accentuation of strength in his entries, however, does not imply his endorsement of a white patriarchal manhood typified by one's domination of those who have dominated him. Jefferson does not stoop to the level of denigrating his detractors to prove his unimagined strength. Rather, he writes about drawing inner strength and love from the support of his Black community—from visits made by the Black schoolchildren whom Grant teaches and from his godmother, Miss Emma (whom he calls "nanan"): "lord have merce sweet jesus mr wigin where all them peple come from when you ax me if some chiren can com up here an speak i didn kno you was meanin all them chiren in yo clas . . . they hadn never don nothin lik that for me before . . . i seen nanan at the table . . . an i tol her i love her *an i tol her i was strong*."[86] Jefferson's reflections on the spiritual and relational strength that he receives and gives during these visits precede his many declarations of "im strong" and "im gon stay strong" in the last half of his diary. Jefferson's strength, that is to say, is constituted by the self-knowledge that he discovers through the conversational empowerment that he receives from his Black community. Because of the meaningful dialogues that he shares with the schoolchildren and his "nanan," Jefferson is better able to express an awareness of his inner strength and thus better able to reject literarily the myth of Black political impotence and dismantle slavery's logic of unchecked racialized discipline as it persists in the Jim Crow South: "im strong." Jeffrey B. Leak excellently discusses this point in his reading of this section of Jefferson's diary: "While its design and ultimate objective is to eradicate the last vestiges of one's manhood, the prison has served as the site of transformation for Jefferson. . . . Jefferson's transformation of consciousness manifests itself in the relationships he affirms before his execution."[87]

Jefferson continues to express his relationship-centered "transformation of consciousness" in later entries by declaring "im somebody" and making a self-assured charge to Grant and all of his future readers: "tell *them* im strong tell *them* im a man."[88] Jefferson uses the plural pronoun "them" not only to refer to those members of the Black community who have helped him to embrace and project a positive self-image but also to serve notice on whites who have mistaken his verbal silence for political weakness. Jefferson's *written* "tell *them* im strong tell *them* im a man" is, in other words, a public record of his response to a white supremacist "them" whom Grant has previously identified as the racist inscribers of Jefferson's "official" story: "[Jefferson,] . . . the white people out there are saying . . . that you're a hog, not a man. . . . You can prove *them* wrong."[89] Jefferson's documented response to Grant's call in his diary—"tell *them* im strong tell *them* im a man"—refutes his representation in the courtroom proceedings as mindless, controllable, and expendable. Writing has thus facilitated Jefferson's attainment of voice and the realization of his potential for social transformation. As Valerie Babb has observed, "Through his language[, Jefferson] is able to . . . pass judgments on the judicial system that has convicted him."[90] Through his revolutionary pronoun usage, Jefferson has spoken truth to proponents of white supremacist state power. He has lambasted a justice system whose personnel and officers are disproportionately white, male, and racist while also literarily dismantling the essentialist and stereotypical conceptions of Black identity that they have perpetuated to preserve slavery's logic of racialized discipline in prison and in Jim Crow society.

Jefferson's death row diary also exemplifies the third element of a revivifying narrative: in his entries, Jefferson also radically refashions his stigmatized identity. First, it is important to emphasize that Jefferson's refashioned identity surpasses his transcendence from "hog" to "man." Jefferson reveals throughout his diary that he also transforms from apolitical conformist to politically awakened authority. This transformation can be most fully understood in the context of an early scene in the novel in which Jefferson not only repeatedly refers to himself as "old hog" but also refuses to respond when Grant frames the state's presentation of him as "hog" within the framework of a larger political confrontation:

> [Jefferson] knelt down on the floor and put his head inside the bag and started eating, without using his hands. He even sounded like a hog. . . . "That's how a old hog eat," he said, raising his head and grinning at me. . . . "Are you trying to hurt me, Jefferson?" I asked him. "Are you trying to make me feel guilty for your being here? You don't want me to come back here anymore?" [Jefferson's] expression didn't change—as though someone had chiseled that painful, cynical grin on his face. "That man out there doesn't want me up here, either. . . . He said I will never be able to make you understand anything. He said I'm just wasting my time coming up here now. . . . *What do you want? You want me to stay away and let him win? The white man? You want him to win?*" [Jefferson's] expression remained the same—cynical, defiant, painful.[91]

Throughout this scene, Jefferson neither replies to Grant's questions about the racial-political struggle before him nor responds to Grant's ensuing request that he offer a word of appreciation to Miss Emma, who has prepared the fried chicken, sweet potatoes, biscuits, and candy that he eats in hog-like fashion. Jefferson seems too psychically wounded to actualize the full political potential of his small freedoms, which include the opportunity to have meaningful dialogue and contact visits with Grant, Miss Emma, and members of the Black community who desire to affirm his humanity in the waning days of his death row incarceration. Jefferson, in other words, deliberately disengages at the prospect of political self-actualization by donning a "cynical" expression and projecting additional body language that conveys detachment: "Jefferson was not looking at me anymore; he had lain back down on the bunk, facing the wall. . . . I turned to Jefferson again. He was facing the wall, his back to me."[92] In sum, Jefferson's self-mocking speech, his mimicry of a hog, and his unresponsiveness to Grant bespeak apolitical conformity to the racialized social control strategy of the state.

Jefferson writes himself out of this apolitical conformist identity by acknowledging in his diary his attainment of a measure of agency. Jefferson becomes politically awakened not only by making the deliberate and repeated decision to write but also by expressing his realization of the political stakes of that decision: "mr wigin you say rite something but i dont kno what to rite an you say i must be thinking about things i aint tellin nobody . . . but i aint never rote a leter in all my life . . . *you say jus say whats on my mind so one day you can be save an you can save the chiren . . . i aint done this much thinkin and this much writin in all my life befor.*"[93] Jefferson articulates his implicit agreement not to "let [the white man] win"—not to comply with the penal institution's objectives of voice dispossession and apoliticality, as Grant had failed to dissuade him of earlier. Jefferson's repetitious labors of "much thinkin" and "much writin"—especially when understood as interdependent acts that function to teach Grant so that he "can save the chiren"—constitute a strategy of political resistance against a penal institution and racial caste system committed to his educational deprivation, political passivity, and premature death. Every time that Jefferson chooses to write, he *politically* revivifies himself and—since this is a diary that he imparts to his Black community—provides a blueprint for how his fellow Jim Crow detainees can politically affirm themselves while confined within a white supremacist society.

Moreover, even as Jefferson confesses that he "aint never rote a letter in all [his] life," his death row diary becomes both the letter he has never written and the insurgent act he has never taken. Along these lines, Jefferson concludes his final entry with a formal salutation that one associates with letter writing—"sincely jefferson"—and by emphasizing that he has charged the white Deputy Paul Bonin with delivering the diary to Grant and the Black schoolchildren: "im gon ax paul if he can bring you this."[94]

Jefferson also refashions his identity from apolitical conformist to politically awakened authority by using the content of his diary to call into question the moral legitimacy of white male proponents of the justice system (with the important exception of Deputy Bonin). In one of his most intriguing entries, Jefferson writes: "ole clark . . . i can see in his face he aint no good . . . paul . . . is the only one rond yer kno how to talk like a youman to people i kno you paul an i kno ole clark an i kno you too shef guiry an you mr picho and mr mogan an all the rest of yall i jus never say non of this before but i know ever las one of yall."[95] Here, in a few short phrases, Jefferson does far more than expose the "no good" character of Deputy Clark and (by brilliantly subversive parallel structure extension) Sheriff Guidry, Mr. Pichot, and Mr. Morgan—white men who have aided and abetted his subjection to particularly horrid conditions of confinement and his expedited execution date. Through the force of his own words, Jefferson also transforms himself from one who is fixed and objectified by a panoptic, racialized gaze to one who has the moral authority to oversee those who seek to facilitate his political passivity and hasten his premature death. As Jefferson repeats "i kno you" and calls the roll of these white male proponents of Jim Crow justice, he actually trades positions with them: he becomes the antipanoptically expressive judge on the page who he is prevented from being in the courtroom and on death row.[96]

Jefferson's on-the-page assumption of this role of moral judge—and his refashioned identity as politically awakened authority—continues in a follow-up entry that he composes when Sheriff Guidry orders Jefferson to write glowingly of his and other white state officials' treatment of him in his diary. It is clear from what Jefferson has previously written about Guidry that he has refused to comply with the sheriff's mandate ("i kno you too shef guiry"). To conceal his genuine feelings, Jefferson appropriates a derisively repetitious "yesir" phraseology while in Guidry's presence, a phraseology that calls to mind the Black expressive culture practice of guised mockery that Paul Laurence Dunbar famously articulates in his poem "We Wear the Mask." Jefferson writes: "shef guiry . . . say i ain't never pik up yo tablet an look in it an he axe me what all i been ritin and i tol him just things an he say aint he done tret me rite and i tol him yesir an he say aint his deptis done tret me fair an i tol him yesir . . . an he say good *put that down in yo tablet i tret you good all the time you been yer.*"[97] Juxtaposed with the passage that I discussed above in which Jefferson thunders "i kno you too shef guiry," Jefferson's repeated "yesir"—which he curiously does not repeat after Guidry asks him to record in his diary that "i tret you good all the time you been yer"—is a politically empowering use of verbal irony. Jefferson's nonstop "yesir" is, in truth, an obscured "no sir." Of course, Jefferson's previous entry, in which he dismisses the moral superiority of Guidry along with that of other white men in power who make it their business to ensure his apoliticality and speedy electrocution ("i know you too shef guiry") reveals that he sees himself as the judge of Guidry and a fundamentally racist criminal justice system. Death row diary writing thus affords Jefferson the perspectival freedom, distance, and privacy that he needs to refashion his stigmatized identity and discredit the justice system that so callously discredited him. In the twilight of his living-death life, Jefferson transforms from apolitical conformist to politically awakened authority. Moreover, by writing and releasing from death row a diary critical of the justice system, Jefferson politically revivifies himself and the Black community at the precise moment that the state intends for him and them to die.

Willie Francis's Revivifying Narrative

I turn our attention now to a second revivifying narrative—a narrative whose content and socially transformative reach mirrors the first. Just as the political reinvigoration of Gaines's fictional Black community depended on a young Black male convict writing and releasing to free society a death row diary, so, too, did real, historical Black people in Willie Francis's segregated hometown need the twice-death-sentenced Francis to use his voice to politically empower them. Francis and the Black community of 1940s-era St. Martinsville, Louisiana, were also captives of a Jim Crow racial caste system that stringently enforced their physical and social immobility. The local Black Catholic priest Maurice Rousseve described the daily experiences of Blacks in St. Martinville as economically exploitative and physically injurious: "Many of the whites around here don't want Negroes to be educated. They want them to work on the plantations. . . . St. Martinville was always prejudiced. . . . [In] St. Martinville, they used to whip . . . Negro prisoners at night till you could hear it."[98] Deborah Denno adds that the white editor of the city's newspaper made a point of printing articles in which he repetitiously referred to Blacks as "niggers" and that such stigmatization was reinforced institutionally by St. Martinville's expressed commitment to Black children's systemic under-education: "The St. Martin Parish School Board noted, matter-of-factly, without apology, that there were no high schools for blacks and that white teachers were paid roughly twice as much as 'negro' teachers."[99] The state's commitment to institutionalizing harm on Black bodies and Black psyches in St. Martinville was not extraordinary but ordinary—crucial, in fact, to the maintenance of a cheap Black plantation labor force, Black illiteracy, and the social control logic of Jim Crow. Yet because Willie Francis produced and published a pamphlet critical of the justice system in the waning months of his life, he would, like Gaines's Jefferson, literarily destabilize this system of racialized discipline and transform himself and others from apolitical conformists to politically awakened authorities.

The stammering and semiliterate Francis, whom local reporters described as indifferent to his racially discriminatory murder conviction in 1945 ("Throughout the trial the negro was uninterested and showed very little emotion"),[100] spent the early months of 1947 energized as he wrote and published, with the assistance of his amanuensis Sam Montgomery, a pamphlet titled *My Trip to the Chair*. This revivifying narrative is a rare document that researchers have been able to access only recently.[101] *My Trip to the Chair* actually traces its origins to replies to letters that Francis wrote after surviving the torment of a malfunctioning electric chair on May 3, 1946. Francis's botched electrocution made sense to no one. As Denno has observed, "People everywhere were entranced by Willie's survival" and by his zeal to educate prison outsiders about the nature of execution, even while the state was pushing for his second electrocution.[102] While his defense lawyer, Bertrand DeBlanc, appealed his case to the U.S. Supreme Court, Francis tirelessly responded to letters from sympathizers who ran the gamut in terms of race, class, gender, and age. In so doing, he laid the groundwork for what he would do in *My Trip to the Chair*: undermine, by way of his own written words from death row, his subjection to a condition of voice dispossession.

Francis displays this first element of a revivifying narrative in a particularly illuminating way in his pamphlet's opening paragraph:

They tell me this is the first time anyone ever had a chance to tell the story of how it feels to go to the electric chair and know that you might have to go back there. This is the first time I ever told the whole story and I hope that by at last telling it people will understand what it means to go through what I went through. . . . *I know how it felt to have them read a death warrant to me. I know how it feels to sit in a cell waiting for the day they will lead me to the chair again. I sure know how it feels to sit in that chair and have them strap me in and put a mask on my eyes. I know how it feels to have the shock go through me and think I am dead but find out I am not.* I do not like to talk about it at all, but if it will help other people to understand each other, I want to tell everything.[103]

During an epoch in which Jim Crow laws and a racist justice system functioned interdependently to silence Black voices, Francis—an adolescent Black convict with a third-grade education—transformed himself from systemically silenced death row prisoner to nationally heeded pedagogue through these carefully chosen, public record-contesting words.[104] Francis refuted the "official" stories about his failed execution circulated by the state, the courts, and the news media. His testimony counters the report of the coroner (which he curiously wrote without any input from Francis), who asserted that with the exception of a quickened heart rate, he "found nothing wrong with [Willie]," and calls into question the statements of news reporters who intimated that Francis was gleeful during and after the botched electrocution: "Negro Slayer Cheats Death."[105] Francis's testimonial use of anaphora in this paragraph—his recurring, defiant "I know" at the start of successive sentences—reveals in preacher-like cadence the great distance between what the coroner and news reporters *perceived* regarding his near-execution and the painfully lived gospel truth: "*I sure know* how it feels to sit in that chair and have them strap me in and put a mask on my eyes. *I know* how it feels to have the shock go through me and think I am dead but find out I am not." Francis thus begins the work of undermining his subjection to a condition of voice dispossession with every "I know" he utters in his published story about the botched execution.

In Francis's concluding "I know," he expresses that some electricity was, in fact, introduced into his body during his first execution. He thus makes apparent the weightiness of the political-pedagogical intervention he is making by writing *My Trip to the Chair*. As Denno aptly notes, Francis's account of encountering and surviving execution made him, in 1947, *the only known person in the United States capable of experientially educating the world about the physical and psychological torture exemplified by a failed electrocution*: "Time and again, Willie attempted in his comments to juxtapose how people . . . told him the electrocution would feel and how it really did feel. . . . In *The Chair*, Willie left no question that the execution attempt caused acute pain."[106] Ironically, then, Francis gets the opportunity to conduct a literary dialogue with a national audience who, by their very act of reading, implicitly affirms his humanity while he is on death row again—while he is contained in a setting in which the state has re-restricted his access to human contact and rescheduled his appointment with state-sanctioned lethal violence and institutionalized expulsion from human existence.

Moreover, like Gaines's Jefferson, Francis begins to undermine his condition of voice dispossession when he seizes his unjust sentencing as an opportunity to illuminate the systemic nature of his sufferings and those of his fellow Jim Crow prisoners at one and same time. In the early pages of his pamphlet, Francis reveals how the ordinariness of white supremacist social control in St. Martinville disciplined him and other Blacks into silent acquiescence to substandard living conditions:

> I was born in St. Martinville, Louisiana. It's just a little town where everybody knows everybody else. We have two sections, one for the white people and the other for the colored, and *everybody gets along fine.* The white tend to their business and the colored tend to theirs. . . . We lived in the colored section at 800 Washington Street. It is a little house dull gray in color and faces north. It has thirteen of us kids running through it all the time. . . . When you live in a house with that many people in it, things aren't as crowded as you would think. *All my brothers and sisters got along fine together because we had to.*[107]

Of particular importance here is Francis's attention to how he and his thirteen siblings and two parents "got along fine together because they had to": Francis and his family would endanger their livelihood if the prison-like "little house" they overcrowded became a source of Black complaint overheard in the white section of town. Francis shows, in other words, that in segregated St. Martinville, life is *not* such that "everybody gets along fine," just as his encounter with the electric chair was not his painless way of "cheating death"—as the state and news media had represented. Rather, with telltale verbal irony, Francis emphasizes that he and his twelve siblings and parents are representative Black sufferers in a Jim Crow town in which the disciplinary logic of white supremacy subjected them to substandard living conditions.

Francis also displays the first element of a revivifying narrative by using the second-person pronoun, *you*, to undermine his voice dispossession. With his recurring *you*, Francis makes clear that he is not the object of knowledge that the penal institution would have him be but, rather, the one who produces, defines, and disseminates knowledge to an attentive, participatory audience. He writes, "At the beginning of April the Sheriff came to tell me that I had to go to the electric chair at the beginning of May. He said the Governor had written my death warrant. . . . *Boy, you sure feel funny when you know you're going to die; almost like you know something only God should know.*"[108] With his frequent inclusion of "you" in his recollection of a state-manufactured encounter with death, Francis brings his free-world readers into direct contact with the unsettling world of death row. Indeed, when it is no longer just Francis but also a "you"—a non-imprisoned reader—who is made to feel the agony of knowing "when you know you're going to die," the anguish produced by a sentence to social isolation and premature death is, in a sense, halved. By incessantly employing this "you" here and throughout his pamphlet, Francis is no longer alone in feeling the ungodliness of state-systematized death: Francis's "you"-implicated readers also feel, at least for a moment, that they know "something only God should know."

Francis is relentless in using "you" to push his readers to connect empathetically with his and their shared, tenuous corporeality:

> It is one of the hardest things to make *yourself* learn how to die right. . . . I'm telling *you* that chair sure isn't full of feathers. I guess people have the idea it tickled the way *you* feel when *you* laugh. . . . It felt like a hundred and a thousand needles and pins were pricking in me all over and my left leg felt like somebody was cutting it with a razor blade. I could feel my arms jumping at my sides and I guess my whole body must have jumped straight out. . . . I thought I was dead.[109]

As Francis boldly declares what he is telling "you"—the non-imprisoned reader who has now, on multiple occasions, become Francis's fellow sufferer—he radically undermines his condition of voice dispossession on death row. Francis transforms himself, in a sense, from silenced prisoner to speaking pedagogue. Because of his testimonial expressivity and community-building use of the second-person pronoun "you" throughout *My Trip to the Chair,* he very clearly demonstrates the first element of a revivifying narrative.

Francis's pamphlet also demonstrates the final two elements of a revivifying narrative: in *My Trip to the Chair,* Francis dismantles slavery's logic of racialized discipline and radically refashions his stigmatized identity. On the one hand, Francis does not explicitly refute the degrading constructions of his identity created by the state and reinforced by the news media, as Gaines's Jefferson does early in his diary with his interrogation of his lawyer's and the state's depiction of him as a hog/criminal/post-slavery slave. Moments after Francis left the electric chair alive, a white onlooker outside the death chamber initiated the town's commentary on Francis's survival by insisting that Francis—whom white lawyers and reporters had deemed either "mentally subnormal" or a callous "Negro murderer" in the wake of his sentencing—was *still* "a black bastard."[110] In the ensuing days and weeks, journalists continued this racialized denigration by implying that Francis's survival of electrocution was somehow part of an elaborate, premeditated scheme: "The Lad Who Cheated the Chair" and "Negro Slayer [Who] Cheats Death" were but two of the newspaper headlines that stereotypically cast Francis as a born criminal.[111] Complicating matters further, Francis's own defense lawyer, a white man named Bertrand DeBlanc, deemed Francis "a beaten animal" in a majority white Louisiana courtroom in a desperate (but nonetheless racially stigmatizing) attempt to evoke sympathy for him.[112] In his pamphlet, Francis does not directly contest these courtroom and media representations of him—representations that ultimately reinforced Francis's and all Blacks' designated place of powerlessness and voicelessness in Jim Crow society.[113]

Seen from another angle, though, Francis dismantles these racially stigmatizing representations of his identity by refusing to devote page space to considering them. In the second paragraph of *My Trip to the Chair*, Francis bluntly disregards his construction by the state and the press as a "Negro Murderer" who, true to his "nature," maliciously shot and killed the white Cajun pharmacist Andrew Thomas: "I don't want to talk about the killing of Mr. Thomas. When they asked me to write this story, I said I would only [write] if I didn't have to say anything about that part. . . . *But I will tell you about the electrocution.*"[114] Francis makes very clear that he will write about only those images of himself that *he* finds worthy of consideration. His statement reinforces his previous insistence that his identity could not be reduced to the crime that he allegedly committed: Francis had inscribed "OF COURSE I AM NOT A KILLER" on the wall of his cell.[115]

Rather than contest the white public's construction of him as a "Negro Murderer," Francis focuses his energy on radically refashioning his stigmatized identity. Francis accomplishes this by offering a counter-narrative in *My Trip to the Chair*, a complex life narrative in which he, as authorial architect, transforms himself from criminal to Christ figure. As Francis chronicles his two confrontations with capital punishment in this counter-narrative, he alludes to Jesus Christ's confrontation with public condemnation and unjust, state-funded premature death as recorded in the Bible. As with Gaines's Jefferson, who imagines himself as approaching execution with the self-assured strength of the falsely convicted Christ—"He never said a mumbling word. . . . That's how I want to go"—the writing act affords Francis the opportunity to frame his racially discriminatory conviction and two trips to the electric chair in the context of Christian martyrdom.[116] Although state records show that Francis spoke no words before his executioners pulled the switch at his first

The death row author Willie Francis takes a moment to glance at his writing on the wall of a prison cell on May 4, 1946. (Associated Press photograph/Bill Allen.)

electrocution, Francis's pamphlet reveals the words that he *meant* to say: "I was thinking about saying I didn't blame anyone for what they were doing to me."[117] Francis was an especially voracious reader of the Bible, so his allusion to the words of Christ in Luke 23:34—"Father, forgive them, for they know not what they do"—is, at one level, unsurprising.[118] But I am interested in just how convincingly Francis—a condemned Black male youth—appropriates the identity of the Hebrew messiah/miscreant, who, bleeding profusely during his execution on an old rugged cross, responded with mindboggling compassion toward those who had sentenced him to death, mocked, and beaten him: "Father, forgive them, for they know not what they do."

On the one hand, Francis's death sentence, like Christ's, is an unjust punishment meted out by a repressive state. Francis was, after all, coerced by white policemen to write a murder confession, tried before an all-white jury without the benefit of sufficient legal counsel, and sentenced to death even though there was no defined motive to kill and no fingerprints or other incriminating evidence on the weapon used in the crime. Yet I argue that what makes Francis's biblical allusion a provocative one is that Francis, like the Christ whom Gospel writers depict as forgiving the very soldiers who nearly flogged him to death *before* his agonizing crucifixion, projects an image of himself as forgiving executioners who, moments later, would torture him to the point of near-death with electric current. Francis's intended statement—"I didn't blame anyone for what they were doing to me"—thus takes on Christ-like significance. Moreover, Francis depicts himself as being sacrificially joyful in the moments after surviving the electrocution when he receives a new death threat from one of his executioners. He writes that he declared, "God is Always good!" just minutes after both events transpired.[119]

Ultimately, then, Francis did not write *My Trip to the Chair* to refute the state's and press's construction of him as a cold-blooded "Negro Murderer." He did not write to make a political statement about who he was *not*. Rather, Francis vernacularized the biblical crucifixion narrative—one of the most sacred discourses of the dominant, white culture—so that he could radically refashion his identity and express who he really was, or could be. In this way, the revivifying narrative that Francis wrote and imparted to the reading public resembles the one that Jefferson gave to Grant Wiggins and the Black community in Gaines's novel. Francis's revivifying narrative, like Jefferson's death row diary, offers documented counterevidence of Blacks' allegedly "natural" racial inferiority and hope for radical social transformation. Francis's *My Trip to the Chair* is yet another midnight-hour re-transcription of the public record that attests to the reality of a death row prisoner's in-tellectualism and communal ties to a denigrated people. Yes, like Gaines's Jefferson, Francis is an imprisoned radical intellectual, a solitary cell educator who seizes both of his racially discriminatory death sentences and the written word to remind a white supremacist social order that Blacks can and do revivify themselves within Jim Crow and prison regimes that have historically functioned to funnel Blacks toward political passivity and premature death.

Conclusion: Lessons in "youman" Discourse

> With the closing of each entry in the diary[,] Jefferson slowly moves from victim to survivor.
>
> —Anne Gray Brown, "Writing for Life"

This chapter has shown that Gaines's characterization of Jefferson as an imprisoned radical intellectual and his creation of the "Jefferson's Diary" chapter in *Lesson* demonstrate his amplification of the voices of condemned men, as well as his sympathetic engagement with the plight and "stand" of Willie Francis. *Lesson* is also instructive for contemporary critical explora-tions of wrongful incarceration and wrongful execution. As of June 2017, 350 formerly imprisoned people (disproportionately, men of color) have been exonerated with the help of the Innocence Project through forensic DNA testing, which is a tool of exculpation that has been used since 1989 in cases where blood, bone, or hair from the crime scene is available.[120] The high number of exonerees in these biological evidence cases alone signifies that our epoch is one in which proof of wrongful conviction, imprisonment, and execution is undeniable and more common than generally imagined. Mainstream stories about these recurring travesties of justice, however, are rarely told from the perspectives of those who experience them. On the one hand, groups that oppose the death penalty, such as the Innocence Project, the American Civil Liberties Union's Capital Punishment Project, and the Death Penalty Information Center, must be applauded for their efforts in making apparent in their literature the racial bias that so often surrounds wrongful incarceration and execution. Their efforts are rare, urgent, and incredibly necessary, not least because the literature they produce exposes the injustice and harm to human lives that result from the state's endorsement of "tough on crime" laws, racially discriminatory judicial practices, and capital punishment and often helps to absolve falsely accused people from criminal convictions. Yet the reports, pamphlets, and online articles that these advocacy groups create and circulate on wrongful incarceration and wrongful execution tend to focus more on the ways in which unjustly criminalized people are viewed by the criminal justice system than on how these people critique such views and the system responsible for their construction.[121]

This is where *Lesson* demonstrates its radical utility.[122] In the novel, Gaines depicts a wrongfully convicted Black death row convict who uses his own written words to pass judgment on a racist justice system and dismantle the racially prejudiced way in which he is viewed by that system. Gaines's literary examination of wrongful conviction and his spotlighting of political content in the death row diary entries of a falsely accused young Black man reveal the capacity that any person under a death sentence has to resituate critically how she or he is seen by Jim Crow society, the court system, and a prison administration through how she or he sees herself or himself. In the case of Gaines's Jefferson, of course, this critical reframing is summed up in his declaration, "tell them im strong tell them im a man."[123] Again, Gaines's novel not only shows how a young Black man's wrongful incarceration and execution reflect the workings of a racist justice system and a white supremacist social order. It also pushes us to see how this young Black man transforms his unjust conviction into an opportunity to critique the justice system and engage in identity refashioning, racial uplift, and radical social transformation. Jeffrey J. Folks has picked up on this important nuance in his reading of *Lesson*:

> Jefferson . . . is a dynamic character who . . . becomes a center of agency in the novel by virtue of his decision to reject a victimized status. . . . Gaines begins his novel with a conventional narrative of victimization, structuring his plot around an innocent black man who, without adequate legal representation, is convicted by an all-white jury of murdering . . . a [white] Cajun storeowner; yet Gaines's

interest centers less on this injustice than on the restoration of Jefferson's human dignity.[124]

Jefferson's diary entries thus contrast sharply with more conventional narratives of wrongful conviction that appear as reports by human rights journalists at the Innocence Project, Capital Punishment Project, and Death Penalty Information Center. These narratives tend to foreground the harrowing reality of wrongful conviction over the subjectivity of the wrongly convicted. Moreover, these narratives are typically published in objectivist third-person point of view to make their content appear more legible and legitimate and to establish affective appeal for "victimized" convicts before the eyes of prospective justice advocates.

Consider, for instance, the Death Penalty Information Center's report *Innocence and the Crisis in the American Death Penalty* (2004), which was written by the center's former executive director, Richard Dieter. The report—which includes Dieter's quantitative and qualitative assessments of recent exonerations and provocative criticisms of capital punishment—offers vital analysis on wrongful incarceration and wrongful execution. Yet I argue that his thinking would have benefited greatly from the commentary of several of the Black male exonerees whose stories he features. Dieter's reconstruction of one of these exonerees' stories, in light of my previous discussion of how deftly Jefferson dismantles his construction as hog by his defense lawyer, is particularly noteworthy:

[Ronald] Jones was a homeless man when he was convicted of the rape and murder of a Chicago woman. He maintained that he signed a confession only after a lengthy interrogation during which he was beaten by police. *Prosecutors described him as a "cold brutal rapist" who "should never see the light of day."* But DNA testing revealed that Jones was not the rapist, and there was no evidence that more than one person had committed the crime. The Cook County state's attorney filed a motion asking the Illinois Supreme Court to vacate Jones's conviction in 1997. In May 1999, the state dropped all charges against Jones.[125]

Here, while Dieter superbly makes clear that state violence preceded and predetermined Jones's wrongful conviction—he writes that Jones "signed a confession only after a lengthy interrogation during which he was *beaten by police*"—he also chooses to emphasize how DNA testing, rather than Jones himself, revealed that he "was not the rapist." To be fair, DNA evidence is indeed the tool of exculpation for cases such as Jones's. Yet Jones's own assessments of his construction as a "cold brutal rapist" by prosecutors do not appear in Dieter's report. Unlike Jefferson, who, as I previously discussed, Gaines reveals as thoughtfully critiquing his construction as hog by his defense lawyer and Sheriff Guidry, we get no sense in Dieter's report of how Jones responds to a state-manufactured identity—an identity ascription that similarly functions to project his crime as being tied to his "nature."

My purpose here is not to criticize Dieter so much as it is to recognize the narrative limitations that arise as a result of conventions specific to the field of human rights literature. As Kay Schafer and Sidonie Smith discuss in *Human Rights and Narrated Lives*, human rights reporters often strategically edit or omit narratives of systemic injustice offered by the falsely accused: "Testimonies can be reduced to forensic evidence, denuded of emotion, and removed from the individual lives and experiences of suffering and trauma. They can be excerpted and joined to other excerpts to produce corroborative evidence."[126] Literary writing, however, as a medium of representation that is invested in getting readers thinking about actual and imagined people's interior lives, helps us to see not only how wrongfully convicted people have been viewed by the criminal justice system but also how they have critiqued those views. As I have shown throughout this book, the neo-abolitionist novel, by virtue of its depiction of the clandestine and insurgent literary practices of characters that are or have been confined to sites of racialized discipline and punishment, is uniquely positioned to illuminate how people who have been defined by their alleged crimes find subversive ways to redefine themselves through the power of their own, antipanoptically expressive words.

I am arguing, then, that what Gaines's death row protagonist accomplishes through writing diary entries far exceeds his sound dismissal of his hog/criminal/post-slavery slave status. Jefferson comes into a fuller knowledge of not only who he is not but also who he is and who he can be, even while Sheriff Guidry continues to call him a "hog" as his execution day nears. Repeatedly, Jefferson uses the written word to reconceptualize himself as a person whose identity cannot be reduced to his "framing" by the Jim Crow justice system that predetermined his wrongful incrimination, punitive isolation, and premature death. Jefferson uses his own written words to express to his Black community, his white supremacist aggressors, and free society that he can—even in a racist criminal justice system; even in an intensely segregated, racially repressive rural Louisiana sharecropping culture—be the person that he desires and aspires to be: "im strong," "im somebody," "im a man."[127] In our contemporary epoch in which the state punitively restricts imprisoned people's attempts to write and publish, non-imprisoned neo-abolitionist novelists who are critical of the justice system—in this case, Gaines and his "Jefferson's Diary" chapter in *Lesson*—help us see the falsely accused as so many of them see themselves: as *people* with agency, as human beings who show the world through the power of their own antipanoptically expressive words that their identities are limited neither to the state's "framing" discourses nor to their obvious victimhood.

In the end, then, we who examine literary works in the so-called free world must become better readers. We must remember how Jefferson, after writing the first entry in his diary, demands that Grant read him. Jefferson's insistence is intended as much for Grant as it is for those who work the fields of the novel's plantation community, his court-appointed white defense lawyer, the courts, Sheriff Guidry—and those of us who might make the tragic mistake of reading Gaines's revivified protagonist as a victim only: "I'm *youman*, Mr. Wiggins. But nobody didn't know that 'fore now."[128] Jefferson's pedagogical respelling—"*you*man" as "human"—recurs throughout the pages of his death row diary, for the most fundamental lesson that Jefferson imparts before dying is that he knows he shares with Grant and others who reside in the so-called free world their humanity and *agency*.[129] Jefferson, a locked-up and electric chair–bound Black man who has literarily liberated himself and others from the disciplinary logic of slavery's past and a contemporary white supremacist sentence of civil, social, and biological death, knows that he possesses and expresses a voice that no justice advocate gave him. It is past time that we, as fellow "youmans," read him and so many other revivifying imprisoned writers as they desire to be read.

Epilogue

The Prison Classroom and
the Neo-Abolitionist Novel

The overwhelming numbers of black men imprisoned in the United States makes them by far the most threatened members of society when it comes to the new form of enslavement being implemented through the prison system.[1]

With well over two million people in prison in the United States, America is not only the world leader in imprisonment; it is also, as the mainstream news media belatedly conceded in 2012, "a nation of incarceration," a country whose collective identity remains bound to a long history of capitalistic investment in mass-based (in)human confinement.[2] In light of my reading of Gaines's *A Lesson Before Dying* as a neo-abolitionist novel, however, what I find even more disturbing than this observation is the fact that Angela Y. Davis's comments in 2001 on the mass-production of racialized social control through the criminal justice system remain as relevant to us now—nearly two full decades into the new millennium—as they were then. In addition to what appears in the block quotation above, Davis had also then stated, "The extent to which black men today function as the main human raw material for the Prison Industrial Complex only highlights the many ways in which the prison system in the United States in general resembles and recapitulates some of the most abhorrent characteristics of the slavery and convict lease system."[3] Indeed, the Sentencing Project reported that in 2010, one in ten Black men in the thirty to thirty-nine age range was in prison or jail on any given day, and, as the Harvard Law School professor Charles Ogletree compellingly argues in *The Presumption of Guilt: The Arrest of Henry Louis Gates, Jr., and Race, Class, and Crime in the United States,* such statistics do not reflect Black men's tendency to engage in criminal activity, but, rather, the way in which racism—from racial profiling to racially discriminatory courtroom proceedings and racist sentencing practices—functions as a social ordering logic in the criminal justice system and in the nation at large. Relatedly, Davis illustrates in her scholarship how the impunity and terror that slaveholders relied on to control slave populations that far outnumbered them now constitute ordinary tools of discipline that contemporary prison employees unleash on an expanding prison population that is disproportionately Black and male. In *Are Prisons Obsolete?* Davis discusses an incident that occurred in 1996 at Brazoria Detention Center, a private prison in Texas where unarmed men in custody—mostly Black men— became the unsuspecting objects of guards' racial slurs, boot kicking, cattle-prod beatings, and police-dog attacks. In a scene that calls to mind the routine and sadistic racial violence that George Jackson confronted, combated, and conceptualized as slavery in California prisons (as I discussed in Chapter 1), Davis recounts: "The inmates, forced to crawl on the floor, also were being shocked with stun guns, while guards—who referred to one black prisoner as '*boy*'—shouted 'Crawl faster!'"[4] Davis concludes that the experience of prisoner abuse at Brazoria was not only cruel but also intentionally racist, for in a nationally broadcast video clip of the incident, "Black male prisoners were seen to be the primary targets of the guards' attacks," and, as one imprisoned man later quipped, "What you saw on tape wasn't a fraction of what happened that day."[5]

Let me be absolutely clear. I have made the case in this book—especially in Chapter 2, on the skyrocketing number of women in state custody who report acts of sexual intimidation and rape by officials and employees in jails, prisons, juvenile facilities, and immigration detention centers—that Black men are not (and never have been) the only group subjected to a justice system whose mass-based social control practices in today's jails and prisons perpetuate the Middle Passage and slavery's white supremacist logic and violence. I am well aware that the American Civil Liberties Union has shown that women make up the fastest growing prison population in the United States. Indeed, women have been incarcerated at nearly twice the rate of men since 1985, owing in large part to the expansion of the so-called War on Drugs.[6] Moreover, I have argued, following Davis and others, that sexualized state violence in women's jails, prisons, and detention centers represents "a proven technique of discipline and power" that must also be understood as calculated, *racialized* harm—harm meted out disproportionately against Black women and girls in state custody.[7] As Davis reminds us, the repressed, routine, and largely unpunished rape of incarcerated women has ironically functioned to reinforce racist perceptions about the allegedly hypersexual "nature" of criminal women—especially Black women, who are overrepresented in prison. More fundamentally, I have argued that male corrections officers' unsupervised supervision of incarcerated women is a practice of male supremacist containment that traces its roots both to Title VII of the Civil Rights Act of 1964 (which ironically sanctioned the stationing of male correctional officers in women's facilities at the same time that it opened the door for female correctional officers to work in men's correctional settings) and to a purportedly bygone Middle Passage epoch in which white male captains and crewmen on slave ships exploited the maritime environment to practice disciplinary rape on the bodies of African women they had kidnapped and stowed away in slave vessels. So I reiterate: the Middle Passage and slavery exist in a real and abiding way in the everyday lives of incarcerated women, and their continued presence in women's facilities demands that people outside prison join jailed and imprisoned women and girls in abolitionist resistance. Still, one issue persists throughout our current mass incarceration epoch that has loomed large throughout U.S. penological history: from the late nineteenth-century era of convict leasing to the present, the massive disappearance of Black men has occurred through the racist machinery of the criminal justice system, and the continuing disproportionate nature of such disappearance is a haunting reminder that the Middle Passage and slavery's centuries-spanning grip on both the racializiation and gendering of American punishment is still very much with us.

In 2015, a *New York Times* article titled "1.5 Million Missing Black Men" tracked a series of recent studies that have considered the role of the prison-industrial complex in the mass-production of Black men's disappearance in the United States. The article's authors concluded that, in recent times, it has not been Black men's high death rates but, rather, their commonplace experience of civil death, social death, and premature death via incarceration that has been the primary cause of their so-called disappearance from society. They wrote:

> Since the 1990s, death rates for young black men have dropped more than for rates for other groups. . . . Both homicides and H.I.V. related deaths, which disproportionately afflict black men, have dropped. Yet the prison population has soared since 1980. In many communities, rising numbers of black men spared an early death have been offset by rising numbers [of black men] behind bars. . . . The missing-men phenomenon will not disappear anytime soon. There are more missing African-American men nationwide than there are African-American men residing in . . . Los Angeles, Philadelphia, Detroit, Houston, Washington, and Boston, combined.[8]

As I am a Black male professor who teaches in prison classrooms that are always overpopulated with Black male students, the idea that more than six major cities' worth of Black men have been disappeared into the nation's prison system saddens me more than it surprises me. The imprisoned men whom I have had the privilege to teach and learn from—Black men, white men, Latino men, and Native American men—are all very alive to me. They have been institutionally disappeared, for sure, but they are not "missing." Yet the fact that these men are not only reduced to state-assigned numbers inside the prison but also myopically categorized as "missing" by people outside the prison is precisely why I go to them. I reiterate: these men are not "missing." They are part of my community. And especially since U.S. Department of Justice statistics have shown that at least 95 percent of them will eventually be released and, moreover, since more than 650,000 imprisoned men and women return to so-called free society each year, I contend that they are *all* part of our national community.[9] Their imprisoned (Black) lives matter. So do their minds. That said, my final argument in this book is that our contemporary prison system's mass-based institutionalization of Black men's disappearance from the status of citizen—a during- and after-incarceration phenomenon that the legal scholar Michelle Alexander has conceptualized as a reinstatement of the Jim Crow racial caste system—has been perniciously reinforced by the slavery-era harm of state-sanctioned mental decomposition.[10] The disproportionate numbers of Black men and boys locked up in an increasingly abusive prison system perpetually confront—in addition to the pre-Emancipation forms of terror that Davis describes in her scholarship—the same kind of dehumanizing condition that the Black male slave Frederick Douglass faced in the nineteenth century and Gaines's Black male prisoner-slave Jefferson faced in the twentieth: the institutionalization of educational deprivation.

From start to finish, Gaines's *Lesson* blurs past and present in its depiction of the racialized social control technique of educational deprivation espoused by a jail administration focused solely on punishment. Published in 1993, Gaines's *Lesson* implicitly provides historical context for the nation's enforcement of systemic under-education in the Jim Crow past and a New Jim Crow present in which an overrepresented population of young Black men encounter not only the psychic agony of indefinite solitary confinement in supermax facilities, Security Housing Units, and death rows but also the systemic withholding of educational opportunities in lower-security "correctional" centers. Concerning the latter, we must remember that when Congress eliminated Pell Grants for imprisoned students by passing the Violent Crime Control and Law Enforcement Act in 1994, it effectively ended higher education in prison. Joan Petersilia recalls the swift and staggering impact of this decision:

In 1990, there were 350 higher education programs for inmates [in the United States]. *By 1997, there were just eight. . . . [H]igher education for inmates now faces "virtual extinction."* Several states . . . have no state-financed college programs for inmates. In most others, the programs generally serve only a small fraction of the prison population and tend to rely on charitable donations or the inmates themselves for financial support.[11]

With the nation's swift defunding of postsecondary prison education in 1994, all people confined within a rapidly expanding prison-industrial complex—including a population of Blacks in state custody that surpassed the population of whites for the first time in recorded history—confronted a new terrain of abusive punishment: the institutionalization of educational deprivation.[12] Interestingly, just a few years before Congress passed the bill that would eliminate Pell Grants for imprisoned people, the United Nations issued a statement that its members (who, of course, include the United States) viewed access to educational opportunity as also an acknowledgment of the essential humanness of all people—even those who are in prison. The United Nations' "Basic Principles for the Treatment of Prisoners" resolution of 1990 states: "All prisoners shall retain the human rights and fundamental freedoms set out in the Universal Declaration of Human Rights. . . . *All prisoners shall have the right to take part in cultural activities and education aimed at the full development of the human personality.*"[13] That the U.S. federal government passed the bill in 1994 that has facilitated the widespread systemic withholding of higher education for people behind bars must be understood as a serious breach of international human rights standards for people in state custody. Given the overwhelmingly Black racial composition of the nation's prison population, I add that this mind-numbing disciplinary practice also amounts to *racialized* prisoner abuse.

Gaines's *Lesson*, published just one year before the bill's passage, seems preoccupied with this institutionalization and racialization of educational deprivation. Much of *Lesson*'s plot revolves around whether state officials will grant the college-educated Black instructor, Grant, the opportunity to teach Jefferson during his incarceration—especially given the relatively short span of months between Jefferson's sentencing and his execution. Soon after Grant is essentially commissioned by Miss Emma and his aunt, Tante Lou, to be Jefferson's death row educator, he waits on his feet for hours to meet with Sheriff Guidry to discuss the possibility of receiving permission to teach. In the first of many attempts to dissuade Grant from that endeavor, Sheriff Guidry postpones the last-minute meeting that he has scheduled with Grant and eventually sends his wife out to meet with Grant.

She also puts him off, saying, "I hear you would like the privilege of visiting Jefferson? . . . Well, I'll have to leave that up to you and the sheriff. . . . He'll talk to you after supper."[14] Grant's endurance is tested again and again. Grant comes to understand that for white men such as Sheriff Guidry, the political stakes of prison education are high because such learning can be, for the prisoner-slave Jefferson, what it was for the self-described slave-turned-man Frederick Douglass during the antebellum era: an opportunity for antipanoptic expressivity, a chance to express critical literacy development, mental freedom, and an alternative identity while confined within a system of educational deprivation aimed at his and other Blacks' mental decomposition, identity erasure, and political passivity. In sum, Sheriff Guidry and the jail administration perceive that Grant's repeated requests for makeshift teaching sessions with Jefferson pose a threat to their slavery-reminiscent agenda of mind control: "I hear from people around here you want to make him a man. A man for what, at this time? . . . You think that's a good idea? . . . There ain't a thing that you can put in that skull that ain't there already."[15]

The jail administration proceeds to make it nearly impossible for Grant to visit with Jefferson, but after Grant persists (reluctantly, at first) with Tante Lou and Miss Emma in securing educational visitation time with Jefferson, a counterculture of uninhibited learning begins to undermine the mind-numbing monotony and isolation of Jefferson's life on death row. The solitary cell becomes a dialogic classroom. In time, a bond is forged between teacher and student, and their roles often reverse. Semiliterate Jefferson pushes himself to think critically, expand his vocabulary, and make regular use of the pencil and notebook that Grant has given him. Although he had previously spent his days lifelessly slumped in the corner of his cell, Jefferson, by novel's end, has thrown himself into a regimen of writing and critical reflection. Jefferson has literarily revivified himself, and aided by the pedagogical presence of Grant—a recipient and imparter of higher education's ideal of critical thinking—he is no longer the "missing" or otherwise prematurely dead Black man that the state intends for him to be. Rather, under Grant's tutelage Jefferson has begun to see himself and speak about himself as a "man" who lives in the face of racialized premature death—a "*you*man" who understands himself as a human being in relation to other human beings through his defiant act of distributing his journal to a Black community that loves and supports him before, during, and after his unjust execution.[16] Moreover, as a result of the undercover education sessions (masked as visitation time) that he experiences with and through Grant, the unlettered Jefferson also becomes a sly, astute critic of the justice system, as I discussed in my analysis of his death row diary in Chapter 4.

It should come as no surprise that *Lesson* is a popularly requested novel among the many Black male students I teach in the prisons of the U.S. South. Embedded in *Lesson*'s many lessons about (Black) carceral life is an anti-panoptic rallying cry that Black men can achieve mental liberation—even if only temporarily—in a U.S. prison system whose vanishing educational opportunities threaten to expedite their premature death or prolong their living death. LeJhoyn Holland, a Black male student I had the pleasure to teach and learn from at Orange Correctional Center (OCC) in Hillsborough, North Carolina, underscored this point in his close readings of Gaines's Jefferson and Grant: "These are people who had it hard anyway from the beginning. . . . Us being in prison, we can relate to [these characters] because the struggle is still before us."[17] Indeed it is. Gaines's neo-abolitionist novel offers imprisoned readers critical language for articulating what so many of them already know: that their being targeted or misread by the state is an issue that too often precedes and predetermines their experiences with criminalization, incarceration, brutalization, and systemic under-education. Jefferson's story, it turns out, is not all that different from theirs. Yet Gaines's characterization of Jefferson in *Lesson* as a prisoner-slave who is engaged in liberationist struggle against premature death—even at the level of his intellectual wellness—seems to offer the imprisoned students I have taught a neo-abolitionist model whereby they, like him, can find ways to think critically, speak boldly, write freely, and build desired community even while enduring (among other things) the institutionalization of educational deprivation. Yes, by teaching Gaines's *Lesson* behind bars, I aim to do much more than (re)acquaint an overlooked audience of readers with the narrative techniques of one of the African American literary tradition's finest authors. Whenever I have the privilege of joining these intellectually adventurous learning communities, I facilitate discussions on *Lesson* that, I hope, help each student to speak his own antipanoptically expressive "tell them im strong tell them im a man" truth to proponents of institutional power and to free-worlders who often too narrowly view them as "missing."[18]

It is my hope that this book will inspire more interdisciplinary scholarship on mass incarceration, particularly work that continues to intersect the fields of literary studies and critical prison studies. I agree with Megan Sweeney, who has made the point that the literary imagination is rife with possibilities for conceptualizing and combating the expansion and existence of the prison-industrial complex. Sweeney writes:

> Literary scholars working within prison studies can perform crucial work by exploring the tropes, symbols, images, narrative patterns, language forms, affects, and structures of feeling that characterize

LeJhoyn Holland (left) shares a poem in a course that he took with me (right) in which he and other imprisoned postsecondary students studied Ernest Gaines's novel *A Lesson Before Dying*. Holland was a participant in the inaugural class of Stepping Stones, a community-sponsored college preparatory program that I co-founded in 2007 with men imprisoned at Orange Correctional Center (OCC) and the Orange County Literacy Council in response to a wide range of educational needs that college and pre-college students at OCC had identified, including poise and proficiency in critical thinking, academic writing, literary critical discussion, and public speaking. (Duke University News and Communication photograph.)

historical and contemporary representations of prisons and prisoners. We have only just begun to explore the manifold ways in which literature and the literary imagination might serve as resources for challenging current penal practices.[19]

The neo-abolitionist novel, as I have discussed here and in the previous chapters, is one such resource for "challenging current penal practices." There are a wealth of prison classroom discussions and imprisoned lives that can be enhanced by attention to the neo-abolitionist fiction of late twentieth-century writers of Black Atlantic or African American literature whose works I do not examine in this book—writers such as Caryl Phillips and John A. Williams. With works such as "The Cargo Rap" (1989) and *Clifford's Blues* (1999), Phillips and Williams have continued the urgent labor of incorporating slavery-to-prison models of prisoner abuse in fictional form, and in so doing, they have also continued to expose the facts of centuries-spanning terror in U.S. prisons in ways that can inspire radical reform of the criminal justice system and prison abolition.[20] Regardless of which side of the razor wire we currently occupy, may our sorely needed explorations of the neo-abolitionist novel continue.

Notes

INTRODUCTION

1. George Jackson, *Blood in My Eye* (Baltimore: Black Classic, 1972), 7.

2. James Baldwin, qtd. in George Jackson, *Soledad Brother: The Prison Letters of George Jackson* (1970); repr. ed. (Chicago: Lawrence Hill, 1994), x.

3. Dan Berger, *Captive Nation: Black Prison Organizing in the Civil Rights Era* (Chapel Hill: University of North Carolina Press, 2014), 112, 176. *Prison-industrial complex* was a term coined by the social historian Mike Davis, but the scholar and anti-prison activist Angela Y. Davis has popularized it. Following Davis, the term refers to a method of conceptualizing imprisonment in the late twentieth century and early twenty-first century as an industry shaped increasingly by private investment. The supply of raw materials for this "punishment industry"—disproportionately criminalized Black, Brown, and poor bodies—is made available by social factors that cannot be reduced to crime, especially ideologies of racism and corporate agendas premised on global capitalism. For more, see Angela Y. Davis, *Are Prisons Obsolete?* (New York: Seven Stories Press, 2003), 84–104.

4. For more, see Billy X Jennings, "Special Assignment: George Jackson Funeral," *San Francisco Bay View National Black Newspaper*, 27 July 2014, http://sfbayview .com/2014/07/special-assignment-george-jackson-funeral/, accessed 30 June 2016.

5. For more, see Randall Kenan, ed., *The Cross of Redemption: Uncollected Writings* (New York: Pantheon, 2010), 121.

6. James Baldwin, *The Fire Next Time* (New York: Dial, 1963), 23.

7. Jackson, *Soledad Brother*, 251.

8. James Baldwin, "Speech from the Soledad Rally," in Kenan, *The Cross of Redemption*, 121, 124, emphasis mine.

9. Jackson, *Blood in My Eye*, 7.

10. Human Rights Watch, "Prisoner Abuse: How Different Are U.S. Prisons?" 13 May 2004, https://www.hrw.org/news/2004/05/13/prisoner-abuse-how-different-are-us-prisons, accessed 30 June 2015; Adam Liptak, "1 in 100 U.S. Adults Behind Bars, New Study Says," NYTimes.com, 28 February 2008, http://www.nytimes.com/2008/02/28/us/28cnd-prison.html?_r=0&pagewanted=print, accessed 30 June 2015; Thoai Lu, "Michelle Alexander: More Black Men in Prison than Were Enslaved in 1850," *Colorlines*, 30 March 2011, http://www.colorlines.com/articles/michelle-alexander-more-black-men-prison-were-enslaved-1850, accessed 30 June 2015.

11. For more, see Margo V. Perkins, *Autobiography as Activism: Three Women of the Sixties* (Jackson: University Press of Mississippi, 2000); Joy James, "Framing the Panther: Assata Shakur and Black Female Agency," in *Want to Start a Revolution? Radical Women in the Black Freedom Struggle*, ed. Dayo F. Gore, Jeanne Theoharis and Komozi Woodard (New York: New York University Press, 2009), 138–160; Michael Hames-García, *Fugitive Thought: Prison Movements, Race, and the Meaning of Justice* (Minneapolis: University of Minnesota Press, 2004); Dylan Rodríguez, *Forced Passages: Imprisoned Radical Intellectuals and the U.S. Prison Regime* (Minneapolis: University of Minnesota Press, 2006); Berger, *Captive Nation*; Mechthild Nagel, "Angela Y. Davis and Assata Shakur as Women Outlaws: Resisting U.S. State Violence," *Wagadu* 13 (Summer 2015): 43–78; Lisa M. Corrigan, *Prison Power: How Prison Influenced the Movement for Black Liberation* (Jackson: University Press of Mississippi, 2016).

12. Tara T. Green, "Introduction," in *From the Plantation to the Prison: African-American Confinement Literature*, ed. Tara T. Green (Macon, GA: Mercer University Press, 2008), 6.

13. My use of the term *mass incarceration* here and throughout the book follows the thinking of the legal scholar Michelle Alexander. *Mass incarceration* refers not only to the rapid and racially discriminatory expansion of a massive system of U.S. imprisonment currently warehousing 2.3 million people "but also to the larger web of laws, rules, policies, and customs that control those labeled criminals both in and out of prison": Michelle Alexander, *The New Jim Crow: Mass Incarceration in the Age of Colorblindness* (New York: New Press, 2010), 13.

14. Avery F. Gordon, *Ghostly Matters: Haunting and the Sociological Imagination* (Minneapolis: University of Minnesota Press, 1997), xvi.

15. Dennis Childs, *Slaves of the State: Black Incarceration from the Chain Gang to the Penitentiary* (Minneapolis: University of Minnesota Press, 2015), 28–29.

16. Ibid., 29, 31.

17. David Oshinsky, *Worse than Slavery: Parchman Farm and the Ordeal of Jim Crow Justice* (New York: Free Press, 1996), 4.

18. For more on the University of Mississippi Prison-to-College Pipeline Program (PTCPP), see Jerry Mitchell, "Professors Making Investments in Future," *Clarion Ledger*, 25 October 2015, http://www.clarionledger.com/story/news/2014/10/25/profs-making-investments-future/17938855, accessed 30 June 2015; Edwin Smith, "UM Program Transforms Incarcerated Men into College Students," *University of Mississippi News*, 18 September 2015, http://news.olemiss.edu/um-program-transforms-incarcerated-men-college-students, accessed 1 December 2015. For more on how critical pedagogy and a counter-hegemonic prison education paradigm inspire the way in which Pickett and I listen to and for our students' perspectives on historical and literary texts and incorporate them into the curriculum, discussions, and writing in the PTCPP, see Patrick Elliot Alexander, "'To live and remain outside of the barb[ed] wire and fence': A Prison

Classroom, African American Literature, and the Pedagogy of Freedom," *Reflections* 11.1 (2011): 88–108.

19. Fannie Lou Hamer, "Testimony Before the Credentials Committee at the Democratic National Convention, Atlantic City, New Jersey, August 22, 1964," in *The Speeches of Fannie Lou Hamer*, ed. Maegan Parker Brooks and Davis W. Houck (Jackson: University Press of Mississippi, 2011), 45.

20. Ishmael Reed, "Foreword," in David Matlin, *Prisons: Inside the New America from Vernooykill Creek to Abu Ghraib* (Berkeley, CA: North Atlantic, 2005), xv.

21. Brenda V. Smith, "Sexual Abuse of Women in United States Prisons: A Modern Corollary of Slavery," *Fordham Urban Law Journal* 33 (2006): 571–608; Kim Shayo Buchanan, "Impunity: Sexual Abuse in Women's Prisons," *Harvard Civil Rights–Civil Liberties Law Review* 42 (2007): 45–87; Colin Dayan, *The Story of Cruel and Unusual* (Cambridge, MA: MIT Press, 2007).

22. Portions of Christian Parenti's *Lockdown America* provide a sense of this base-level definition of prisoner abuse: Christian Parenti, *Lockdown America: Police and Prisons in the Age of Crisis* (New York: Verso, 1999), 170–174, 190–193.

23. For more, see Anne-Marie Cusac, "Abu Ghraib, USA," in Anne-Marie Cusac, *Cruel and Unusual: The Culture of Punishment in America* (New Haven, CT: Yale University Press, 2009), 244–252; Seymour M. Hersch, "Torture at Abu Ghraib," *New Yorker*, 10 May 2004, http://www.newyorker.com/magazine/2004/05/10/torture-at-abu-ghraib, accessed 30 June 2015.

24. H. Bruce Franklin, "The Inside Stories of the Global American Prison," *Texas Studies in Literature and Language* 50.3 (2008): 236, 238. Relatedly, see H. Bruce Franklin, "The American Prison and the Normalization of Torture," in *Torture, American Style*, ed. Margaret Power, May 2006, http://www.historiansagainstwar.org/resources/torture/brucefranklin.html, accessed 16 December 2011; Cusac, *Cruel and Unusual*.

25. Although the practice of "extrajudicial execution by law enforcement"—and the ongoing work of the national organization #BlackLivesMatter in opposition to its prevalence—represents another facet of state terror and another source of political struggle in our current epoch, its presence in a locale beyond prison means that my analysis of it is beyond the scope of this book. I do argue in Chapter 1, however, that intimidation and violence by the police are white supremacist practices of social control that, like extrajudicial execution by law enforcement, must be understood as intimately interconnected with the disciplinary deployment of racialized state violence on the bodies of the disproportionately Black populations that languish in the locality of the contemporary U.S. prison. For more on #BlackLivesMatter, see http://blacklivesmatter.com/about.

26. Dayan, *The Story of Cruel and Unusual*, 7–8, 16.

27. John Edgar Wideman, *Brothers and Keepers* (New York: Mariner, 2005), 187, 189.

28. Rodríguez, *Forced Passages*, 81–86.

29. H. Bruce Franklin, *The Victim as Criminal and Artist: Literature from the American Prison* (New York: Oxford University Press, 1978), 124–178.

30. Rubin Carter, *The Sixteenth Round: From Number 1 Contender to Number 45472* (Toronto: Macmillan, 1974); Angela Y. Davis, *Angela Davis: An Autobiography* (New York: International Publishers, 1974); Assata Shakur, *Assata: An Autobiography* (Chicago: Lawrence Hill, 1987); Mumia Abu-Jamal, *Live from Death Row* (New York: HarperCollins, 1995); Robert Hillary King, *From the Bottom of the Heap: The Autobiography of Black Panther Robert Hillary King* (Oakland, CA: PM Press, 2008).

31. Joy James, "Introduction: Democracy and Captivity," in *The New Abolitionists: (Neo)Slave Narratives and Contemporary Prison Writings*, ed. Joy James (Albany: State University of New York Press, 2005), xxxii.

32. My conception of "confined people" here is indebted to the work of Tara T. Green, who argues that confinement, as experienced and represented in African American literature and culture, operates on a racialized carceral continuum that links slave plantations, Jim Crow societies, and prisons because confinement "describes the status of persons who are imprisoned and [persons] who are unjustly relegated to a social and political status that . . . render[s] them powerless and subject to the rules of those who have assumed a position of authority": Green, "Introduction," 3. My understanding of white supremacy as a "disciplinary logic" is indebted to the important work of Rodríguez, who begins *Forced Passages* by troubling common conceptions of prisons as geographic sites for the disciplinary containment of criminals. He makes the case that the massive, hyper-punitive, and abusive prison system that has emerged over the past half century may be best understood as the most recent manifestation of a centuries-old "condition of direct and unmediated confrontation with technologies of state and state-sanctioned (domestic) warfare." The social-ordering nature of this "contemporary U.S. 'prison regime,'" for Rodríguez, is as old as slavery, for the most recent innovations in the state's surveillance, capture, and containment practices (and resistance to them) function within a disciplinary logic of white supremacy that is "historically derived from the socially constitutive American production of white life/mobility through black, brown, and indigenous death/immobilization": Rodríguez, *Forced Passages*, 2, 14.

33. In *Autobiography as Activism*, Perkins uses the term *political autobiography* (following Angela Davis's coining of the term in her autobiography) to make evident the extent to which Davis's and Shakur's autobiographies accomplish radical political, personal, and pedagogical work by offering a Black radical woman's counter-narrative to the racially discriminatory discourse of the news media and fundamentally sexist histories of state-sanctioned political repression and gendered social control in the criminal justice system and the U.S. carceral state. In Perkins's words, "Their narratives invite readers to interrogate hegemonic ways of knowing and understanding. Writing autobiography is a way for them to document their experiences, to give voice to the voiceless, to amend the historical record, and to expose the repressive tactics of the state": Perkins, *Autobiography as Activism*, 149.

34. Michel Foucault, *Discipline and Punish: The Birth of the Prison* (New York: Vintage, 1976), 200.

35. Ibid., emphasis mine.

36. Cristina Rathbone, *A World Apart: Women, Prison, and Life Behind Bars* (New York: Random House, 2005), xii.

37. Ibid., xiii.

38. Franklin, "The Inside Stories of the Global American Prison," 235.

39. Michael Collins, "The Antipanopticon of Etheridge Knight," *PMLA* 123.3 (2008): 581–582, 595.

40. Joy James, *Resisting State Violence: Radicalism, Gender and Race in U.S. Culture* (Minneapolis: University of Minnesota Press, 1996), 27. Recently, Rashad Shabazz has echoed James and extended her critique in his fascinating study of racialized carceral power *Spatializing Blackness: Architectures of Confinement and Black Masculinity in Chicago* (Urbana: University of Illinois Press, 2015).

41. Rodríguez, *Forced Passages*, 47.

42. Hamer, "Testimony Before the Credentials Committee at the Democratic National Convention," 45.

43. Maegan Parker Brooks has offered the most sustained analysis of Hamer's famous testimony, but her rhetorical lens is one that does not take into consideration the combined force of racialized carceral power and the panoptic gaze against which Hamer speaks. For more, see Maegan Parker Brooks, *A Voice That Could Stir an Army: Fannie Lou Hamer and the Rhetoric of the Black Freedom Movement* (Jackson: University Press of Mississippi, 2014), 86–120.

44. All text citations in this paragraph are to Hamer, "Testimony Before the Credentials Committee at the Democratic National Convention," 44–45.

45. Ibid., 44.

46. For more see, Chana Kai Lee, *For Freedom's Sake: The Life of Fannie Lou Hamer* (Urbana: University of Illinois Press, 1999), 89.

47. All text citations in this paragraph are to Hamer, "Testimony Before the Credentials Committee at the Democratic National Convention," 44–45, emphasis mine.

48. For more, see Victoria Law, *Resistance Behind Bars: The Struggles of Incarcerated Women* (Oakland, CA: PM Press, 2009).

49. Davis conceives of *prison abolition* as a coalitional movement to dismantle the existing prison-industrial complex and seek alternatives to address the social problems that mass-produce prisons and prisoners. Non-imprisoned people are to supportively follow the lead of imprisoned men and women in crowding out the hyper-punitive prison system with institutions focused on life skills development, educational improvement, drug treatment, and entrepreneurship. For more, see Davis, *Are Prisons Obsolete?* 103–115.

50. Lynn Orilla Scott, *James Baldwin's Later Fiction: Witness to the Journey* (East Lansing: Michigan State University Press, 2002), 20–61; Aaron Oforlea, "Remaking and Marking Tradition: Black Male Subjectivity in Baldwin's *Tell Me How Long the Train's Been Gone*," *Obsidian* 9.2 (2008): 62–76; D. Quentin Miller, *A Criminal Power: James Baldwin and the Law* (Columbus: Ohio State University Press, 2012), 103–135.

51. Scott, *James Baldwin's Later Fiction.*

52. James Baldwin, *Tell Me How Long the Train's Been Gone* (New York: Dial Press, 1968), 231–233.

53. Ibid., 233.

54. Ibid.

55. Ibid., emphasis mine.

56. Ibid.

57. Ibid., 234.

58. Ibid., 233–234.

59. Ibid., 236–237.

60. Ibid., 239.

61. Kay Schaffer and Sidonie Smith, *Human Rights and Narrated Lives: The Ethics of Recognition* (New York: Palgrave, 2004), 183.

62. Bernard Bell, *The Afro-American Novel and Its Tradition* (Amherst: University of Massachusetts Press, 1987), 289.

63. Ashraf H. A. Rushdy, *Neo-Slave Narratives: Studies of the Social Logic of a Literary Form* (New York: Oxford University Press, 1999), 3.

64. Elizabeth Ann Beaulieu, *Black Women Writers and the American Neo-Slave Narrative: Femininity Unfettered* (Westport, CT: Greenwood, 1999), 4.

65. Angelyn Mitchell, *The Freedom to Remember: Narrative, Slavery, and Gender in Contemporary Black Women's Fiction* (New Brunswick, NJ: Rutgers University Press, 2002), 4.

66. Arlene R. Keizer, *Black Subjects: Identity Formation in the Contemporary Narrative of Slavery* (Ithaca, NY: Cornell University Press, 2004), 4.

67. My theory of the neo-abolitionist novel can be understood as an admiring rejoinder to Childs's recent conception of Morrison's *Beloved* as a *narrative of neoslavery*, a term he has coined to describe "prison and chain-gang centered soundings, writings, testimonies and social practices in which the unsettling continuities of slavery and freedom are brought into overt relief": Childs, *Slaves of the State*, 29–39.

68. Ernest Gaines, *A Lesson Before Dying* (New York: Vintage, 1993), 34.

CHAPTER 1

1. David Leeming, *James Baldwin: A Biography* (New York: Knopf, 1994), 323, emphasis mine. A notable exception to my claim is an excellent essay by D. Quentin Miller that examines Baldwin's relationship to his imprisoned friend Tony Maynard: D. Quentin Miller, "'On the Outside Looking In': White Readers of Nonwhite Prison Narratives," in *Prose and Cons: Essays on Prison Literature in the United States,* ed. D. Quentin Miller (Jefferson, NC: McFarland, 2005), 15–32.

2. James Baldwin, "Equal in Paris" in James Baldwin, *Notes of a Native Son* (Boston: Beacon, 1955), 138.

3. James Baldwin, *No Name in the Street* (New York: Dial, 1972), 100–149, 196.

4. Leeming, *James Baldwin*, 292–294, 304. Baldwin also wrote the foreword to Bobby Seale's autobiography, *A Lonely Rage: The Autobiography of Bobby Seale* (New York: Bantam, 1979).

5. James Baldwin, "An Open Letter to My Sister, Angela Davis," in *The Cross of Redemption: Uncollected Writings*, ed. Randall Kenan (New York: Pantheon, 2010), 259.

6. Leeming, *James Baldwin*, 321.

7. James Baldwin, "A Letter to Prisoners," in Kenan, *The Cross of Redemption*, 261.

8. Miller has begun this important labor: see D. Quentin Miller, *A Criminal Power: James Baldwin and the Law* (Columbus: Ohio State University Press, 2012).

9. Baldwin, *No Name in the Street*, 115.

10. James Baldwin, *The Fire Next Time* (New York: Dial, 1963), 23.

11. James Baldwin, *Go Tell It on the Mountain* (New York: Dial, 1953), 167.

12. Ibid., 171.

13. Ibid.

14. Ibid., 170.

15. The Fourth Amendment to the U.S. Constitution protects citizens from "unreasonable searches and seizures." The Eighth Amendment prohibits the practice of "cruel and unusual punishments" by state officials.

16. Baldwin, *The Fire Next Time*, 33–34.

17. Mortimer Belden, qtd. in H. Bruce Franklin, *The Victim as Criminal and Artist: Literature from the American Prison* (New York: Oxford University Press, 1978), 131.

18. James Baldwin, *Early Novels and Stories* (New York: Literary Classics of the United States, 1998), 936.

19. Harriet Jacobs, *Incidents in the Life of a Slave Girl* (Mineola, NY: Dover, 2001), 41.

20. James Baldwin, *Tell Me How Long the Train's Been Gone* (New York: Dial, 1968), 64.

21. George Jackson, *Soledad Brother: The Prison Letters of George Jackson* (1970), repr. ed. (Chicago: Lawrence Hill, 1994), 251.

22. Leeming, *James Baldwin*, 323.

23. Trudier Harris-Lopez, *South of Tradition: Essays on African American Literature* (Athens: University of Georgia Press, 2002), 138; Horace A. Porter, *Stealing the Fire: The Art and Protest of James Baldwin* (Middletown, CT: Wesleyan University Press, 1989), 12.

24. James Baldwin, "It's Hard to Be James Baldwin" (interview by Herbert R. Lottman), *Intellectual Digest*, July 1972, 67–68.

25. For more on COINTELPRO, see Ward Churchill and Jim Vander Wall, *Agents of Repression: The FBI's Secret Wars Against the Black Panther Party and the American Indian Movement* (Boston: South End, 1988), xii, 37–99; James Baldwin, qtd. in George Goodman Jr., "For James Baldwin, a Rap on Baldwin," *New York Review of Books,* 26 June 1972, http://www.nytimes.com/books/98/03/29/specials/baldwin-rap.html, accessed 29 October 2011.

26. Richard Majors and Janet Mancini Billson, *Cool Pose: The Dilemmas of Black Manhood in America* (New York: Lexington, 1992), 3, 8.

27. Trudier Harris, "The Eye as Weapon in *If Beale Street Could Talk*," *MELUS* 5.3 (1978): 54–66.

28. James Baldwin, *If Beale Street Could Talk* (New York: Dial, 1974), 172.

29. Maurice Wallace, *Constructing the Black Masculine: Identity and Ideality in African American Men's Literature and Culture, 1775–1995* (Durham, NC: Duke University Press, 2002), 32.

30. Baldwin, *If Beale Street Could Talk*, 37.

31. Ibid., 6.

32. For more, see, Malcolm X, "The Harlem Hate-Gang Scare," in *Malcolm X Speaks: Selected Speeches and Statements*, ed. George Breitman (New York: Grove, 1965), 66–71.

33. Baldwin, *If Beale Street Could Talk*, 9, 55, 144. My reading of this section of Baldwin's novel is informed by my engagement with Foucault's discussion of Panopticism: Michel Foucault, *Discipline and Punish: The Birth of the Prison* (New York: Vintage, 1976), 195–228.

34. Baldwin, *If Beale Street Could Talk*, 12, 11, 106, 108, 171, 141.

35. Ibid., 135–136.

36. Ibid., 137–138.

37. Ibid., 138.

38. Ibid., 139, 137.

39. Ibid., 116–117.

40. For more, see Houston A. Baker Jr., "The Embattled Craftsman: An Essay on James Baldwin," *Journal of African-Afro-American Affairs* 1.1 (1977): 28–51, and in *Critical Essays on James Baldwin*, ed. Fred Stanley and Nancy V. Burt (Boston: G. K. Hall, 1988): 66–77.

41. Jared Sexton, "Racial Profiling and the Societies of Control," in *Warfare in the Homeland: Policing and Prison in a Penal Democracy*, ed. Joy James (Durham, NC: Duke University Press, 2007), 197–218.

42. Angela Y. Davis, "Political Prisoners, Prisons, and Black Liberation," in *If They Come in the Morning: Voices of Resistance*, ed. Angela Y. Davis (New Rochelle, NY: Third Press, 1971), 22, emphasis mine.

43. Jackson, *Soledad Brother*, 184–185. I do not dismiss a point raised by many scholars that traces of the story of the abused prisoner Tony Maynard, Baldwin's friend, are

present in Fonny's plight. However, the tendency of scholars such as Carolyn Wedin Sylvander, William J. Weatherby, and Lynn Orilla Scott to imagine Maynard as Baldwin's sole or primary influence for depicting Fonny's predicament or his persona seems, in light of my research on Baldwin's abiding fascination with George Jackson, a bit shortsighted.

44. Leeming, *James Baldwin*, 311; Baldwin, "An Open Letter to My Sister, Angela Davis," 254–260; James Baldwin, "Speech from the Soledad Rally," in Kenan, *The Cross of Redemption*, 120–125; Baldwin, *No Name in the Street*, 197.

45. Lee Bernstein, *America Is the Prison: Arts and Politics in Prison in the 1970s* (Chapel Hill: University of North Carolina Press, 2010), 4.

46. Jackson, *Soledad Brother*, 110.

47. Brian Conniff, "The Prison Writer as Ideologue: George Jackson and the Attica Prison Rebellion," in Miller, *Prose and Cons*, 150.

48. Churchill and Vander Wall, *Agents of Repression*, 98; Baldwin, qtd. in Jackson, *Soledad Brother*, x.

49. Kenan, *The Cross of Redemption*, 121.

50. Jackson, *Soledad Brother*, 4, emphasis mine.

51. Tara T. Green, "Introduction," in *From the Plantation to the Prison: African-American Confinement Literature,* ed. Tara T. Green (Macon, GA: Mercer University Press, 2008), 1.

52. Dylan Rodríguez, *Forced Passages: Imprisoned Radical Intellectuals and the U.S. Prison Regime* (Minneapolis: University of Minnesota Press, 2006), 120, emphasis mine.

53. Jackson, *Soledad Brother*, 250. For more context, see Min S. Yee, *The Melancholy History of Soledad Prison: In Which a Utopian Scheme Turns Bedlam* (New York: Harper's Magazine Press, 1973), 124–125.

54. Jackson, *Soledad Brother*, 251–252.

55. Ibid., 213, 174.

56. Ibid., 252.

57. Ibid., 111, 4.

58. Ibid., 3, 10.

59. For more, see Joy James, *Imprisoned Intellectuals: America's Political Prisoners Write on Life, Liberation, and Rebellion*, ed. Joy James (Lanham, MD: Rowman and Littlefield, 2003), 84–87; Joy James, ed., *The New Abolitionists: (Neo)Slave Narratives and Contemporary Prison Writings* (Albany: State University of New York Press, 2005), 227.

60. Jackson, *Soledad Brother*, 6.

61. Maya Angelou, *I Know Why the Caged Bird Sings* (New York: Random House, 1969), 170.

62. Jackson, *Soledad Brother*, 10.

63. Ibid.

64. Ibid.

65. Ibid., 9.

66. Rodríguez, *Forced Passages*, 117, emphasis mine.

67. Jackson, *Soledad Brother*, 18, 19.

68. Ibid., 99–100.

69. Yee, *The Melancholy History of Soledad Prison*, 127.

70. Jackson, *Soledad Brother*, 79.

71. Eric Mann, *Comrade George: An Investigation into the Life, Political Thought, and Assassination of George Jackson* (New York: Harper and Row, 1972), 26–27.

72. For more, see Gregory Armstrong, "Preface," in George L. Jackson, *Blood in My Eye* (Baltimore: Black Classic, 1990), xii.

73. Jackson, *Soledad Brother*, 53, 115, 121, 247.

74. Ibid., 178.

75. See Terry A. Kupers, "Mental Health in Men's Prisons," in *Prison Masculinities*, ed. Don Sabo, Terry A. Kupers, and Willie London (Philadelphia: Temple University Press, 2001), 192–197.

76. Jackson, *Soledad Brother*, 157.

77. Ibid., 184–185.

78. Ibid., 16.

79. Dan Berger, *Captive Nation: Black Prison Organizing in the Civil Rights Era* (Chapel Hill: University of North Carolina Press, 2014), 99.

80. Jackson, *Soledad Brother*, 143, 208.

81. Ibid., 233–234, emphasis mine.

82. A San Quentin official's report to prison warden L. S. Nelson on September 3, 1971, includes the books I mention among a list of ninety-nine that were "taken from the cell of George Jackson . . . following Adjustment Center incident at San Quentin."

83. Official, qtd. in Yee, *The Melancholy History of Soledad Prison*, 128, emphasis mine.

84. Allan Mancino, qtd. in Mann, *Comrade George*, 55. See also Berger, *Captive Nation*, 133.

85. Jackson, *Soledad Brother*, 251, 252.

86. James, *Warfare in the Homeland*, 21.

87. For more, see Yee, *The Melancholy History of Soledad Prison*, 134–135.

88. Lynn Orilla Scott, *James Baldwin's Later Fiction: Witness to the Journey* (East Lansing: Michigan State University Press, 2002), 116.

89. Baldwin, *If Beale Street Could Talk*, 36.

90. Ibid., 35.

91. Scott, *James Baldwin's Later Fiction*, 115; Baldwin, *If Beale Street Could Talk*, 36, emphasis mine.

92. Baldwin, *If Beale Street Could Talk*, 36.

93. Brady Thomas Heiner and Ariana Mangual, "The Repressive Social Function of Schools in Racialized Communities," in *States of Confinement: Policing, Detention, and Prisons*, ed. Joy James (New York: Palgrave, 2000), 223, 227. More recently, the legal scholar Michelle Alexander has made the similar observation that "schools located in ghetto communities more closely resemble prisons than places of learning, creativity, or moral development": Michelle Alexander, *The New Jim Crow: Mass Incarceration in the Age of Colorblindness* (New York: New Press, 2010), 167.

94. Baldwin, *If Beale Street Could Talk*, 36.

95. Ibid., 36–38.

96. Ibid., 65, 37. Relatedly, in his essay "A Report from Occupied Territory," Baldwin states, "'Bad niggers,' in America, as elsewhere, have always been watched and have usually been killed": Baldwin, *Early Novels and Stories*, 729.

97. Jackson, *Soledad Brother*, 4, 251.

98. Harris, "The Eye as Weapon in *If Beale Street Could Talk*," 59–60.

99. Baldwin, *If Beale Street Could Talk*, 94.

100. Ibid., 120.

101. Ibid., 191–193.

102. Ibid., 4.

103. Kim Shayo Buchanan, "Our Prisons, Ourselves: Race, Gender, and the Rule of Law," *Yale Law and Policy Review* 29.1 (2010): 4.

104. Baldwin, *If Beale Street Could Talk*, 174.

105. Ibid., 103.

106. Ibid., 138.

107. Ibid., 171, 172.

108. Ibid., 173–174, emphasis mine.

109. Ibid., 174.

110. Angela Y. Davis, "Reflections on the Black Woman's Role in the Community of Slaves," in *The Angela Y. Davis Reader*, ed. Joy James (Malden, MA: Blackwell, 1998), 124. This essay was first published in *Black Scholar* in December 1971.

111. Baldwin, "An Open Letter to My Sister, Angela Davis," 256.

112. Baldwin, *If Beale Street Could Talk*, 173–174.

113. Ibid., 7.

114. Ibid., 196.

115. Ibid., 162.

116. Baldwin, *No Name in the Street*, 172.

117. For more on We Charge Genocide's notably testimonial, narrative, activist-centered organizing against racialized state violence, see http://wechargegenocide.org.

118. Amnesty International, *United States of America: Police Brutality and Excessive Force in the New York City Police Department* (London: Amnesty International, 1996); Human Rights Watch, *Shielded from Justice: Police Brutality and Accountability in the United States*, 1 July 1998, accessed 29 October 2011; Andrea J. Ritchie and Joey L. Mogul, "In the Shadows of the War on Terror: Persistent Police Brutality and Abuse of People of Color in the United States," April 2006, http://www.ushrnetwork.org/sites/ushrnetwork.org/files/shadow_report_to_cat_on_police_brutality_final.pdf, accessed 29 October 2011.

119. Amnesty International, *United States of America*, 12–13.

120. Kay Schaffer and Sidonie Smith, *Human Rights and Narrated Lives: The Ethics of Recognition* (New York: Palgrave, 2004), 43–44.

121. The suspension points in this essay title are reprinted as they appear in the original.

122. Houston A. Baker Jr., "Scene . . . Not Heard," in *Reading Rodney King: Reading Urban Uprising*, ed. Robert Gooding Williams (New York: Routledge, 1993), 39–40.

123. Recently, the *New York Times*, Grio.com, and Bitch Media have helped to productively undermine this underrepresentation in the news media of Black women's subjection to racialized and sexualized police intimidation. See Wendy Ruderman, "For Women in Street Stops, Deeper Humiliation," NYTimes.com, 6 August 2012, http://www.nytimes.com/2012/08/07/nyregion/for-women-in-street-stops-deeper-humiliation.html?pagewanted=all&_r=2&, accessed 8 December 2014; Lily Workneh, "Stop-and-Frisk: Women Who Are Stopped Feel Deeper Embarrassment," TheGrio.com, 3 May 2013, http://thegrio.com/2013/05/03/stop-and-frisk-women-who-are-stopped-feel-deeper-embarrassment/#, accessed 8 December 2014; Victoria Law, "Remembering the Black Women Killed by Police," *Bitch Media*, 20 August 2014, http://bitchmagazine.org/post/gender-and-race-and-police-violence-women-ferguson-michael-brown, accessed 8 December 2014. In scholarly discourse, Andrea J. Ritchie's work on the women of color's confrontations with state violence is, similarly, an important contribution: Andrea J. Ritchie, "Law Enforcement Violence Against Women of Color," in *The Color of Vio-*

lence: The Incite! Anthology, ed. INCITE! Women of Color Against Violence (Boston: South End, 2006), 138–156. Also, the renowned critical race theory scholar and law professor Kimberlé Crenshaw, who is the executive director of the African American Policy Forum, has explained how the recently formed #SayHerName movement also undermines this underrepresentation by the news media of Black women's subjection to racialized and sexualized police intimidation. "Although Black women are routinely killed, raped, and beaten by the police, their experiences are rarely foregrounded in popular understandings of police brutality. Yet, inclusion of Black women's experiences in social movements, media narratives, and policy demands around policing and police brutality is critical to effectively combating racialized state violence for Black communities and other communities of color": http://www.aapf.org/sayhername.

124. Baldwin, *If Beale Street Could Talk*, 138.

125. Ibid., 174.

126. Ibid., 63, 197.

CHAPTER 2

1. Toni Morrison, *Beloved* (New York: Plume, 1987), 180, emphasis mine.

2. Ibid., 104, 199, emphasis mine.

3. Ibid., 68, 199.

4. Ibid., 245, emphasis mine.

5. Ibid., 119, emphasis mine.

6. Ibid., 235, emphasis mine.

7. Ibid., 119, emphasis mine.

8. Silja J. A. Talvi, *Women Behind Bars: The Crisis of Women in the U.S. Prison System* (Emeryville, CA: Seal, 2007), 57.

9. For more, see "Incarcerated Women" fact sheet, Sentencing Project, http://sentencingproject.org/doc/publications/cc_Incarcerated_Women_Factsheet_Dec2012final.pdf.

10. Brenda V. Smith, "Sexual Abuse of Women in United States Prisons: A Modern Corollary of Slavery," *Fordham Urban Law Journal* 33 (2006): 571.

11. Saidiya Hartman, *Scenes of Subjection: Terror, Slavery, and Self-Making in Nineteenth-Century America* (New York: Oxford University Press, 1997), 79–112.

12. For more on Black women's representational constraints in abolitionist print culture, see France Smith Foster, "'In Respect to Females': Differences in the Portrayals of Women by Male and Female Narrators," *Black American Literature Forum* 15.2 (Summer 1981): 66–70.

13. Breea C. Willingham, "Black Women's Prison Narratives and the Intersection of Race, Gender, and Sexuality in U.S. Prisons," *Critical Survey* 23.3 (2011): 56.

14. The following essays on *Beloved* suggest that the novel is "a resurrection of disremembered people, experiences, expressive cultures, and architectures from the Middle Passage and slavery": Ashraf H. A. Rushdy, "Daughters Signifyin(g) History: The Example of Toni Morrison's *Beloved*," *American Literature* 64.3 (1992): 567–597; Jan Furman, "Remembering the 'Disremembered': *Beloved*," in Jan Furman, *Toni Morrison's Fiction* (Columbia: University of South Carolina Press, 1996), 67–84; Avery F. Gordon, "Not Only the Footprints but the Water Too and What Is Down There," in Avery F. Gordon, *Ghostly Matters: Haunting and the Sociological Imagination* (Minneapolis: University of Minnesota Press, 1997), 136–190; Angeletta KM Gourdine, "Hearing Reading and Being 'Read' by *Beloved*," *NWSA Journal* 10 (1998): 13–31; Mae Gwendolyn Henderson, "Toni

Morrison's *Beloved*: Re-Membering the Body as Historical Text," in *Toni Morrison's Beloved: A Casebook*, ed. William L. Andrews and Nellie Y. McKay (New York: Oxford University Press, 1999), 79–106; Linda Krumholz, "The Ghosts of Slavery: Historical Recovery in Toni Morrison's *Beloved*," in Andrews and McKay, *Toni Morrison's* Beloved, 107–125; Nancy Jesser, "Violence, Home, and Community in Toni Morrison's *Beloved*," *African American Review* 33.2 (1999): 325–345; Carole E. Henderson, "Dis-Membered to Remember: Bodies, Scars and Ritual in Toni Morrison's *Beloved*," in Carole E. Henderson, *Scarring the Black Body: Race and Representation in African American Literature* (Columbia: University of Missouri Press, 2002), 81–110; Dennis Childs, "'You Ain't Seen Nothin' Yet': *Beloved* and the Middle Passage Carceral Model," in Dennis Childs, *Slaves of the State: Black Incarceration from the Chain Gang to the Penitentiary* (Minneapolis: University of Minnesota Press, 2015), 25–55.

The following essays on *Beloved* suggest that the novel is "a reconstruction of U.S history and historical fiction": Barbara Christian, "'Somebody Forgot to Tell Somebody Something': African-American Women's Historical Novels," in *Wild Women in the Whirlwind: Afro-American Culture and the Contemporary Literary Renaissance*, ed. Joanne M. Braxton and Andrée Nicola McLaughlin (New Brunswick, NJ: Rutgers University Press, 1990), 326–341; Emily Miller Budick, "Absence, Loss, and the Space of History in Toni Morrison's *Beloved*," *Arizona Quarterly* 48.2 (Summer 1992): 117–138; Caroline Rody, "Toni Morrison's *Beloved*: History, 'Rememory,' and a 'Clamor for a Kiss,'" *American Literary History* 7.1 (1995): 92–119; Kimberly Chabot Davis, "'Postmodern Blackness': Morrison's *Beloved* and the End of History," *Twentieth-Century Literature* 44.2 (1998): 242–260.

The following essays on *Beloved* suggest that the novel is "a testament to African cosmology and culture": Barbara Christian, "Fixing Methodologies: *Beloved*," *Cultural Critique* 24 (Spring 1993): 5–15; Karla FC Holloway, "*Beloved*: A Spiritual," in Andrews and McKay, *Toni Morrison's* Beloved, 67–78; Kathryn Rummell, "Toni Morrison's *Beloved*: Transforming the African Heroic Epic," *The Griot* 21.1 (Spring 2002): 1–15.

More recently, Melanie Anderson argued that the novel "conjure[s] African American history through a spectral guide. . . . This bridge of personal and historical memory is the ghost: Beloved": Melanie R. Anderson, "'What Would It Be Like to Be on the Other Side?' History as a Spectral Bridge in *Beloved* and *Paradise*," in Melanie R. Anderson, *Spectrality in the Novels of Toni Morrison* (Knoxville: University of Tennessee Press, 2013), 65.

15. Sabine Sielke, *Reading Rape: The Rhetoric of Sexual Violence in American Literature and Culture, 1790–1990* (Princeton, NJ: Princeton University Press, 2002), 152.

16. Henderson, *Scarring the Black Body*, 82.

17. Pamela E. Barnett, "Figurations of Rape and the Supernatural in *Beloved*," *PMLA* 112 (1997): 418, 420.

18. Barnett offers an important discussion of how the white male guards Morrison depicts in *Beloved* subject Black male characters—specifically, Paul D and the forty-five other Black men who are chain gang captives in Alfred, Georgia—to institutionalized sexual violence. These captive Black men are forced to fellate the guards at gunpoint: ibid., 419, 423–425.

19. Morrison, *Beloved*, 23.

20. Ibid., 223.

21. Ibid., 70.

22. It is worth stating here that I am referring to slavery's "*ostensible* abolishment in 1865 with the passage of the Thirteenth Amendment" because the amendment's excep-

tion clause effectively reinstates slavery for people who are convicted of crime: "Neither slavery nor involuntary servitude, *except as a punishment for crime*, whereof the party shall have been duly convicted, shall exist within the United States, or any place subject to their jurisdiction."

23. Toni Morrison, "The Pain of Being Black," *Time*, May 22, 1989: 20, emphasis mine.

24. Krumholz, "The Ghosts of Slavery," 109.

25. Dan Berger, *Captive Nation: Black Prison Organizing in the Civil Rights Era* (Chapel Hill: University of North Carolina Press, 2014), 206.

26. Angela Y. Davis, *Angela Davis: An Autobiography* (New York: International Publishers, 1974), 5.

27. Ibid., 5–6, emphasis mine.

28. Angela Y. Davis, *Are Prisons Obsolete?* (New York: Seven Stories, 2003), 68.

29. Angela Y. Davis, "Angela Davis on Solitary Confinement, Immigration Detention, and '12 Years a Slave,'" *Democracy Now*, 6 March 2014, http://www.democracynow.org/blog/2014/3/6/part_2_angela_davis_on_solitary, accessed 13 February 2015. Davis made this observation primarily to make evident the historical continuities between the capital-driven racialized social control logic that characterized slavery and the similar logic that characterized the post–Civil War convict lease system, which has led to the resurfacing of this social control logic in the current prison-industrial complex.

30. Barnett, "Figurations of Rape and the Supernatural in *Beloved*," 420.

31. "Abuse: Guard Not Prosecuted for Sexual Attacks," *Orange County Register*, July 29, 1990.

32. Eric Harrison, "Nearly 200 Women Have Told of Being Raped, Abused in a Georgia Prison Scandal So Broad Even Officials Say It's . . . : A 13-Year Nightmare," *Los Angeles Times*, 30 December 1992, http://articles.latimes.com/print/1992-12-30/news/vw-2637_1_women-prisoners, accessed 13 February 2015.

33. Human Rights Watch Women's Project, *All Too Familiar: Sexual Abuse of Women in U.S. State Prisons* (Washington, DC: Human Rights Watch, 1996), 236–237.

34. Human Rights Watch, "Summary," in Human Rights Watch, *Nowhere to Hide: Retaliation Against Women in Michigan State Prisons*, July 1998, http://www.hrw.org/legacy/reports98/women/Mich.htm#P37_769, accessed 13 February 2015.

35. Talvi, *Women Behind Bars*, 59.

36. Michelle Chen, "Groups Press Justice Department on Prison Rape," *Colorlines*, 18 August 2010, http://www.colorlines.com/articles/groups-press-justice-department-prison-rape, accessed 13 February 2015.

37. Kim Severson, "Troubles at Women's Prison Test Alabama," NYTimes.com, 1 March 2015, http://www.nytimes.com/2014/03/02/us/troubles-at-womens-prison-test-alabama.html?_r=0, accessed 1 June 2015; Kim Chandler, "Alabama, Feds Reach Agreement over Alleged Prison Sex Abuse," *Tampa Tribune*, 31 May 2015, http://tbo.com/ap/alabama-feds-reach-agreement-over-alleged-prison-sex-abuse-20150531, accessed 1 June 2015.

38. Human Rights Watch and the American Civil Liberties Union, *Custody and Control: Conditions of Confinement in New York's Juvenile Prisons for Girls* (New York: Human Rights Watch and the American Civil Liberties Union, 2006); Amnesty International, *Broken Bodies, Shattered Minds: Torture and Ill-Treatment of Women* (London: Amnesty International, 2001); Nick Hudson, Bob Lilal, and Andrew Strong, "Private Prison Scandals from Texas," in *Considering a Private Jail, Prison, or Detention Center? A Resource for Community Members and Public Officials*, 2d ed., 16 September 2009,

http://www.grassrootsleadership.org/Texas%20resources/CPJ%20Second%20Edition
.pdf, accessed 13 February 2015; Assata Shakur, *Assata: An Autobiography* (Chicago:
Lawrence Hill, 1987); Women + Prison: A Site for Resistance, http://www.womenand
prison.org; Talvi, *Women Behind Bars*; Victoria Law, *Resistance Behind Bars: The Struggles of Incarcerated Women* (Oakland, CA: PM Press, 2009); Jodie Michelle Lawston
and Ashley E. Lucas, eds., *Razor Wire Women: Prisoners, Activists, Scholars, and Artists*
(Albany: State University of New York Press, 2011); Robin Levi and Ayelet Waldman,
eds., *Inside This Place, Not of It: Narratives from Women's Prisons* (San Francisco: Mc-
Sweeney's and Voice of Witness, 2011).

39. Gayl Jones, *Eva's Man* (1976), repr. ed. (Boston: Beacon, 1987); Angela Y. Davis,
Angela Davis: An Autobiography (New York: International Publishers, 1974).

40. Dan Berger notes Morrison's presence in Davis's jail time as a visitor, writing,
"At the Marin County Jail, Davis received a parade of well-known visitors that included
Maya Angelou, Nina Simone, Toni Morrison, and Ralph Abernathy": Berger, *Captive
Nation*, 206.

41. Megan Sweeney makes the important point that "while allowing Ku Klux Klan
publications such as *Negro Watch* and *Jew Watch*, the Texas penal system has banned
Toni Morrison's novel *Paradise*, on the grounds that it contains 'information of a racial nature' that seems 'designed to achieve a breakdown of prisons'": Megan Sweeney,
The Story Within Us: Women Prisoners Reflect on Reading (Urbana: University of Illinois Press, 2012), 2. The Texas Department of Criminal Justice has also stated that
Morrison's novel *Paradise* (1997) is a "publication [that] contains material that a reasonable person would construe as written solely for the purpose of communicating information designed to achieve a breakdown": Kaitlyn Greenidge, "The Riotous Power
of Toni Morrison," *Virginia Quarterly* 91.2 (2015), http://www.vqronline.org/fiction-
criticism/2015/04/riotous-power-toni-morrison. Accessed 1 June 2015.

42. Toni Morrison and Angela Davis, "Toni Morrison and Angela Davis on Friendship and Creativity," interviewed by Dan White, *University of California Santa Cruz
Review*, 29 October 2014, http://news.ucsc.edu/2014/10/morrison-davis-q-a.html, accessed 13 February 2015. In this same interview, Davis discusses how she has treasured
the literary exchanges that have characterized her friendship with Morrison, especially
as it emerged in the years surrounding Davis's incarceration: "It was quite an amazing
experience for me to have [Toni] as my mentor. . . . I had the opportunity to read *The
Bluest Eye* before most people I know were exposed to it."

43. Davis, *Angela Davis*, 64–65.

44. Ibid., 67.

45. Ibid., 68, emphasis mine.

46. Angela Y. Davis, "A Letter from Angela to Ericka," in *If They Come in the Morning: Voices of Resistance*, ed. Angela Y. Davis (New Rochelle, NY: Third Press Publishers,
1971), 125–126.

47. Angela Y. Davis, *Abolition Democracy: Beyond Empire, Prisons, and Torture*
(New York: Seven Stories Press, 2005), 81.

48. Davis, *Angela Davis*, 68, emphasis mine.

49. Ibid., 69.

50. Morrison, *Beloved*, 140.

51. Ibid., 16–17.

52. Ibid., 17.

53. Ibid., emphasis mine.

54. Ibid., 200.

55. Ibid., 251.

56. Ibid., 119.

57. Ibid.

58. Toni Morrison, qtd. in Marsha Darling, "In the Realm of Responsibility: A Conversation with Toni Morrison," *Women's Review of Books* 5 (March 1988): 5.

59. Gordon, *Ghostly Matters*, 140. Relatedly, Carol E. Henderson states, "In making Beloved *flesh*, Morrison makes [a] historical moment *tangible* as Beloved's physical frame becomes a material symbol of those bodies unaccounted for—those [epigraphic] sixty million or more lost on various sea voyages between Africa and America. [Beloved] is the conduit through which these disembodied victims of the Middle Passage gain a literate voice": Henderson, *Scarring the Black Body*, 89.

60. Gordon, *Ghostly Matters*, xv.

61. Ibid., xvi.

62. Ibid., xvi.

63. Ibid., xvi.

64. Morrison, *Beloved*, 275.

65. Ibid., 241, emphasis mine. I am not alone in reading this scene and others in Morrison's novel as direct references to Black female characters' *routine* sexual abuse on the slave ship. See, for instance, Angelyn Mitchell, *The Freedom to Remember: Narrative, Slavery, and Gender in Contemporary Black Women's Fiction* (New Brunswick, NJ: Rutgers University Press, 2002), 96–97.

66. Morrison, *Beloved*, 241, emphasis mine.

67. Ibid., 210, 212, emphasis mine. Throughout this chapter, spacing within quotations is re-created as it appeared in the original.

68. Ibid., 215.

69. Ibid., 62.

70. Gordon, *Ghostly Matters*, 183, emphasis mine.

71. Smith, "Sexual Abuse of Women in United States Prisons," 579, 582–583, 586, emphasis mine. The legal scholar Kim Shayo Buchanan has also chronicled the evolution of institutionalized rape from the carceral locale of the slave plantation to the current era's women's prison: see Kim Shayo Buchanan, "Impunity: Sexual Abuse in Women's Prisons," *Harvard Civil Rights–Civil Liberties Law Review* 42 (2007): 45–87.

72. Davis, *Are Prisons Obsolete?* 77–78; Talvi, *Women Behind Bars*, 54–78; Law, *Resistance Behind Bars*, 59–76.

73. Alan Elsner, *Gates of Injustice: The Crisis in America's Prisons* (Upper Saddle River, NJ: Prentice Hall, 2006), 148–150; Terry Kupers, "The Role of Misogyny and Homophobia in Prison Sexual Abuse," *UCLA Women's Law Journal* 18 (Fall 2010): 107–111. The Prisoner Litigation Reform Act (PLRA) of 1996 declares that imprisoned people *may* be granted the right to sue prison personnel only after filing complaints through all levels of a facility's grievance system, even though, almost across the board, the grievance system demands the direct involvement of those prison personnel members who have harmed or abused the imprisoned person(s) filing a complaint: Human Rights Watch, *No Equal Justice: The Prison Litigation Reform Act in the United States* (New York: Human Rights Watch, 2009).

74. Regarding the "United States' tolerance of torture," Joy James remarks, "Although the Convention Against Torture, which the United States ratified in 1994, defines rape of women in custody by a correctional officer as 'torture,' the United States government has engaged in virtually no monitoring of the human rights conditions and situations of imprisoned women": Joy James, "Introduction," in *States of Confinement:*

Policing, Detention, and Prisons, ed. Joy James (New York: Palgrave, 2000), xi. Also to this point, Christian Parenti writes, "In America's booming private for-profit dungeons, the rape crisis is even worse, because officials and COs are less accountable to prisoners or the public. Inmates in corporate penitentiaries are often sent far from their home state and thus have few (if any) local contacts to help expose abuse": Christian Parenti, *Lockdown America: Police and Prisons in the Age of Crisis* (New York: Verso, 1999), 191.

75. Barbara Owen, "Women's Prisons," in *Encyclopedia of Prisons and Correctional Facilities*, ed. Mary Bosworth (Thousand Oaks, CA: Sage, 2005), 1051–1056.

76. Morrison, *Beloved*, 241.

77. Anannya Bhattacharjee, "Private Fists and Public Force: Race, Gender, and Surveillance," in *Policing the National Body: Sex, Race, and Criminalization*, ed. Jael Sillman and Anannya Bhattacharjee (Cambridge, MA: South End, 2002), 26.

78. For more, see Talvi, *Women Behind Bars*, 54–78.

79. Marcus Rediker, *The Slave Ship: A Human History* (New York: Penguin, 2007), 7, 188, emphasis mine. See also David Brion Davis, *Inhuman Bondage: The Rise and Fall of Slavery in the New World* (New York: Oxford University Press, 2006), 92–93.

80. Jean Wyatt, "Giving Body to the Word: The Maternal Symbolic in Toni Morrison's *Beloved*," *PMLA* 108.3 (1993): 480; Robert Broad, "Giving Blood to the Scraps: Haints, History, and Hosea in *Beloved*," *African American Review*, 28.2 (1994): 191; J. Brooks Bouson, *Quiet as It's Kept: Shame, Trauma, and Race in the Novels of Toni Morrison* (Albany: State University of New York Press, 2000), 154; Kristin Boudreau, "Pain and the Unmaking of Self in Toni Morrison's *Beloved*," *Contemporary Literature* 36.3 (1995): 452.

81. Morrison, *Beloved*, 198.

82. Toni Morrison, "The Site of Memory," in *Out There: Marginalization and Contemporary Cultures*, ed. Russell Ferguson, Martha Gever, Trinh T. Minh-ha, and Cornel West (New York: New York Museum of Contemporary Art, 1990), 299–305.

83. Christian, "Fixing Methodologies," 6.

84. Cynthia Hamilton, "Revisions, Rememories, and Exorcisms: Toni Morrison and the Slave Narrative," *Journal of American Studies* 30.3 (1996): 430.

85. Mae Gwendolyn Henderson, "Speaking in Tongues: Dialogics, Dialectics, and the Black Woman Writer's Literary Tradition," in *Changing Our Own Words: Essays on Criticism, Theory, and Writing by Black Women*, ed. Cheryl A. Wall (New Brunswick, NJ: Rutgers University Press, 1989), 16–37.

86. Hamilton, "Revisions, Rememories, and Exorcisms," 435.

87. Hartman, *Scenes of Subjection*, 66.

88. Morrison, *Beloved*, 198–199.

89. Ibid., 199.

90. Danielle Maestretti, "Breaking Free: Prisoners Publish Their Stories in Zines," *Utne Reader*, March–April 2010, http://www.utne.com/Media/Breaking-Free-Prisoners-Publish-Their-Stories-in-Zines.aspx, accessed 1 June 2015.

91. Law, *Resistance Behind Bars*, 139.

92. Danielle L. McGuire, *At the Dark End of the Street: Black Women, Rape, and Resistance—a New History of the Civil Rights Movement from Rosa Parks to the Rise of Black Power* (New York: Knopf, 2010), xvii–xx, 218–220.

93. Geneva Smitherman, *Talkin' and Testifyin': The Language of Black America* (Boston: Houghton Mifflin, 1977), 150.

94. Michelle Alexander, "Foreword," in Levi and Waldman, *Inside This Place, Not of It*, 11–13.

95. Morrison, *Beloved*, 62.

96. Ibid.

97. James Olney, "'I Was Born': Slave Narratives, Their Status as Autobiography and Literature," *Callaloo* 20 (Winter 1984): 46–73; John Sekora, "Black Message/White Envelope: Genre, Authenticity, and Authority in the Antebellum Slave Narrative," *Callaloo* 32 (Summer 1987): 482–515; William L. Andrews, "The Novelization of Voice in Early African American Narrative," *PMLA* 105 (1990): 23; Molly Abel Travis, "Speaking from the Silence of the Slave Narrative: *Beloved* and African-American Women's History," *Texas Review* 13 (1992): 73.

98. John Newton, qtd. in Rediker, *The Slave Ship*, 241, emphasis mine.

99. Claudine Raynaud, "The Poetics of Abjection in *Beloved*," in *Black Imagination and the Middle Passage*, ed. Maria Diedrich, Henry Louis Gates Jr., and Carl Pedersen (New York: Oxford University Press, 1999), 74.

100. Bibi Bakare-Yusuf, "The Economy of Violence: Black Bodies and the Unspeakable Terror," in *Feminist Theory and the Body: A Reader*, ed. Janet Price and Margrit Shildrick (New York: Routledge, 1999), 318. Also relevant here is a similar observation made by Anne Bailey that "the termination of unwanted pregnancies by slave women was also viewed by some [as] an act of defiance, as they thereby deprived the master of yet another child born into slavery": Anne C. Bailey, *African Voices of the Atlantic Slave Trade: Beyond the Silence and the Shame* (Boston: Beacon, 2005), 98.

101. For more on "natal alienation," see Orlando Patterson, *Slavery and Social Death: A Comparative Study* (Cambridge, MA: Harvard University Press, 1985).

102. Stephanie Smallwood, *Saltwater Slavery: A Middle Passage from Africa to American Diaspora* (Cambridge, MA: Harvard University Press, 2007), 124.

103. Ibid., 125.

104. Deborah Gray White, *Ar'n't I a Woman? Female Slaves in the Plantation South* (New York: W. W. Norton, 1985), 63.

105. Ibid., 63.

106. Victoria Law, *Invisibility of Women Prisoner Resistance*, n.d., http://acap.in terference.cc/wp-content/uploads/invisibility-of-women-prisoner-resist-zine-final.pdf; http://womenandprison.org/contributors/view/barrilee_banniste, accessed 1 June 2015.

107. Law, *Resistance Behind Bars*, 141.

108. Judy Peet, "N.J. Inmates Tell Their Own Stories of Abuse," *Star-Ledger*, 23 May 2004, http://www.nj.com/news/ledger/stories/specialprojects/womenprison01.html, accessed 1 June 2015.

109. Marianne Brown, "Making History Inside Prison Walls," *Tenacious* 21 (Fall 2010): 11–12.

110. Anne Folwell Stanford, "Lit by Each Other's Light: Women's Writing at Cook County Jail," in *Interrupted Life: Experiences of Incarcerated Women in the United States*, ed. Rickie Solinger, Paula C. Johnson, Martha L. Raimon, Tina Reynolds, and Ruby C. Tapia (Berkeley: University of California Press, 2010), 165.

111. Morrison, *Beloved*, 210, 211.

112. Ibid., 212.

113. See, e.g., Wyatt, "Giving Body to the Word," 474–488; Broad, "Giving Blood to the Scraps," 189–196; Bouson, *Quiet as It's Kept*, 131–162.

114. Morrison, *Beloved*, 241, emphasis mine.

115. Ibid., 210.

116. Ibid., 200, 205.

117. Ibid., 211.

118. Ibid., 210–212.

119. Smallwood, *Saltwater Slavery*, 152.

120. For a notable exception, see Vincent Brown, "Social Death and Political Life in the Study of Slavery," *American Historical Review* 114 (2009): 1231–1249.

121. Morrison, *Beloved*, 211.

122. Ibid., 210.

123. Ibid.

124. Smallwood, *Saltwater Slavery*, 122.

125. Law, *Resistance Behind Bars*, 140.

126. Diana Block, Urszula Wislanka, Cassie Pierson, and Pam Fadem, "*The Fire Inside*: Newsletter of the California Coalition for Women Prisoners," *NWSA Journal* 20.2 (Summer 2008): 48–49.

127. Laura Gottesdiener, "California Women Prisons: Inmates Face Sexual Abuse, Lack of Medical Care and Unsanitary Conditions," *Huffington Post*, 3 June 2011, http://www.huffingtonpost.com/2011/06/03/california-women-prisons_n_871125.html, accessed 1 June 2015; Talvi, *Women Behind Bars*, 57.

128. Beverly Herny, qtd. in Gottesdiener, "California Women Prisons."

129. Johanna Hudnall, "Prison Rape," in Lawston and Lucas, *Razor Wire Women*, 165.

130. M.S., "Abu Ghraib Torture Began at Home," *The Fire Inside* 28 (Summer 2004): 1 June 2015, http://www.womenprisoners.org/fire/000511.html, emphasis mine. (Permission granted by California Coalition for Women Prisoners, 1540 Market #490, San Francisco, CA 94102.)

131. See Luke Harding, "Focus Shifts to Jail Abuse of Women," *The Guardian*, 12 May 2004, https://www.theguardian.com/world/2004/may/12/iraq.usa, accessed 26 April 2011; Duncan Gardham, "Abu Ghraib Photos 'Show Rape,'" *The Telegraph*, 9 May 2009, http://www.telegraph.co.uk/news/worldnews/northamerica/usa/5395830/Abu-Ghraib-abuse-photos-show-rape.html, accessed 26 April 2011. Relatedly, Mechthild Nagel remarks that "the mass media did not focus on Iraqi women prisoners who had also been sexually abused, raped, humiliated, and even disappeared, as . . . human rights groups . . . have charged. Such 'disappearance' of women is disturbing, especially in light of the dramatic display of U.S. personnel's torture against Iraqi male detainees": Mechthild Nagel, "Angela Y. Davis and Assata Shakur as Women Outlaws: Resisting U.S. State Violence," *Wagadu* 13 (Summer 2015): 45.

132. Sharon Daniel, *Public Secrets*, http://vectors.usc.edu/issues/4/publicsecrets/; Law, *Resistance Behind Bars*; Lawston and Lucas, *Razor Wire Women*; Levi and Waldman, *Inside This Place, Not of It*; Beth E. Richie, *Arrested Justice: Black Women, Violence, and America's Prison Nation* (New York: New York University Press, 2012); Solinger et al., *Interrupted Life*; Women + Prison: A Site for Resistance, http://www.womenandprison.org.

133. Megan Sweeney, *Reading Is My Window: Books and the Art of Reading in Women's Prisons* (Chapel Hill: University of North Carolina Press, 2010), 6. Daniel Burton-Rose provides a useful example of how imprisoned female survivors of sexual abuse are represented as "silent objects of cultural and political discourse," writing, "While incarcerated in a for-profit prison in Arizona, Christina Foos says she was attacked by a guard, Ernesto Rivas, as she stepped out of the shower in March 1997. Christina told *Prison Legal News* that she was startled by the sight of him, standing there with his exposed erection in hand. Before she could think of what to do, she says, Rivas ordered her to bend over the bed in her cell and he raped her. She says he returned two hours later to repeat the

act": Daniel Burton-Rose, "Our Sisters' Keepers," in *Prison Nation: The Warehousing of America's Poor*, ed. Tara Herivel and Paul Wright (New York: Routledge, 2003), 258.

134. Law, *Resistance Behind Bars*, 4, 127.

135. Ibid., 128.

136. Ibid., 4.

137. Foster, "'In Respect to Females . . . ,'" 67.

138. Deborah E. McDowell, "Negotiating Between Tenses: Witnessing Slavery after Freedom—*Dessa Rose*," in *Slavery and the Literary Imagination*, ed. Deborah E. McDowell and Arnold Rampersad (Baltimore: Johns Hopkins University Press, 1989), 146.

CHAPTER 3

1. Charles Johnson, *Middle Passage* (New York: Plume, 1990), 25–26.

2. Ibid., 26, emphasis mine.

3. Ibid.

4. Ibid., 26–27.

5. Ibid. It is worth noting here that my reading of Captain Falcon's rape of Tommy as being routine is qualified by a remark that Cringle makes later in the book: "[Captain Falcon] always watches for a [ship]man's weaknesses once he's signed on. He knows mine is Tommy, that I cannot stand his treatment of the boy": ibid., 63.

6. Ibid., 25.

7. Ibid., 27.

8. Ibid., 30.

9. Mumia Abu-Jamal, *Jailhouse Lawyers: Prisoners Defending Prisoners v. the U.S.A.* (San Francisco: City Lights, 2009), 233.

10. Bill Mears, "High Court Dismisses Ruling on Abu-Jamal Death Sentence," CNN.com, 19 January 2010, http://www.cnn.com/2010/CRIME/01/19/scotus.abu.jamal, accessed 30 June 2015; Jorge Rivas, "Mumia Abu-Jamal Will No Longer Face Death Penalty," *Colorlines*, 7 December 2011, http://www.colorlines.com/articles/mumia-abu-jamal-will-no-longer-face-death-penalty, accessed 30 June 2015. Also relevant here are John Edington, dir., *Mumia Abu-Jamal: A Case for Reasonable Doubt?* documentary film, Otmoor Productions, Oxford, UK, 1998, and Stephen Vittoria, dir., *Long Distance Revolutionary: A Journey with Mumia Abu-Jamal*, documentary film, Street Legal Cinema, Los Angeles, 2013.

11. Brian Conniff, "Mumia Abu-Jamal's *Live from Death Row* as Post-legal Prison Writing," in *Literature and Law*, ed. Michael J. Meyer (New York: Rodopi, 2004), 160, emphasis mine.

12. Abu-Jamal, *Jailhouse Lawyers*, 233, emphasis mine.

13. Ibid.

14. Johnson, *Middle Passage*, 26, emphasis mine.

15. Ibid., 74.

16. Ibid.

17. See Phillis Wheatley's poem "On Being Brought from Africa to America," in *Poems on Various Subjects, Religious and Moral* (London: A. Bell, 1773). In the poem's seventh line, the phrase "Remember, *Christians, Negros*, black as *Cain*," links the dominant white/European (and Christian) culture's preoccupation with enslaved Africans' dark skin color with the immoral or sinful behavior of Cain. According to the Book of Genesis in the Bible, Cain is the first murderer in Christian discourse, so Wheatley shows how the dominant white/European culture's frequent comparisons of Africans to Cain implicitly brands Af-

ricans as "naturally" criminal—and violently criminal at that. Africans are thus seen as descendants of Cain, the first man God cursed for criminal behavior.

18. Abu-Jamal, *Jailhouse Lawyers*, 233.

19. Human Rights Watch, "Prison Conditions in the United States," 1 November 1991, http://www.hrw.org/report/1991/11/01/prison-conditions-united-states, accessed 30 June 2015; Mumia Abu-Jamal, *Live from Death Row* (New York: HarperCollins, 1995), 74, emphasis mine.

20. Lorna A. Rhodes, *Total Confinement: Madness and Reason in the Maximum Security Prison* (Berkeley: University of California Press, 2004), 4–5.

21. Angela Y. Davis, "Race, Gender, and Prison History: From the Convict Lease System to the Supermax Prison," in *Prison Masculinities*, ed. Don Sabo, Terry A. Kupers, and Willie London (Philadelphia: Temple University Press, 2001), 44.

22. Leena Kurki and Norval Morris, "The Purposes, Practices and Problems of Supermax Prisons," *Crime and Justice* 28 (2001): 385.

23. For more, see Laurie Jo Reynolds and Stephen F. Eisenman, "Tamms Is Torture: The Campaign to Shut Down an Illinois Supermax Prison," *Truthout*, 8 May 2013, http://www.truth-out.org/news/item/16241-tamms-is-torture-the-campaign-to-close-an-illinois-supermax-prison, accessed 15 March 2016.

24. George Pawlacyzk and Beth Hundsdorfer, "Trapped in Tamms: Investigation Reveals Truth Behind Mental Health Issues in Supermax Prison," *Southern Illinoisian*, 9 August 2009, http://thesouthern.com/news/trapped-in-tamms-investigation-reveals-truth-behind-mental-health-issues/article_9c217943-9381-5fa9-813e-b5f72c96fd38.html, accessed 20 December 2016.

25. Lance Tapley, "Mass Torture in America: Notes from the Supermax Prisons," in *The United States and Torture: Interrogations, Incarceration, and Abuse*, ed. Marjorie Cohn (New York: New York University Press, 2011), 219, emphasis mine. Relatedly, while I wholeheartedly follow thinking of critical prison studies scholars such as Dylan Rodríguez who argues that "torture . . . should be understood as an essential element of American statecraft, not its corruption or deviation," I do agree with Robert M. Pallitto's nuanced conception of torture as reflecting "in some senses the most egregious [manifestations] of state violence": Dylan Rodríguez, *Forced Passages: Imprisoned Radical Intellectuals and the U.S. Prison Regime* (Minneapolis: University of Minnesota Press, 2006), 47; Robert M. Pallitto, "Introduction," in *Torture and State Violence in the United States: A Short Documentary History*, ed. Robert M. Pallitto (Baltimore: John Hopkins University Press, 2011), 8.

26. Michael James, qtd. in Lance Tapley, "Torture in Maine's Prison," *Portland Phoenix*, 11–17 November 2005, http://www.portlandphoenix.com/features/top/ts_multi/documents/05081722.asp, accessed 12 March 2012; Terry Kupers, "Mental Health in Men's Prisons," in Sabo et al., *Prison Masculinities*, 192–197.

27. Abu-Jamal, *Live from Death Row*, 82–84.

28. Robert Perkinson, "Shackled Justice: Florence Federal Penitentiary and the New Politics of Punishment," *Social Justice* 21.3 (Fall 1994): 121.

29. Johnson, *Middle Passage*, 26.

30. Ibid., 65, 106. According to Daniel Mears, as of 2005 forty-four states had supermax prisons, housing more than twenty-five thousand prisoners. This represents an exponential (and unsettling) expansion: the first U.S. supermax prison opened in Marion, Illinois, in 1983: Daniel P. Mears, *Evaluating the Effectiveness of Supermax Prisons* (Washington, DC: Urban Institute, 2006).

31. Avery F. Gordon, *Ghostly Matters: Haunting and the Sociological Imagination* (Minneapolis: University of Minnesota Press, 1997), xvi.

32. Alan Elsner, *Gates of Injustice: The Crisis in America's Prisons* (Upper Saddle River, NJ: Prentice Hall, 2006), 154.

33. Colin Dayan, *The Law Is a White Dog: How Legal Rituals Make and Unmake Persons* (Princeton, NJ: Princeton University Press, 2011), 64, 65, emphasis mine.

34. Ibid., 72.

35. Johnson, *Middle Passage*, 32.

36. Hortense J. Spillers, "Mama's Baby, Papa's Maybe: An American Grammar Book," *Diacritics* 17.2 (1987): 68.

37. Johnson, *Middle Passage*, 34.

38. 32.

39. Ibid., 32–33. The suspension points in this sentence are reprinted as they appear in the original.

40. Johnson, *Middle Passage*, 33.

41. Vincent Woodard, *The Delectable Negro: Human Consumption and Homoeroticism Within U.S. Slave Culture* (New York: New York University Press, 2014), 41–42.

42. Johnson, *Middle Passage*, 66.

43. Ibid., 120, emphasis mine.

44. Ibid., 23.

45. Ibid., 32, emphasis mine.

46. Ibid., 132.

47. In Agamben's model, concentration camps are confinement spaces that are fundamentally constructed by a governing of human life and death that surpasses juridical notions of crime. These netherworld zones of controlled human debilitation are "born not out of ordinary law . . . but out of a state of exception." Further, actions like those of Falcon and his crew that I have highlighted—their routine rape of enslaved women, beating of enslaved men and women to the point of profuse bleeding, castration of enslaved men—would be possible to comprehend as *legal* crimes following Agamben's logic: Giorgio Agamben, *Homo Sacer: Sovereign Power and Bare Life*, trans. Daniel Heller-Roazen (Stanford, CA: Stanford University Press, 1998), 166–167.

48. Dayan, *The Law Is a White Dog*, 98. Also relevant here is an observation by Tapley, "The suffering that occurs in a supermax prison . . . does not arise from lawful sanctions. It is a consequence of an administrative decision, not a court's and the inmate has little ability to lawfully challenge his or her placement in supermax conditions because of the severe restrictions placed on inmate lawsuits by the 1996 Prisoner Litigation Reform Act": Lance Tapley, "Mass Torture in America: Notes from the Supermax Prisons," in *The United States and Torture: Interrogations, Incarceration, and Abuse*, ed. Marjorie Cohn (New York: New York University Press, 2011): 219.

49. Rodríguez, *Forced Passages*, 223.

50. Marcus Rediker, *The Slave Ship: A Human History* (New York: Penguin, 2007), 45; Rodríguez, *Forced Passages*, 234.

51. Rodríguez, *Forced Passages*, 46, emphasis mine. The distinction that I am making here between the unabashedly repressive genealogy of mass-based detention that Rodríguez outlines and the history of the modern penitentiary has been discussed well by Angela Davis, who writes: "Given the recent emergence of supermaximum-security prisons and the increasingly punitive character of prisons in the United States in general—which are being divested of educational, recreational, and other programs histori-

cally associated with rehabilitation projects—it is important to recall that, ironically, in their early history, prisons were proposed as radical alternatives to horrendous bodily pain that then constituted the dominant mode of punishment. The penitentiary . . . was conceived architecturally and theoretically as a form for the moral reformation of the individual": Davis, "Race, Gender, and Prison History," 37.

52. Rodríguez, *Forced Passages*, 239, 223.

53. Ibid., 224, 231, 239.

54. Lisa Guenther, *Solitary Confinement: Social Death and Its Afterlives* (Minneapolis: University of Minnesota Press, 2013), 162.

55. Ibid., 162–163.

56. Rodríguez, *Forced Passages*, 233.

57. Ibid., 239.

58. Ibid., 227.

59. Vincent O'Keefe, "Reading Rigor Mortis: Offstage Violence and Excluded Middles 'in' Johnson's *Middle Passage* and Morrison's *Beloved*," *African American Review* 30.4 (1996): 640; Elizabeth Muther, "Isadora at Sea: Misogyny as Comic Capital in Charles Johnson's *Middle Passage*," *African American Review* 30.4 (1996): 654.

60. Johnson, *Middle Passage*, 172, 208.

61. Ibid., 124–125.

62. Ibid., 32.

63. Ibid., 105–106, emphasis mine.

64. Ibid., 120, emphasis mine.

65. Ibid., 124–125, emphasis mine.

66. Ibid., 125.

67. Ibid., 74.

68. For more, please see http://www.whatthefolly.com/2011/08/30/transcript-rev-william-mcgarveys-testimony-on-the-harmful-impacts-of-solitary-confinement-practices-at-california%E2%80%99s-secure-housing-units-shu-prison-facilities.

69. Johnson, *Middle Passage*, 133–134, emphasis mine.

70. Ibid., 134.

71. Ibid., 155, emphasis mine.

72. Etheridge Knight, "Preface," in *Black Voices from Prison*, ed. Etheridge Knight (New York: Pathfinder, 1970), 5, emphasis mine.

73. For more on Rodríguez's conceptions of "the contemporary U.S. prison regime" and "domestic war zones," see Rodríguez, *Forced Passages*, 1–74.

74. Knight, "Preface," 9.

75. Ibid.

76. Etheridge Knight, qtd. in Michael S. Collins, *Understanding Etheridge Knight* (Columbia: University of South Carolina Press, 2012), 63.

77. James Weaver, "Rehabilitative Storytelling: The Narrator-Narratee Relationship in J. California Cooper's *Family*," *MELUS* 30.1 (2005): 109.

78. Ibid., 112, 129.

79. Melvin Farmer, *The New Slave Ship: A Ship That Does Not Sail* (Los Angeles: Milligan, 1998), 5, 16.

80. Rashi'd Qawi' Al-Ami'n, "I Say Today I Recognized a Slave Ship," *Cell Door Magazine* 5.1 (March 2003), http://www.lairdcarlson.com/celldoor/00501/Al-Ami'n00501SlaveShip.htm, accessed 12 March 2012.

81. Knight, "Preface," 9.

82. Ibid., 6.

83. Ibid., 9–10, emphasis mine.

84. Ibid., 10, emphasis mine. The suspension points in this sentence are reprinted as they appear in the original.

85. Ibid., 10.

86. George Jackson, *Soledad Brother: The Prison Letters of George Jackson*, repr. ed. (Chicago: Lawrence Hill, 1994 [1970]), 154.

87. Ibid., 233–234.

88. Ibid., 213.

89. Johnson, *Middle Passage*, 60.

90. Ibid., 24.

91. Ibid., 82, 87, 91.

92. Ibid., 91, emphasis mine.

93. Ibid., 30.

94. Ibid., 146, emphasis mine.

95. Ibid.

96. Ibid., 51, emphasis mine.

97. Ibid., 200–201, emphasis mine.

CHAPTER 4

1. Ernest Gaines, "Writing *A Lesson Before Dying*," in *Mozart and Leadbelly: Stories and Essays*, ed. Marcia Gaudet and Reggie Young (New York: Knopf, 2005), 52.

2. Herman Beavers, "Prodigal Agency: Allegory and Voice in Ernest J. Gaines's *A Lesson before Dying*," in *Contemporary Black Men's Fiction and Drama*, ed. Keith Clark (Urbana: University of Illinois Press, 2001), 149; Gaines, "Writing *A Lesson Before Dying*," 52–53. Also relevant here is Michael DeRell Hill's recent assertion that Gaines's *Lesson* is typified by a "preoccupation with marquee themes of the African American protest literature" which, following Claudia Tate and others, he defines as literature that "centrally engages Anglo-America's inhumanity to its domestic black population": Michael DeRell Hill, *The Ethics of Swagger: Prizewinning African American Novels, 1977–1993* (Columbus: Ohio State University Press, 2013), 71.

3. Maya Schenwar, "America's Plantation Prisons," *Truthout*, 28 August 2008, http://www.globalresearch.ca/america-s-plantation-prisons/10008, accessed 12 February 2015.

4. Dennis Childs, *Slaves of the State: Black Incarceration from the Chain Gang to the Penitentiary* (Minneapolis: University of Minnesota Press, 2015), 94.

5. For more, see Dennis Childs, "Angola, Convict Leasing, and the Annulment of Freedom: The Vectors of Architectural and Discursive Violence in the U.S. Slavery of Prison," in *Violence and the Body: Race, Gender, and the State*, ed. Arturo J. Aldama (Bloomington: Indiana University Press, 2003), 189–208; Robert Hillary King, *From the Bottom of the Heap: The Autobiography of Black Panther Robert Hillary King* (Oakland, CA: PM Press, 2008); Wilbert Rideau, *In the Place of Justice: A Story of Punishment and Redemption* (New York: Vintage, 2011).

6. Beavers, "Prodigal Agency," 149, 151, emphasis mine.

7. Marcia Gaudet, "Storytelling and the Law: Variants of Justice in Ernest J. Gaines's *A Lesson Before Dying*," *Interdisciplinary Humanities* 17.2 (2000): 125. Gaudet adds, "Gaines says he did not set out to write a 'legal' novel nor to write an indictment of the death penalty. He did, however, meet with a former District Attorney in Lafayette about a death penalty case in Louisiana and about his experiences when executions still took place in the individual parishes": ibid., 133.

8. Darrell Bourque, "*Poesis*, the Law, and the Notebook," *Interdisciplinary Humanities* 17.2 (2000): 145.

9. John Lowe, "Transcendence in the House of the Dead: The Subversive Gaze of *A Lesson Before Dying*," in *The World Is Our Home: Society and Culture in Contemporary Southern Writing*, ed. Jeffrey J. Folks and Nancy Summers Folks (Lexington: University Press of Kentucky, 2000), 147–148, emphasis mine.

10. Ernest Gaines, qtd. in John Lowe, ed., *Conversations with Ernest Gaines* (Jackson: University Press of Mississippi, 1995), 310. In interviews, Gaines candidly makes the same connections between slavery's past and the post-slavery present that he depicts in his fiction. In an interview with Gregory Fitzgerald in 1969, he discusses how racism undergirded the planters' exploitation of Black prisoners' labor in mid-twentieth-century Louisiana:

> I went in the fields when I was about the age of eight. . . . I . . . stayed there until I was about fifteen. So . . . I knew a lot about the work and life on a plantation. For instance, in [my] novel [*Of Love and Dust*] . . . the plantation owner bond[s] my young killer out of jail and put[s] him to work in his field. This was a normal thing in the forties. Some of our best southern gentlemen did it; this was still going on in the fifties. And as late as 1963, when I was [back] in Louisiana, a friend of mine pointed out a black youth who had killed another black youth and had been bonded out and put to work only a few days later. The . . . prisoner . . . usually spent twice as much time on the plantation than he would have spent in the penitentiary. Many times he found himself working just as hard, and maybe even harder, and there was nothing he could do about it, because the day he decided to run, the white man was going to put the sheriff on his trail again. (Ibid., 7)

11. Gaines's representation of the racialization of such social control practices in the post-slavery U.S. South in his fictional works reflects his engagement with a condition that scholars have called "worse than slavery," "the slavery of prison," or "slavery by another name." For more, see David Oshinsky, *Worse than Slavery: Parchman Farm and the Ordeal of Jim Crow Justice* (New York: Free Press, 1996); Angela Y. Davis, "From the Prison of Slavery to the Slavery of Prison," in *The Angela Y. Davis Reader*, ed. Joy James (Malden, MA: Blackwell, 1998), 74–95; Douglas A. Blackmon, *Slavery by Another Name: The Re-enslavement of Black Americans from the Civil War to World War II* (New York: Anchor, 2008).

12. Ernest Gaines, *Bloodline* (New York: Dial, 1968), 147, emphasis mine.

13. Ibid., 150.

14. Ibid., emphasis mine.

15. Ibid., 151–152.

16. Gaines, qtd. in Lowe, *Conversations with Ernest Gaines*, xv. Katherine Daley and Carolyn M. Jones offer a helpful gloss of Gaines's discourse of standing, writing, "Standing, for Gaines, means responsibility, striving, and exhibiting grace under pressure. From his aunt and from Hemingway, Gaines comes to understand what 'dignity under pressure' and 'survival with dignity' mean. Standing—and in *Lesson*, the additional act of kneeling—is done in a situation of oppression, of confinement. These acts call for integrity, reliability, strength, and determination—all of which make one good and contribute to community": Katherine Daley and Carolyn M. Jones, "Ernest J. Gaines's *A Lesson Before Dying*: Freedom in Confined Spaces," in *From the Plantation*

to the Prison: African-American Confinement Literature, ed. Tara T. Green (Macon, GA: Mercer University Press, 2008), 84–85.

17. Ernest Gaines, *Of Love and Dust* (New York: W. W. Norton, 1967), 31.

18. Ibid.

19. Ibid., 225, emphasis mine.

20. Ibid., 25.

21. Ernest Gaines, *A Lesson Before Dying* (New York: Vintage, 1993), 7–8, emphasis mine.

22. Ibid., 191.

23. Ibid., 4.

24. Ernest Gaines, "A Literary Salon: Oyster/Shrimp Po'Boys, Chardonnay, and Conversation with Ernest J. Gaines" (interview by Marcia Gaudet and Darrel Bourque), in *Mozart and Leadbelly: Stories and Essays*, ed. Marcia Gaudet and Reggie Young (New York: Knopf, 2005), 152.

25. Gaines, qtd. in Lowe, *Conversations with Ernest Gaines*, 239–240.

26. Gaines, *A Lesson Before Dying*, 234.

27. In my reading of Gaines's *Lesson*, I wish to acknowledge the important scholarship that has emerged that takes up the "Jefferson's Diary" chapter of the novel and push critical thought on that chapter in new directions.

On the one hand, some scholars have been interested mostly in how Jefferson's diary production is a personally redemptive act—an act that Jefferson undertakes to accept or overcome the reality of premature death, engage in self-actualization, or reject the many racially stigmatizing and psychically injurious conceptions of his identity that state lawyers have entered into the public record: see, e.g., Valerie Babb, "Old-Fashioned Modernism: 'The Changing Same' in *A Lesson Before Dying*," in *Critical Reflections on the Fiction of Ernest J. Gaines*, ed. David C. Estes (Athens: University of Georgia Press, 1994), 250–264; Philip Auger, "A Lesson about Manhood: Appropriating 'The Word' in Ernest Gaines's *A Lesson Before Dying*," *Southern Literary Journal* 27.2 (1995): 74–85; Karen Carmean, *Ernest J. Gaines: A Critical Companion* (Westport, CT: Greenwood, 1998), 118–121; Bourque, "Poesis, the Law, and the Notebook," 137–145; Mary Ellen Doyle, *Voices from the Quarters: The Fiction of Ernest J. Gaines* (Baton Rouge: Louisiana State University Press, 2002), 223–225; Daley and Jones, "Ernest J. Gaines's *A Lesson Before Dying*," 92–103.

On the other hand, another field of *Lesson* scholarship is interested mostly in how outside community expectations, community responsibility, and an overarching narrative of community-inspired racial uplift surround the production of Jefferson's diary: see, e.g., Jeffrey J. Folks, "Communal Responsibility in Ernest J. Gaines's *A Lesson Before Dying*," *Mississippi Quarterly* 52.2 (1999): 259–271; Gaudet, "Storytelling and the Law," 125–135; Beavers, "Prodigal Agency," 135–154; Carlyle Van Thompson, *Black Outlaws: Race, Law, and Male Subjectivity in African American Literature and Culture* (New York: Peter Lang, 2010), 135–178; Jason Stupp, "Living Death: Ernest Gaines's *A Lesson before Dying* and the Execution of Willie Francis," in *Demands of the Dead: Executions, Storytelling, and Activism in the United States*, ed. Katy Ryan (Iowa City: University of Iowa Press, 2012), 45–58.

A notable exception to these trends in criticism on the "Jefferson's Diary" chapter is an essay by Anne Gray Brown in which she argues that the fact and content of Jefferson's diary writing undermine the ordinary operation of racialized social control on both sides of the chain-link fence. She writes, "Writing gives Jefferson a temporary measure of superiority over an oppressive system which deems him incapable of rational thought and behavior. As he writes in the journal, he subtly observes his surroundings, and quietly studies the character of the men [in power] in his [prison] environment. . . . He remains the prisoner in the cell, but he also becomes the gatekeeper of his space. . . . As he continues writing, the racial dynamics at the jail slowly begin to change . . . the intensity with which Jefferson writes alters the social terrain and, to a small degree, transforms the people upon whom he is dependent. The physical presence of notebook places him in a position of command over his oppressors": Anne Gray Brown, "Writing for Life: 'Jefferson's Diary' as Transformative Text in Ernest J. Gaines's *A Lesson Before Dying*," *Southern Quarterly* 47.1 (2009): 33.

On the whole, little critical attention has been paid to the penal-historical and political-intellectual significance of Jefferson's acts of writing and clandestinely distributing a death row diary to free society. Gaines scholarship has yet to assess deeply the socially transformative significance of Jefferson's calling into question the organizing logic of the penal institution and Jim Crow by writing against white supremacy *from a site of incarceration*. It is this lacuna in the criticism on the "Jefferson's Diary" chapter that I address here.

28. Gaines, "Writing *A Lesson Before Dying*," 61.

29. Gaines, *A Lesson Before Dying*, 227.

30. Ibid., 234.

31. For more, see Willie Francis (as told to Sam Montgomery), *My Trip to the Chair* (Lafayette, LA: Self-published, 1947), Afro-American Pamphlets, Part 3 (1827–1948), Rare Books and Special Collections Reading Room, U.S. Library of Congress, Washington, DC, repr. in *Demands of the Dead: Executions, Storytelling, and Activism in the United States*, ed. Katy Ryan (Iowa City: University of Iowa Press, 2012): 33–44; George Jackson, *Soledad Brother: The Prison Letters of George Jackson* (1970), repr. ed. (Chicago: Lawrence Hill, 1994); Rubin "Hurricane" Carter, *The Sixteenth Round: From Number 1 Contender to Number 45472* (1974), repr. ed. (Chicago: Chicago Review Press, 2011).

32. Critical prison studies is an emerging interdisciplinary field that perhaps has been made most visible terminologically by the American Studies Association's Critical Prison Studies caucus: http://www.theasa.net/caucus_prison_studies. In broad terms, critical prison studies encompasses humanistic studies (including literary, legal, and ethnic studies, history, sociology, and geography) that draw on cross-disciplinary analyses of race, class, gender, and sexuality to critically examine domestic and international regimes of criminalization, captivity, and punishment. Particular emphasis is placed on investigating the centrality of global capitalism, racism, and gender discrimination in the mass-production of crime and criminals (i.e., the emergence of the prison-industrial complex) and the sanctioning and normalization of state violence and state terror. Scholarship in this field also emphasizes the importance of conceptualizing coalitional strategies for prison abolition. Representative texts include Christian Parenti, *Lockdown America: Police and Prisons in the Age of Crisis* (New York: Verso, 1999); Angela Y. Davis, *Are Prisons Obsolete?* (New York: Seven Stories, 2003); Tara Herivel and Paul Wright, eds., *Prison Nation: The Warehousing of America's Poor* (New York: Routledge, 2003); Dylan Rodríguez, *Forced Passages: Imprisoned Radical Intellectuals and the U.S. Prison Regime* (Minneapolis: University of Minnesota Press, 2006); Victoria Law, *Resistance Behind Bars: The Struggles of Incarcerated Women* (Oakland, CA: PM Press, 2009); Jodie Michelle Lawston and Ashley E. Lucas, eds., *Razor Wire Women: Prisoners, Activists, Scholars, and Artists* (Albany: State University of New York Press, 2011).

33. Rodríguez, *Forced Passages*, 2, 7. Also relevant here is critical prison studies scholar Joy James's discussion of "imprisoned intellectuals" in an introductory essay to her edited volume on the writings of imprisoned intellectuals: Joy James, "Introduction,"

in Joy James, *Imprisoned Intellectuals: America's Political Prisoners Write on Life, Libera-tion, and Rebellion* (Lanham, MD: Rowman and Littlefield, 2003), 3–27.

34. Gaines, qtd. in Lowe, *Conversations with Ernest Gaines*, 307; Ernest Gaines, "Er-nest J. Gaines: *A Lesson Before Dying*," interview by Dan Stone for the NEA Big Read, 16 August 2007, http://www.neabigread.org/books/lessonbeforedying/readers-guide, ac-cessed 16 February 2012.

35. The distinction that I am drawing here between Gaines's *Lesson* and Wright's most famous novel, *Native Son*, can be understood in relation to an important point raised by Marcia Gaudet, who has interviewed Gaines and written on his oeuvre ex-tensively. She writes, "Gaines's fiction, particularly *A Lesson Before Dying*, may be foregrounded in the consequences of the law, but the most important theme is not the debilitating effects of the law. It is the potential capacity of African Americans . . . to transcend the humiliation of the law and maintain their dignity—in spite of a legal system designed to deny them not only their dignity, but their very humanity—their personhood": Gaudet, "Storytelling and the Law," 132.

Also relevant here are observations made by Jeffrey Folks and Reggie Scott Young. From Folks's perspective, "Gaines has never been content to replay the naturalistic mode of representation of other late capitalist texts, for beneath the sensuous detail of his novels rests the author's vision of social change . . . Gaines has frequently stressed that he is writ-ing with the self-conscious intention of examining the course of American social history, not merely to represent this history in naturalistic terms but to change it": Folks, "Com-munal Responsibility in Ernest J. Gaines's *A Lesson Before Dying*," 260. Young importantly adds that Gaines has been explicit in not naming Wright as an ancestor or influence for his literary production, including *Lesson*, writing, "Based on Gaines's discussion of the research he did before writing [*Lesson*] . . . none of it involved reading Wright's *Native Son*. However . . . Madelyn Jablon declares that [*Lesson*] was set in an earlier decade (the 1940s) because of the influence of Wright's novel. . . . Her attempt to create an influential link between *A Lesson Before Dying* and *Native Son* ignores prior statements by Gaines concerning the actual influences of the work": Reggie Scott Young, "Theoretical Influ-ences and Experimental Resemblances: Ernest J. Gaines and Recent Critical Approaches to the Study of African American Fiction," in *Contemporary African American Fiction: New Critical Essays*, ed. Dana A. Williams (Columbus: Ohio State University Press, 2009), 24.

36. Gaines, *A Lesson Before Dying*, 69, 76, 81.

37. Stupp, "Living Death," 45, 51, emphasis mine.

38. Gaines, *A Lesson Before Dying*, 5–6.

39. Carmean, *Ernest J. Gaines*, 118.

40. Gaines, *A Lesson Before Dying*, 9, 22.

41. Thompson, *Black Outlaws*, 135–178.

42. Gaines, *A Lesson Before Dying*, 7–8, emphasis mine.

43. Ibid., 242.

44. Ibid., 157–158.

45. Ibid., 83.

46. Ibid., 71.

47. Ibid., 134.

48. Daley and Jones, "Ernest J. Gaines's *A Lesson Before Dying*," 89, emphasis mine.

49. Gaines, *A Lesson Before Dying*, 31.

50. Rodríguez, *Forced Passages*, 105, 110.

51. Gaines, "Ernest Gaines, *A Lesson Before Dying*," interview by the Academy of Achievement, 4 May 2001, http://www.achievement.org/autodoc/printmember/

gai0int-1, accessed 16 February 2012. It is also worth stating here that Gaines's fiction reflects his attentiveness to the voices and life experiences of not only death row prisoners but also a whole range of people who have spent time behind bars. In interviews, Gaines speaks of well-known and less well-known imprisoned men as inspiring the characters that he creates in his work. For instance, in the interview with Gaudet and Bourque, Gaines remarks that listening to Huddie "Leadbelly" Ledbetter and witnessing an imprisoned man endure hard labor provided him with rich context for character and plot development in some of his novels, saying, "[From] Leadbelly singing about the prisons—at Angola or the prisons in Texas. I get a good feeling of what prison life was like. . . . When I wrote *Of Love and Dust*, a man was put on the farm to work his time out. That had an influence on me": Gaines, "A Literary Salon," 132–133.

52. Gaines, transcript of "A Conversation with Lawrence Bridges," interview by Lawrence Bridges for the NEA Big Read, 16 August 2007.

53. Gaines, "Ernest J. Gaines" (Stone interview).

54. "Ernest Gaines, *A Lesson Before Dying*" (Academy of Achievement interview).

55. Stupp, "Living Death," 45–58; Gilbert King, *The Execution of Willie Francis* (New York: Basic Civitas, 2008), xi, 18, 89–90.

56. King, *The Execution of Willie Francis*, 70, 86–88; Deborah W. Denno, "When Willie Francis Died: The 'Disturbing' Story Behind One of the Eighth Amendment's Most Enduring Standards of Risk," in *Death Penalty Stories*, ed. John H. Blume and Jordan M. Steiker (New York: Foundation Press, 2009), 32–34.

57. Gaines, "Writing *A Lesson Before Dying*," 53–54, emphasis mine.

58. Ibid., 53.

59. Ibid., 52.

60. Gaines, qtd. in Lowe, *Conversations with Ernest Gaines*, 199.

61. Rodríguez, *Forced Passages*, 3.

62. Gaines, *A Lesson Before Dying*, 14.

63. Sharon Patricia Holland, *Raising the Dead: Readings of Death and (Black) Subjectivity* (Durham, NC: Duke University Press, 2000), 3–4.

64. What I here outline as a revivifying narrative can be imagined, as I discuss in the Introduction, to be related to what Joy James defines as a "contemporary insurrectionist penal-slave narrative." James coins the term *contemporary insurrectionist penal-slave narrative* to identify how hyper-punitively imprisoned Black autobiographers such as Assata Shakur and Mumia Abu-Jamal literarily situate their experiences with racial bias, indefinite solitary confinement, and racialized prisoner abuse in the larger historical experience of slavery in the Americas and, through their writings that are critical of the criminal justice system, undermine the politically repressive agenda of premature death devised for them by the penal institution and the state. For more, see Joy James, "Introduction: Democracy and Captivity," in *The New Abolitionists: (Neo)Slave Narratives and Contemporary Prison Writings*, ed. Joy James (Albany: State University of New York Press, 2005), xxi–xlii.

65. Gaines, *A Lesson Before Dying*, 192–193.

66. Ibid., 20–21.

67. Gaines, "Writing *A Lesson Before Dying*," 57.

68. Gaines, *A Lesson Before Dying*, 13.

69. Ibid., 193. See also page 94, where Grant makes a similar confession to his girlfriend Vivian: "I wish I could just run away from this place."

70. Ibid., 193, emphasis mine.

71. Gaines, *A Lesson Before Dying*, 191.

72. Ibid.

73. Ibid., 193.

74. Gates writes, "The production of literature was taken to be the central arena in which persons of African descent could, or could not, establish and redefine their status within the human community. Black people . . . had to represent themselves as 'speaking subjects' before they could even begin to destroy their status as objects, as commodities, within Western culture. In addition to all of the myriad reasons for which human beings write books, this particular reason seems to have been paramount to the black slave. At least since 1600, Europeans had wondered aloud whether or not the African 'species of men' as they most commonly put it, could ever create formal literature, could ever master the arts and sciences. If they could, then, the argument ran, the African variety of humanity and the European variety were fundamentally related. If not, then it seemed clear that the African was destined by nature to be a slave": Henry Louis Gates Jr., *The Signifying Monkey: A Theory of African American Literary Criticism* (New York: Oxford University Press, 1988), 129.

It is also worth stating who Gates brings up in this discussion as an educated white American writer who rejected the thought of Black rationality: Thomas Jefferson, whose last name, in a verbally ironic twist, is the first name of Gaines's death-sentenced Black protagonist (Jefferson). Several scholars have offered provocative insights on the significance of Jefferson's name: see, e.g., Michael DeRell Hill, "*A Lesson Before Dying* as Style Guide," in Hill, *The Ethics of Swagger*, 70–89; Thompson, *Black Outlaws*, 135–178; Beavers, "Prodigal Agency," 135–154.

75. Gaines, *A Lesson Before Dying*, 194.

76. Ibid., 222–225, emphasis mine.

77. Ibid., 225.

78. Ibid. Mary Ellen Doyle eloquently articulates this role reversal as Grant "slowly yet at last willingly becoming his student's student." For Doyle, this moment is one in which Grant recognizes that "Jefferson, the semiliterate condemned man . . . will teach and liberate all the . . . people [and] . . . direct the whole community toward life": Doyle, *Voices from the Quarters*, 205, 213.

79. Gaines, *A Lesson Before Dying*, 220.

80. Frederick Douglass, *Narrative of the Life of Frederick Douglass, an American Slave, Written by Himself*, ed. Angela Y. Davis (San Francisco: City Lights, 2010), 136, emphasis mine.

81. Craig W. Snyde, "An Old Fashioned Hog Slaughter," *Mother Earth News*, 1 September 1982, http://www.motherearthnews.com/Sustainable-Farming/1982-09-01/An-Old-Fashioned-Hog-Slaughter.aspx, accessed 16 February 2012.

82. Gaines, *A Lesson Before Dying*, 7–8, emphasis mine.

83. Ibid., 7–8.

84. Beyond the article by Thompson mentioned earlier in this chapter, my conception of Jefferson as a lynched subject in this scene is indebted to the work of Robyn Wiegman and L. V. Gaither. Wiegman argues that "in severing the black male's penis from his body, either as a narrative account or a material act, the mob aggressively denies the particular sign and symbol of the masculine, interrupting the privilege of the phallus and thereby reclaiming, through the perversity of dismemberment, the black male's (masculine) potentiality of citizenship": Robyn Wiegman, *American Anatomies: Theorizing Race and Gender* (Durham, NC: Duke University Press, 1995), 83. Gaither writes

that "the lynching of blacks was a means of terrorizing an oppressed group, suppressing their political and economic aspirations, reaffirming and reinforcing their group marginalization from the mainstream of 'society,' and it was carried out in pogrom fashion. . . . Eventually the lynching of African Americans became institutionalized within the criminal justice system as a form of ultimate punishment": L. V. Gaither, *Loss of Empire: Legal Lynching, Vigilantism, and African American Intellectualism in the 21st Century* (Trenton, NJ: Africa World Press, 2006), 6.

85. Gaines, *A Lesson Before Dying*, 83, 231–234.

86. Ibid., 230–231, emphasis mine.

87. Jeffrey B. Leak, *Racial Myths and Masculinity in African American Literature* (Knoxville: University of Tennessee Press, 2005), 85.

88. Gaines, *A Lesson Before Dying*, 232–234, emphasis mine.

89. Ibid., 191, emphasis mine.

90. Babb, "Old Fashioned Modernism," 262. Also relevant here is a similar observation that Brown makes in her reading of Jefferson's death row diary. She writes, "[Jefferson's] use of the pronoun 'them' not only references the people in his emotional circle—his godmother and Tante Lou, specifically—but also those persons who are responsible for proclaiming him guilty and declaring his fate: the all-white jury, and, by extensions, the entire racist system of injustice": Brown, "Writing for Life," 39.

91. Gaines, *A Lesson Before Dying*, 83–84, emphasis mine.

92. Ibid., 84–85.

93. Ibid., 226, 228–229, emphasis mine.

94. Ibid., 234.

95. Ibid., 230.

96. My (anti)panoptic reading of this particular entry from Gaines's "Jefferson's Diary" chapter is informed by my critical reframing of Foucault's discussion of Panopticism that I outlined in the Introduction. For more, see Michel Foucault, *Discipline and Punish: The Birth of the Prison* (New York: Vintage, 1976), 195–228.

97. Gaines, *A Lesson Before Dying*, 233, emphasis mine.

98. King, *The Execution of Willie Francis*, 100, 142.

99. Denno, "When Willie Francis Died," 22.

100. Ibid., 38. In the months following his initial sentencing to death, Francis revealed the extent of his apathy and apoliticality by scrawling the following letter to the white sheriff who had coerced him to write the murder confession that would convict him: "*I'm a negro, I killed a white man. I know that you are trying to give me a death penalty. I don't mind at all*": ibid., 40.

101. I am indebted to Eric Frazier of the Rare Books and Special Collections Division of the U.S. Library of Congress, Washington, DC, for providing me access to Francis's *My Trip to the Chair* in the earliest stage of this chapter's development in 2011. Gilbert King, a historian who published a study of Francis's execution in 2008, emphasizes just how hard it has been, until very recently, to access *My Trip to the Chair*. Before a representative from the Library of Congress followed up with King, King writes, the "only known copy [of the pamphlet] had been catalogued in a file of rare African American pamphlets at the Library of Congress in Washington, but it had been missing for almost two decades": King, *The Execution of Willie Francis*, xi.

102. Denno, "When Willie Francis Died," 45.

103. Francis, *My Trip to the Chair*, 33, emphasis mine.

104. King, *The Execution of Willie Francis*, 20.

105. Denno, "When Willie Francis Died," 44; King, *The Execution of Willie Francis*, 32.

106. Denno, "When Willie Francis Died," 46–47.

107. Francis, *My Trip to the Chair*, 33–34, emphasis mine.

108. Ibid., 35–36, emphasis mine.

109. Ibid., 36, 41, emphasis mine.

110. Denno, "When Willie Francis Died," 27; King, *The Execution of Willie Francis*, 17, 29.

111. King, *The Execution of Willie Francis*, 30.

112. Ibid., 162.

113. Ibid., 120.

114. Francis, *My Trip to the Chair*, 33, emphasis mine.

115. King, *The Execution of Willie Francis*, 150. King notes that scholars continue to struggle with the full meaning of this phrase in connection with others on Francis's wall that would seem to point to his involvement in some kind of encounter—but not necessarily a murder—with Andrew Thomas.

116. Gaines, *A Lesson Before Dying*, 223.

117. Francis, *My Trip to the Chair*, 40–41, emphasis mine.

118. My reference here is to the King James Version of the Bible. In addition to telling his *My Trip to the Chair* readers outright that he would read his Bible for hours on end—"I read in my Bible until the sun went down"—Francis also informs his audience that he asked to be pictured reading his Bible and offers them an image of its frequent use, writing, "One day [my father] brought me a Bible my mother gave him for me. It's pretty well worn out now": Francis, *My Trip to the Chair*, 35–36.

119. Francis, *My Trip to the Chair*, 42.

120. For more, see the Innocence Project's website at http://www.innocenceproject.org/know.

121. A notable exception to this trend in human rights reporting is the national organization Witness to Innocence, based in Philadelphia, which has foregrounded the voices of wrongfully convicted people. In videos posted online, people who have endured wrongful convictions provide brief first-person narratives in which they show themselves to be not only victims but also survivors of systemic racial injustice in the justice system. See http://www.witnesstoinnocence.org/index.html

122. I like to think of *Lesson*, with its emphasis on the voice and critical thinking of a wrongfully convicted Black man on death row, as a fictional narrative that has served as an important precursor to the important work of playwrights and documentarians who have recently helped to amplify the voices and critical thinking of wrongfully convicted men and women who are currently on death row or have been previously confined to death row. That is to say, I imagine Gaines's "Jefferson's Diary" chapter as African American fiction's forerunner to Jessica Blank and Erik Jensen's award-winning play *The Exonerated* (2002); Jessica Sanders's award-wining documentary *After Innocence* (2005); and Rickie Stern and Anne Sunberg's acclaimed HBO documentary, *The Trials of Daryl Hunt* (2006).

123. Gaines, *A Lesson Before Dying*, 234.

124. Folks, "Communal Responsibility in Ernest J. Gaines's *A Lesson Before Dying*," 261–262.

125. Richard C. Dieter, *Innocence and the Crisis in the American Death Penalty*, September 2004, http://www.deathpenaltyinfo.org/innocence-and-crisis-american-death-penalty, accessed 16 February 2012, emphasis mine.

126. Kay Schaffer and Sidonie Smith, *Human Rights and Narrated Lives: The Ethics of Recognition* (New York: Palgrave, 2004), 44.

127. Gaines, *A Lesson Before Dying*, 232, 234.

128. Ibid., 224, emphasis mine.

129. I concur with much of the criticism on *Lesson* that Jefferson's rendering of the word *youman* in his death row diary is a pedagogical gesture. See, e.g., Carmean's reading, "Jefferson's spelling of 'human' as 'youman' emphasizes his kinship to all members of the community, including his jailers": Carmean, *Ernest J. Gaines*, 121.

EPILOGUE

1. Angela Y. Davis, "Race, Gender, and Prison History: From the Convict Lease System to the Supermax Prison," in *Prison Masculinities*, ed. Don Sabo, Terry A. Kupers, and Willie London (Philadelphia: Temple University Press, 2001), 43.

2. For more, see Martha Teichner, "The Cost of a Nation of Incarceration," CBS News, 22 April 2012, http://www.cbsnews.com/8301-3445_162-57418495/the-cost-of-a-nation-of-incarceration, accessed 10 July 2015.

3. Davis, "Race, Gender, and Prison History," 43.

4. Angela Y. Davis, *Are Prisons Obsolete?* (New York: Seven Stories, 2003), 96, emphasis mine.

5. Ibid.

6. For more, see American Civil Liberties Union: "Facts about the Over-incarceration of Women in the United States," https://www.aclu.org/facts-about-over-incarceration-women-united-states.

7. Davis, *Are Prisons Obsolete?* 77–78; Angela Y. Davis, *Abolition Democracy: Beyond Empire, Prisons, and Torture* (New York: Seven Stories, 2005), 115.

8. Justin Wolfers, David Leonhardt, and Kevin Quealy, "1.5 Million Missing Black Men," NYTimes.com, 10 April 2015, http://www.nytimes.com/interactive/2015/04/20/upshot/missing-black-men.html?_r=0, accessed 31 May 2016.

9. Joan Petersilia, *When Prisoners Come Home: Parole and Prisoner Reentry* (New York: Oxford University Press, 2003), 3. For more, see https://www.justice.gov/archive/fbci/progmenu_reentry.html.

10. For more, see Michelle Alexander, *The New Jim Crow: Mass Incarceration in the Age of Colorblindness* (New York: New Press, 2010).

11. Petersilia, *When Prisoners Come Home*, 34, emphasis mine. See also Zaid Jilani, "How Congress Killed One of the Few Lifelines for Former Prisoners—and Why It's Time to Bring It Back," *AlterNet* 3 June 2015, https://www.prisonactivist.org/alerts/how-congress-killed-one-few-lifelines-former-prisoners-and-why-its-time-bring-it-back, accessed 10 July 2015.

12. H. Bruce Franklin notes, "By 1994, the incarceration rate for African-American males had soared to seven times that for white males, and for the first time the number of African-American prisoners exceeded the number of white prisoners": H. Bruce Franklin, "Introduction," in *Prison Writing in 20th Century America*, ed. H. Bruce Franklin (New York: Penguin, 1998), 15.

13. United Nations, *Basic Principles for the Treatment of Prisoners*, 14 December 1990, http://www.ohchr.org/EN/ProfessionalInterest/Pages/BasicPrinciplesTreatment OfPrisoners.aspx, accessed 10 July 2015, emphasis mine.

14. Ernest Gaines, *A Lesson Before Dying* (New York: Vintage, 1993), 45.

15. Ibid., 49–50.

16. Ibid., 224, 234, emphasis mine.

17. LeJhoyn Holland, quoted in James Todd, "Student's Prison Course Yields Liter-

ary Insights," *Duke Today*, 24 September 2010, https://today.duke.edu/2007/10/patrick
.html, accessed 10 July 2015.

18. Gaines, *A Lesson Before Dying*, 233.

19. Megan Sweeney, "Legal Brutality: Prisons and Punishment, the American Way,"
American Literary History 22.3 (2010): 702.

20. Caryl Phillips, "The Cargo Rap" in Caryl Phillips, *Higher Ground: A Novel in
Three Parts* (New York: Vintage, 1989): 61–172; John A. Williams, *Clifford's Blues* (Minneapolis, MN: Coffee House, 1999).

Bibliography

Abu-Jamal, Mumia. *Death Blossoms: Reflections from a Prisoner of Conscience.* Cambridge, MA: South End, 1996.
———. *Jailhouse Lawyers: Prisoners Defending Prisoners v. the U.S.A.* San Francisco: City Lights, 2009.
———. *Live from Death Row.* New York: HarperCollins, 1995.
Agamben, Giorgio. *Homo Sacer: Sovereign Power and Bare Life,* trans. Daniel Heller-Roazen. Stanford, CA: Stanford University Press, 1998.
Al-Ami'n, Rashi'd Qawi'. "I Say Today I Recognized a Slave Ship." *Cell Door Magazine* 5.1 (March 2003). Web. http://www.lairdcarlson.com/celldoor/00501/Al-Ami'n00501Slave Ship.htm. Accessed 12 March 2012.
Alexander, Michelle. "Foreword." In *Inside This Place, Not of It: Narratives from Women's Prisons,* ed. Robin Levi and Ayelet Waldman. San Francisco: McSweeney's and Voice of Witness, 2011, 11–14.
———. *The New Jim Crow: Mass Incarceration in the Age of Colorblindness.* New York: New Press, 2010.
Alexander, Patrick Elliot. "'To live and remain outside of the barb[ed] wire and fence': A Prison Classroom, African American Literature, and the Pedagogy of Freedom." *Reflections* 11.1 (2011): 88–108.
Amnesty International. *Broken Bodies, Shattered Minds: Torture and Ill-Treatment of Women.* London: Amnesty International, 2001.
———. *United States of America: Police Brutality and Excessive Force in the New York City Police Department.* London: Amnesty International, 1996.
Anderson, Melanie R. *Spectrality in the Novels of Toni Morrison.* Knoxville: University of Tennessee Press, 2013.
Andrews, William L. "The Novelization of Voice in Early African American Narrative." *PMLA* 105 (1990): 23–34.

Angelou, Maya. *I Know Why the Caged Bird Sings.* New York: Random House, 1969.

Auger, Philip. "A Lesson about Manhood: Appropriating 'The Word' in Ernest Gaines's *A Lesson before Dying.*" *Southern Literary Journal* 27.2 (1995): 74–85.

Babb, Valerie. "Old Fashioned Modernism: 'The Changing Same' in *A Lesson Before Dying.*" In *Critical Reflections on the Fiction of Ernest J. Gaines,* ed. David C. Estes. Athens: University of Georgia Press, 1994, 250–264.

Bailey, Anne C. *African Voices of the Atlantic Slave Trade: Beyond the Silence and the Shame.* Boston: Beacon, 2005.

Bakare-Yusuf, Bibi. "The Economy of Violence: Black Bodies and the Unspeakable Terror." In *Feminist Theory and the Body: A Reader,* ed. Janet Price and Margrit Shildrick. New York: Routledge, 1999, 311–323.

Baker, Houston A., Jr. "The Embattled Craftsman: An Essay on James Baldwin," *Journal of African-Afro-American Affairs* 1.1 (1977): 28–51, and in *Critical Essays on James Baldwin,* ed. Fred L. Standley and Nancy V. Burt. Boston: G. K. Hall, 1988, 66–77.

———. "Scene . . . Not Heard." In *Reading Rodney King: Reading Urban Uprising,* ed. Robert Gooding Williams. New York: Routledge, 1993, 38–48.

Baldwin, James. *Early Novels and Stories.* New York: Literary Classics of the United States, 1998.

———. *The Fire Next Time.* New York: Dial, 1963.

———. *Go Tell It on the Mountain.* New York: Dial, 1964.

———. *If Beale Street Could Talk.* New York: Dial, 1974.

———. "It's Hard to Be James Baldwin" (interview with Herbert R. Lottman). *Intellectual Digest,* July 1972, 67–68.

———. "A Letter to Prisoners." In *The Cross of Redemption: Uncollected Writings,* ed. Randall Kenan. New York: Pantheon, 2010, 261–263.

———. *No Name in the Street.* New York: Dial, 1972.

———. *Notes of a Native Son.* Boston: Beacon, 1955.

———. "An Open Letter to My Sister, Angela Davis." In *The Cross of Redemption: Uncollected Writings,* ed. Randall Kenan. New York: Pantheon Books, 2010, 254–260.

———. "Speech from the Soledad Rally." In *The Cross of Redemption: Uncollected Writings,* ed. Randall Kenan. New York: Pantheon Books, 2010, 120–125.

———. *Tell Me How Long the Train's Been Gone.* New York: Dial, 1968.

Barnett, Pamela E. "Figurations of Rape and the Supernatural in *Beloved.*" *PMLA* 112 (1997): 418–427.

Beaulieu, Elizabeth Ann. *Black Women Writers and the American Neo-Slave Narrative: Femininity Unfettered.* Westport, CT: Greenwood, 1999.

Beavers, Herman. "Prodigal Agency: Allegory and Voice in Ernest J. Gaines's *A Lesson before Dying.*" In *Contemporary Black Men's Fiction and Drama,* ed. Keith Clark. Urbana: University of Illinois Press, 2001, 135–154.

Bell, Bernard. *The Afro-American Novel and Its Tradition.* Amherst: University of Massachusetts Press, 1987.

Berger, Dan. *Captive Nation: Black Prison Organizing in the Civil Rights Era.* Chapel Hill: University of North Carolina Press, 2014.

Bernstein, Lee. *America Is the Prison: Arts and Politics in Prison in the 1970s.* Chapel Hill: University of North Carolina Press, 2010.

Bhattacharjee, Anannya. "Private Fists and Public Force: Race, Gender, and Surveillance." In *Policing the National Body: Sex, Race, and Criminalization,* ed. Jael Sillman and Anannya Bhattacharjee. Cambridge, MA: South End Press, 2002, 1–54.

Blackmon, Douglas A. *Slavery by Another Name: The Re-enslavement of Black Americans from the Civil War to World War II*. New York: Anchor Books, 2008.

Block, Diana, Urszula Wislanka, Cassie Pierson, and Pam Fadem. "*The Fire Inside*: Newsletter of the California Coalition for Women Prisoners." *NWSA Journal* 20 (Summer 2008): 48–70.

Boudreau, Kristin. "Pain and the Unmaking of Self in Toni Morrison's *Beloved*." *Contemporary Literature* 36.3 (1995): 447–465.

Bourque, Darrell. "*Poesis*, the Law, and the Notebook." *Interdisciplinary Humanities* 17.2 (2000): 137–145.

Bouson, J. Brooks. *Quiet as It's Kept: Shame, Trauma, and Race in the Novels of Toni Morrison*. Albany: State University of New York Press, 2000.

Broad, Robert. "Giving Blood to the Scraps: Haints, History, and Hosea in *Beloved*." *African American Review* 28.2 (1994): 189–196.

Brooks, Maegan Parker. *A Voice That Could Stir an Army: Fannie Lou Hamer and the Rhetoric of the Black Freedom Movement*. Jackson: University Press of Mississippi, 2014.

Brown, Anne Gray. "Writing for Life: 'Jefferson's Diary' as Transformative Text in Ernest J. Gaines's *A Lesson Before Dying*." *Southern Quarterly* 47.1 (2009): 23–46.

Brown, Marianne. "Making History Inside Prison Walls." *Tenacious* 21 (Fall 2010): 11–17.

Brown, Vincent. "Social Death and Political Life in the Study of Slavery." *American Historical Review* 114 (2009): 1231–1249.

Buchanan, Kim Shayo. "Impunity: Sexual Abuse in Women's Prisons." *Harvard Civil Rights–Civil Liberties Law Review* 42 (2007): 45–87.

———. "Our Prisons, Ourselves: Race, Gender, and the Rule of Law." *Yale Law and Policy Review* 29.1 (2010): 1–82.

Budick, Emily Miller. "Absence, Loss, and the Space of History in Toni Morrison's *Beloved*." *Arizona Quarterly* 48.2 (Summer 1992): 117–138.

Burton-Rose, Daniel. "Our Sisters' Keepers." In *Prison Nation: The Warehousing of America's Poor*, ed. Tara Herivel and Paul Wright. New York: Routledge, 2003, 258–261.

Carmean, Karen. *Ernest J. Gaines: A Critical Companion*. Westport, CT: Greenwood Press, 1998.

Carter, Rubin. *The Sixteenth Round: From Number 1 Contender to Number 45472* (1974), repr. ed., Chicago: Chicago Review Press, 2011.

Chandler, Kim. "Alabama, Feds Reach Agreement over Alleged Prison Sex Abuse." *Tampa Tribune*, 31 May 2015. Web. http://tbo.com/ap/alabama-feds-reach-agreement-over-alleged-prison-sex-abuse-20150531. Accessed June 2015.

Chen, Michelle. "Groups Press Justice Department on Prison Rape." *Colorlines*, 18 August 2010. Web. http://www.colorlines.com/articles/groups-press-justice-department-prison-rape. Accessed 13 February 2015.

Childs, Dennis. "Angola, Convict Leasing, and the Annulment of Freedom: The Vectors of Architectural and Discursive Violence in the U.S. Slavery of Prison." In *Violence and the Body: Race, Gender, and the State*, ed. Arturo J. Aldama. Bloomington: Indiana University Press, 2003, 189–208.

———. *Slaves of the State: Black Incarceration from the Chain Gang to the Penitentiary*. Minneapolis: University of Minnesota Press, 2015.

Christian, Barbara. "Fixing Methodologies: *Beloved*." *Cultural Critique* 24 (Spring 1993): 5–15.

———. "'Somebody Forgot to Tell Somebody Something': African-American Women's Historical Novels." In *Wild Women in the Whirlwind: Afro-American Culture and the Contemporary Literary Renaissance*, ed. Joanne M. Braxton and Andrée Nicola McLaughlin. New Brunswick, NJ: Rutgers University Press, 1990, 326–341.

Churchill, Ward, and Jim Vander Wall. *Agents of Repression: The FBI's Secret Wars Against the Black Panther Party and the American Indian Movement*. Boston: South End, 1988.

Collins, Michael S. "The Antipanopticon of Etheridge Knight." *PMLA* 123.3 (2008): 580–597.

———. *Understanding Etheridge Knight*. Columbia: University of South Carolina Press, 2012.

Conniff, Brian. "Mumia Abu-Jamal's *Live from Death Row* as Post-legal Prison Writing." In *Literature and Law*, ed. Michael J. Meyer. New York: Rodopi, 2004, 160–171.

———. "The Prison Writer as Ideologue: George Jackson and the Attica Prison Rebellion." In *Prose and Cons: Essays on Prison Literature in the United States*, ed. D. Quentin Miller. Jefferson, NC: McFarland, 2005, 147–173.

Corrigan, Lisa M. *Prison Power: How Prison Influenced the Movement for Black Liberation*. Jackson: University Press of Mississippi, 2016.

Cusac, Anne-Marie. *Cruel and Unusual: The Culture of Punishment in America*. New Haven, CT: Yale University Press, 2009.

Daley, Katherine, and Carolyn M. Jones. "Ernest J. Gaines's *A Lesson Before Dying*: Freedom in Confined Spaces." In *From the Plantation to the Prison: African-American Confinement Literature*, ed. Tara T. Green. Macon, GA: Mercer University Press, 2008, 83–117.

Darling, Marsha. "In the Realm of Responsibility: A Conversation with Toni Morrison." *Women's Review of Books* 5 (March 1988): 5–6.

Davis, Angela Y. *Abolition Democracy: Beyond Empire, Prisons, and Torture*. New York: Seven Stories, 2005.

———. *Angela Davis: An Autobiography*. New York: International Publishers, 1974.

———. "Angela Davis on Solitary Confinement, Immigration Detention, and '12 Years a Slave.'" *Democracy Now*, 6 March 2014. Web. http://www.democracynow.org/blog/2014/3/6/part_2_angela_davis_on_solitary. Accessed 13 February 2015.

———. *Are Prisons Obsolete?* New York: Seven Stories, 2003.

———. "From the Prison of Slavery to the Slavery of Prison." In *The Angela Y. Davis Reader*, ed. Joy James. Malden, MA: Blackwell Publishing, 1998, 74–95.

———. "A Letter from Angela to Ericka." In *If They Come in the Morning: Voices of Resistance*, ed. Angela Y. Davis. New Rochelle, NY: Third Press, 1971, 123–127.

———. "Political Prisoners, Prisons, and Black Liberation." In *If They Come in the Morning: Voices of Resistance*, ed. Angela Y. Davis. New Rochelle, NY: Third Press, 1971, 27–43.

———. "Race, Gender, and Prison History: From the Convict Lease System to the Supermax Prison." In *Prison Masculinities*, ed. Don Sabo, Terry A. Kupers, and Willie London. Philadelphia: Temple University Press, 2001, 35–45.

———. "Reflections on the Black Woman's Role in the Community of Slaves." In *The Angela Y. Davis Reader*, ed. Joy James. Malden, MA: Blackwell, 1998.

Davis, David Brion. *Inhuman Bondage: The Rise and Fall of Slavery in the New World*. New York: Oxford University Press, 2006.

Davis, Kimberly Chabot. "'Postmodern Blackness': Morrison's *Beloved* and the End of History." *Twentieth-Century Literature* 44.2 (1998): 242–260.

Dayan, Colin. *The Law Is a White Dog: How Legal Rituals Make and Unmake Persons*. Princeton, NJ: Princeton University Press, 2011.

————. *The Story of Cruel and Unusual*. Cambridge: Massachusetts Institute of Technology Press, 2007.

Denno, Deborah W. "When Willie Francis Died: The 'Disturbing' Story Behind One of the Eighth Amendment's Most Enduring Standards of Risk." In *Death Penalty Stories*, ed. John H. Blume and Jordan M. Steiker. New York: Foundation Press, 2009, 17–94.

Dieter, Richard C. *Innocence and the Crisis in the American Death Penalty*. September 2004. Web. http://www.deathpenaltyinfo.org/innocence-and-crisis-american-death-penalty. Accessed 16 February 2012.

Douglass, Frederick. *Narrative of the Life of Frederick Douglass, an American Slave, Written by Himself*, ed. Angela Y. Davis. San Francisco: City Lights Books, 2010.

Doyle, Mary Ellen. *Voices from the Quarters: The Fiction of Ernest J. Gaines*. Baton Rouge: Louisiana State University Press, 2002.

Elsner, Alan. *Gates of Injustice: The Crisis in America's Prisons*. Upper Saddle River, NJ: Prentice Hall, 2006.

Farmer, Melvin. *The New Slave Ship: A Ship That Does Not Sail*. Los Angeles: Milligan, 1998.

Folks, Jeffrey J. "Communal Responsibility in Ernest J. Gaines's *A Lesson Before Dying*." *Mississippi Quarterly* 52.2 (1999): 259–271.

Foster, Frances Smith. "'In Respect to Females . . . ': Differences in Portrayals of Women by Male and Female Narrators." *Black Literature Forum* 15.2 (Summer 1981): 66–70.

Foucault, Michel. *Discipline and Punish: The Birth of the Prison*. New York: Vintage, 1976.

Francis, Willie (as told to Sam Montgomery). *My Trip to the Chair* (Lafayette, LA: Self-published, 1947). Afro-American Pamphlets, Part 3 (1827–1948), Rare Books and Special Collections Reading Room, U.S. Library of Congress, Washington, DC, repr. in *Demands of the Dead: Executions, Storytelling, and Activism in the United States*, ed. Katy Ryan. Iowa City: University of Iowa Press, 2012, 33–44.

Franklin, H. Bruce. "The American Prison and the Normalization of Torture." In *Torture, American Style*, ed. Margaret Power. May 2006. Web. http://www.historiansagainstwar.org/resources/torture/brucefranklin.html. Accessed 16 December 2011.

————. "The Inside Stories of the Global American Prison." *Texas Studies in Literature and Language* 50.3 (2008): 235–242.

————. "Introduction." In *Prison Writing in 20th Century America*, ed. H. Bruce Franklin. New York: Penguin, 1998, 1–18.

————. *The Victim as Criminal and Artist: Literature from the American Prison*. New York: Oxford University Press, 1978.

Furman, Jan. "Remembering the 'Disremembered': *Beloved*." In Jan Furman, *Toni Morrison's Fiction*. Columbia: University of South Carolina Press, 1996, 67–84.

Gaines, Ernest. *Bloodline*. New York: Dial, 1968.

————. "Ernest Gaines, *A Lesson Before Dying*" (interview by the Academy of Achievement). 4 May 2001. Web. http://www.achievement.org/autodoc/printmember/gai0int-1. Accessed 16 February 2012.

————. "Ernest J. Gaines: *A Lesson Before Dying*" (interview by Dan Stone), NEA Big Read. 16 August 2007. Web. http://www.neabigread.org/books/lessonbeforedying/readers-guide. Accessed 16 February 2012.

————. *A Lesson Before Dying*. New York: Vintage, 1993.

————. "A Literary Salon: Oyster/Shrimp Po'Boys, Chardonnay, and Conversation with Ernest J. Gaines" (interview by Marcia Gaudet and Darrel Bourque). In *Mozart and Leadbelly: Stories and Essays*, ed. Marcia Gaudet and Reggie Young. New York: Knopf, 2005, 131–159.

———. *Of Love and Dust*. New York: W. W. Norton, 1967.

———. Transcript of "A Conversation with Ernest Gaines" (interview by Lawrence Bridges). NEA Big Read. 16 August 2007.

———. "Writing *A Lesson Before Dying*." In *Mozart and Leadbelly: Stories and Essays*, ed. Marcia Gaudet and Reggie Young. New York: Knopf, 2005, 52–62.

Gaither, L. V. *Loss of Empire: Legal Lynching, Vigilantism, and African American Intellectualism in the 21st Century*. Trenton, NJ: Africa World Press, 2006.

Gardham, Duncan. "Abu Ghraib Photos 'Show Rape.'" *The Telegraph*, 9 May 2009. Web. http://www.telegraph.co.uk/news/worldnews/northamerica/usa/5395830/Abu-Ghraib-abuse-photos-show-rape.html. Accessed 26 April 2011.

Gates, Henry Louis, Jr. *The Signifying Monkey: A Theory of African American Literary Criticism*. New York: Oxford University Press, 1988.

Gaudet, Marcia. "Storytelling and the Law: Variants of Justice in Ernest J. Gaines's *A Lesson Before Dying*." *Interdisciplinary Humanities* 17.2 (2000): 125–135.

Goodman, George, Jr. "For James Baldwin, a Rap on Baldwin." *New York Review of Books*, 26 June 1972. Web. http://www.nytimes.com/books/98/03/29/specials/baldwin-rap.html. Accessed 29 October 2011.

Gordon, Avery F. *Ghostly Matters: Haunting and the Sociological Imagination*. Minneapolis: University of Minnesota Press, 1997.

Gottesdiener, Laura. "California Women Prisons: Inmates Face Sexual Abuse, Lack of Medical Care and Unsanitary Conditions." *Huffington Post*, 3 June 2011. Web. http://www.huffingtonpost.com/2011/06/03/california-women-prisons_n_871125.html. Accessed 1 June 2015.

Gourdine, Angeletta KM. "Hearing Reading and Being 'Read' by *Beloved*." *NWSA Journal* 10.2 (1998): 13–31.

Green, Tara T. "Introduction." In *From the Plantation to the Prison: African-American Confinement Literature*, ed. Tara T. Green. Macon, GA: Mercer University Press, 2008, 1–7.

Greenidge, Kaitlyn. "The Riotous Power of Toni Morrison." *Virginia Quarterly* 91.2 (2015) Web. http://www.vqronline.org/fiction-criticism/2015/04/riotous-power-toni-morrison. Accessed 1 June 2015.

Guenther, Lisa. *Solitary Confinement: Social Death and Its Afterlives*. Minneapolis: University of Minnesota Press, 2013.

Hamer, Fannie Lou. "Testimony Before the Credentials Committee at the Democratic National Convention, Atlantic City, New Jersey, August 22, 1964." In *The Speeches of Fannie Lou Hamer*, ed. Maegan Parker Brooks and Davis W. Houck. Jackson: University Press of Mississippi, 2011, 42–45.

Hames-García, Michael. *Fugitive Thought: Prison Movements, Race, and the Meaning of Justice*. Minneapolis: University of Minnesota Press, 2004.

Hamilton, Cynthia. "Revisions, Rememories, and Exorcisms: Toni Morrison and the Slave Narrative," *Journal of American Studies* 30.3 (1996): 429–445.

Harding, Luke. "Focus Shifts to Jail Abuse of Women." *The Guardian*, 12 May 2004. Web. https://www.theguardian.com/world/2004/may/12/iraq.usa. Accessed 26 April 2011.

Harris, Trudier. "The Eye as Weapon in *If Beale Street Could Talk*." *MELUS* 5.3 (1978): 54–66.

Harris-Lopez, Trudier. *South of Tradition: Essays on African American Literature*. Athens: University of Georgia Press, 2002.

Harrison, Eric. "Nearly 200 Women Have Told of Being Raped, Abused in a Georgia

Prison Scandal So Broad Even Officials Say It's . . . : A 13-Year Nightmare." *Los Angeles Times*, 30 December 1992. Web. http://articles.latimes.com/print/1992-12-30/news/vw-2637_1_women-prisoners. Accessed 13 February 2015.

Hartman, Saidiya. *Scenes of Subjection: Terror, Slavery, and Self-Making in Nineteenth-Century America*. New York: Oxford University Press, 1997.

Heiner, Brady Thomas, and Ariana Mangual. "The Repressive Social Function of Schools in Racialized Communities." In *States of Confinement: Policing, Detention, and Prisons*, ed. Joy James. New York: Palgrave, 2000, 222–229.

Henderson, Carole E. *Scarring the Black Body: Race and Representation in African American Literature*. Columbia: University of Missouri Press, 2002.

Henderson, Mae Gwendolyn. "Speaking in Tongues: Dialogics, Dialectics, and the Black Woman Writer's Literary Tradition." In *Changing Our Own Words: Essays on Criticism, Theory, and Writing by Black Women*, ed. Cheryl A. Wall. New Brunswick, NJ: Rutgers University Press, 1989, 16–37.

———. "Toni Morrison's *Beloved*: Re-Membering the Body as Historical Text." In *Toni Morrison's* Beloved: *A Casebook*, ed. William L. Andrews and Nellie Y. McKay. New York: Oxford University Press, 1999, 79–106.

Herivel, Tara, and Paul Wright, eds. *Prison Nation: The Warehousing of America's Poor*. New York: Routledge, 2003.

Hersch, Seymour M. "Torture at Abu Ghraib." *New Yorker*, 10 May 2004. Web. http://www.newyorker.com/magazine/2004/05/10/torture-at-abu-ghraib. Accessed 30 June 2015.

Hill, Michael DeRell. *The Ethics of Swagger: Prizewinning African American Novels, 1977–1993*. Columbus: Ohio State University Press, 2013.

Holland, Sharon Patricia. *Raising the Dead: Readings of Death and (Black) Subjectivity*. Durham, NC: Duke University Press, 2000.

Holloway, Karla FC. "*Beloved*: A Spiritual." In *Toni Morrison's* Beloved: *A Casebook*, ed. William L. Andrews and Nellie Y. McKay. New York: Oxford University Press, 1999, 67–78.

Hudnall, Johanna. "Prison Rape." In *Razor Wire Women: Prisoners, Activists, Scholars, and Artists*, ed. Jodie Michelle Lawston and Ashley E. Lucas. Albany: State University of New York Press, 2011, 165–167.

Hudson, Nick, Bob Lilal, and Andrew Strong. "Private Prison Scandals from Texas." *Considering a Private Jail, Prison, or Detention Center? A Resource for Community Members and Public Officials*, 2d ed. 16 September 2009. Web. http://www.grassroots leadership.org/Texas%20resources/CPJ%20Second%20Edition.pdf. Accessed 28 December 2010.

Human Rights Watch. *No Equal Justice: The Prison Litigation Reform Act in the United States*. New York: Human Rights Watch, 2009.

———. *Nowhere to Hide: Retaliation Against Women in Michigan State Prisons*. July 1998. Web. http://www.hrw.org/legacy/reports98/women/Mich.htm#P37_769. Accessed 13 February 2015.

———. "Prison Conditions in the United States." 1 November 1991. Web. http://www.hrw.org/report/1991/11/01/prison-conditions-united-states. Accessed 30 June 2015.

———. "Prisoner Abuse: How Different Are U.S. Prisons?" 13 May 2004. Web. https://www.hrw.org/news/2004/05/13/prisoner-abuse-how-different-are-us-prisons. Accessed 30 June 2015.

———. *Shielded from Justice: Police Brutality and Accountability in the United States*. 1 July 1998. Web. http://www.hrw.org/legacy/reports/reports98/police/uspo99.htm. Accessed 29 October 2011.

Human Rights Watch and the American Civil Liberties Union. *Custody and Control: Conditions of Confinement in New York's Juvenile Prisons for Girls*. New York: Human Rights Watch and the American Civil Liberties Union, 2006.

Human Rights Watch Women's Project. *All Too Familiar: Sexual Abuse of Women in U.S. State Prisons*. Washington, DC: Human Rights Watch, 1996.

Jackson, George. *Blood in My Eye*. Baltimore: Black Classic, 1990.

———. *Soledad Brother: The Prison Letters of George Jackson* (1970), repr. ed. Chicago: Lawrence Hill, 1994.

Jacobs, Harriet. *Incidents in the Life of a Slave Girl*. Mineola, NY: Dover, 2001.

James, Joy. "Framing the Panther: Assata Shakur and Black Female Agency." In *Want to Start a Revolution? Radical Women in the Black Freedom Struggle*, ed. Dayo F. Gore, Jeanne Theoharis, and Komozi Woodard. New York: New York University Press, 2009, 138–160.

———. *Imprisoned Intellectuals: America's Political Prisoners Write on Life, Liberation, and Rebellion*, ed. Joy James. Lanham, MD: Rowman and Littlefield, 2003.

———. "Introduction: Democracy and Captivity." In *The New Abolitionists: (Neo) Slave Narratives and Contemporary Prison Writings*, ed. Joy James. Albany: State University of New York Press, 2005, xxi–xlii.

———, ed. *The New Abolitionists: (Neo)Slave Narratives and Contemporary Prison Writings*. Albany: State University of New York Press, 2005.

———. *Resisting State Violence: Radicalism, Gender and Race in U.S. Culture*. Minneapolis: University of Minnesota Press, 1996.

———, ed. *States of Confinement: Policing, Detention, and Prisons*. New York: Palgrave, 2000.

———. *Warfare in the Homeland: Policing and Prison in a Penal Democracy*. Durham, NC: Duke University Press, 2007.

Jennings, Billy X. "Special Assignment: George Jackson Funeral." *San Francisco Bay View National Black Newspaper*, 27 July 2014. Web. http://sfbayview.com/2014/07/special-assignment-george-jackson-funeral. Accessed 30 June 2016.

Jesser, Nancy. "Violence, Home, and Community in Toni Morrison's *Beloved*." *African American Review* 33.2 (1999): 325–345.

Jilani, Zaid. "How Congress Killed One of the Few Lifelines for Former Prisoners—and Why It's Time to Bring It Back." *AlterNet*, 3 June 2015. Web. https://www.prisonactivist.org/alerts/how-congress-killed-one-few-lifelines-former-prisoners-and-why-its-time-bring-it-back. Accessed 10 July 2015.

Johnson, Charles. *Middle Passage*. New York: Plume, 1990.

Jones, Gayl. *Eva's Man*. Boston: Beacon, 1976.

Keizer, Arlene R. *Black Subjects: Identity Formation in the Contemporary Narrative of Slavery*. Ithaca, NY: Cornell University Press, 2004.

Kenan, Randall, ed. *The Cross of Redemption: Uncollected Writings*. New York: Pantheon, 2010.

King, Gilbert. *The Execution of Willie Francis*. New York: Basic Civitas, 2008.

King, Robert Hillary. *From the Bottom of the Heap: The Autobiography of Black Panther Robert Hillary King*. Oakland, CA: PM Press, 2008.

Knight, Etheridge, "Preface." In *Black Voices from Prison*, ed. Etheridge Knight. New York: Pathfinder, 1970, 5–10.

Krumholz, Linda. "The Ghosts of Slavery: Historical Recovery in Toni Morrison's *Beloved*." In *Toni Morrison's* Beloved: *A Casebook*, ed. William L. Andrews and Nellie Y. McKay. New York: Oxford University Press, 1999, 107–125.

Kupers, Terry. "Mental Health in Men's Prisons." In *Prison Masculinities*, ed. Don Sabo, Terry A. Kupers, and Willie London. Philadelphia: Temple University Press, 2001, 192–197.

———. "The Role of Misogyny and Homophobia in Prison Sexual Abuse." *UCLA Women's Law Journal* 18 (Fall 2010): 107–130.

Kurki, Leena, and Norval Morris. "The Purposes, Practices and Problems of Supermax Prisons." *Crime and Justice* 28 (2001): 385–424.

Law, Victoria. *Invisibility of Women Prisoner Resistance*. n.d. Web. http://acap.interference .cc/wp-content/uploads/invisibility-of-women-prisoner-resist-zine-final.pdf. Accessed 1 June 2015.

———. "Remembering the Black Women Killed by Police." *Bitch Media*, 20 August 2014. Web. http://bitchmagazine.org/post/gender-and-race-and-police-violence-women-ferguson-michael-brown. Accessed 8 December 2014.

———. *Resistance Behind Bars: The Struggles of Incarcerated Women*. Oakland, CA: PM Press, 2009.

Lawston, Jodie Michelle, and Ashley E. Lucas, eds. *Razor Wire Women: Prisoners, Activists, Scholars, and Artists*. Albany: State University of New York Press, 2011.

Leak, Jeffrey B. *Racial Myths and Masculinity in African American Literature*. Knoxville: University of Tennessee Press, 2005.

Lee, Chana Kai. *For Freedom's Sake: The Life of Fannie Lou Hamer*. Urbana: University of Illinois Press, 1999.

Leeming, David. *James Baldwin: A Biography*. New York: Knopf, 1994.

Levi, Robin, and Ayelet Waldman, eds. *Inside This Place, Not of It: Narratives from Women's Prisons*. San Francisco: McSweeney's and Voice of Witness, 2011.

Liptak, Adam. "1 in 100 U.S. Adults Behind Bars, New Study Says." NYTimes.com, 28 February 2000. Web. http://www.nytimes.com/2008/02/28/us/28cnd-prison.html?_r=0&pagewanted=print. Accessed 30 June 2015.

Lowe, John, ed. *Conversations with Ernest Gaines*. Jackson: University Press of Mississippi, 1995.

———. "Transcendence in the House of the Dead: The Subversive Gaze of *A Lesson before Dying*." In *The World Is Our Home: Society and Culture in Contemporary Southern Writing*, ed. Jeffrey J. Folks and Nancy Summers Folks. Lexington: University Press of Kentucky, 2000, 142–162.

Lu, Thoai. "Michelle Alexander: More Black Men in Prison than Were Enslaved in 1850." *Colorlines*, 30 March 2011. Web. http://www.colorlines.com/articles/michelle-alexander-more-black-men-prison-were-enslaved-1850. Accessed 30 June 2015.

Maestretti, Danielle. "Breaking Free: Prisoners Publish Their Stories in Zines." *Utne Reader*. March–April 2010. Web. http://www.utne.com/Media/Breaking-Free-Prisoners-Publish-Their-Stories-in-Zines.aspx. Accessed 1 June 2015.

Majors, Richard, and Janet Mancini Billson. *Cool Pose: The Dilemmas of Black Manhood in America*. New York: Lexington, 1992.

Mann, Eric. *Comrade George: An Investigation into the Life, Political Thought, and Assassination of George Jackson*. New York: Harper and Row, 1972.

McDowell, Deborah E. "Negotiating Between Tenses: Witnessing Slavery after Freedom—*Dessa Rose*." In *Slavery and the Literary Imagination*, ed. Deborah E. McDowell and Arnold Rampersad. Baltimore: Johns Hopkins University Press, 1989, 144–163.

McGuire, Danielle L. *At the Dark End of the Street: Black Women, Rape, and Resistance—a New History of the Civil Rights Movement from Rosa Parks to the Rise of Black Power*. New York: Knopf, 2010.

Mears, Bill. "High Court Dismisses Ruling on Abu-Jamal Death Sentence." CNN.com, 19 January 2010. Web. http://www.cnn.com/2010/CRIME/01/19/scotus.abu.jamal. Accessed 30 June 2015.

Mears, Daniel P. *Evaluating the Effectiveness of Supermax Prisons.* Washington, DC: Urban Institute, 2006.

Miller, D. Quentin. *A Criminal Power: James Baldwin and the Law.* Columbus: Ohio State University Press, 2012.

———. "'On the Outside Looking In': White Readers of Nonwhite Prison Narratives." In *Prose and Cons: Essays on Prison Literature in the United States*, ed. D. Quentin Miller. Jefferson, NC: McFarland, 2005, 15–32.

Mitchell, Angelyn. *The Freedom to Remember: Narrative, Slavery, and Gender in Contemporary Black Women's Fiction.* New Brunswick, NJ: Rutgers University Press, 2002.

Mitchell, Jerry. "Professors Making Investments in Future." *Clarion Ledger*, 25 October 2015. Web. http://www.clarionledger.com/story/news/2014/10/25/profs-making-investments-future/17938855. Accessed 30 June 2015.

Morrison, Toni. *Beloved.* New York: Plume, 1987.

———. "The Pain of Being Black." *Time*, May 22, 1989.

———. "The Site of Memory." In *Out There: Marginalization and Contemporary Cultures*, ed. Russell Ferguson, Martha Gever, Trinh T. Minh-ha, and Cornel West. New York: New York Museum of Contemporary Art, 1990, 299–305.

Morrison, Toni, and Angela Davis. "Toni Morrison and Angela Davis on Friendship and Creativity" (interview by Dan White). *University of California Santa Cruz Review*, 29 October 2014. Web. http://news.ucsc.edu/2014/10/morrison-davis-q-a.html. Accessed 13 February 2015.

M.S. "Abu Ghraib Torture Began at Home." *The Fire Inside* 28 (Summer 2004). Web. http://www.womenprisoners.org/fire/000511.html. Accessed 1 June 2015.

Muther, Elizabeth. "Isadora at Sea: Misogyny as Comic Capital in Charles Johnson's *Middle Passage*." *African American Review* 30.4 (1996): 649–658.

Nagel, Mechthild. "Angela Y. Davis and Assata Shakur as Women Outlaws: Resisting U.S. State Violence." *Wagadu* 13 (Summer 2015): 43–78.

Oforlea, Aaron. "Remaking and Marking Tradition: Black Male Subjectivity in Baldwin's *Tell Me How Long the Train's Been Gone*." *Obsidian* 9.2 (2008): 62–76.

O'Keefe, Vincent. "Reading Rigor Mortis: Offstage Violence and Excluded Middles 'in' Johnson's *Middle Passage* and Morrison's *Beloved*." *African American Review* 30.4 (1996): 635–647.

Olney, James. "'I Was Born': Slave Narratives, Their Status as Autobiography and Literature." *Callaloo* 20 (Winter 1984): 46–73.

Oshinsky, David. *Worse than Slavery: Parchman Farm and the Ordeal of Jim Crow Justice.* New York: Free Press, 1996.

Owen, Barbara. "Women's Prisons." In *Encyclopedia of Prisons and Correctional Facilities*, ed. Mary Bosworth. Thousand Oaks, CA: Sage, 2005, 1051–1056.

Pallitto, Robert M. "Introduction." In *Torture and State Violence in the United States: A Short Documentary History*, ed. Robert M. Pallitto. Baltimore: John Hopkins University Press, 2011, 1–18.

Parenti, Christian. *Lockdown America: Police and Prisons in the Age of Crisis.* New York: Verso, 1999.

Patterson, Orlando. *Slavery and Social Death: A Comparative Study.* Cambridge, MA: Harvard University Press, 1985.

Pawlacyzk, George, and Beth Hundsdorfer. "Trapped in Tamms: Investigation Reveals Truth

Behind Mental Health Issues in Supermax Prison." *Southern Illinoisian*, 9 August 2009. Web. http://thesouthern.com/news/trapped-in-tamms-investigation-reveals-truth-behind-mental-health-issues/article_9c217943-9381-5fa9-813e-b5f72c96fd38.html. Accessed 20 December 2016.

Peet, Judy. "N.J. Inmates Tell Their Own Stories of Abuse." *Star-Ledger*, 23 May 2004. Web. http://www.nj.com/news/ledger/stories/specialprojects/womenprison01.html. Accessed 1 June 2015.

Perkins, Margo V. *Autobiography as Activism: Three Black Women of the Sixties*. Jackson: University Press of Mississippi, 2000.

Perkinson, Robert. "Shackled Justice: Florence Federal Penitentiary and the New Politics of Punishment." *Social Justice* 21.3 (Fall 1994): 117–132.

Petersilia, Joan. *When Prisoners Come Home: Parole and Prisoner Reentry*. New York: Oxford University Press, 2003.

Phillips, Caryl. "The Cargo Rap." In Caryl Phillips, *Higher Ground: A Novel in Three Parts*, 61–172. New York: Vintage, 1989.

Porter, Horace A. *Stealing the Fire: The Art and Protest of James Baldwin*. Middletown, CT: Wesleyan University Press, 1989.

Rathbone, Cristina. *A World Apart: Women, Prison, and Life Behind Bars*. New York: Random House, 2005.

Raynaud, Claudine. "The Poetics of Abjection in *Beloved*." In *Black Imagination and the Middle Passage*, ed. Maria Diedrich, Henry Louis Gates Jr., and Carl Pedersen. New York: Oxford University Press, 1999, 70–85.

Rediker, Marcus. *The Slave Ship: A Human History*. New York: Penguin, 2007.

Reed, Ishmael. "Foreword." In David Matlin, *Prisons: Inside the New America from Vernooykill Creek to Abu Ghraib*. Berkeley: North Atlantic, 2005, xi–xv.

Reynolds, Laurie Jo, and Stephen F. Eisenman. "Tamms Is Torture: The Campaign to Shut Down an Illinois Supermax Prison." *Truthout*, 8 May 2013. Web. http://www.truth-out.org/news/item/16241-tamms-is-torture-the-campaign-to-close-an-illinois-supermax-prison. Accessed 15 March 2016.

Rhodes, Lorna A. *Total Confinement: Madness and Reason in the Maximum Security Prison*. Berkeley: University of California Press, 2004.

Richie, Beth E. *Arrested Justice: Black Women, Violence, and America's Prison Nation*. New York: New York University Press, 2012.

Rideau, Wilbert. *In the Place of Justice: A Story of Punishment and Redemption*. New York: Vintage, 2011.

Ritchie, Andrea J. "Law Enforcement Violence Against Women of Color." In *The Color of Violence: The Incite! Anthology*, ed. INCITE! Women of Color Against Violence. Boston: South End, 2006, 138–156.

Ritchie, Andrea J., and Joey L. Mogul. "In the Shadows of the War on Terror: Persistent Police Brutality and Abuse of People of Color in the United States," April 2006. http://www.ushrnetwork.org/sites/ushrnetwork.org/files/shadow_report_to_cat_on_police_brutality_final.pdf. Accessed 29 October 2011.

Rivas, Jorge. "Mumia Abu-Jamal Will No Longer Face Death Penalty." *Colorlines*, 7 December 2011. Web. http://www.colorlines.com/articles/mumia-abu-jamal-will-no-longer-face-death-penalty. Accessed 30 June 2015.

Rodríguez, Dylan. *Forced Passages: Imprisoned Radical Intellectuals and the U.S. Prison Regime*. Minneapolis: University of Minnesota Press, 2006.

Rody, Caroline. "Toni Morrison's *Beloved*: History, 'Rememory,' and a 'Clamor for a Kiss.'" *American Literary History* 7.1 (1995): 92–119.

Ruderman, Wendy. "For Women in Street Stops, Deeper Humiliation." NYTimes.com, 6 August 2012. Web. http://www.nytimes.com/2012/08/07/nyregion/for-women-in-street-stops-deeper-humiliation.html?pagewanted=all&_r=2&. Accessed 8 December 2014.

Rummell, Kathryn. "Toni Morrison's *Beloved*: Transforming the African Heroic Epic." *The Griot* 21.1 (Spring 2002): 1–15.

Rushdy, Ashraf H. A. "Daughters Signifyin(g) History: The Example of Toni Morrison's *Beloved*." *American Literature* 64.3 (1992): 567–597.

———. *Neo-Slave Narratives: Studies of the Social Logic of a Literary Form*. New York: Oxford University Press, 1999.

Schaffer, Kay, and Sidonie Smith. *Human Rights and Narrated Lives: The Ethics of Recognition*. New York: Palgrave, 2004.

Schenwar, Maya. "America's Plantation Prisons." *Truthout*, 28 August 2008. Web. http://www.globalresearch.ca/america-s-plantation-prisons/10008. Accessed 12 February 2015.

Scott, Lynn Orilla. *James Baldwin's Later Fiction: Witness to the Journey*. East Lansing: Michigan State University Press, 2002.

Seale, Bobby. *A Lonely Rage: The Autobiography of Bobby Seale*. New York: Bantam, 1979.

Sekora, John. "Black Message/White Envelope: Genre, Authenticity, and Authority in the Antebellum Slave Narrative." *Callaloo* 32 (Summer 1987): 482–515.

Severson, Kim. "Troubles at Women's Prison Test Alabama." NYTimes.com, 1 March 2015. Web. http://www.nytimes.com/2014/03/02/us/troubles-at-womens-prison-test-alabama.html?_r=0. Accessed 1 June 2015.

Sexton, Jared. "Racial Profiling and the Societies of Control." In *Warfare in the Homeland: Policing and Prison in a Penal Democracy*, ed. Joy James. Durham, NC: Duke University Press, 2007, 197–218.

Shabazz, Rashad. *Spatializing Blackness: Architectures of Confinement and Black Masculinity in Chicago*. Urbana: University of Illinois Press, 2015.

Shakur, Assata. *Assata: An Autobiography*. Chicago: Lawrence Hill, 1987.

Sielke, Sabine. *Reading Rape: The Rhetoric of Sexual Violence in American Literature and Culture, 1790–1990*. Princeton, NJ: Princeton University Press, 2002.

Smallwood, Stephanie. *Saltwater Slavery: A Middle Passage from Africa to American Diaspora*. Cambridge, MA: Harvard University Press, 2007.

Smith, Brenda V. "Sexual Abuse of Women in United States Prisons: A Modern Corollary of Slavery." *Fordham Urban Law Journal* 33 (2006): 571–608.

Smith, Edwin. "UM Program Transforms Incarcerated Men into College Students." *University of Mississippi News*, 18 September 2015. Web. http://news.olemiss.edu/um-program-transforms-incarcerated-men-college-students. Accessed 1 December 2015.

Smitherman, Geneva. *Talkin' and Testifyin': The Language of Black America*. Boston: Houghton Mifflin, 1977.

Snyde, Craig W. "An Old Fashioned Hog Slaughter," *Mother Earth News*, 1 September 1982. Web. http://www.motherearthnews.com/Sustainable-Farming/1982-09-01/An-Old-Fashioned-Hog-Slaughter.aspx. Accessed 16 February 2012.

Solinger, Rickie, Paula C. Johnson, Martha L. Raimon, Tina Reynolds, and Ruby C. Tapia, eds. *Interrupted Life: Experiences of Incarcerated Women in the United States*. Berkeley: University of California Press, 2010.

Spillers, Hortense J. "Mama's Baby, Papa's Maybe: An American Grammar Book." *Diacritics* 17.2 (1987): 64–81.

Stanford, Anne Folwell. "Lit by Each Other's Light: Women's Writing at Cook County Jail." In *Interrupted Life: Experiences of Incarcerated Women in the United States*, ed. Rickie Solinger, Paula C. Johnson, Martha L. Raimon, Tina Reynolds, and Ruby C. Tapia. Berkeley: University of California Press, 2010, 165–177.

Stupp, Jason. "Living Death: Ernest Gaines's *A Lesson Before Dying* and the Execution of Willie Francis." In *Demands of the Dead: Executions, Storytelling, and Activism in the United States*, ed. Katy Ryan. Iowa City: University of Iowa Press, 2012, 45–58.

Sweeney, Megan. "Legal Brutality: Prisons and Punishment, the American Way." *American Literary History* 22.3 (2010): 698–713.

———. *Reading Is My Window: Books and the Art of Reading in Women's Prisons*. Chapel Hill: University of North Carolina Press, 2010.

———. *The Story Within Us: Women Prisoners Reflect on Reading*. Urbana: University of Illinois Press, 2012.

Talvi, Silja J. A. *Women Behind Bars: The Crisis of Women in the U.S. Prison System*. Emeryville, CA: Seal, 2007.

Tapley, Lance. "Mass Torture in America: Notes from the Supermax Prisons." In *The United States and Torture: Interrogations, Incarceration, and Abuse*, ed. Marjorie Cohn. New York: New York University Press, 2011, 215–238.

———. "Torture in Maine's Prison." *Portland Phoenix*, 11–17 November 2005. Web. http://www.portlandphoenix.com/features/top/ts_multi/documents/05081722.asp. Accessed 12 March 2012.

Teichner, Martha. "The Cost of a Nation of Incarceration." CBS News, 22 April 2012. Web. http://www.cbsnews.com/8301-3445_162-57418495/the-cost-of-a-nation-of-incarceration. Accessed 10 July 2015.

Thompson, Carlyle Van. *Black Outlaws: Race, Law, and Male Subjectivity in African American Literature and Culture*. New York: Peter Lang, 2010.

Todd, James. "Student's Prison Course Yields Literary Insights." *Duke Today*, 24 September 2010. Web. https://today.duke.edu/2007/10/patrick.html. Accessed 10 July 2015.

Travis, Molly Abel. "Speaking from the Silence of the Slave Narrative: *Beloved* and African-American Women's History." *Texas Review* 13 (1992): 69–81.

United Nations. *Basic Principles for the Treatment of Prisoners*. 14 December 1990. Web. http://www.ohchr.org/EN/ProfessionalInterest/Pages/BasicPrinciplesTreatmentOfPrisoners.aspx. Accessed 10 July 2015.

Wallace, Maurice. *Constructing the Black Masculine: Identity and Ideality in African American Men's Literature and Culture, 1775–1995*. Durham, NC: Duke University Press, 2002.

Weaver, James. "Rehabilitative Storytelling: The Narrator-Narratee Relationship in J. California Cooper's *Family*." *MELUS* 30.1 (2005): 109–134.

Wheatley, Phillis. "On Being Brought from Africa to America." In Phillis Wheatley, *Poems on Various Subjects, Religious and Moral*, 18. London: A. Bell, 1773, repr. ed., Charleston, SC: CreateSpace, 2016.

White, Deborah Gray. *Ar'n't I a Woman? Female Slaves in the Plantation South*. New York: W. W. Norton, 1985.

Wideman, John Edgar. *Brothers and Keepers*. New York: Mariner, 2005.

Wiegman, Robyn. *American Anatomies: Theorizing Race and Gender*. Durham, NC: Duke University Press, 1995.

Williams, John A. *Clifford's Blues*. Minneapolis, MN: Coffee House, 1999.

Willingham, Breea C. "Black Women's Prison Narratives and the Intersection of Race, Gender, and Sexuality in U.S. Prisons." *Critical Survey* 23.3 (2011): 55–66.

Wolfers, Justin, David Leonhardt, and Kevin Quealy. "1.5 Million Missing Black Men." NYTimes.com, 10 April 2015. Web. http://www.nytimes.com/interactive/2015/04/20/upshot/missing-black-men.html?_r=0. Accessed 31 May 2016.

Woodard, Vincent. *The Delectable Negro: Human Consumption and Homoeroticism Within U.S. Slave Culture*. New York: New York University Press, 2014.

Workneh, Lily. "Stop-and-Frisk: Women Who Are Stopped Feel Deeper Embarrassment." TheGrio.com, 3 May 2013. Web. http://thegrio.com/2013/05/03/stop-and-frisk-women-who-are-stopped-feel-deeper-embarrassment/#. Accessed 8 December 2014.

Wyatt, Jean. "Giving Body to the Word: The Maternal Symbolic in Toni Morrison's *Beloved*." PMLA 108.3 (1993): 474–488.

X, Malcolm. *Malcolm X Speaks: Selected Speeches and Statements*, ed. George Breitman. New York: Grove Press, 1965.

Yee, Min S. *The Melancholy History of Soledad Prison: In Which a Utopian Scheme Turns Bedlam*. New York: Harper's Magazine Press, 1973.

Young, Reggie Scott. "Theoretical Influences and Experimental Resemblances: Ernest J. Gaines and Recent Critical Approaches to the Study of African American Fiction." In *Contemporary African American Fiction: New Critical Essays*, ed. Dana A. Williams. Columbus: Ohio State University Press, 2009, 11–36.

Index

PATRICK ELLIOT ALEXANDER is Assistant Professor of English and African American Studies at the University of Mississippi and co-founder of the University of Mississippi Prison-to-College Pipeline Program at Parchman/Mississippi State Penitentiary.